P9-DHE-128

Keywords for Asian American Studies

Keywords for Asian American Studies

Edited by Cathy J. Schlund-Vials, Linda Trinh Võ, *and* K. Scott Wong

NEW YORK UNIVERSITY PRESS *New York and* London

NEW YORK UNIVERSITY PRESS
New York and London
www.nyupress.org

© 2015 by New York University
All rights reserved

References to Internet websites (URLs) were accurate at the time
of writing. Neither the author nor New York University Press is
responsible for URLs that may have expired or changed since the
manuscript was prepared.

ISBN: 978-1-4798-7453-8 (hardback)

ISBN: 978-1-4798-0328-6 (paperback)

For Library of Congress Cataloging-in-Publication data, please contact
the Library of Congress.

New York University Press books are printed on acid-free paper, and
their binding materials are chosen for strength and durability. We
strive to use environmentally responsible suppliers and materials to
the greatest extent possible in publishing our books.

Manufactured in the United States of America

10 9 8 7 6 5 4 3 2 1

Also available as an ebook

Contents

Acknowledgments

First and foremost, we want to publicly thank all the contributors to this *Keywords for Asian American Studies* volume, whose work renders visible the capaciousness, strength, and growth of the field. They patiently worked with us through our requests for revisions to make this a cohesive project and it is through their immense scholarly contributions to the field that we are able to produce this collection.

We likewise owe much to Eric Zinner, who had the foresight to envision the need for such a volume; without hesitation and with considerable consistency, he provided indefatigable support and offered invaluable advice from the planning stage to the production phase. Alicia Nadkarni at NYU Press in comparative fashion ushered us through all facets of the process. This volume benefits greatly from anonymous readers, who productively pushed us to reconsider and reevaluate the overall scope of the project.

In a more local vein, *Keywords for Asian American Studies* would not be possible without the careful eyes of Laura A. Wright, who vetted citations and kept the project on track in its first phase; we are also appreciative of Patrick S. Lawrence, who made sure the manuscript was thoroughly prepared for final submission. Last, but certainly not least, we want to acknowledge those who make what we do possible via their hourly and daily support:

Cathy is thankful to her parents, Charles and Ginko Schlund, along with her twin brother, Charles; they have offered unfaltering support and guidance. She is forever indebted to Christopher Vials, who is a true partner in all respects.

Linda appreciates her parents, Thuy and Bob, and sister, Christine, and her family for their constant sustenance and encouragement. She is thankful for her children, Aisha and Kian, and partner, John, and his children, Bronson and Carly, who bring her immeasurable enjoyment and fulfillment.

Scott is grateful for the wonderful support he has received over the years from his parents, Henry and Mary Wong, his brothers, Kenny, Keith, and Christopher, and his wife, Carrie, and daughter, Sarah, as well as his friends and colleagues who sustain him with love, companionship, good food, and music.

Finally, it is to our students, mentors, and colleagues that we dedicate this collection for enriching our pedagogical capacities and reminding us of the vitality of Asian American studies.

Introduction

Cathy J. Schlund-Vials, Linda Trinh Võ, and
K. Scott Wong

Born out of the civil rights and Third World liberation movements of the 1960s and 1970s, Asian American studies has grown considerably over the past four decades, both as a distinct field of inquiry and as a potent site of critique. In the late nineteenth century, most of what was written about the Asian presence in America was by those who sought to impede the immigration of Asians or to curtail the social mobility of Asians already in the country. This tendency in the literature of the time, and subsequent scholarship on Asians and Asian Americans that appeared into the late 1960s, led Roger Daniels to observe, "Other immigrant groups were celebrated for what they had accomplished, Orientals were important for what had been done to them" (1966, 375). As the field developed starting in the late 1960s, more emphasis was placed upon the lived experiences of Asian Americans, in terms of what they have endured, accomplished, and transformed. In the early stages of the development of Asian American studies as an academic field of inquiry, more attention was paid to the history and experiences of Chinese, Japanese, and to some extent, Filipinos in the United States.

Among the first foundational texts in Asian American studies were edited collections that included contributions by an eclectic group of Asian American activists, artists, and academics. *Roots: An Asian American Reader* (Tachiki et al. 1971) was intent on going to the "root" of the issues facing Asians in America and included three

sections—"Identity," "History," and "Community"—focusing on the "imperative that their voices be heard in all their anger, anguish, resolve and inspiration" (vii). *Counterpoint: Perspectives on Asian America* (Gee 1976) questioned the "self-image of America as a harmonious, democratic, and open society," calling for a reexamination of the mistreatment of Asian Americans to deepen "their understanding of their own past and present political, economic, and social position in American society" (xiii). While some of the authors in these two collections, published by the Asian American Studies Center at the University of California, Los Angeles, had established careers, many of them were emerging community activists, writers, and academics who would become the important first generation of noted Asian Americanists. Although they came from different backgrounds, they were committed to bringing the Asian American experience to the foreground, in order to stress how they had been marginalized in the dominant narrative of our nation's history, society, and culture. The articles and essays in these two publications represent themes that would dominate the field for years: labor exploitation, immigration policies, racial stereotypes and oppression, community development, gender inequalities, social injustices, U.S. imperialism in Asia, struggles of resistance, and the formation of Asian American identities. The Immigration Act of 1965 and the end of the Vietnam War in 1975 drastically changed the demographics of the Asian American population, bringing ethnic Chinese from the diaspora as well as expanding the number of Filipinos, Koreans, and Asian Indians and adding refugees from Cambodia, Laos, and Vietnam, and these ongoing shifts have created new scholarly directions for the field.

In private and public institutions across the country, Asian American studies courses, emanating from these tumultuous histories of struggles, are now an identifiable and often integral part of university and college curricula. Most notable was the creation of the only College of Ethnic Studies at San Francisco State College (now San Francisco State University) in 1969, which incorporated Asian American studies. Currently, some courses in Asian American studies are offered by traditional departments, while others are in American studies or ethnic studies, with some campuses creating Asian American programs or centers and others establishing Asian American studies departments. The expansion of the field led to the creation of the Association for Asian American Studies in 1979, whose first conference was held the following year. Faculty and scholarship that focus on Asian Americans are found in a range of fields including anthropology, art, communications, economics, education, history, literature, political science, psychology, law, public health, public policy, religion, sociology, theater, urban studies, and women's and gender studies. This has created a robust discipline that has broadened its scope in ways that were unimaginable when the field first began to take form, but it has also generated varying pedagogical directions and competing theoretical frameworks. The nature and tenor of Asian American studies have shifted dramatically since student strikes and undergraduate demand instigated its formation.

As recent scholarship underscores, Asian American studies is presently characterized by transnational, transpacific, and trans-hemispheric considerations of race, ethnicity, migration, immigration, gender, sexuality, and class. On the one hand, the pervasiveness of "trans" as a legible methodological prefix highlights the ways in which scholars in the field divergently evaluate the intersections between politics, histories, and subjectivities. On the other hand, such interdisciplinary approaches, ever attentive to past/present histories of racialization, social formation, imperialism, capitalism, empire, and commodification, engage a now-familiar set of what cultural critic Raymond Williams famously defined as "keywords." These terms, which constitute "the vocabulary of a crucial area of social and cultural discussion" (1976, 24), serve as a foundation for *Keywords for Asian American Studies*.

Some of the essays included in *Keywords for Asian American Studies* demarcate the origins of the field as well as critique its scholarly development. Certainly essays on "education" and "incarceration" speak to what has happened to Asian Americans as well as address critical transformations in the field. Essays on "diaspora" and "community" examine how Asian Americans have navigated their way around the world and established themselves in the United States, indirectly reshaping the field in the process. As significant, essays about "memory," "terrorism," and "postcolonialism" signal the field's intimate yet nevertheless expansive engagement with U.S. imperialism and American war making.

Like *Keywords for American Cultural Studies* (edited by Bruce Burgett and Glenn Hendler) and the other volumes in the series, *Keywords for Asian American Studies* is not an encyclopedia. Instead, *Keywords for Asian American Studies* is repeatedly guided by Williams's provocative assertion that such a vocabulary "has been inherited within precise historical and social conditions" that nevertheless must "be made at once conscious and critical" (1985, 24). Expressly, the keywords included in this collection—central to social sciences, humanities, and cultural studies—reflect the ways in which Asian American studies has, in multidisciplinary fashion, been "shap[ed] and reshap[ed], in real circumstances and from profoundly different and important points of view" (1985, 25). Attentive to the multiple methodologies and approaches that characterize a dynamic field, *Keywords for Asian American Studies* contains established and emergent terms, categories, and themes that undergird Asian American studies and delineate the contours of Asian America as an imagined and experienced site. On one level, such "imagined" and "experienced" frames highlight what Sucheng Chan evocatively characterized in *Asian Americans: An Interpretive History* (1991) as distinctly racialized modes of hostility via "prejudice, economic discrimination, political disenfranchisement, physical violence immigration exclusion, social segregation, and incarceration" (45). On another level, Chan's use of "interpretive" as a disciplinary modifier functions as a theoretical touchstone and methodological foundation for *Keywords for Asian American Studies*.

As field interpreters, the collection's contributors contextualized and situated their keywords according to their disciplines, points of entry, and critical engagement, while being simultaneously attuned to the fluidity and trajectories of the field. Determining the selection of keywords has been an organic progression. In terms of structuring the collection, we initially envisioned and prioritized keywords that capture the contours of multiple scholarly disciplines and that resonate with our pedagogical methodologies. As editors, we established few parameters for the contributors; however, we had the difficult task of assigning varying lengths to each keyword, recognizing that spatial limitations would be the major challenge for all authors, most of whom have written books related to their respective keywords. Strategically, we did not inform the contributors of the other entries, with the intent of allowing them to develop their keywords unencumbered, although as editors we suggested revisions so that the collection would be comparative in scope and tangentially cohere.

Additionally, we were interested in exploring core terms that suggestively demarcated distinctive Asian American histories, curricula, and pedagogies. While some of these keywords, such as "assimilation," "citizenship," and "trauma," may be universal terms applied to immigrants in general, our contributors were observant to their specific application in Asian American studies, and mindful of the need to shift dominant paradigms that have been exclusionary. As the project moved from proposal to completed manuscript, our original purview grew to encapsulate divergent approaches, nomenclatural shifts, and disciplinary variations. For example, while "internment" remains a recognizable term within the field, it nevertheless fails to contain (as Lane Ryo Hirabayashi productively notes) the racial, gendered, and classed dimensions analogously associated with present-day understandings of "incarceration." Armed with the editorial desire to represent spheres of knowledge and diverse methodologies, we deliberated over terms such as "capitalism," "democracy," and "prostitution," which are fundamentally subsumed or embedded within other terms (hence, their omission in this iteration). We were similarly attentive to parsing out keywords that are often considered synonymous (for example, "gender," "sexuality," and "queer"). At the same time, we recognized the need to include terms that are foundational to the field, such as "labor," "exclusion," "identity," "ethnicity," "immigration," and "war." Last, but certainly not least, we encouraged contributors to engage the heterogeneity of Asian Americans in their respective essays, so analyses were not limited to one ethnicity or a singular historical moment.

This capaciousness frames the overall collection, which features interconnected references between keywords, includes overlapping examples, and involves reiterated events (such as the Chinese Exclusion Act, the incarceration of Japanese Americans, the civil rights movement, the Vietnam War, and the ongoing War on Terror). The derived meaning or relevance and justifications or reasons for these events have transformed over time for both the populations they have impacted as well as for the critical scholarship they have generated. Although there may be repetitions of some concepts or events in these essays, they are illuminated by differing perspectives and contextualized through varying lenses. The transforming demographics of the involved populations continue to contribute to fundamental debates regarding the racial positioning of Asian Americans and this has impacted the crucial terms and concepts in the field. In some instances, the emergence of a particular keyword within the field (e.g., "genocide" and "refugee") is due to history and policy more closely tied to a specific ethnic group (for example, Southeast Asian Americans). Yet we encouraged authors to move beyond the expected boundaries of ethnic containment and address how their keywords are historically, ideologically, or empirically interconnected to various groupings. Following suit, the collection's contributors demonstrate the ways these diverse groups, in the face of colonial histories and imperial structures, have resisted cumulative pressures by creating their own dynamic identifications.

Although directed to consider the field's expansiveness, contributors were purposely provided latitude in analyzing the formulation and tone of their keywords to more aptly represent the genealogies in which ideas and ideologies traverse theoretical and disciplinary insularities. Even with these intentional coherences, each essay illustrates variations in approach and relevancy in articulating the significance or utilization of a keyword. Correspondingly, while Asian American studies remains an interdisciplinary field, its practitioners nevertheless bear the mark of their respective disciplines with regard to terminology and emphasis. Rather than serve as a limitation, these disciplinary linkages make visible new ways not only of seeing established fields but also of rethinking seemingly familiar topics.

Set adjacent to this editorial context, two terms that admittedly do not appear as specific entries in this collection serve as an implicit point of entry for each contributor: "Asian" and "American." Encompassing geographical sites, political affiliations, and ethnoracial categories, both "Asian" and "American" are incontrovertibly qualified terms that syntactically operate as modifiers (e.g., adjectives) and subjects (specifically, nouns). As John Kuo Wei Tchen previously argued in *Keywords for American Cultural Studies*, "Asian" (along with "Asia" and—more problematically—"Asiatic") is necessarily "loaded with particular spatial orientations rooted in temporal relationships" that are anthropological, geopolitical, and cartographic in scope (2007, 22). These concepts have been constructed as antagonistic to or in competition with one another, evidenced by the political conflicts in the Pacific, or in the cultural juxtapositions of the oppositional identifiers "traditional" and "modern" associated with each. Concomitantly, "American," as an analogously overburdened concept, encompasses cultural, social, and political understandings of citizenship. Within the dominant U.S. imagination, these senses of belonging—fixed to characterizations of the United States as a "nation of immigrants"—correspond to assimilative and euphemistic claims of *e pluribus unum* ("out of many, one") selfhood. Notwithstanding the encumbered nature of each word, the term "Asian American" (which pairs continent and country) upholds Yuji Ichioka's intent when he coined it to replace such derogatory labels as "Asiatic" and "Oriental" and envisioned its politicized possibilities. On one level, the adjectival use of "Asian" as a descriptor for "American" accentuates the degree to which the field reflects multiple coordinates (in East, South, and Southeast Asia, and the United States). On another level, "Asian American" as an identifiable ethnoracial category underscores the migration histories of variegated peoples whose experiences divergently involve overt exclusion, aversive discrimination, and paradoxical incorporation.

In sum, this collection is a gathering of scholarship by those who have dedicated their careers to creating what is now an established field of knowledge, which has been remarkably dialogic in nature and fostered meaningful collaborations. The field emerged under conditions of contestation and resistance and it has generated controversies regarding its epistemological legitimacy, direction, and purpose. The essays are not intended to be definitive, but to encourage readers to creatively engage with the multilayered historical and contemporary debates and the vexing contradictions that reflect the shifting and evolving terrain of Asian American studies. Our expectation is that this collection will provide intellectual stimulation for the seasoned scholar and activist as well as a critical tool for those initially encountering the field to further their inquiry and research.

1

Adoption

Catherine Ceniza Choy

In Asian American studies, the word "adoption" is increasingly significant for elucidating the breadth and depth of Asian American demographics, cultural expression, contemporary issues, and history. In the late twentieth and early twenty-first centuries, the sight of an Asian child with white American parents has become a new social norm. Between 1971 and 2001, U.S. citizens adopted 265,677 children from other countries, and over half of those were from Asian countries. In 2000 and 2001, China was the leading sending country of adoptive children to the United States. South Korea, Vietnam, India, Cambodia, and the Philippines were among the top twenty sending countries (Evan B. Donaldson Adoption Institute 2013). Thus, the terms "international adoption," "intercountry adoption," and "transnational adoption" are used to describe the global dimensions of Asian adoption in the United States (Volkman 2005; Eleana Kim 2010).

A related keyword is "diaspora," which acknowledges the broader histories of Asian international adoption across time and space. Since the end of the Korean War, approximately two hundred thousand Korean children have been sent to the United States for adoption and an additional fifty thousand have been sent to Europe (Yuh 2005). Because white Americans predominantly adopt these children, the words "transracial" and "cross-cultural" are additional key modifying terms for describing this phenomenon (A. Louie 2009; Davis 2012). However, Asian Americans have also adopted children from Asia. The phenomenon of "transethnic" and "multiethnic" adoption (wherein one or both of the parents is Asian American) thus deserves further study.

American adoptive parents and adult Asian American adoptees have made a mark on American national culture by spearheading organizations, such as Families with Children from China and Also-Known-As, that expand the traditional boundaries of kinship and community. They have created specialized virtual networks, print media, and heritage camps, which provide resources and support to other adoptive families and potential adoptive parents. In doing so, they participate in "global family making," the process through which people create and sustain a family by consciously crossing national and often racial borders (Choy 2013). These "global families" are well known to the general public through mainstream news stories about celebrities as well as ordinary Americans adopting children from Asia. These narratives typically portray the phenomenon as a virtuous example of contemporary U.S. multiculturalism and a desirable way to create a family.

The international and transracial adoption of Asian children is also highly controversial. Since the late 1990s, anthologies, documentary films, and memoirs by Korean American adoptees about their upbringing emphasize the themes of American racism and alienation (Bishoff and Rankin 1997; Borshay Liem 2000; Borshay Liem 2010; Trenka 2003; Trenka 2009). The popularity of the seemingly positive stereotype of Asian Americans as "model minorities" in relation to negative "less than model" stereotypes of African Americans adds further complexity to issues of race in Asian international adoption. Some scholars have argued that these stereotypes undergird a racial preference for Asian children over African American children (Dorow 2006).

Furthermore, the decreasing supply of white babies in the United States that began in the second half of the twentieth century—a result of factors including the creation of the birth control pill, the legalization of abortion, and the increasing social legitimacy of single parenting—contributes to the commodification of Asian children for an international adoption market. Charges of "baby selling" and child abduction have resulted in suspensions of international adoptions from Vietnam and Cambodia. Some scholars have strongly criticized international adoption, characterizing it as a global market that transports babies from poorer to richer nations and likening it to a form of forced migration and human trafficking (Hubinette 2006).

These controversies have a longer history rooted in the post–World War II and Cold War presence of the U.S. military in Asia. Americans adopted Japanese and Korean war orphans, but their adoption of mixed-race Japanese, Korean, and Vietnamese children (popularly known as Amerasians), a population fathered by U.S. servicemen with Asian women, captured the hearts and minds of the general public. The distinctive racial features of these mixed Asian-and-American children made them visible targets for abuse. And the lack of U.S. and Asian governmental support, and desertion by their American fathers, influenced their mothers' decisions to abandon them, creating a group of children available for adoption.

International adoption from China is popularly conceived as a recent history, beginning in the late 1980s and early 1990s with the emergence of China's "one-child policy" and its increasing standardization of international adoption. While the policy may have eased the pressure of rapid population growth on Chinese communities, it has been widely criticized for motivating Chinese families, living in a patriarchal society with a marked cultural preference for boys, to relinquish baby girls for adoption. However, an earlier period of Chinese international adoption took place in the 1950s and 1960s under the auspices of the "Hong Kong Project," through which Chinese American and white American families adopted hundreds of Chinese boys and girls who had been relinquished by refugee families fleeing communist mainland China.

Individual advocates who had themselves adopted children internationally—most notably Oregon farmer Harry Holt, Pulitzer Prize–winning writer Pearl S. Buck, and Hollywood actress Jane Russell—and international social service agencies, such as the International Social Service–United States of America (ISS-USA) branch, popularized and facilitated Asian international adoption in the United States. While Russell's WAIF (World Adoption International Fund) worked with the ISS-USA, Harry Holt organized the Holt Adoption Program (now known as Holt International) and Pearl S. Buck founded Welcome House, which continues to facilitate international adoptions. In the 1950s and 1960s, competition between social service agencies and individuals over who should oversee international adoption processes, and the controversy over proxy adoptions—through which adoptive parents adopted a child "sight unseen" through a third party abroad—dominated their interactions. In later years, more cooperative relations would prevail.

Until recently, the history of Asian international adoption was a topic markedly absent from Asian American studies. In the past decade, however, a critical mass of scholarship has emerged. The leadership of Korean adoptee artists and scholars has been pivotal in making Asian adoptee concerns integral to the field. Under the executive directorship of filmmaker and producer Deann Borshay Liem, NAATA (National Asian American Telecommunications Association, now the Center for Asian American Media) showcased films about Asian international adoption. The Association for Asian American Studies (AAAS) features an Asian Adoptee section, which Kim Park Nelson founded in 2007. At the groups's annual meetings, scholarly panels regularly feature recent research on Asian international adoption.

Finally, the keyword "adoption" has enabled political as well as scholarly projects that are critical of the dominant narrative about Asian international adoption, which casts the phenomenon as the humanitarian rescue of Asian children by white American families. Scholars and activists have called attention to the global inequities that persist in Asian international adoption, the significance of birth families, the social reality of *adult* adoptees, and the historical and political ties that bind international adoptees to immigrants. They emphasize that Asian international adoption is a unique phenomenon deserving of scholarly attention on its own terms as well as a generative lens through which we can view our increasingly global society.

2

Art

Margo Machida

Whereas all human societies have developed visual idioms, the idea of Art (with a capital "A") is elusive, much debated, and often closely entwined with social and class hierarchies, and subjective matters of value, taste, and sensibility. Its historic application as a cultural category and definitions of what constitutes visual art have varied significantly from culture to culture, across different historic periods, and according to the background, position, and perception of the viewer. Especially in the modern West, distinctions have typically been drawn between "high" or "fine" art, and crafts or applied arts. "Fine" art has been conceived as a specialized, elevated focus of aesthetic activity with its own intellectual history, professional principles, standards of judgment, and notions of individual "genius." By contrast, crafts, design, and vernacular practices deemed as "tribal," "primitive," "folk," or "outsider" art were often treated as lesser. While the Western tradition of visual art once referred mainly to painting, sculpture, drawing, and graphics, the invention of groundbreaking technologies— photography, film, television, the computer—and the appearance of new practices including video, digital, mixed media, web-based, conceptual, installation, performance, body, land, and earth art have repeatedly enlarged and complicated the ways in which visual artistic activity is understood and utilized. Moreover, as distinctions continue to erode between the realms of the "fine" arts, visual and material culture, and everyday life, it is more commonplace for artists to draw upon and integrate methods and materials from a range of sources, including craft, commercial, and industrial processes.

The term "Asian American art," like "Asian American," first came into general usage as a discrete subject of interest in the late 1960s and 1970s with the contemporaneous rise of the Asian American movement and establishment of ethnic studies as an academic field, beginning on the West Coast. Fueled by broad-based protest, identity, and counterculture movements, this turbulent moment witnessed the potent convergence of heightened ethnic awareness, cultural activism, and politically inspired cultural production. Activist scholars and writers published the first critical writings that sought to frame constituent elements of a distinct Asian American identity and culture. This emergent panethnic formulation was premised on the belief that despite their many differences and longstanding antagonisms, Asian groups shared common struggles and aspirations to establish themselves in the face of a difficult domestic history marked by racism, discrimination, exclusion, and economic exploitation.

Exposure to ethnic studies programs also galvanized members of this generation to use art to promote social change. Consequently, the 1970s witnessed the nationwide formation of grassroots organizations by loose groupings of artists, writers, scholars, college students, and cultural activists that played a foundational role in the Asian American community arts movement (Wei 1993; Louie and Omatsu 2001). Pioneering organizations were established with a strong visual arts component like Basement Workshop in New York, and Kearny Street Workshop and Japantown Art and Media Workshop in San Francisco. Activist artists produced large-scale public murals, silk-screened posters, prints, and illustrations intended to impart clear messages that could be apprehended by the broadest possible audience (Cockcroft, Weber, and Cockcroft 1977). Cuban graphics, Cultural Revolution–era Chinese political posters, the Chicano art movement, and Mexican murals influenced these efforts as expressions of solidarity with liberatory struggles against racism and imperialism in the U.S. and the Third World (Machida 2008). Similarly, in the early 1970s, visual art regularly appeared in the Asian American alternative press—including periodicals such as *Aion* and *Gidra* in California, and *Bridge* magazine in New York—as illustrations, comics, photography, and portraits of people and community life.

During the early years of the Asian American movement, a highly politicized approach to cultural development influenced by writings such as Mao Zedong's 1942 "Talks at the Yan'an Forum on Literature and Art" prevailed. Its advocates conceived of art as a force for revolutionary transformation and emphasized the artist's social and political responsibility to produce work of relevance to a community identified chiefly with the Asian American working class and immigrants. In conjunction with highlighting social problems, and crafting empowering images to counter distortive representations imposed by the dominant culture, activist artists sought to envision a distinctive Asian American culture. However, their efforts to articulate a definitive aesthetic and, by extension, something that could legitimately be called "Asian American art" proved problematic. The issue would lead to perennial debates over whether the term "Asian American art" refers to the background of the maker or to a particular subject matter—that is, work that directly addresses some historic, social, or political aspect of Asian American experience. With conceptions of Asian American art shifting substantially after the 1970s, a wide spectrum of opinion subsequently arose about how, or if, an Asian American visual aesthetic should be defined (A. Tam 2000). Reflective of a variety of ideological and intellectual orientations, these views have ranged from prescriptive formulations inflected by political doctrines to deconstructive critiques of the term itself.

The intensifying interest in Asian American artists likewise led to the emergence of Asian American arts writing, critical discourse, curatorial projects, and archival efforts in the 1970s. Such developments converged with wider efforts by activist scholars and critics, under the umbrella term "multiculturalism," to challenge the strictures of Eurocentric art historical and aesthetic canons and bring forward art by nonwhite groups in U.S. society (Lippard 1990). These allied practices would contribute to the gradual formation of Asian American art history over the ensuing decades. Such ventures, in which seminal community-based Asian American arts organizations played a generative role, understandably associated Asian American art with the groups that comprised the largest domestic Asian populations of the period: peoples of East, Southeast, and South Asian descent. The imprint of that era, as manifested in many exhibitions throughout the 1980s, would exert a significant influence on extant discourses about what constitutes Asian American art. The 1990s witnessed an unprecedented number of museum and gallery exhibitions organized under either an Asian American frame or ethnic-specific rubrics such as Japanese American, Chinese American, Korean American, Filipino American, and Vietnamese American art. Many of these shows centered on identity, sociopolitical, and historic issues related to the transpacific trajectory of U.S. involvement in Asia, including the pervasive, multigenerational effects on U.S. Asian communities of war in Korea and Southeast Asia, the colonization of the Philippines, and the World War II internment of Japanese Americans (Machida 2009).

Yet by the late 1970s, conceptions of Asian American art were ripe for a radical realignment due to the demographic transformation of the U.S. Asian population, resulting from changes in inequitable federal immigration laws, and an expanding backlash against multiculturalism and identity politics. Due to the 1965 abolition of restrictions that severely limited Asian immigration to the U.S., along with refugee statutes enacted after the Vietnam War, new entrants had begun to outstrip the U.S.-born generations whose forebears had mostly settled by the early twentieth century. Beyond the profound impact of this new wave of immigration and transnational circulation on the internal landscape of Asian America, the so-called "culture wars" were also rapidly gaining momentum. Not only was ethnoracial difference as a defining concept under widespread attack in America by the 1980s, but also due to parallel intellectual challenges to discourses of identification and strategies of representation, categories such as nation, race, ethnicity, and gender, and even unitary conceptions of the self were being reconceived as multidimensional, shifting, contingent, and discontinuous (Trinh 1992).

Ever more resistant to being labeled as Asian Americans, by the 1990s younger artists, curators, critics, and scholars perceived that identity, especially when filtered through the lens of race and autobiography, had virtually become a new delimiting canon for minoritized artists. In this move away from rhetorics of race and identity politics, formulations like "post-racial" and "post-identity" art gained increasing currency. As any interest in cultural specificity and affiliation risked being associated with a confining essentialism, those who continued to characterize their subject as "Asian American" art inevitably found themselves treading through a dense political and intellectual minefield. Moreover Asian American art, unlike other disciplines in ethnic studies that were firmly established before the 1980s, was still a subject-in-formation when it ran afoul of this polarizing climate (Elaine Kim 2003).

Visual art, moreover, was largely overlooked as a research priority in Asian American studies, unlike other aspects of visual culture such as film, television, and print media. The paucity of serious and sustained Asian Americanist scholarly writing on the subject is attributed to conditions specific to the genesis and ideological roots of a field concerned with ongoing struggles with racism and marginalization (G. Chang 2008). The role of visual art in the everyday lives of Asian communities was seldom mentioned until the 1990s, given Asian American scholarship's emphasis on bottom-up approaches to social history and labor studies. Indeed the subject was often viewed with ambivalence, due to its presumptive links to elite and elitist interests with no relevance to the lives and circumstances of the Asian American masses. Visual representation was also scrutinized for its function in providing dominant culture with a means to negatively stereotype and suppress Asian efforts to claim a place for themselves in this nation.

Another powerful influence in repositioning Asian American art and cultural criticism—as framed through an array of scholarly and curatorial projects—has come via the accelerating influx of Asian artists and intellectuals to the U.S. during the post-1965 era, which has increasingly placed Asian American art and artists in dynamic conversation with art and ideas emerging from Asian nations and global overseas Asian communities (A. Yang 1998). As identity- and nation-based rhetorics are relativized by discourses of diaspora, transnationality, and globalization, the idea of diaspora, while sometimes criticized for its links to nationalism, provides a basis for the comparative study of distinct yet multivalent identifications that transcend dichotomous

notions of domestic identity (DeSouza 1997). By utilizing a diasporic lens, and by positing an "aesthetics of diaspora," visual art by Asians in the U.S. was reconceived as part of a broad continuum of Asian and Asian diasporic artistic production. These included interstitial frames like "transexperience" and "intersecting communities of affinities" that were respectively applied to jointly position work by overseas Chinese artists residing in three Western nations (the United States, Australia, and France) (M. Chiu 2006), and to trace the formation and artistic production of mixed Asian American and Asian artist collectives in New York and Tokyo (A. Chang 2008). More recent pandiasporic exhibitions organized both domestically and abroad would similarly emphasize international connections by juxtaposing artists in Asia with their ethnic counterparts in Asian diasporas, among them a Korean biennial that brought together works by Korean and Korean diasporic artists from the U.S., Kazakhstan, China, Brazil, and Japan (Y. S. Min 2002).

Overall, the past two decades have proved to be an especially fertile period, distinguished by an upsurge of publications, research initiatives, and thematic and survey exhibitions on and of Asian American art, including projects by scholars in Asia and the Pacific. Much as the foundational work in this field has simultaneously proceeded inside and outside the academy, it is due to the combined efforts of curators, critics, artists, academics, art museums, alternative spaces, community arts and artist-run groups, and historical societies that the scope of the contemporary discourse on Asian American art continues to expand. Tracing individual artists' creative and personal trajectories, these projects variously reveal intricately configured circuits of cultural production and differing contexts in which artistic work is produced, displayed, interpreted, and marketed. Amid these expansive conceptions of contemporary Asian American participation in ongoing flows of artists, ideas, and cultural influences between Asia, Oceania, the Americas, Europe, Africa, and the Caribbean, there is rising interest in artists of mixed ancestry (Kina and Dariotis 2013), and in artistic efforts that occurred prior to the 1960s (Chang, Johnson, and Karlstrom 2008; Johnson 2013). Recent publications shed fresh light on works by Yun Gee, Miné Okubo, and Yasuo Kuniyoshi (A. Lee 2003; Robinson and Tajima Creef 2008; S. Wang 2011). These explorations allow for a clearer understanding of the continuum of concerns and standpoints that have engaged visual artists of Asian heritages working in the U.S., including their historic contributions to the development of an internationalized modernism.

As this area of inquiry continues to evolve, some cultural critics are also revisiting the value of framing and promoting art as "Asian American." While they may harbor reservations about "bounded" notions of identity associated with such a term, they also acknowledge the potential elasticity of the rubric in broadly delineating positions that arise from a common presence in this nation. Moreover, they continue to grapple with how to account for the significance of conceptions of race and the particular effects of domestic racialized exclusion on Asians and other nonwhite groups. To the extent, they argue, that the experiences, histories, and cultural contributions by Asian groups in the U.S. society remain obscured, neglected, or even actively denied, platforms for collective representation remain strategically necessary (S. Min 2006).

With contemporary Asian American visual artists embracing virtually every medium, stylistic exploration, and intellectual current, and drawing upon the full range of representational and critical strategies, no single discourse, critical perspective, ideological stance, or theme can be taken as definitive. Approached this way, the use of the umbrella term "Asian American art"—like the heterogeneous construct of Asian America itself—maintains its utility as an angle of view that allows for the work of artists of diverse Asian heritages to be situated and compared, irrespective of visual idiom, formal approach, or subject matter.

3

Assimilation

Lisa Sun-Hee Park

The definition of "assimilation" and its subsequent usage has long been a contentious issue in American scholarship. Fundamentally, assimilation raises difficult questions about the social composition of a society or culture. More specifically, the debates around the term address the adaptation of those populations or individuals understood as outside or different from mainstream society. The *New Oxford American Dictionary* defines "assimilate" as a verb meaning to "take in (information, ideas, or culture) and understand fully" and "absorb and integrate."

The dispute over the meaning of assimilation follows the intertwined history of racial formation, immigration politics, and national identity in the United States. In 1897, W.E.B. Du Bois published "The Conservation of Races," in which he argued against assimilation. Du Bois pushed for the substantive retention of racial difference, beyond that of physical difference, in acknowledgment of distinct, racial experiences and their particular contributions to society. In this way, to assimilate was understood as meaning to absorb into white America, which requires the negation of black experience and knowledge. He asked, "Have we in America a distinct mission as a race—a distinct sphere of action and an opportunity for race development, or is self-obliteration the highest end to which Negro blood dare aspire?" (1897, 12). Du Bois's argument rests on the assertion that African Americans were already Americans; thereby raising the question of "assimilation into what?" If one is already an American, then assimilation efforts are normative measures to center whiteness as the national identity during a historic era of transnational migration that brought significant racial and national challenges. With substantial agreement in political ideals and social engagement, Du Bois saw no need for assimilation: "there is no reason why, in the same country and on the same street, two or three great national ideals might not thrive and develop, that men of different races might not strive together for their race ideals as well, perhaps even better, than in isolation" (1897, 13). In other words, racial difference was not the problem; it was the racism, or the assumption of racial inferiority, that marginalizes African Americans which was the problem.

Later, Robert E. Park further solidified the connection between racial anxiety and assimilation. However, unlike Du Bois, Park viewed assimilation as a solution to racial difference, which he understood as a social problem. Park's views were more in line with those of another important African American figure of the time, Booker T. Washington, for whom Park worked as press secretary for seven years at the Tuskegee Institute in Alabama (see H. Yu 2001, 38). Park would later become the most prominent member of the Chicago School of sociology and the influence of his time with Washington and their framing of assimilation as a solution is evident within sociology generally. Park and Ernest Burgess's canonical 1921 work, *Introduction to the Science of Sociology*, established Park's theory of interaction, according to which two different social groups follow a cycle of progressive stages of interaction. This was understood as a universal, natural process that begins with competition and ends with assimilation. Assimilation, then, was understood as inevitable, though there were significant barriers to achieving this outcome. Park and his protégés went on to produce studies of these barriers—prejudice and isolation in particular—that would define the foundations of U.S. sociology in general and research on immigrants specifically.

Since then, sociology has fluctuated in its usage and acceptance of the term. More recently, Richard Alba and Victor Nee have argued for the continued legitimacy of assimilation as a social scientific concept by "reformulating" the term apart from some of the most disagreeable elements of the past. They write, "As a state-imposed normative program aimed at eradicating minority cultures, assimilation has been justifiably repudiated" (1997, 827). In addition, they acknowledge the limitation of this concept as a universal outcome measure but contend that assimilation remains the single best theoretical framework from which "to understand and describe the integration into the mainstream experienced across generations by many individuals and ethnic groups" (1997, 827).

Parallel to this social scientific progression, the concept of assimilation has been interrogated in other ways. Building upon new knowledge of power and the role of the state, scholars have criticized the continued assumption of assimilation as a taken-for-granted process of immigrant incorporation in which the state holds a universal and implicitly benign presence. As DeWind and Kasinitz note in their review of immigrant adaptation, whether this concept of assimilation is "segmented" (see Portes and Zhou 1993) or encounters other "bumps in the road," "[t]he world may well be more complicated than the straight line model of assimilation implies" (1997, 1099). Alba and Nee and others continue to treat assimilation as a natural (meaning spontaneous and unintentional) occurrence derived from interpersonal interaction, largely devoid of state interference. Implicit in this assumption is an understanding of the state as a top-down, readily observable social force. But, as scholarship on power has shown, the state has multiple faces, many of them hidden. A "state-imposed normative program aimed at eradicating minority cultures" can come in multiple forms in the age of hegemonic governmentality, in which the domination and subordination of particular classes take place on a "multiplicity of fronts" (Gramsci 1971, 247) and bureaucratic forms of recognition and identification enforce "the way in which the conduct of individuals or groups might be directed" (Foucault 1982, 21).

This is particularly so within neoliberal conditions in which the state maintains both a fluid and pervasive presence. And while Alba and Nee are careful to note that their definition "does not assume that one group must be the ethnic majority; assimilation can involve minority groups only, in which case the ethnic boundary between the majority and the merged minority groups presumably remains intact" (1997, 863), their analysis lacks an understanding of multiple forms of power. Assimilation is not a haphazard event. Governmental programs, with the enforcement of controlling images, are structured in specific ways to promote assimilation into a particular citizen subject (see L. Park 2011).

It is an aspirational process and, as such, the point or value of assimilation is not necessarily to achieve it. Its usefulness resides in its nebulous state as a distant goal rather than as a reality. In this regard, the main issue of contention with respect to assimilation is not its definition but its intention. A critical perspective, derived from an interdisciplinary analysis that combines the theoretical and methodological tools of feminist/queer, ethnic, transnational, and postcolonial studies, approaches assimilation or, more to the point, the wish to assimilate as a powerful normative, disciplinary tool. This perspective is based in an analysis of power that moves away from a state-centric approach. It is an effort to decenter normative or dominant understandings of migration, which often unquestioningly mimic the goals of national economic and political rationalities.

A case in point is the model minority myth, which is assimilation exemplified. The idea of Asian Americans as the "model minority" is a myth—meaning, untrue. However, the myth remains strongly entrenched in the U.S. narrative of its national origins as a liberal democracy with equal opportunity. It holds up Asian Americans as models for other minorities based on measures of income, education, and public benefit utilization rates (see Cheng and Yang 2000; L. Park 2008). Just recently, the myth was promoted in a Pew Research Center publication (P. Taylor et al. 2012). Disregarding data that shows vast variations in income and employment experiences across Asian immigrant groups in the U.S., the Pew report in question states that Asian Americans have made tremendous progress from a century ago, when most were "low-skilled, low-wage laborers crowded into ethnic enclaves and targets of official discrimination" (P. Taylor et al. 2012, 1). And, now, these same immigrants are "the most likely of any major racial or ethnic group in America to live in mixed neighborhoods and to marry across racial lines." As an example, the report states, "When newly minted medical school graduate Priscilla Chan married Facebook founder Mark Zuckerberg last month, she joined the 37% of all recent Asian-American brides who wed a non-Asian groom" (P. Taylor et al. 2012, 1).

According to this report, Asian Americans are models of assimilation, enjoying high educational achievement, good (white) neighborhoods, and interracial marriages to whites. On its face, the model minority myth is a seemingly positive image of personal success and social integration that promotes a moral narrative of "pull yourself up by your bootstraps." Absent from this progress narrative are the many Asian Americans who live in poverty and experience intense and direct racism. The murder of six Sikhs in Milwaukee by a white supremacist two months after the Pew report's

publication is just one graphic reminder. In addition, this assimilationist narrative focuses on just six of the largest and wealthiest subgroups (Chinese, Filipino, Indian, Vietnamese, Korean, and Japanese Americans), which obscures not only the composition of the poverty that exists within Asian American communities but the history of Asian migration to the United States. The privileged Asian Americans of today are not the same Asian Americans of a century ago. They are not the generations descended from the low-wage laborers, in keeping with a simplistic individual progress narrative of assimilation. Instead, today's Asian Americans represent a dramatically bifurcated immigration system that separates the "high skilled" from the "low," and success or lack thereof in the U.S. is, in no small part, indicative of one's access to Western education and other forms of human capital prior to migration (see Park and Park 2005 and Hing 1993 for detailed discussions of immigration policy). However, the significant role of the state in structurally determining who gets ahead remains hidden within a linear, ahistorical progression toward cultural assimilation.

A critical assessment, then, brings the state to the fore by asking, "assimilation into what?" Similar to "capitalist discipline" as defined by Aihwa Ong, assimilationist narratives promote the "enforced and induced compliance" of Asian Americans with specific political, social, and economic objectives (1987, 5). According to Yến Espiritu, the objective is a well-rehearsed patriotic drama of American rescue, cleansed from the messy realities of conquest and colonization (2003, 208). These narratives represent a double-edged sword for Asian Americans. Lisa Lowe explains that Asians in the U.S. hold an impossible position in which they are simultaneously projects of inclusion and exclusion (1996, 4). She argues that this contradiction is rooted in the paradoxical nature of American citizenship, in which the state presents itself as a democratic, unified body where all subjects are granted equal access, while it also demands that differences—of race, class, gender, and locality—be subordinated in order for those subjects to qualify for membership (1996, 162). Assimilation, then, is required for inclusion. But assimilation into what? For Asian Americans, it is the position of the perpetual foreigner/victim who must be rescued, welcomed, and domesticated (i.e., assimilated) again and again (see Tuan 1999). The logic is paradoxical by design. Asian Americans, as a marginalized racial minority, are compelled to adapt their history to fit into an Orientalist drama that requires they play the outsiders repeatedly, all in an effort to establish their legitimate role as insiders. In essence, Asian Americans must be foreign in order to fit into the United States (see L. Park 2005).

Some of the most influential work on Asian America illustrates how the notion of a model minority does not imply full citizenship rights but, rather, a secondary set of rights reserved for particular minorities who "behave" appropriately and stay in their designated subsidiary space without complaint (see Y. Espiritu 2003; L. Lowe 1996; Glenn 2004; Ong 1999; Palumbo-Liu 1999). This subsidiary space is a socially marginal one in which Asian Americans despite their legal citizenship continue to hold foreigner status (see C. Kim 2000). In this way, assimilation actually reinforces established racial inequalities and imposes on even subsequent generations of Asian Americans born in the U.S. a precarious defensive dilemma in which they must constantly prove their worth as "real" Americans.

The foundational disputes regarding racial formation, immigration politics, and national identity associated with assimilation continue. For example, Nadia Kim's (2007) contemporary critique of assimilation as a form of racialization into whiteness is strongly reminiscent of Du Bois's more than a century ago. Over the years, scholarly contestations regarding assimilation as a measurement of Americanization conveyed the fluctuating composition of social citizenship and its deeply intertwined connection to historical formations of racial difference. It remains to be seen whether assimilation as a concept can be convincingly recuperated from its imperial tendencies. As Iris Marion Young has argued, this would require the transformation of institutions and norms to no longer express dominant interests but function according to neutral rules that do not disadvantage those deemed "different" (1990, 266). What is clear, however, from these many years of contemplation is that assimilation is neither simple nor "natural."

4

Brown

Nitasha Tamar Sharma

"Brown" is a term from 11th-century Old English (*brun*) and Middle English (*broun*) referring to a color, meaning "duskiness, gloom." With regard to people, the *Oxford English Dictionary* describes a brown person as "having the skin of a brown or dusky colour: as a racial characteristic." "Brown"'s work as an adjective ("brown bird"), verb ("to brown"), and noun parallels its references to multiple groups of people, including those from Africa, Asia, Europe, the Pacific, and Latin America. Given that many people have "brown" skin, "Brown" of course refers to much more than skin color and phenotype: like the terms "Black" (used to refer to people of African descent), "Yellow" (often referring to East Asians), and "Red" (indigenous peoples of the Americas), it refers not to a thing or person as much as to the processes through which these are given meaning.

The unsettled and untethered uses of "Brown" illustrate the ambiguity and contestation that define its history. "Yellow" is often the expected terminology with which to discuss Asian Americans, as it has long been the American referent for the "Yellow peril" formerly known as "Orientals." The U.S. conflation of Asia with East Asia arises from immigration histories and geopolitical relations. The Chinese and Japanese were the first to arrive in substantial numbers, followed by Filipinos and South Asians, who were also considered "Asiatics," albeit Brown ones. Under the umbrella of "Brown," members of various ethnicities (e.g., Filipinos, Indians,

Pakistanis) arrived with distinct colonial and military histories and cultures that shaped their ethnic politics and experiences in the United States. For instance, Vijay Prashad highlights how Orientalists developed a dominant conception of South Asians, or desis—the "Brown" in his title *The Karma of Brown Folk*—as neither White nor Black others who are viewed by Americans through the lenses of spirituality and culture vis-à-vis British colonization. The direct colonial and military history of U.S.-Philippine relations, on the other hand, shaped Filipinos' distinct earlier legal status as U.S. nationals (rather than as aliens ineligible for citizenship) who were viewed as a sexual-economic threat. Brown and Yellow Asians, therefore, have been racialized as perpetual foreigners, outsiders to the nation. Their social locations are to be understood in relation to the foundational Black-White binary rooted in U.S. slavery and to indigeneity. As a racial category forged through racialist ideologies and colonization, Brown often reflects the intermediary hierarchal position of those who are neither Black nor (fully) White.

The institutions of science and law have defined who and what is Brown through categorizing and fixing populations to justify colonialism abroad and exclusion at home. At the turn of the 19th century, race scientists such as Johann Friedrich Blumenbach referred to people from Southeast Asia and the Pacific, including Filipinos, as belonging to the "Malay" or "Brown" race. During the 1900s, White colonialists distinguished themselves from their Filipino and Indian subjects. Filipinos in the Philippines and the U.S. were bestialized as "Brown monkeys" and South Asians were patronized, as they were by the British, as "little Brown brothers" and "Brown cousins." U.S. courts used Blumenbach's taxonomy of five races when they added "Malay" to the list of races prohibited from marrying Whites, further distinguishing Brown Malays from Yellow Mongolians.

Yet law and science have often disregarded one another. The Supreme Court case *United States v. Thind* (1923) shifted the categorization of South Asians from "Caucasian" (and therefore legally "White") to non-White (and thus Brown), upon which they became "aliens ineligible for citizenship."

The ambiguous and shifting nature of this term continues to reveal tensions and alliances across groups. Some populations that fall within the umbrella of "Asian American" identify with "Brown" to distinguish themselves from Whites as well as East Asians and yet they may be misrecognized as Latino or assumed to be Muslims. In late-20th-century U.S. popular representations, "Brown" referred to Latinos and more specifically to Mexicans in the Southwest. Hernandez (2010) proposes "Mexican Brown" as a conceptual and rhetorical tool that reflects the racial lumping of a denigrated caste of Mexican migrants who have been constructed as "illegal" noncitizens. Since 9/11, both the Wars on Terror and the Arab Spring have shifted yet again the always-under-construction lines of "Brown," so that it now refers to people from the Middle East and North Africa and more broadly to the religion of Islam. That these multiple populations representing transnational geographies identify with the same word does not mean they identify with each other as belonging to a single "race." Thus, "Brown" as a reference to a people's phenotype, like "Black," is not merely descriptive or U.S. based—it is political and global.

The rise of subfields in Asian American studies has led to an interrogation of the heterogeneity and hierarchies of knowledge production within the field. Since the 1990s, Filipino American (Tiongson et al. 2006), Southeast Asian (Schlund-Vials 2012a), South Asian American (Prashad 2000; Prashad 2002), and Pacific Island studies (Camacho 2011) scholars have expanded Asian American studies. These subfields highlight the deeply local yet diasporic formations of Brownness and the relational dynamics among communities of color across territorial boundaries. Events since the millennium have encouraged these scholars to consider the locations and intersections of Asian Americans with Arab and Muslim Americans as fellow subjects of U.S. empire and militarization (Maira and Shihade 2006). Other scholars have drawn intellectual and ethnographic links between Brown and Black populations that illustrate models of interminority solidarity. Scholars in Asian American studies have expanded upon Paul Gilroy's (1993) diasporic notion of the Black Atlantic in their attention to queer and female subjectivity formation (Gopinath 2005) and racio-religious terror (Rana 2002) within South Asian diasporas. Critical histories (Fujino 2005; Fujino 2012) have articulated the impacts of Black struggles (e.g., *Brown v. BOE*, 1954) and racial models of Blackness upon Asian American identity and political formation (Wang 2006).

"Brown" at the turn of the 21st century is not simply an imposed identity; it also reflects the racial consciousness of those who self-identify with the term. Various groups in the U.S. have taken to claiming "Brown pride" as a politicized expression of non-Whiteness, akin to Black pride. Post-9/11, "Brown" (Sharma forthcoming) operates as a political and diasporic identity among people across the globe in response to the Wars on Terror and changing U.S.–Middle East relations. This expression of Brownness as a political concept and identity in the 21st century is evidenced in communities that have arisen through global social networks and in hip hop music that discusses surveillance and oppression that links Arabs, South Asians, North Africans, and Muslims—and those mistaken for them—in their homelands and across diasporas.

"Brown" is both part of and expands beyond Asian America. Referring to Latinos, Filipinos, South and

Southeast Asians, Arabs, "Muslim-looking" people, and others, its flux reminds us to question the seemingly fixed boundaries of all racial categories. Racial formation is an always incomplete process of contestation and negotiation, of hegemony and resistance, and of imposition and adoption. This category, crafted by racial scientists to impose (their) order upon the world has also been a self-selected identity. The identifications of people around the world as Brown—whether racially, politically, or religiously—demonstrate that Brown will "stick around" as an expansive and global category infused with power relations.

5

Citizenship
Helen Heran Jun

"Citizenship" has been a key foundational term within modern liberal definitions of rights since the 18th century. In the most basic sense, citizenship is a legal status accorded to subjects of a nation that confers to its members a host of rights, protections, and obligations. Citizenship is the institution through which states may grant or deny such rights and duties to the inhabitants of a national territory, and thereby positions the state as the ultimate arbiter and guarantor of equality and justice. With the rise of the nation-state form, citizenship became a necessity for realizing what had been imagined as inalienable human rights, insofar as these rights could be practically claimed and administered only if recognized by a nation-state entity (Arendt 1968).

At the very heart of the modern idea of citizenship is a universality that is both its emancipatory promise and limit. For example, all subjects who have secured U.S. citizenship status, regardless of the specific particulars of their economic standing, gender, race, religion, national origin, etc., have equal standing before the law and are formally equivalent to one another. Hence, all U.S. citizens can participate in electoral politics, operating *as if* they were equivalent to one another. Critiques of citizenship maintain that this universalism is a false abstraction since citizens participate in an imaginary political sphere of equality and formal equivalence, while their material lives are in fact constituted by substantive inequalities that define the economic and social spheres. In other words, political emancipation via citizenship replaces and displaces possibilities for actual emancipation. Marx noted how the elimination of religion and property ownership as preconditions for citizenship did not eliminate the power of these institutions over people's everyday conditions, but rather, intensified the reach of religion and class position, which were now falsely bracketed as private matters so that the citizen-subject can emerge as an imaginary "universal." While the liberal position maintains that this abstract equality is the grand substance of citizenship, critics maintain that this imaginary universalism is designed to offer merely abstract equality—the law will treat you *as if* you were all equal to one another—to ensure the reproduction of vast existing inequality.

Ethnic studies scholars have observed that the Marxist critique of citizenship as abstract and illusory does not adequately account for the contradictions that inhere to racialized citizenship. For nonwhites in the United States, historical processes of racialization are not easily confined to the privatized domain of an individual "particular" and racial difference institutionally emerges in contradiction to the universality promised by political emancipation through citizenship. Lisa Lowe notes that while Marx regarded abstract labor in the economic sphere as underwriting abstract citizenship, "capital has maximized its profits not through rendering labor 'abstract,' but precisely through the social production of 'difference,' marked by race, nation, geographical origins, and gender" (1996, 27–28). In other words, the classical Marxist critique has not accounted for modalities of differentiation as being crucial to the development of capitalism. Like other racialized minorities within the United States, Asians have neither been abstract labor nor abstract citizens, "but have been historically formed in contradiction to both the economic and the political spheres" (L. Lowe 1996, 28). This point might seem a familiar one for students of Asian American studies, but it is crucial to contextualize the stakes of this intervention, which is not a simple negation of the Marxist critique of citizenship but rather a deepening of that critique through an understanding of how racialization can produce a productively antagonistic contradiction to the institution of citizenship.

Citizenship has been a primary analytic of Asian American discourse (and within ethnic studies, generally), with an emphasis on both its denial and negation. The early history of Asian American racial formation has been a history of the incorporation of Asian labor in the West while those workers were rendered more exploitable through the systematic denial of citizenship status through legislation that deemed Asian immigrants ineligible for citizenship. From the 1790 Naturalization Act, which deemed only "free white persons" eligible for naturalized citizenship, to the systematic exclusion of new Asian emigrants (Chinese in 1882, Asian Indians in 1917, Japanese and Koreans in 1924, and Filipinos in 1934), and finally to Alien Land laws that prohibited Asians already in the United States from owning property, these acts of legislation are concrete manifestations of how Asians were constituted as not only nonwhite but as antithetical to the U.S. citizen. The history of Asian Americans is indeed, generally narrated as the denied access to U.S. citizenship. For those born to Asian immigrants in the United States and therefore U.S. citizens by birth (what Mai Ngai [2000] refers to as "alien citizenship"), we can observe the practical irrelevance and disregard of that legal status, such as in the mass internment of Japanese American citizens.

We understand this history of exclusion from citizenship as the product of competing interests and institutions, including capital (which has historically embraced Asian immigrant labor), white labor interests (which has historically organized to prohibit Asian immigrant labor), Asian nation-states with varying degrees of geopolitical influence, and the U.S. state, which both passes and reverses exclusionary legislation in the effort to manage the political crises that have arisen due to the threat (or alternately, the "promise") of Asian labor in the United States. In many ways, the 19th-century exclusion of Asian immigrant workers from citizenship was also a reaction to the formal inclusion of African Americans into citizenship in 1868 following the abolition of slavery, a political concession that capital, labor, and the U.S. state were not eager to repeat (Saxton 1975; Du Bois 2008).

After World War II, however, the needs of the U.S. labor market, geopolitical ideological demands, and mass civil rights mobilization led by African Americans and others brought an eventual end to exclusionary legislation directed against Asian immigrants (Melamed 2011; L. Lowe 1996; S. Chan 1991). One feature of the post–civil rights era has been Asian American incorporation into U.S. citizenship via liberalized immigration policies resulting from the Immigration and Naturalization Act, or Hart-Celler Act, of 1965 (Ngai 2000). Indeed, with the passage of civil rights legislation that same year, African Americans (who were formally granted U.S. citizenship via the 14th Amendment almost a century earlier) and all other racialized groups also finally experienced full formal equality and equal rights, that is, full equality in the realm of the law. However, as the Marxist critique of citizenship underscores, legal equality and political emancipation (*as if* we were equal) will necessarily fail to resolve the brutal racialized inequality that constitutes our social formation. The ethnic studies critique of Marx's inability to account for the imbrication of race and class retains this crucial understanding that under liberal capitalism, citizenship is constituted in relation to the sanctity of property rights that the political state is founded to protect. While an ethnic studies critique

of citizenship recognizes the historical racialization of citizenship in the United States, it also simultaneously recognizes that citizenship and the achievement of rights can never abolish the exploitative systems that they were in fact designed to protect and reify. Rather, the charge for a critical ethnic studies analytic has been to better understand how the imbrication of race and class yields an entire range of contradictions for racialized subjects who can be situated in contradictory antagonism to the mandates of both the state and capital.

For Asian Americans who have been racialized as alien to the national body, but who have been otherwise incorporable as exploited workers, as bourgeois professionals, and as capitalists, it is crucial to clarify the multiple implications of how Asian American racial difference emerges in contradiction to citizenship. Bearing out the materialist critique, we can see, since 1965, that securing civil rights instantiated racial equality in the United States, but only in the legal realm of abstract formal equivalence. While such legal equality enabled partial socioeconomic mobility on the part of U.S. racial minorities, institutionalized racial exploitation continues to materialize in racialized ghettoization, uneven mortality rates and unequal access to functioning public education, a racialized, gendered labor market, and subjection to state violence and detention.

One aspect of contradiction that has been familiar terrain within Asian American discourse underscores how, despite access to citizenship, Asian Americans continue to signify within the national imaginary as racially particular and as foreign to the national culture. We can see how Asian American racial difference is a particularity that does not simply dissolve into the universality promised by political representation through the institution of citizenship. Hence, even economically privileged Asian Americans are read not as "universal" U.S. citizens, but regarded through the laudatory terms of their racial difference as model minorities. While members of the educated Asian American professional class may continue to signify as culturally foreign despite their citizenship and economic status, such examples of exclusion do not negate or displace the vast differences in life opportunities that radically distinguish the lives of the Asian American poor from those of their economically mobile professional counterparts.

Therefore, what is often referred to as the construction of the Asian as the "forever foreigner"—the deferred promise of full inclusion into the national body that Asian Americans are yet to enjoy—cannot be interpreted as the ultimate crisis and horizon of what Asian Americans must both claim and aspire to. Such a positioning situates the Asian American critique as a perpetual lament of never being recognized as a "true" American, a grievance that one is continually (mis)recognized as a foreigner rather than citizen. For the Asian American poor, the consequences of such Othering can mean the naturalization of violence and exploitation of, say, immigrant garment workers or the lack of resources for displaced Southeast Asian refugees after Katrina, while for the Asian American elite, it can manifest as a bittersweet night of winning the Miss America pageant or the difficulty of securing political office in a non-Asian district. While all of these instances can be taken up as yet another sign of the enduring "disenfranchisement" of Asian Americans, there is much at stake for Asian American studies in recognizing that full inclusion for the latter group—that is, when professional Asian Americans can unquestionably be regarded as representative of America—will not resolve the violent material deprivation of the Asian American poor.

Given the history of Asian American studies and its commitment to critiquing the exploitation of 19th- or 21st-century Asian/American workers, opposing imperialist wars waged in Asia (and beyond), or waging antieviction campaigns on the behalf of the Asian American elderly, there is strong reason to believe that despite the institutionalization of Asian American studies, it is possible that in the distance or disruption produced by Asian American racialization, something other than the lamenting desire for inclusion into existing institutions might emerge to interrupt the endless loop of denial and desire constituted by citizenship. In other words, even middle-class or elite Asian American disaffection/alienation can potentially be the basis for a critique of citizenship with different political horizons that would be transformative of the brutal conditions endured by the racialized poor in this country and beyond. Race is the locus in which multiple contradictions—economic, gender, sexual—variously cohere and assemble in specific contexts, and hence it is a locus of myriad tensions that must be kept in productive relation with a critical understanding of global capitalism (Hall 1980; L. Lowe 1996).

As with other racialized immigrants, citizenship is one of the most crucial mediating institutions in the formation of Asian Americans, irrespective of specific legal statuses. Whether as U.S.-born citizens, green-card holders, H-1B workers, or those granted refugee status, the institution of citizenship dictates the terms of access to the labor market and to a host of state-regulated resources, including housing, healthcare, and education. In this context, we can recognize the clear importance of pressuring the state to make good on its promises of abstract rights, whether in the instance of challenging state surveillance of U.S. Muslim communities, seeking benefits for Filipino World War II veterans, or securing safer housing for Southeast Asian refugees. At the same time, it is critical to simultaneously recognize how a rights-based discourse narrows the parameters and terms of what can be claimed and imagined as politically possible.

Predictably for the most privileged under globalized capitalism, Asian American displacement from national culture may cease to even resonate as crisis, particularly for the members of a bourgeois Asian cosmopolitan class less invested in signifying as "American" so long as they have the access secured by multiple passports and dual citizenship (Ong 1999; Appadurai 2000; Miyoshi 1993). The globalization of capital has significantly altered the meaning of citizenship as neoliberal rhetoric and economic policies have dismantled the welfare state and the very notion that citizenship entails "entitlements"; there is, instead, an obsessive trumpeting of a discourse of "individual responsibility" that works to displace any traditional notion of the social. Stuart Hall and David Held contend that, while traditional critics might have regarded citizenship rights as a kind of "bourgeois fraud" in the post-Thatcher/Reagan era, there are renewed stakes to working out "the individual vs. the social dimensions of citizenship rights," the latter of which is negated by a neoliberal rhetoric that asserts that the common good can be realized only by private individuals engaging in a capitalist free market, unencumbered by state intervention (Hall and Held 1989). As Thatcher famously declared, "there is no such thing as society, only individual men and women and their families," an extraordinary call that seeks to obliterate the very notion of a larger social good or collective beyond the heteronormative nuclear family.

This neoliberal emphasis and recognition of the normative "family" as the only legible social unit also suggests that the dominant construction of Asian Americans since 1965 as hardworking, self-reliant, and family-oriented subjects is part of a neoliberal rhetoric that has refashioned the modern discourse of citizenship of entitlements and state obligations—to provide access to housing, public education, health care, and employment—into an individuated narrative of private competition in the free market and diminished state capacity (with the exception of policing and the military). In other words, in the post–civil rights era, discourses of Asian American racial difference are consistently in the service of constituting a new conception of citizenship defined through both normativity and individual competition, while explicitly undermining and eroding principles of reciprocity, obligation, and social contract that have constituted the most compelling social dimensions of citizenship.

6

Class
Min Hyoung Song

The meaning of "class" in Asian American studies formed in conversation with Marxism, with the former building on the latter's insights while seeking to find ways to exceed its perceived limitations. For instance, Lisa Lowe starts her groundbreaking book *Immigrant Acts: On Asian American Cultural Politics* by insisting, "Understanding Asian immigration to the United States is fundamental to understanding the racialized foundations of both the emergence of the United States as a nation and the development of American capitalism" (1996, ix). In the equally groundbreaking *Everybody Was Kung Fu Fighting: Afro-Asian Connections and the Myth of Racial Purity*, Vijay Prashad observes, "White supremacy emerged in the throes of capitalism's planetary birth to justify the expropriation of people off their lands and the exploitation of people for their labor" (2001, x–xi). In both these examples, race plays a larger role in the development of capitalism than Marx himself ever considered. This is so because, for Marx, capitalism could best be explained as a process of valorization produced by the inequality between those who own the means of production and those who own only their ability to work. To keep this discussion as simple as possible, we can refer to these two fundamental socioeconomic classes as capitalists and workers. While other classes did exist for Marx, he understood them as having become less relevant as capitalism replaced preexisting economic arrangements. For scholars like Lowe and Prashad, such

a claim has been significantly supplemented by an acknowledgement of the importance of race, as well as gender, sexuality, and other markers of difference, in sustaining unequal access to wealth, and indeed to the very means of sustaining life itself.

As Marx was quite aware, history does not unfold with the dialectical neatness that his insistence on the primacy of capital and labor suggests. Moments of revolutionary possibility do not always, or often, lead to changes that directly benefit workers. The outcome of any struggle is intrinsically unpredictable. There are at least two major ways in which the capitalist class can keep the working class in check regardless of the historic circumstances, frustrating or even foiling what might have turned into a revolution. First, it can deploy what Louis Althusser calls—in an essay that has been widely quoted and critiqued in Asian American studies circles (J. Ling 1998, 159–60; V. Nguyen 2002, 144; M. Chiang 2009, 27)—a "repressive state apparatus," which is a combination of laws, courts, police, and military that work more or less in concert against the interests of the working class. Unfortunately for the capitalist class, relying on repression alone is expensive and inefficient. Being nakedly repressive also leaves capitalists unable to keep workers, such as individual police officers, serving in roles that require them to inflict physical harm on others of the same class. Before long, such workers can begin to think of themselves openly *as* part of the working class and join the very people they are supposed to keep in line. Under such circumstances, capitalists have no choice but to employ the lumpenproletariat, a subclass of loafers who neither have any access to the means of production nor care to use their labor to perform any useful work. They are as a result more inclined to crime and other unproductive behavior than anyone else. Employing the lumpenproletariat as hired thugs is a dangerous move, however, because by definition they are untrustworthy and might easily decide to turn their weapons of repression on their employers with the hope that they can usurp their position.

Hence, finding an alternative way to prevent workers from engaging in revolutionary activity is of paramount importance if the capitalist class wants to maintain its dominance. The most significant method involves confusion, via what Althusser called the "ideological state apparatus." For instance, workers may be convinced by various means that what truly ails them are undocumented workers whose illegal presence in their country steals jobs away from those like themselves, who are law abiding. In this way, such workers may be convinced that their real enemies are not the owners of the means of production but a subgrouping within their own class who reap unmerited rewards, who unfairly hog resources, and who are somehow a threat to their way of life. As this example suggests, the task of confusion is easier to accomplish if workers are divided along racial, ethnic, gendered, and national lines, and taught to feel superior because they are not the Other. Hence, for those who study Asian Americans, a keen awareness of how race coincides with the interests of capital might stress, as Mae Ngai does, how this concept "is always historically specific. At times, a confluence of economic, social, cultural, and political factors has impelled major shifts in society's understanding (and construction) of race and its constitutive role in national identity formation" (2004a, 7).

Given how essential this second method of social control is, we might say that there are two levels of relationships that organize capitalist societies. There is the "base" or "infrastructure," which refers specifically to the relationship between capital and labor that forms "the economic conditions of production" (Marx 1978, 5). It is necessarily structured by inequality, without which wealth would not be possible and capitalist societies would fall apart. Overlaid on top of this all-important structure of inequality are the efforts capitalists employ to confuse workers and make them unable to band together into a revolutionary force. We can call this layer of misinformation, deception, and trickery the "superstructure," an epiphenomenon of ideological manipulation that actively frustrates workers' attempt to make sense of their real interests even as it may also act as a crucial domain for these same workers to grasp intellectually changes occurring to the base that can lead them to revolt. The fact that the superstructure can simultaneously obfuscate and provide insight suggests that while the base is ultimately what drives history forward, there remains a fluid and heuristic relationship between the two. Despite Marx's tacit recognition that the base is not always and only determinant, many leftists have conceived of the cultural work they should engage in as tantamount to showing how what we believe to be important is an illusion, a part of the superstructure, that inhibits us from firmly making sense of what is actually important, the base.

As Asian American studies scholars have pointed out, many of the activists who first considered themselves Asian Americans in the early 1970s modeled their struggles on black power (Maeda 1999; Omatsu 2000; Fujino 2005). This means that while they often employed the language of Marxism, they were also engaged in a sharp departure from its preoccupation with class, especially when it privileges this category of analysis over all others. There were of course several prominent activists who maintained the centrality of class in their thinking, such as Grace Lee Boggs (although she did so specifically with an attention to the experiences of an African American working class), but others who turned explicitly to race as a basis of organizing tended to be skeptical of such privileging. Some, for instance, turned to the Black Panther Party for inspiration, and in doing so adopted the very un-Marxist view that the lumpenproletariat was revolution's "vanguard" (Pulido 2006, 142).

In general, most early self-conscious Asian Americans understood revolution less as the overturning of a class relation and more as a struggle against inequalities of many kinds. It was only by coordinating such struggles, they reasoned, that a broad coalition could be built to help upset the status quo into social forms more respectful of the complexities of peoples' actual lives. This kind of thinking had little room to grant class the kind of primacy it once enjoyed, and has instead led to understandings of class and race, alongside gender, sexuality, and increasingly disability, as dynamically intersectional concepts (Hong 2006, xxvi). In their foundational book *Racial Formation in the United States: From the 1960s to the 1990s*, Michael Omi and Howard Winant state this view with unequivocal clarity: "Racial dynamics must be understood as determinants of class relationships and indeed class identities, not as mere consequences of these relationships" (1994, 34). Other thinkers such as Chandan Reddy (2011, 33–34), Junaid Rana (2011, 157), and Lisa Marie Cacho (2012, 99–100) have since turned to Foucault, who in "Society Must Be Defended" suggests that class may be an epiphenomenon of race: "After all, it should not be forgotten that toward the end of his life, Marx told Engels in a letter written in 1882 that '[y]ou know very well where we found our idea of class struggle; we found it in the work of the French historians who talked about the race struggle'" (2003, 79).

For the most part, debate about the importance of class has largely been settled in Asian American studies in favor of intersectional thinking. Class is now widely understood to be one of several important forms of inequality around which we understand how modern American society, as well as societies in general, are structured. Indeed, anyone who advocates for giving primacy to class at the expense of attention to these other forms is likely to stir suspicion, as such an approach is a sure sign that one is not taking the struggles of racial minorities, women, queers, and the disabled seriously enough. This view also conjures past working-class movements that have defined the worker explicitly as white, male, heteronormative, and able-bodied.

One consequence of this consensus is the discomfort it has generated for those who insist that class must remain at the center of all socially responsible thought. The prominent American literature scholar Walter Benn Michaels exemplifies this discomfort when he writes, "we like the difference between black people and white people or between whites and Asians much more than we like the difference between the rich kids and the poor ones" (2011, 1023). As this quotation suggests, when class is understood as the primary social relationship around which all others are of secondary importance, attention to racial difference, gender, sexual orientation, the disabled, or the nation can be easily understood as a sideshow. Worse, becoming fixated on anything other than class can mean that one has become a counterrevolutionary, someone so blinded by the buzz of the superstructure that one ends up preventing others from engaging in meaningful political struggle. Indeed, so blind has Asian American studies been in its commitment to everything but class, it has, according to Michaels, become focused on fostering "a world in which the fundamental conflicts have less to do with wealth than with race, space, gender, and sexuality. . . . This is the world of neoliberalism, the world in which identity and inequality have both flourished" (2011, 1029).

For many in the field of Asian American studies, the demand that scholars must choose between paying attention to race *or* class can feel impossible to satisfy. As Sunaina Maira reports, for instance: "an African American woman who lived in the North Wellford [pseudonym] apartments once told me that all the South Asian families were middle class, if not well off, and she observed that they were quick to move out of the high-rise apartments and buy their own houses. What she did not see was that many of these family members worked, possibly even without wages, in family businesses and so did not earn much individually and that several family units were crowded into small apartments where they shared one or two bedrooms" (2009, 141). Being Asian American in the mind of this African American woman, as in Michaels's article, has become synonymous with upward mobility, mysterious access to wealth, and social distance. At the same time, Maira's explanation of the invisible struggles South Asian American family members endure reveals how tirelessly working class they are and how *within* the family unit class cleavages emerge. Some members are workers whose exploitation is nearly total, so that they work only for the cost of their basic physical maintenance, while other members reap the benefits of their labor to concentrate wealth and invest in schemes for more accumulation. In this example, Asian immigrants become both capital and labor, and as a result capable of economic mobility while simultaneously remaining workers with only their ability to work to sell. Because of this apparent class paradox, they also seem racially different from their African American neighbors, who somehow can't—and wouldn't want to?—achieve the same feat. Clearly, more attention to the way class entangles ideas of race, and the way race does the same to class, is needed.

One approach that many scholars have already taken (Parreñas 2001; Park and Park 2005; Zhou and Gatewood 2007) is to consider how successive immigration laws have given birth to an hourglass, and often transnational, class structure within Asian America itself that is also often ethnically marked. At the top, there are relatively large numbers of materially well-off college-educated professionals and skilled international workers on specialized visas who are gaining a lot of attention, and setting the pace for what is popularly understood as Asian American. While few in this group can be said to own the means of production, and many may lead modestly precarious lives (in the sense that should they ever lose their jobs, they could quickly fall into economic and other kinds of trouble), they do enjoy an impressive access to wealth and the kind of pleasures such access can afford. At the bottom, there are an equally large, if not larger, number of working poor, the undocumented, refugees, and so forth who struggle everyday with little wealth to sustain themselves at a high level of precarity. Now, more than ever, "Asian America" names a paradox of "class" that makes the latter term resonate with urgent meaning.

7

Commodification

Nhi T. Lieu

In *Capital*, Volume One, Marx was highly critical of commodification, a process that occurs under capitalism whereby things are assigned an exchange value in the marketplace. He observed that when the use-value of commodities are given economic or exchange values, these commodities subsequently *modify* social relationships. Building upon these ideas, Marxist scholars such as Arjun Appadurai (1986), Stuart Hall (1992), and Donald Lowe (1995) have complicated the studies of commodification to argue that the social values of commodities are highly contested and firmly immersed in their cultural, social, and political contexts. In her thought-provoking article "Eating the Other," bell hooks (1992) contends that racial and ethnic expressions of difference by minoritized groups can be co-opted, sold, and consumed in the dominant marketplace. In this essay, I explore the various ways in which capitalism makes commodification practices manifest through culture, ethnicity, and the racialized body. I suggest that histories of colonialism and Orientalism shape various forms of commodification as it pertains to Asians and Asian Americans. Following complex human migratory paths, the social lives of objects, bodies, cultural forms, and practices are animated by transnational market exchanges. Commodification thus occurs as a dynamic process in the service of capitalist expansion. It functions to transform racial and ethnic difference by repackaging, exoticizing, and making cultural forms and practices more palatable for mainstream consumption.

In addressing the historical commodification of race, Mae Ngai considers the enterprising ways in which Chinese merchants acted as social agents who capitalized on the exoticism of racial difference in world's fairs and insists that we examine such interactions as "products of translation and negotiation" (2004a, 61). Likewise, Sabina Haenni notes in her close readings of commercial leisure in Chinatowns that Chinese immigrants played an active role in "self-Orientalization" as a way to seek "cultural legitimation" (2008, 146).

As did the early immigrants who vied for cultural legitimacy, Asian immigrants who arrived later invested in cultural commodification for different purposes, transforming meanings of cultural nationalism and cultural practice as well as ethnic identity. One of the most public displays of culture is embodied through dress, but clothing and fashion are contested terrains of commodification. For example, adorning women in traditional ethnic dress such as the ao dai, cheongsam, hambok, kimono, and sari visually renders them as cultural bearers of different Asian nations. Vietnamese refugees commodified the national dress, the ao dai, to consolidate an identity of exile by claiming it as an authentic piece of Vietnamese culture (Lieu 2001). The maintenance of exclusive claim to a commodified object is however elusive, particularly as traditional material objects become highly desirable fashion pieces that reinterpret meanings of class, ethnicity, and gender. Thuy Linh Tu's evocative study of Asian American fashion designers "threads" together "design as an Asian American practice and Asianness as a fashionable commodity" (2010, 6). Tu troubles the complex web of intimacies between Asian immigrant labor and Asian American fashion designers who are defined by their positioning as a racialized creative class. Tu's work illuminates the trend in late capitalist globalization in which commodification frequently erupts in popular culture and Orientalist tropes still resonate in fashion and design.

Advances in technology from the 1990s onward in media such as satellite television and digital video have facilitated this circulation of Orientalist images in contemporary popular culture. In her work on the emergence of "Indo-chic" and "Asian cool," Sunaina Maira argues that the popularization of Asian cultural practices such as the application of henna by American models, actress, and celebrities including Madonna and Gwen Stefani commercializes and evacuates them of their specific cultural meanings. More specifically, her studies of the mainstream embrace and cooptation of mehndi, bindis, yoga, and belly dancing (2007; 2008) demonstrate the fluidity of these cultural forms as they become palatable to and commodified by middle-class women. She writes, "Indo-chic does the political and symbolic work of domesticating difference, extracting not just profit but the very signs of difference from South Asian immigrant workers and South Asian Americans at large. This commodification of the threat of difference is even more apparent as the 'war on immigrants' of the 1980s and 1990s has extended into the 'war on terror,' affecting Muslim, Arab, and South Asian immigrants, as well as undocumented immigrants more generally" (2007, 237). Confronted with cultural and racial difference, dominant groups thus commodify "others" to manage what is deemed as unfamiliar.

While the commodification of cultural practices renders ethnic and immigrant communities subject to other forms of commodification, Marilyn Halter (2000) has demonstrated that immigrant groups have the power to gain economic security when they reinforce their ethnic identities. This was most pertinent between the 1990s and early 2000s, when multiculturalism flourished as a profitable marketplace phenomenon. Today, in an era perceived as "post-racial," there remains a profitable "ethnicity" enterprise that seeks to tweak and refashion old products and invent new ones to contribute to the discourse of American exceptionalism. As such, embodied racial hybridity has become valuable in the marketplace, particularly in a society that claims to value diversity but is slow to respond to social policies that promote it.

With the expansion of global capitalism, the dominance of new media, and the advancement in digital technology, we are witnessing not only the commodification of ethnicity, but of bodies, food, music, and anything that can be marketed, made available for economic exchange, and consumed by those with access to capital. Ethnic immigrant communities have participated in self-commodification as a strategy to assuage the social fears of alien others. While this introduced the mainstream to "foreign cultures," the drawback to commodification remains that it renders humans as objects to be desired. Moreover, the racial structure does not allow for Asians and Asian Americans to have control over consumption. It is important to note what bell hooks reminds us, that the consumption of the other is legitimated by a racial structure that positions others to be consumed. The danger lies not in commodification itself but, as Marx would caution, in the fetishism of commodities.

8

Community

Linda Trinh Võ

"Community," or "communities," is an amorphous keyword in Asian American studies that has evolved along with societal transformations, and its meaning is highly contested. The *Oxford English Dictionary* defines "community" as a "body of people organized into a political, municipal, or social unity"; it can be characterized as those "who have certain circumstances of nativity, religion, or pursuit, common to them, but not shared by those among whom they live." In Asian American studies, the term is most often associated with bounded, geographic localities that incorporate people, places, and institutions that have an affinity to one another or intricate connections. Additionally, communities are interpreted as non-territorial spaces, formed by individuals residing in various locations who share similar interests or objectives. They can be created as a result of people being excluded or treated interchangeably, thereby compelling them to come together, or they can be forged by internal notions of sameness, as a result of which aggregates cohere and differentiate themselves from those outside certain territorial or ideological boundaries. For Asian Americans, these collectivities are often projected as welcoming and unified; however, they also can be exclusionary and divided, so in certain contexts the term has a beneficial and affirming connotation, while in other cases it is perceived as oppressive and constrictive.

Studies of Asian Americans have focused on them as victims of racial discrimination and involuntary segregation. They were unwelcomed in an American republic that espoused a fervent nationalism and nation-state based on white supremacy. The 1790 Naturalization Act bestowed citizenship on "free white persons," thereby excluding Asians, who were classified as "aliens ineligible for citizenship," from the body politic, which relegated them to the status of perpetual foreigners. U.S. colonial projects in Asia and domestic policies based on ideologies of Manifest Destiny reified their subordinate position in the racial hierarchy. Cultural stereotypes and pseudo-scientific constructions of them as inferior, uncivilized, and inassimilable affirmed that they were a peril to national unity. Xenophobia and fears of Asian laborers as economic competitors created exclusionary immigration policies, particularly concerning women, and repatriation programs, which were implemented to prevent the formation of permanent geographic settlements. The ethnic spaces they managed to form were alleged to be sites of contagious diseases and aberrant sexuality, "vice-filled opium dens," and as such, threats to public health and Protestant morality (N. Shah 2001). They endured mob violence and massacres as well as the arson of their residences and neighborhoods.

Scholars have also recouped a celebratory history of Asian American pioneers who contributed to the nation, capturing the materialization of their communities and their engagement in acts of resistance. Ostracized from mainstream America, early immigrants forged their own economic and cultural spaces in both rural and urban areas (Takaki 1989; S. Chan 1991; Matsumoto 1993). Attracted by economic opportunities, they labored in agricultural production, railroad construction, fishing industries, service sector economies, and light manufacturing, with some owning small farms or businesses. In their pocket areas, they managed to create economic niches for survival, devoid of interracial competition and governmental interference. They relied on kin and non-kin networks with those who shared the same dialect, home village, region, and religion to find housing and employment. As a result of legislation, such as the Alien Land Laws, and later racially restrictive covenants, Asian immigrants were prohibited from purchasing land or property, but they managed to establish roots by registering property in their U.S.-born children's names, signing long-term leases, or finding neighborhoods willing to accommodate their presence (Brooks 2012). The Asian women who were permitted entry, such as merchant's wives and picture brides, contributed to the family labor and the formation of permanent settlements.

In these positive references to community, cluster spaces are narrativized as safe havens where Asians found a refuge from mistreatment. Scholars analyzed how members created their own associations and institutions, some of which paralleled mainstream ones. As a form of resistance to their exclusion, they demarcated their communities by establishing markets, stores, restaurants, pool halls, schools, and religious sites that served co-ethnics. For residents and migratory laborers, these ethnic hubs allowed those who were homesick to absorb the sights, sounds, and smells of their homeland. In the earlier historical period, the predominantly male population created a bachelor subculture and engaged in leisure activities in these shared homosocial spaces. With the arrival of a diverse range of immigrants following the 1965 Immigration Act and refugees at the end of the Viet Nam War in the post-1975 era, ethnic sites provide opportunities for newcomers to participate in communal activities and construct a collective ethnic identity (Bonus 2000; Rudruppa 2004). This perspective conceives of community as a favorable place for ethnic solidarity, since it promotes ethnic retention and the transmission of traditional cultural practices (Wong and Chan 1998; L. Kurashige 2002).

In addition to "community," ethnic districts have been identified with terms such as "barrio," "colonia," "enclave," "ghetto," "inner city," and "slums," which can have negative or positive connotations depending on the context (Y. Chang 2010). Ethnic succession or ecological models developed by Chicago School sociologists theorized that ethnic concentrations are gateway spaces for first-generation immigrants to transition and eventually assimilate into American society (H. Yu 2002). Although other terms have been employed, "ethnic enclave" is typically associated with Asian American community formation and many scholars depict such ethnic concentrations as places that provide opportunities for immigrants to find employment, build networks, become incorporated, and ultimately, be socioeconomically mobile (Zhou 1995). In contrast, other scholars argue that enclaves are isolating and counterproductive to assimilating immigrants or enhancing their civic engagement (Peter Kwong 1996). Additionally, critics of neoliberalism argue that ethnic enclaves reproduce conditions of inequality and poverty, and that their insularity allows the state to relinquish its social and fiscal obligations. Immigrant enclaves are reliant on an informal economy characterized by fierce competition, slim profit margins, and a flexible labor pool (Hum 2014). As such, they produce labor market segmentation in the light manufacturing industries, retail and service sectors, and small businesses, which can lead to unemployment and underemployment as well as co-ethnic labor exploitation that is often unmonitored or unregulated.

The concept of community is not only used synonymously to reference an ethnic group, such as Filipino American or Korean American, it is also substituted for the broader label "Asian American." In the late 1960s, the term "Asian American," coined by Yuji Ichioka, was adopted by activists who articulated their shared interests, in parallel with the formation of Asian American studies (Y. Espiritu 1992). Benedict Anderson observes that nations are *imagined communities* in which members "will never know most of their fellow-members, meet them or even hear of them, yet in the mind of each lives the image of their communion," so this usage of "community" is symbolic and instrumental (2006, 6). Given that they were externally lumped together, activists during the Yellow Power movement embraced this racialized identity and intentionally constructed a collective history that focused on their commonalties in terms of the discrimination they encountered domestically and the oppression they faced as colonized subjects from "Third World" nations (Maeda 2011). By masking their cultural, ethnic, historical, linguistic, and ideological variances to outsiders and forming a coalition or community of interest, Asian American activists continue to enlarge their numerical representation in their struggle for scarce resources. Using a strategic essentialism model, advocates often use broad generalizations or summative statements about the state or condition of this population to impact public policies (Spivak 1996). For example, using the latest U.S. Census reports that Asian Americans have surpassed Latinos as the fastest-growing minority group, increasing by over 43 percent in the last decade to more than 17 million, analysts attempt to tactically parlay this demographic growth into political power.

Critics note that the deployment of an imagined homogeneity to garner resources or political clout can reinforce a precarious interchangeability. The model minority label, which stereotypes Asian Americans as hardworking, highly educated, successful, and lacking social problems, has been utilized to deny them public services as well as to exclude them from remedial programs. Activists attempting to counter this myth have continually pushed for the collection of disaggregated data, broken down particularly by ethnic groups, in order to understand the distinct educational, health-care, and socioeconomic needs of each population. For example, Southeast Asian refugee groups tend to have more English-language learners and lower socioeconomic status and educational achievement than other Asian Americans. Internal debates continue about the practicality or political efficacy of mobilizing under a collective rubric when the community is so divergent, with emergent ethnicities—such as Bhutanese, Burmese, Indonesian, Nepalese, and Thai—adding new complexity to the grouping, and there are also divergencies within each subgroup. Some aver that regardless of how individuals or groups identify themselves, if outsiders continually perceive them as interchangeable, then it is beneficial for them to forge multiethnic and multiracial alliances to effectively protect the interest of their collectivity (F. Wu 2003). These contentious debates mirror ongoing discursive and programmatic negotiations within the academy regarding the structure of Asian Americans as a field of study, since it requires articulating the interconnections between and convergences of multiple groupings, disciplines, theories, and methods.

The meaning of the word "community" often minimizes dissimilarities and accentuates cohesiveness, when de facto, communities are fragile and fractured collectivities (Võ and Bonus 2002). Its usage is modified from Raymond Williams's definition in his *Keywords: A Vocabulary of Culture and Society*, in which he states, "What is most important, perhaps, is that unlike all other terms of social organization (state, nation, society, etc.) it [community] seems never to be used unfavourably" (1983, 76). Ideological differences were evident during World War II when Japanese Americans were divided on how to respond to their forced relocation from the West Coast and incarceration as well as whether they should agree to serve in the U.S. military after their imprisonment. Those who served were praised for displaying Japanese American patriotism, while those who refused to enlist in U.S. military service were denounced as disloyal and shunned by co-ethnics. In retrospect, those who challenged the incarceration orders and rejected enlistment are applauded for standing up for their civil rights and upholding the tenets of American democratic ideals. Allegiances to a racialized grouping were enforced during the turbulent 1960s and 1970s when Asian American activists were asked to choose their political allegiances along binaries, such as women being encouraged to join their Asian American brothers to fight racial discrimination over aligning with their feminist sisters in the struggle against gender oppression (Maeda 2009). Some ethnics prefer to hide their social problems, such as domestic violence, arguing that publicizing them disrupts community harmony and reinforces negative perceptions of the community among outsiders (Abraham 2000). Additionally, scholars have examined urban struggles that have strained interethnic relations and impacted solidarities or antagonisms with other racialized communities (Abelman and Lie 1997; S. Kurashige 2008).

As the population became more diverse, disagreements over inclusion in this assemblage or "community" became more pronounced, and scholars increasingly focused on affective ties or feelings of belonging and the elasticity of boundaries. For example, studies have examined how Asian Americans who are gay, lesbian, bisexual, queer, and transgender have subverted and countered their marginalization and created alternative, politicized spaces (Manalansan 2003). Other studies have critiqued the monoracial constructions of Asian America, delineating the saliency of interracial sexual contact and relations in Asia as well as in America and the existence of multiracial or mixed-race children, which necessitates shifting the definitions of

community (Williams-León and Nakashima 2001). As generations move away from ethnic neighborhoods, do not maintain traditional cultural practices, and cannot speak the heritage language, vexing questions arise about their authenticity as ethnics as well as their membership in the collectivity (Portes and Rumbaut 2001). The assumption is that ethnic identity will disappear if individuals intermarry or are socioeconomically incorporated. However, this ethnic-option or dissipation model is more applicable to white immigrants who can blend more easily into the mainstream; it is not so facile for individuals who are racialized.

During the late 1960 and early 1970s, urban renewal projects were initiated to redevelop areas that were designated as blighted, which often included ethnic concentrations in inner cities. These targeted areas of gentrification became contested terrain between residents, public and private investors, urban planners, and civic and political leaders. Since the 1970s, there have been concerted efforts to preserve and reinvent areas identified as historic Chinatown, Japantown/Little Tokyo, and Filipinotown/Manilatown (Laguerre 2000; Mabalon 2013). In other cases, contemporary immigrants and refugees have rejuvenated established neighborhoods, but they also have created new distinctive areas, such as Cambodia Town, Koreatown, Thai Town, Little Bangladesh, Little India, Little Saigon, and Little Taipei (Khandelwal 2002; A. Chung 2007; Aguilar-San Juan 2009; Vergara 2009). These efforts at place making attempt to designate an ethnic space by preserving landmark buildings, establishing festivals or other cultural events, and reviving the space with ethnic residents and businesses (Habal 2007; J. Lin 2011). However, there are controversies over appropriation and representation in demarcating and claiming geographic spaces.

Efforts to revitalize ethnic concentrations reflect the debates over what constitutes a community and whom it should benefit (Võ 2004). While some ethnic concentrations cater almost exclusively to co-ethnics, others focus on finding a balance between serving residents and nonresidents, as well as marketing themselves to tourists. A designation as a tourist site brings voyeuristic elements and involves catering to customers seeking exotic eateries and curio shops, making ethnic residents uncomfortable. Ethnic entrepreneurs maintain that tourism supports small business owners and creates employment opportunities for new immigrants or refugees, which infuses more revenue into the local economy. With empty storefronts, some ethnic areas adapt by attracting Asians from various ethnicities and non-Asians who open up music venues, art galleries, and specialty shops, catering to a bohemian crowd seeking entertainment in alternative spaces. Other ethnic areas have been abandoned by the younger generation and it is the ethnic elders that remain, so the fundamental question arises as to the necessity of preserving these areas and the value of refabricating them into commercially driven, "Orientalized" attractions merely for the tourism trade.

The suburbanization process has led to the abandonment of ethnic concentrations in the urban core and to the establishment of ethnic neighborhoods and commercial centers in the suburbs, redefining perceptions of ethnic communities. In recent decades, socioeconomically mobile Asian Americans and affluent immigrants began relocating to once predominantly wealthier, white suburbs, which were established in the post–World War II years. Earlier theories of cultural assimilation applied to European immigrants are not applicable, since these Asian suburbanites began recreating ethnic communities with clusters of ethnic businesses and institutions. Some engaged in dramatic reconfigurations of the suburban landscape by remodeling mini-malls or building shopping centers, erecting religious centers, and revamping once bland spaces into destinations for co-ethnics. This commodification has lead to more expansive notions of ethnic communities and the creation of new terms such as "satellite communities" and "ethnoburbs" to describe these ethnic spaces (W. Li 2009). As immigrant populations expand their commercial or residential presence, even in areas that they regenerate, these newcomers often face accusations that they are displacing or encroaching on established neighborhoods and attracting excessive numbers of "foreigners," which has fueled antigrowth movements and English-only campaigns (Saito 1998). In the post-9/11 era, with the War on Terror campaign, religious and racial intolerance in the U.S. has led to protests against the building of Muslim mosques and Sikh gurdwaras or temples, which are intended to prevent the establishment of South Asian communities.

The circulation of transnational capital and people is transforming once racially segregated spaces and reimagining them as alluring, international spaces (J. Lin 1998). Local ethnic leaders as well as city planners and politicians are turning to foreign financiers, real estate developers, and corporations to invest in urban residential, commercial, and entertainment projects. Historically, as a result of restrictive immigration policies, immigrants from Asia maintained homeland connections and split-family households. The majority of Asians in America are first-generation immigrants and refugees, some of whom continue to maintain close contacts and networks with co-ethnics in their homeland and throughout the diaspora, and local leaders want to capitalize on their potentially lucrative overseas connections. Asian American community networks are envisioned as key assets for economic recovery and urban modernization, but this is tempered by U.S. fears of increasing economic dominance by China and other Asian nations.

The tensions between capitalism and community are manifested in ethnic localities. In the postindustrial city, international financial investments can be disruptive, bankrupting small ethnic businesses that cannot compete with transnational corporate enterprises and displacing low-income ethnic residents who are unable to afford rising housing costs. In addition, these spaces are conceived of as having fluid and flexible borders that allow for "postcolonial transnational subjects" with dual citizenship to freely navigate between the domestic and international spheres (Ong 1999). However, in contrast to the cosmopolitan jetsetters, who are binational or multinational entrepreneurial and professional elites opting to venture abroad to enrich their opportunities, are transmigrant laborers forced to leave their homelands under conditions of poverty to find employment in the service sector or industrial production and send their modest remittances to support relatives who remain behind. These socioeconomic contrasts speak to the heterogeneity of the community and are evident when Asian owners of garment factories, supermarkets, restaurants, hotels, and other businesses in ethnic districts clash with the local workforce, which is often comprised of Asian and Latino immigrants, over unfair wages or exploitative labor practices. Although it fosters global interconnections, capitalism with its inherent competition-and-profit model produces fragmentation and polarization within communities. This process has led community scholars to reconsider what compelling factors continue to bond seemingly disparate groups.

In the contemporary period, innovations in communication and travel affect time-space compression and facilitate transformative kinds of social networks and affinity groups (D. Harvey 1989), stretching the boundaries of nonspatial or deterritorialized communities (Y. Espiritu 2003; Valverde 2012). Technological advances provide opportunities for immigrants to maintain familial and social ties to their homeland as well as facilitate their transnational business ventures and cultural exchanges. Scholars are examining the ways communication devices such as cell phones and various forms of social media, such as Skype, Facebook, YouTube, Twitter, and blogs, create new virtual communities (Davé, Nishime, and Oren 2005; Nakamura 2008). For example, YouTube has allowed Asian American artists who have been bypassed by traditional and even alternative marketing venues to create virtual fan bases, domestically and internationally (Schlund-Vials 2012b). These interactive platforms facilitate the sharing of gossip, information, and news, enabling Asians and Asians Americans to forge instantaneous relations and connections that were once unimaginable. The Internet has been instrumental in mobilizing geographically dispersed Asians around political interests and social justice causes. Future modernizations will alter the economic, cultural, and political linkages between individuals, groups, and institutions, which will have profound effects on conceptualizations of community.

9

Coolie

Kornel Chang

The etymology of the word "coolie" was for a long time thought to have Tamil—*kuli* (wages)—Urdu—*quli* (hireling)—or Chinese—*kuli* (bitter strength)—origins (Tinker 1974; Tsai 1976; Irick 1982; M. Jung 2006). More recently, Mae Ngai (2015) has traced the word's origins to a European neologism that was first employed by sixteenth-century Portuguese to describe common native workers on the Indian subcontinent. By the mid-nineteenth century, "coolie" came to be applied specifically to indentured laborers from China and India who were being contracted out to colonial plantations in Southeast Asia and the Americas (Hu-DeHart 1992; W. Lai 1993; Yun 2008). This shift in meaning was inextricably bound up with the abolition of slavery and deepening Euro-American imperial incursions into the Asia-Pacific world. Intensifying Euro-American encroachments in the region generated widening imperial networks through which people from China and South Asia were forcibly transported across the Atlantic to constitute a new colonial labor force in the Americas. As Lisa Lowe has noted, the introduction of the coolie trade in the nineteenth century "marked a significant . . . shift in the management of race and labor in the colonies" (2005, 193).

In the United States, charges of coolieism mainly fixated on Chinese laborers who were being imported to the Americas to take the place of formerly enslaved Africans. The coolie entered the American mainstream vernacular by way of political debates over free and slave labor in the mid-nineteenth century (M. Jung 2006). Prior to emancipation, pro- and antislavery ideologues both considered the Chinese coolie a coerced and degraded figure, but they mobilized this knowledge to advocate diametrically opposed positions on the slavery question, with southern slaveholders citing the evils of the Chinese coolie system to uphold the moral superiority of slavery while abolitionists conflated the Chinese "coolie" with slavery. This consensus around what and who constituted a "coolie" produced a national agreement—the 1862 act to prohibit the coolie trade—that suppressed the importation of Chinese coolie labor. Carrying the law's premise to its logical conclusion, white labor restrictionists on the West Coast pushed for Chinese exclusion a decade and a half later, insisting that all Chinese, as living embodiments of the coolie, should be excluded (Saxton 1971; Chang 2012).

Advocates for Chinese immigration challenged the reasoning that made the Chinese synonymous with servitude. In his 1889 essay "The Chinese Must Stay," Chinese American intellectual and activist Yan Phou Lee declared the Chinese in the United States definitively "not coolies." Emphasizing their volition and agency, he insisted Chinese migrants "all came voluntarily . . . and their purpose in leaving their homes and friends was to get honest work" (476). In taking this line of argument, Lee sought to counter the dominant image of the Chinese as slavish laborers who worked and lived cheaply, which justified their exclusion from the body politic. But if the Chinese were not coolies, the question of what or who was a coolie remained unanswered in Lee's spirited defense, thus leaving the terms of the debate intact.

Early scholarly writings on Chinese immigration reproduced this binary framing of the "coolie" question. The publication of Gunther Barth's *Bitter Strength* reignited the debate about whether or not Chinese immigrants in the United States were in fact "coolies" (Barth

1964). Operating from sociologist Robert Park's concept of the race relations cycle, Barth concluded that Chinese immigrants experienced greater difficulty integrating into American society because they had migrated to the United States under coercion, and thus, unlike Europeans, did not possess a self that was capable of being free. This condition of servitude, along with their perpetual sojourning, accounted for their marginalization and exclusion from mainstream (white) American society.

By the 1980s, scholars, especially in the emerging field of Asian American studies, contested Barth's characterization of the Chinese and his implication that they were responsible (at least in part) for their isolation and alienation. They identified both structural and popular forms of white racism that segregated Chinese immigrants into ethnic ghettos, relegated them to the bottom of a racially stratified labor market, and excluded them socially and culturally from white American society. Like earlier advocates of the Chinese, these scholars also challenged Barth's thesis by insisting that Chinese migrants were not coolies. In attempting to establish the voluntary nature of Chinese immigration to the United States, they drew a sharp distinction between labor systems in North America and those in Latin America and the Caribbean. On colonial plantations in Cuba and Peru, they argued, the Chinese were formally indentured laborers and thus endured slavelike conditions; in the industrial wage-system of the United States and Canada, on the other hand, the Chinese may have been lowly workers but they were "free" immigrant laborers. In this way, scholars in U.S. immigration history and Asian American studies debated the issue almost exactly along the same lines as their historical actors.

Critiquing the terms of the debate, Moon-Ho Jung, in *Coolies and Cane*, forcefully asserted: "No one, in the United States or the Caribbean, was really a coolie, but Asian workers were surely racialized as coolies across the world, including the United States" (2006, 6). By maintaining that the Chinese in the United States were immigrants, and not coolies, Asian American scholars, Jung argued, unwittingly reified coolies and reproduced U.S. exceptionalism by giving credence to the myth of an immigrant nation. Contrasting labor relations in the United States to the coolie system in the Caribbean and Latin America gave the illusion that the management of the North American capitalist economy was enlightened and its system of wage labor was based on voluntary exchange, free from coercion.

To get beyond the stalled and stale debate on whether or not Chinese were coolies in the United States, Moon-Ho Jung, Lisa Lowe, and Mae Ngai have attended to the varied and contradictory work an imagined "coolie" performed in service to nation and empire, showing how it was generative of universalist liberal thought, from the "rights of man" to ideas of free labor, trade, and mobility. From their perspective, the "coolie" was not so much a person or thing as an ideational construct that simultaneously expressed and projected Euro-American imperial visions, myths, and fantasies. This was not to deny that many Chinese (and other Asian) laborers were exploited for their labor and held in conditions of bondage, but so were other groups who yet were never identified as coolies. Recognizing the term as more of a "product of the imaginers rather than the imagined," as Jung exhorts (2006, 6), allows us see the "coolie" as an artifice of nation and empire that helped to produce American exceptionalism and sanitize U.S. imperial ventures in the Americas and across the Pacific as "humanitarian" projects.

10

Cosmopolitanism

Lucy Mae San Pablo Burns

From its inception, Asian American studies has struggled with its ability to attend to, describe, and theorize experiences and ideas that exceed single-nation identification, fixed territorial boundaries, and conditions produced by globalization. Various terms such as "internationalism," "transnationalism," "diaspora," "exile," "flexible citizens," and "extra-nationals" have been mobilized in the field to indicate an Asian American imaginary, identification, and everyday practice that signal more than just Asia and America, more than just Asia, more than just America. This list of terms suggests an embodied and discursive mobility that refuses to settle along distinct and firm borders, particularly national ones. "Cosmopolitanism" belongs to this list of terms.

Cosmopolitanism as an idea, a political philosophy, an identity, and a practice is often attributed in Western political and philosophical discourse to the Greek Stoics and later Immanuel Kant. Its meaning has been equated with world citizenship and world belonging, and with universalism. In this sense, the term always already summons a relationship to the nation, boundaries, vernacularism, and localism, notions against which cosmopolitanism is often defined. The word is mobilized against the constrictions of national boundary, national citizenship, and nationalism. Citizenship construction is imagined through the nation-state—thus to be a citizen entails loyalty and duty to the nation-state, and the nation-state is the primary protector of citizenship.

What, then, does it mean to have world citizenship, to be a citizen of the world?

Frequently, invocations of cosmopolitanism are ahistorical, and it becomes a free-floating word used to advocate benevolent pro-world citizenship, a word with which to rally around a post- or even anti-national identity. To challenge the dominant reference of the term beyond its Greek and Western roots, scholars such as Vinay Dharwadker (2001) and Rajini Srikanth (2004) trace Buddhist and Hindus worldviews, arguing that such religions are inherently cosmopolitan. Walter Mignolo (2000) further complicates these approaches as he staunchly situates the emergence of cosmopolitanism within the project of the twinned formation of modernity and colonialism. Pheah Cheng (1998), in his introduction to the collection *Cosmopolitics*, grounds the often-invoked genealogy of Greek cosmopolitanism and its development by Immanuel Kant (in relation to his idea of "perpetual peace" among nations) within the history of the politics that produced the condition of its emergence as a political thought and practice.

Cosmopolitanism, as it appears in Asian American studies scholarship, variously (and in some vaguely) invokes citizenship as linked and formed through the nation-state. In this sense, Asian American theorizations of cosmopolitanism reformulate citizenship and belonging, attending to the experiences and imaginations of migrants of every status, including dual citizens, refugees, and transnational laborers of all classes. Cosmopolitanism in the writings of literary scholars Rajini Srikanth and Viet Nguyen (2009) takes on an aspirational quality. By aspirational, I mean to suggest that Srikanth and Nguyen theorize cosmopolitanism as a quality and an identity to strive toward; that is, cosmopolitanism is desirable, something to want, something to become. Cosmopolitanism gains some traction in the works of these literary scholars as they attach it to the possibilities and the labor of literature in the making of a sympathetic and empathetic subject, qualities needed, they argue, to make a subject that cares beyond oneself (the self as racialized, gendered, national, and so on). Srikanth's focus on South Asian American writers emphasizes acknowledging difference and "hard work" to arrive at cosmopolitanism (2004, 23). Nguyen, in discussing the Vietnam War and American literature, echoes Srikanth as he theorizes cosmopolitanism as an endeavor to "imagine peace and cope with war's enduring aftermath" (2009, 151).

Some concerns, however, do remain: Does cosmopolitanism have anything to say about Asian American racialization? Conversely, in what ways does Asian American racialization prompt a rethinking of cosmopolitanism? Playwright Velina Hasu Houston's (2002) and scholar Una Chaudhuri's (2001) discussion of theater, racism, and racial formation provide insights to these questions. Houston sets up her cosmopolitan point of view against U.S. monoracialism, ethnocentricity, and racism as she experiences them in theater practice. Making a distinction between her political identity and her identity as an artist, Houston claims theater as a site for cosmopolitanism where she can travel imaginatively, inhabiting various cultures and other identity categories. Houston charges both American mainstream institutions and ethnic-specific theaters with limited vision based on "tribalism and neat categories." She claims to have intimate exposure to diversity because she is a multiracial, multinational artist. Chaudhuri, too, theorizes theater as an observation ground for "the new dynamics of identity-formation, . . . of the ambivalences of the new cosmopolitanisms." Cosmopolitanism, in Chaudhuri's essay, challenges binaries such

as East/West, center/margins, global/local, as well as text/performance and page/stage (2001, 173). Theater, Chaudhuri argues, is not just a place for "accurate and responsible representations of ethnic diversity"; it is equally a site of intervention for discourses on race and ethnicity (2001, 174).

Rather than approach cosmopolitanism as something to aspire to, the collection *New Cosmopolitanisms: South Asians in the U.S.*, edited by Gita Rajan and Shailja Sharma (2006), expands the term to "new cosmopolitanism," which is configured at the "intersections of travel, technology, and labor." Rajan and Sharma render differently what has become a dominant image of a cosmopolite—highly educated, techno-driven, upper-management class—to include figures such as nannies from the Philippines or Sri Lanka who care for the children of rich Arab families or aging Israelis. They address the limits of the word's class bias, offering the phrase "new cosmopolitanism" as a means to consider a "fluid subject position," one that moves laterally and horizontally across national and class lines. This collection theorizes South Asian diasporic cosmopolitanism through ethnography, literary analysis, psychology, and a range of subjects including eating disorders in the context of globalization, Bollywood cinema, religions, and museum displays.

"Cosmopolitanism" is a word that has certainly appeared in Asian American studies scholarship, though its significance in the field is not nearly that of such terms as "transnationalism" or "diaspora." Academic majors, programs, and departments are in the process of redefining Asian American studies as a transnational project, changing names from "Asian American Studies" to "Asian American and Asian Diaspora Studies." In 2010, UC Berkeley announced that its department would be renamed Asian American Studies and Asian Diaspora Studies, underscoring the field's long-standing themes that "have become increasingly visible in recent decades as a result of forces of globalization" (Elaine Kim 2010). In 2012, *The Journal of Transnational American Studies* released a special issue titled "Redefining the American in Asian American Studies: Transnationalism, Diaspora and Representation." No sustained and passionate calls have inspired a "cosmopolitanism turn" in Asian American scholarship, activist, and artistic projects.

11

Culture
Robert G. Lee

Asian American studies began as the intellectual expression of a political and social movement mobilized to answer questions long suppressed, suspended, or foreclosed in a national imaginary shaped by race and empire. The twin tasks of Asian American studies with regard to culture have been to critique the changing cultural formation of empire and to recuperate critical agency for Asian American cultural production. This essay argues that such a critical approach to culture depends on the recognition of the connection between local cultures and the global historical terrain on which they are produced. This is not to claim that the conditions of material life determine each instance of cultural production but rather to simply acknowledge Karl Marx's caution that "men make their own history but they do not make it as just as they please" (1951, 103).

"Culture" is a shape-shifting word that can signify the whole range of human activity in general, the particular way of life of a group of people, the expression of intellectual and aesthetic sensibilities, or the production of goods, tastes, and meaning itself (Eagleton 2000). For an Asian American studies committed to a recuperation of history and agency, culture must be understood as both the expressive production of everyday life and the central site of struggle over the meaning of social identities (Hall 1980; Robert Lee 1999). The Asian American cultural imaginary becomes a terrain on which to interrogate and critique discourses of social practice and politics that construct systems of dominance (L. Lowe 1996).

Since the nineteenth century one common definition of culture has been "the particular way of life of a people living together in a particular place" (Williams 1958, 234). However the very term "Asian America," coined in resistance to imposed Oriental descriptors, gestures toward the hybridity, heterogeneity, and multiplicity that mark continuous circuits of movement and disrupt reassuring narratives of a grounded national culture (L. Lowe 1996). The effort to mark the Oriental as a singular identity of difference continues to operate powerfully within the nation's taxonomy of race. This ideological construction obscures the vast range of historically specific Asian American trajectories and subjectivities (Y. Espiritu 1992).

Asian America is a social formation produced in the confluence of colonialisms, racialized national formations, and local resistances (Bonacich and Cheng 1984). The cultural heterogeneities and hybridities that characterize Asian America are produced across shifting economic, political, and social geographies that have crosscut on global, national, and local scales for four centuries. On the global scale, the circuits of goods, money, and people across and around the Pacific long predate the presence of a sizable population of Asian people in North America (A. Frank 1998; C. Frank 2011; Tchen 2001). Setting aside for the moment that "Asia" and "Asians" are themselves cultural geographic terms with contested histories, it should be recalled that over the past two centuries Asians have arrived in North America from many places other than Asia itself—Vietnamese from Germany, Chinese from Peru, Japanese from Brazil, Koreans from Mexico, and Indians from Uganda are only a few of the most recent associations that add to the heterogeneities and heteroglossias of the many communities gathered under the sign of Asian America. In these spaces of transit as well as in Asia itself, "the Asian" has been imbricated in both empire- and nation-building projects in varying roles as agent, victim, and participant-observer, adding to the deep complications of the ethnic identities and solidarities that are produced in the United States. What kind of Asian American politics might be shared between anticommunist Vietnamese shopkeepers and Bangladeshi labor activists? Do Spanish-speaking Koreans arriving from Mexico or Honduras become Asian American or Latino in the racial landscapes of New York or Los Angeles (Ropp 2000)?

Early attempts to situate Asian American history and culture as an epiphenomenon of proletarianization or to locate an Asian American authenticity in an uncontaminated self collapsed in the face of this demographic diversity (Chin et al. 1974; Chan et al. 1991; Bonacich and Cheng 1984). Neither model could long contain the class contradictions and different lived experiences between for example, the offspring of Sansei-White families who attend Brown University and mobilize as Hapas and Cambodian-Black families who live in inner-city Providence and call themselves Blasians.

Powerful new migration flows, new ethnicities, and class formations have reshaped the Asian American urban landscape with both middle-class ethno-burbs and new ghettos, a result of the penetration of capitalism, the dismantling of socialist and social welfare systems, and the imposition of the neoliberal regimes of accumulation throughout Asia (Ong, Bonacich, and Chang 1994; W. Li 2009; Paul Kwong 1991). The regime of racial exclusion based on the doctrine of indelible cultural difference has been replaced by new, more refined Orientalist discourses and new systems of control and domination. The bio-political power of the state to manage difference is daily enforced through the police, welfare agency, hospital, school, church, and home. These new geographies of power have become the terrain for new modes of resistance and solidarities for Asian garment workers, South Asian feminists, Filipino/a queers, Cambodian refugee families, and Muslim teenagers, among a host of others (M. Louie 2001; Das Gupta 2006; Manalansan 2003; Ong 2003; Maira 2009). The search for an Asian American cultural authenticity must now attend to the quotidian mobilizations around the intersections of immigration, labor, gender, and sexuality. It is on these historically specific terrains that multiple and sometimes contradictory imaginaries are produced and articulate new Asian American identities, critiques, and resistances. While such identities may be newly expressed, they are not without their own histories. A critical Asian Americanist approach to culture must therefore read across the whole history of transpacific colonial and racial formations to account for the different and intersecting trajectories that condition local struggles over meaning (Palumbo-Liu 1999). Such an approach necessarily challenges what Vijay Prashad (2002) has called the "myth of cultural purity" to find authenticity in the actual struggles through which local identities are transformed in relation to each other and enables a self-reflexive Asian American studies that can critique not only European, American, and Asian colonialisms but can equally and comfortably interrogate Asian American sub-colonialisms as well (Azuma 2005; Fujikane and Okamura 2008).

The twenty-first-century transpacific is the new globalized terrain of cultural production, markets, and cultural forms radically restructured by the triumph and hypermobility of financial capital, the rapid growth of Asian capitalisms, and the emergence of a transpacific mass culture. In the neoliberal world market, Asian Americans are everywhere along the globalized chain of production and consumption of culture (Ong, Bonacich, and Chang 1994; Ong 1999).

In the current stage of globalization, unfettered capitalisms generate new neocolonial projects that have intensified radical inequalities both between and within nations. These worldwide flows of capital, technology, and people have challenged the autonomy of national sovereignty, territory, and identity. Mediating between the global and the local, Asian Americans are transnationals in a moment when, in response to globalization, national identity has rebounded as a privileged axis of identification. The Taiwan-born businessmen who commutes from his home in Silicon Valley to factories scattered across the Pearl River delta, the Cambodian OG threatened with forced "return" to a country he has never seen, and the Filipina mothers whose own children grow up in the Philippines while they care for the children of the wealthy in San Francisco, Hong Kong, or Dubai have radically different access to power, but each occupies a liminal and precarious position in the cultural landscape shaped by national identity and structured around citizenship (Ong 1999; Ong 2003; Parreñas 2008). The perennial questions asked of all are, "where are you from, how long are you going to stay, when are you going back?"

The current reassertion of borders and the rise of nationalisms in response to globalization reminds us that contemporary Asian American cultural productions, however distant in time and space from the age of exclusion, cannot be adequately addressed without accounting for the long shadows of empire and race. The popular and legal discourses of the excludable Oriental may no longer be hegemonic, but it is important nonetheless to remember that American national identity has historically been constituted against the contradictory narratives of Asian material productivity and moral poverty (Tchen 2001; Robert Lee 1999). In the American imaginary, *Asia* has been identified as the exceptional cultural space of wealth and power, the *idée fixe* of imperial desire, while *Asians* have been imagined as morally disordered, invasive, and Oriental aliens.

This historically specific imaginary can no longer be directly mapped onto Asian America under the current conditions of globalism, but under the twin signs of the global War on Terror and the global financial crisis new representations of the Oriental alien, as tiger mother or Islamic terrorist, continue to do the ideological work of policing crisis (Chua 2011; Puar 2007). This underscores the continuing need to map the cultural discourses of domination as the terrain on which the politics of Asian American accommodation, imagining, and cultural resistances are fought.

Twenty years ago, lamenting the receding of the Asian American movement some asked where all the Asian American activists had gone. The simple and correct answer was "everywhere" (Aguilar-San Juan 1994b; Liu, Geron, and Lai 2008). Today we can witness Asian American critiques in the most mundane to the most esoteric, in the most ubiquitous to the most unexpected spaces in American culture. In New York, Chinese Americans participate in a Puerto Rican–led multiracial coalition against the toxic pollution of their neighborhoods (Sze 2007). In New Jersey, South Asian women organize against domestic violence (Das Gupta 2006). Over the internet, in magazines, and on TV, "outlaw" Asian American celebrity chefs self-consciously challenge the accepted canons of authenticity and stereotyped masculinity (Huang 2013; Ying 2012). An accounting of these diversities and their global and local trajectories necessarily refuses an easy triumphalism with regard to the "model minority" and opens Asian American culture as a space for the interrogation and critique of the political economy of everyday transnational social practice.

12

Deportation
Bill Ong Hing

According to the *Oxford English Dictionary*, "deportation" (noun) refers to "the action of carrying away; forcible removal, *esp.* into exile; transportation." Connotative of an involuntary relocation and exilic subjectivity, "deportation" as a state policy and legislative practice is by no means limited to Asian immigrants. The very condition of deportation—wherein individuals are, due to shifting politics, contested demographics, and changing cultural dynamics, compulsorily moved out of country—is at the forefront of the expulsion of Spanish Jews in 1492; it is apparent in the forced removal of Native peoples during the seventeenth, eighteenth, and nineteenth centuries per a larger U.S. imperial project. Deportation in the frame of twentieth-century human rights violations is at once manifest in the mandated relocation of European Jews to segregated ghettos and concentration camps during World War II; one could also extend this frame to encompass the contemporaneous evacuation, incarceration, and internment of Japanese Americans. Last, but certainly not least, the post-9/11 deportation of multiple populations (particularly from Muslim and Arab lands, Southeast Asia, and Latin America) underscores the term's present-day resonance.

Set within a U.S. context, deportation—as state practice—coincides with the "discovery" of America by Columbus in 1492; as Native American history underscores, it is a policy that likewise corresponds to the expansion of the United States from colony to colonizing entity. With regard to Asian American history, the wartime experiences of Japanese Americans were necessarily haunted by the threat of deportation under the guise of national security. For Asian American studies then, deportation becomes a primary analytic through which to consider and map coherences between and among diverse groups. Notwithstanding the presence of Asian immigrants prior to the *en masse* arrival of Chinese migrants in the mid-nineteenth century, the issue of deportation as integral to the Asian American experience is arguably first evident in the prohibitions embedded in the 1882 Chinese Exclusion Act, under which Chinese laborers were barred from entering for ten years; anyone apprehended in violation of the law was subject to removal. As is well documented, leaders of the anti-Chinese movement succeeded, over the next dozen years, in promoting a series of treaties and new laws that led to an indefinite ban on Chinese labor immigration in 1904 (S. Chan 1994; Shah 2001). Most notable among them for their increasingly clever techniques and rationales for control and deportation were the Scott Act of 1888 and the Geary Act of 1892. According to the former, Chinese laborers who left the United States could not return; with regard to the latter, Chinese laborers were required to register with immigration officials—those who failed to do so within a year were deportable. Chinese were denied bail and, prior to deportation, any Chinese person not lawfully entitled to be in the United States was imprisoned at hard labor for up to a year.

As many scholars have noted, these prohibitions and limitations—which rendered immigrants deportable—were applied to subsequent Asian subjects, inclusive of those migrating from Japan, Korea, India, and the Philippines. Significantly, Asians did not dutifully accede to the systematic efforts to control their presence in the United States; as a result some were undocumented. Resistance to restrictions was common among immigrants from Japan and India. For instance, many Japanese evaded Japanese regulations on emigration, which were precursors to the Gentlemen's Agreement of 1907, by traveling to Hawai'i and then on to the mainland. As early as 1900, labor brokers in Japan claimed that they procured the entry of as many as four thousand laborers by falsifying passports and other public documents. While the Asian Indian population was declining between 1920 and 1940, an estimated three thousand Sikhs and Hindus crossed the Mexican border to work as farm laborers. At the same time, many Sikhs from Punjab and Muslims from Bengal working as crewmen jumped ship on the Eastern seaboard, although most were apprehended and deported.

Because of their relatively larger numbers, longer stays in the United States, and the hardship of family separation and antimiscegenation laws, Chinese were given to undocumented migration more than any other group. Their gambits were many, and a legion entered after the enactment of exclusion laws under false citizenship claims. A Chinese laborer might assert, for example, that he had been born in San Francisco and that his birth certificate had been destroyed in the 1906 earthquake. Then he would claim, after various trips to China, that his wife there had given birth to children (usually sons) who automatically derived citizenship. In fact, the children were often fictitious, and the few immigration slots were given or sold to others in China; those claiming such fabricated genealogies were not surprisingly known as "paper sons." Some who had valid claims of entry would simply sell their identity to another. Since merchants, students, and teachers were exempted from the first exclusion laws, laborers entered with falsified evidence of membership in one of those classes. Thousands of others, including wives, sneaked across the Canadian or Mexican border. In fact, the Border Patrol that today conjures up images of deportation of Mexicans or the incarceration of unaccompanied children from Central America was established in response to unauthorized entries of Chinese. Any estimate of how many Chinese entered through any of these means would be speculative, but the practice was undoubtedly widespread at one time.

Immigration inspectors grew to distrust Chinese Americans. Consequently, besides the Border Patrol, the government used other enforcement tools against alleged offenders, such as inspection at the notorious detention camp on Angel Island in San Francisco Bay; in addition to Chinese immigrants who arrived at the holding center on ship, Japanese, Indians, and Mexicans were also processed there. Between 1910 and 1940, about fifty thousand Chinese were confined—often for months and years at a time—in Angel Island's bleak wooden barracks, where inspectors would conduct grueling interrogations. Those who did not pass scrutiny were deported back to China. Across the country, raids on private homes, restaurants, and other businesses were also favored by authorities. Initiated at the turn of the century, raids were revived in the 1950s to capture and deport supporters of the new Communist regime in mainland China. It should be noted that such detentions and deportations were by no means limited to the West Coast; indeed, the most famous of U.S. immigration centers—Ellis Island—was dramatically transformed from immigration station to deportation holding center after the passage of the 1924 Johnson-Reed Act, which impacted immigrants from Asia, Eastern Europe, and Southern Europe. The expansiveness of such deportation policies makes visible a wide-ranging xenophobia that corresponds to what Matthew Frye Jacobson (1999) maintains represents the realities of racialized difference and the perils of probationary whiteness.

Nevertheless, many Chinese did have something to hide; moreover, because of the intense level of deportation enforcement directed at them, many Chinese Americans lived in constant fear of immigration authorities. Even those with nothing to hide were forced to constantly look over their shoulder. A "confession program" offered by immigration authorities in the late 1950s for those Chinese desirous of clearing up their immigration histories (since names and family trees had been confused by earlier false claims) made matters worse. The program was purportedly a trade-off for the raids during the Red Scare and was promoted in some quarters as an amnesty program. In fact, it offered only a weak assurance that if a confessed Chinese was eligible for an existing statutory remedy, the paperwork would be processed. Some might now be married to a citizen through whom immigration was possible, others who had entered illegally prior to June 28, 1940, could be eligible for a relief termed "registry," and still others could apply for suspension of deportation if extreme hardship and good moral character could be demonstrated. Because they feared immigration authorities, relatively few Chinese went through the confession program. In San Francisco, the principal residence for Chinese Americans at the time, only about ten thousand Chinese came forward. Many of those actually were deported because they were not eligible for any immigration benefit.

Since the mid-twentieth century, deportation enforcement efforts have been manifested in operations that continue to prey heavily on Asian immigrants. For example, in the summer of 1978, immigration inspectors in Honolulu began a systematic interrogation of elderly Asians who were lawful permanent residents of the United States. They were returning from visits abroad that were generally no more than thirty days. The interrogation went beyond the customary questioning as to purpose and length of stay, focusing, rather, on whether the travelers were or had been recipients of supplemental security income (SSI) public assistance benefits. (SSI is a subsistence program for elderly and disabled poor made available to citizens and lawful resident aliens.) If SSI had been previously received, immigration inspectors took possession of the person's alien card and passport and instructed the person to report for further inspection and interrogation in the district of residence, e.g., Los Angeles, San Diego, Seattle, or San Francisco. At the subsequent inspection these elderly Filipinos, Chinese, Koreans, and Japanese were informed that they were excludable from the United States as public charges. They were given three alternatives: go back to their native country, request an exclusion hearing, or terminate SSI benefits and post a public charge bond of several thousand dollars.

The authority for the INS to reimpose the public charge ground for exclusion each and every time an alien reentered the United States stemmed from the "reentry doctrine" concept. However, the reentry doctrine had traditionally been used to exclude returning criminals, subversives, and other undesirables, and had not been used to exclude returning lawful residents who had received public assistance. There was no question that the person had a right to apply for and to receive SSI. There were not allegations of fraud. If the individuals had not proceeded abroad, the standard deportation laws would not be triggered. Under SSI regulations, they were permitted to leave the country for periods up to thirty days without affecting their SSI eligibility, and in many cases they were informed by SSI representatives prior to departure that there was nothing to worry about. However, they unwittingly walked into the trap of the reentry doctrine. The practice was not stopped until the INS changed the exclusion policy after months of lobbying by community activists. By then, dozens of lawful resident Asian residents were barred from returning.

Such policies underscore not only the consistency of anti-Asian exclusion; they also highlight the ongoing racialization of Asian immigrants notwithstanding their status (as permanent residents). This *deportative* reading of Asian American history is even more apparent in the case of Filipino migrants who—due to colonization—were U.S. subjects; even with this status, they were targeted by migration restriction (via the Tydings-McDuffie Act of 1934) and repatriation (in 1935). As immigration rates from the Philippines began to increase significantly in the 1970s, a noticeably distrustful attitude emerged at the INS toward Filipinos as it had historically toward Chinese. Fueled by allegations of visa fraud in Manila, local INS investigators, examiners, and clerical staff developed a demeaning and insensitive attitude toward Filipinos. As a group, natives of the Philippines continue to be distrusted and interrogated more intensively by immigration inspectors at international airports. In visa cases involving marriage, when one party is from the Philippines, both are subjected to exhaustive questioning far beyond the already humiliating examinations conducted in most marriage cases. Often, as a matter of discretion in visa and citizenship cases, further investigation is requested by the U.S. Consulate in Manila, forcing delays. As a general rule, the validity of documents is questioned, and many deportation hearings demand corroborating evidence beyond that required of non-Filipinos. This is most succinctly captured by a federal immigration judge who stated on the record: "By now, everyone dealing with such matters is well aware that aliens from the Philippines will engage in any fraud to get here and will do anything to stay" (quoted in Hing 1993, 113). As a result of this approach and attitude, Filipinos remain the target for deportation when it comes to alleged visa and marriage fraud.

These frames of fraud and criminality circumscribe and influence the current state of deportation affairs vis-à-vis Asian American communities. The deportation of Chinese gang members (mostly back to Hong Kong) has been going on for decades, and eventually (per the tenets of racialized immigration policy) similar focus was placed on Koreans and Filipinos. In 2002, the United States began deporting Cambodian refugees convicted of crimes back to Cambodia, even though many of the deportees could not speak Khmer, were originally refugees, and had entered the United States as infants and toddlers. Some had never before set foot on Cambodian soil, having been born in Thai refugee camps. Similarly, in 2008, the deportation of Vietnamese immigrants and refugees convicted of crimes commenced, at least for those who entered after 1995. As of this writing, thousands of Cambodians and Vietnamese have faced the prospect of deportation.

While these deportations are seemingly fixed to post-9/11 anxieties (particularly with regard to the post-2001 deportations of Southeast Asians and the detention/deportation of South Asians, Arabs, and Muslims), it is important to note that immigration reforms passed in 1996 contained several categories of crimes that place lawful permanent residents and refugees at risk of deportation, including aggravated felonies and crimes involving moral turpitude. Anyone convicted of an aggravated felony can be deported without the opportunity to demonstrate rehabilitation and hardship to relatives. Prior to 1996, an immigration judge could give these individuals a second chance, but that authority was revoked under the auspices of the Illegal Immigration Reform and Immigrant Responsibility Act. As significant, the use of deportation as a means of criminal sentencing accesses past characterizations of Asian Americans and Latinos as "perpetual foreigners" who threaten the nation as purveyors of vice, disorder, and lawlessness.

As most would expect, aggravated felonies include murder, rape, other crimes of violence, drug trafficking, and money laundering. However, some minor crimes such as selling $10 worth of marijuana or "smuggling" one's little sister across the border also are aggravated felonies. And being convicted of a misdemeanor as opposed to a felony does not automatically preclude aggravated-felon status. For example, several offenses are classified as aggravated felonies once a one-year sentence is imposed. These include theft, burglary, perjury, and obstruction of justice, even though the criminal court may classify such a crime as a misdemeanor.

The causes of criminality in refugee communities are well documented. Refugees' experiences at the camps prior to their entering the United States are challenging. Many parents who survive the trauma of fleeing persecution are in shock and continue to suffer from post-traumatic stress disorder. The rates at which different family members adapt may be poles apart, straining relationships and producing discord. The new environment into which refugees to the United States are thrust could not be more different than those from where they came; gender roles, relationship with elders, and culture are upended. As refugees, many newcomers are poor, which affects, among other things, quality of life, residential neighborhood, and access to good schools. Often the camaraderie of gangs offers a surrogate family for refugee youngsters. They search for acceptance and often find a sense of common understanding with their peers who are experiencing similar feelings of ostracism from the mainstream and adults. Many also join gangs for protection. As a youngster gets picked on, he welcomes the help that others similarly situated can offer. Unfortunately, their activities often become criminal, resulting in deportable convictions. As a result, they fall squarely into enforcement priorities that rank criminal aliens at the top of the list.

In the face of local dynamics, within the context of national politics, and set against a larger global imaginary marked by "War on Terror" anxieties, deportation remains a significant term through which to map not only a racialized history of exclusion and expulsion; it also affords the possibility—as antideportation activists make clear—of cross-ethnic, cross-racial solidarity and resistance (Reddy 2011; Cacho 2012; Kwon 2013). Expressly, Unidad Latina en Accion, an organization focused on workers' and immigration rights, has consistently appealed to the Barack Obama administration to halt further deportations; analogously, the West Coast–based Asian Pacific Islander Youth Promoting Advocacy and Leadership (AYPAL) has staged protests to raise awareness about and engender action against deportation. Such potential coalitions, predicated on the dismantling of the systemic oppression faced by immigrants of color, correspond in many ways to the early history of Asian American studies and ethnic studies, which were formed in solidarity with Third World liberation movements (abroad) and civil rights movements (at home).

13

Diaspora
Evelyn Hu-DeHart

"Diaspora" is now a word in the popular domain, but its popularization presents challenges to the field of diaspora studies, namely how to regain some control over its meaning and parameters before it is totally reduced to a simple and simplistic essentialism denoting any kind of human mobility and scattering, or any kind of sentimental yearning by upper-class exiles. World history has been replete with diasporas, starting with the ancient Greeks who gave us the word "diaspora" (to sow or scatter) with their practice of intentionally planting colonies in other lands for cultural propagation and to advance trade. New ones continuously arise from different corners of the world, or emerge reshaped from the bowels of existing diasporas. From the ancient to the modern world, diaspora has been most frequently associated with the traumatic forced expulsion of Jews from their ancestral homeland of Israel and subsequent worldwide dissemination over the course of centuries (Safran 1991). In the modern world, accompanying the rise of capitalism and its corollary, the colonial reach of Europe to Asia, Africa, and Latin America for markets and raw materials, is the great and terrible African diaspora, created by the traumatic forced removal of tens of millions of men and women of many ethnic groups out of Africa over four centuries, to be dispersed throughout the Americas as chattel slaves. Unified initially by the dehumanizing regime of slavery and later reinforced by the demeaning regime of racism, descendants of slaves identify with each other through race, as "black people," and have created multiple, dynamic expressions and meanings of blackness through culture—music, dance, art, literature—throughout the diaspora.

Next to the African and almost contemporaneously, another great modern diaspora evolved from China, beginning in the mid-sixteenth century of the late Ming. In mapping this diaspora, we see that it shares some of the central characteristics of other large diasporas, but also differs in notable ways. If not among the oldest, it is certainly one of the longest, most persistent, and ongoing mass migrations from one central location, today represented by the estimated twenty-five to fifty million peoples of Chinese descent living outside China. They and their ancestors cannot be said to have been traumatically expelled from China *en masse*, although severe hardships, violent conflicts, and natural disasters played their role in impelling so many to leave home and seek new livelihoods far away in alien lands. To be sure, when out-migration greatly accelerated around the mid-nineteenth century, the Opium Wars, the Taiping Rebellion, and other local and regional peasant uprisings acted as push factors that induced many to leave China. Many more were forced to leave by floods, famines, and the oft-cited demographic growth and subsequent pressure on arable land; still others not necessarily in dire straits left China in search of trade and business opportunities. Their reasons for leaving home were not materially different from those of the Irish, the Lebanese, the Japanese, the Italians, and South Asians of many different ethnicities and religions (R. Cohen 1997).

Following China, Asia has spawned many other diasporas: Japanese, Indian, and South Asian, Hindu, Sikh, Tamil, Muslim, Vietnamese, Filipino, and Southeast Asian, most recently Korean, the proliferation occurring from the late nineteenth, throughout the twentieth, and into the present moment of the twenty-first century. During this tumultuous period, revolutions giving way to civil wars, world wars, anticolonial armed struggles and guerrilla movements ("wars of national liberation"), old empires falling, and new imperial regimes rising have complicated out-migration from homelands, which has manifested in new forms, such as exile, banishment, expulsion, expatriation, and, notably, refugee flows and asylum seeking. In other words, with many and varied reasons for leaving home and staying away for long periods eventually extending into generations, these global migrations have given rise to a "range of phenomenon" that can be said to constitute diasporas (Clifford 1997).

Diasporas are most often defined in terms of race (black), ethnicity (Jewish, Chinese, Lebanese, Vietnamese), nation (Japanese, Indian, Cuban, Mexican), and also religion (Hindu, Muslim, Tibetan Buddhist), region (South Asian, Caribbean), and other categories. Incorporating all these mass human migrations and resettlements over space and time under the expanding rubric of diaspora has given rise to the fast growing academic project of diaspora studies. Precisely because so many of the world's human experiences now qualify as diaspora, it is imperative that diasporas be studied respectively and in their distinct and particular historical contexts in order for this common experience to be appreciated comparatively. The following synopsis of the Chinese experience with migration over time and space illustrates how one might go about studying this ever-growing phenomenon of diaspora.

Since at least the sixteenth century, southern Chinese (from Guangdong and Fujian provinces) had been leaving home to trade, and later, to settle, throughout Southeast Asia—today's Philippines, Indonesia, Malaysia, Singapore, Thailand. Migration to the Americas—North to South and including the Caribbean islands—took off in the nineteenth and early twentieth centuries, consisting overwhelmingly of working-age men, although not necessarily unmarried and without families (Mazumdar 2003). Wives and children were often initially left behind (Qing policy actually prohibited out-migration of Chinese women and children), then later beckoned to join husbands and fathers. Migrants also formed first or secondary families with local women. Furthermore, Chinese men were attracted to a range of frontier and newly developing economic regions of Southeast Asia, the Pacific (the small islands as well as Australia and New Zealand), California and the American West, the borderlands between the U.S. and Mexico, and plantation societies of the Caribbean and Latin America. In all these vibrant spaces, both labor and business opportunities abounded. Whether the places of settlement were still European colonies or recently decolonized, Chinese migrants were introduced as a deterritorialized intermediate sector between natives bound to their land and villages, and colonial and neocolonial masters and administrators determined to extract wealth and maintain social control. Encouraged by the white masters to feel superior by race and civilization to the subjugated and darker-skinned native populations, they were nevertheless denied acceptance as social equals and were rarely accorded metropolitan citizenship no matter how successful or prosperous they may have become.

In European settler societies—the United States, Canada, Australia—which upon shedding their colonized status installed white supremacist social structures, Chinese and other Asian immigrants were denied the political right to citizenship as well as most of the important economic and social rights, such as landownership, interracial marriages, access to education, well-paying jobs, and the professions. The sum of these deprivations sheds light on one of the most common reasons why migrations become diasporas: a tense, troubled, tenuous, and tortuous relationship with the state and key elements of the receiving society with whom migrants interact and compete. When faced with these challenges, Chinese migrant communities have developed ways of overt resistance as well as accommodationist practices, all for the purpose of self-defense, preservation, and survival. This common experience of rejection, marginalization, discrimination, and oppression by host societies encourage diasporic Chinese communities to forge a strong sense of identification and empathy for each other's common plight, and develop mechanisms for quick mobilization in mutual support when one of them comes under vicious nativist attack.

For all of the nineteenth and much of the twentieth centuries, their inability to fully penetrate host societies for social acceptance and political integration has trumped whatever aspiration diasporic Chinese might have harbored to assimilate into another cultural and national identity, ironically the only way they could have ended their sense of displacement and exile. In this diasporic condition, the final reference for home remained their native village and region, the *guxiang* (Sinn 1997), and eventually China itself, which incidentally has never been occupied or destroyed. So for diasporic Chinese, the return-to-homeland yearning and practices unfold in a different context than for Jews, Africans, Palestinians, and Armenians, who must first reconquer and reestablish a home before they can return to one. Instead, Chinese desire to return in order to compensate for their deterrorialization abroad by reterritorializing at home, that is, by strengthening their roots to village and nation.

Chinese diasporics reconnect with home in another significant and now increasingly problematic way: when shut out of citizenship and political participation, they become susceptible to the siren calls of homeland politics. In the case of the U.S., beginning with the fiercely competitive factions of reformers and revolutionaries of the turn-of-the-century plotting to overthrow the Manchu rulers of the Qing dynasty, followed by the bitter and protracted political rivalry between the Kuomingtang regime under Chiang Kai-shek in Taiwan and the Communist regime in China, Chinese in America have found it difficult to distance themselves from such politics (Ma 1990; Tsai 1983). But identification and involvement with homeland politics have come at a costly price for many Chinese communities in the diaspora, for these practices often clashed with other imperatives, fears, and anxieties of the larger societies, notably rising new nationalisms in postcolonial societies such as Indonesia, Malaya (before the split into Chinese-dominated Singapore and Malay-dominated Malaysia), and the Philippines, where even well-established Chinese communities are seen as untrustworthy, undependable allies of the nationalist project.

Because China itself was not lost, diasporic Chinese were always able to make home visits if they had the financial means. For several decades, however, after the Communists took power in 1949, the doors were closed to movements of people and capital in and out of the country, and were not reopened until later in the twentieth century. During this period, the world changed dramatically, highlighted by further decolonization in the Western empires; the challenge of socialism in the Third World and the rise and fall of the Cold War; the triumph of liberal democracies worldwide, accompanied by the dismantling of legal racial segregation and racially exclusive policies in white supremacist societies such as the U.S., Canada, and Australia; and the advent of late-capitalist globalization. These worldwide social transformations brought about conditions in which, for the first time in history, diasporic Chinese everywhere are finally accorded the rights of citizenship and belonging where they have settled. In so doing, the dynamics of their relationship change: instead of guest and host,

it becomes citizen and government. At this moment, we also ask of the Chinese diaspora, is it drawing to a close? It seems that, like diasporic Jews, Chinese overseas are becoming ever more transnational, even as they become more rooted and integrated into host societies. If diaspora is—as Khachig Tölölyan argues in the inaugural issue of *Diaspora: A Journal of Transnational Studies*, which he founded and edits—the classic exemplar of transnationalism (Tölölyan 1991), I would add that transnational practices did not just give rise and shape to diasporas at the point of their formation, but new transnational practices are invented to help them at their points of expiration or transition to a new era.

In the present moment, when most diasporic Chinese are no longer marginalized outsiders but active citizens and aggressive businessmen of multiple nation-states around the world, their traditional voluntary associations (*huiguan*), which had once helped migrants become localized, turned into global instruments of networking, drawing upon deeply seated sub-ethnic identities. For example, Hakka (*kejia*) around the world organize international reunions, Teochow (Chaozhou) people hold international conventions, and not to be outdone, Fujian associations have their own world meetings. The same is true of surname associations such as the Guan clan, which has held its own World Guan Association meeting. These global networks facilitate transnational practices of postcolonial, postmodern Chinese capitalists of the Asia Pacific (Nonini 2001; Hu-DeHart 1999).

Meanwhile, China itself is generating another diasporic spurt, once again sending out migrants in large numbers, and to places where they had not been prominent before, such as Eastern Europe. Not only China, but parts of the original diaspora itself—Taiwan, Hong Kong, Singapore, Indonesia, Vietnam, and Thailand, as well as Cuba and Peru, Jamaica and Guyana—have been leaking ethnic Chinese migrants to other parts of the world, complicating the pattern of migration and disrupting a common association of place of origin with ethnicity. A new immigrant to the U.S. self-identified as "Chinese" may originate from any of a multiplicity of places in addition to China itself, and speak primarily English or Spanish rather than Mandarin, Cantonese, or Fujianese. For their part, much as in the case of most Jews in the world, who have elected not to return to the re-created Israel, the longtime imagined homeland of diasporic desire, so most Chinese are happy only to visit China from many points in the diaspora, and not to stay forever. Diasporic Chinese today are self-identified as such ethnically and maybe culturally as well, but not nationalistically. And the Chinese identities and cultures they have invented in the diaspora are as varied and diverse as the places they have settled; multiple, creolized, flexible, contingent, situational, adaptable, changeable, malleable, these diasporic Chinese identities have been the subject of numerous studies (Ang 2001; Ho 1989; Ong 1999 are three good examples among many).

In the same inaugural issue of *Diaspora*, Tölölyan also proposes that "[w]e use 'diaspora' provisionally to indicate our belief that the term that once described Jewish, Greek, and Armenian dispersion now shares meanings with a larger semantic domain that includes words like immigrant, expatriate, refugee, guest workers, exile community, overseas community, ethnic community. This is the vocabulary of transnationalism" (1991, 4–5). Old diasporas fade while new ones arise, because more than anything, diasporas describe relationships and human drama across time and space, that is, history itself. Nor surprisingly, diasporas reflect and display usual conflicts along class, gender, and generational lines. Moreover, modern diasporas seem to emerge, unfold, move, change, recede, or come alive within successive modes of capitalist production, be they colonialism, new

world slavery and plantation, free market capitalism and imperialism, state and monopoly capitalism, and currently, late capitalist or neoliberal globalization. For this reason, state actions and policies on both the sending and receiving ends of migration play crucial roles in diaspora formations.

One notable example of a new kind of Asian diaspora is the massive, state-sponsored, and state-directed out-migration of Filipino workers, predominately women, to Europe, Asia, and America, a migration, it can be argued, that resembles a guest worker program more than a diaspora. Children remain behind to be raised by grandparents while occasional fathers and many mothers depart under contract to work as maids, nurses, nannies, and other gendered forms of labor (Parreñas 2001). The billions of dollars remitted back to villages and towns in the Philippines sustain entire communities. Because workers often remain overseas on multiple renewed contracts for ten or more years cumulatively, their regular remittances become dependable and concrete links to home; moreover, modern technology such as phone cards and the internet provide additional ways to connect. The Filipino model has motivated Thai, Indonesian, and Bangladeshi women to follow their sisters into overseas contract work. While their work stints are supposedly temporary, marriage with foreign men can make their overseas sojourns permanent.

The explosive breakup of empires has often resulted in voluntary and involuntary departures from unstable, violent, and often corrupt postcolonial societies. Thus we can speak of the out-migration of Caribbean peoples of African and Asian descent (Chinese and South Asians) to Canada, the United States, France, and Spain (Humanities Institute 1987). We can point to the forced removal of South Asians from Idi Amin's Uganda almost half a century ago, only to find them returning decades later, picking up businesses they had once lost, and thriving again. Most diasporic Chinese today, especially those in officially recognized multicultural, pluralistic liberal democracies, assertively exercise their coequal citizenship and political rights alongside other groups, including privileged whites in the U.S., Canada, and Australia, where whites constitute the majority and continue to monopolize wealth and power.

In the case of Singapore with its majority Chinese population and Chinese-controlled government, diasporic Chinese have created an ethnic Chinese nation not controlled by the motherland. Taiwan Chinese would like to achieve the same autonomy, while the moment for Hong Kong Chinese might have passed. In all these places, can we now speak of the Chinese as entering the post-diasporic era, in which they can avail themselves of social capital accumulated in the diaspora to strengthen *guanxi* (connections) and *xinyong* (trust) in order to gain business advantages over competitors under globalization (Nonini 2001; Kiong and Kee 1998), or to reinforce a distinctive Chinese ethnic identity in avowedly multicultural and pluralistic democracies that no longer, at least officially, demand assimilation to a dominant majority culture? At the same time, in these various postcolonial and postmodern environments, are diasporic Chinese not also motivated to engage in a larger dialogue about building civil society along with other ethnic groups?

A notable kind of post-diasporic practice is embracing official multiculturalism. It is telling that when Hakkas gather, for example, the *lingua franca* is more likely to be English (or French) than any of the several Hakka languages, for participants consist of many second and third generations born in the diaspora to societies that have fully integrated them. For example, at Canada's First Annual Conference on Hakka Heritage and Culture, held in Toronto in December 2000, York University Professor of Chinese Studies Pietro Giordan (who is obviously not Hakka) read a poem written in French by a contemporary Mauritian writer of Hakka descent, Joseph Tsang Mang Kin. The poem was appropriately entitled "Le grand chant Hakka" ("The Great Hakka Song"). Officially opening the ceremony in English was Canadian senator Vivienne Poy, whose Hakka sister-in-law, the Canadian television personality Adrienne Poy Clarkson, was even more prominent in her role as the governor-general of Canada, appointed by the prime minister to be the face of Canada to the queen of England and to the vast British Commonwealth that stretches from Canada to the Caribbean, to Asia, and to Africa. These transnational Hakkas are easing effortlessly into the post-diasporic moment in numerous multicultural societies while celebrating their global diasporic ties (Toronto Hakka Heritage and Cultural Conference 2000).

As more and more diasporas come into academic focus, we can begin to identify a growing list of tensions between sets of, if not opposing, then at least contesting forces or tendencies. These tensions define diasporic subjectivity; explain decisions made by individuals, communities, and the state, or delineate their options; and maintain the diasporic condition while also destabilizing diasporas. In random order, some of these tensions can be framed as: tradition and modernity; localization and globalization; territorialization and deterritorialization; belonging and leaving; integration and separation; exile and return; sojourner and citizen; national and transnational; nation-bound and border-crossing; purity and hybridity; ethnicization and assimilation; localism and nationalism; parochialism and cosmopolitanism; displacement and integration; cooperation and competition; rigidity and flexibility. No doubt, students of diasporas will add to this list.

14

Disability

Cynthia Wu

According to the *Oxford English Dictionary*, the first appearance of "disability" occurred in the mid-sixteenth century. Its adjectival form, "disabled," follows shortly thereafter in the linguistic record. It appears that from the beginning, the three definitions of disability that persist today—"a lack of ability (to discharge any office or function)," "a physical or mental condition that limits a person's movements, senses, or activities," and "a restriction framed to prevent any person or class of persons from sharing in duties and privileges which would otherwise be open to them"—coexisted with one another. A now-obsolete meaning, disability as financial hardship, disappeared from use in the nineteenth century.

The field of Asian American studies has seen a recent surge of scholarship that addresses disability. A Modern Language Association convention panel, a special issue of *Amerasia Journal*, and several monographs—all appearing in the past few years—together mark this acceleration of interest. Although ethnic studies was, at first, somewhat slow to initiate dialogue with disability studies, the conversations that scholars have generated of late speaks to the shared intellectual and political commitments of these fields.

Disability studies was founded in the 1990s in ways that reflected the cultural changes in the wake of the Americans with Disabilities Act of 1990. The legislation—which prohibited discrimination based on ability status and mandated reasonable accommodations in education, employment, public facilities, and commercial services for disabled people—actualized a long effort on the part of activists that began during the civil rights era. Disability studies, as a discipline in the humanities, differentiates itself from the fields of rehabilitation medicine (such as physical therapy or occupational therapy) by locating its critique within the social and built environments that create incapacitating barriers for disabled people. Instead of developing therapies to normalize people, the field focuses on the social justice implications of unequal access. Consequently, it adopts a methodology that privileges the cultural meanings of physical, sensory, and neural difference rather than treatment and cure.

Despite the presence of disability—as evidenced in the linguistic record—as a social and cultural entity from the mid-1500s onward, it was not until the advent of modernity that differences marked by ability status were regarded and handled in the manner that is familiar to us now. The standardizing discourses and practices associated with empiricism, urbanization, and industrialization occasioned a shift from a society where human variation was integrated into everyday life to one where forms of intervention and control—linguistic, educational, spatial, medical, and legal—were leveled upon disabled people (Bogdan 1990; Davis 1995; Trent 1995; Baynton 1996; Reiss 2008; Schweik 2010; Rembis 2011; Nielsen 2012). The historical effects of this segregation, forced or coerced therapy, juridical abuse, and cultural erasure are what activists and scholars are still attempting to expose and redress today.

This framework—which posits disability as difference that demands accommodation in the form of institutional change rather than assimilation and integration—would be familiar to scholars of race. The emergence of ethnic studies as an academic discipline in the late 1960s and early 1970s took place in tandem with concurrent social movements outside of the academy that challenged racism, class inequality, and militaristic imperialism. The various racial liberatory movements and the opposition to the Vietnam War marked a departure from the Cold War conformity of the previous generation.

The rise of a sustained panethnic and cross-racial Asian American movement during this era privileged a heteropatriarchal—and, by extension, a nondisabled—subject. The early activists attempted to generate their critiques of social inequality by appealing to standards of normative masculinity. The disavowal of gender and sexual difference in cultural nationalist politics has been well documented in Asian American studies. However, the lack of a corresponding body of work that unpacks ableism in Asian American cultural nationalism is striking, given how closely the discourses of gender, sexuality, and disability are intertwined.

Correspondingly, disability studies has faced critiques of its white normativity (Bell 2006). Its areas of inquiry and the demographic composition of its practitioners have assumed a whiteness that marginalized scholars who maintained intellectual commitments to race. Nevertheless, there are a few seminal texts where we can see the earliest examples of disability and race/ethnicity overlapping and/or mutually constituting each another (Gilman 1985; Gilman 1996; Kraut 1995; Garland-Thomson 1997). This methodology extends itself more explicitly in the work that follows (James and Wu 2006; James 2007; C. Wu 2012; Ho, Lee, and Pan 2013; Minich 2013). The challenge for scholars as this line of inquiry moves forward, especially in the field of Asian American studies, is to explore how these interpretive lenses can be repurposed to go beyond—but not transcend—a predictable archive. Such an approach might follow the dictum that we acknowledge but not hierarchize the tension between seeing matters of political difference as particular to social minorities and seeing difference as integrated into the universality of human experience (Sedgwick 1990) or the proposition that we evacuate the subject of analysis altogether and define our field by mode of critique (Chuh 2003).

Examples of recent work that performs these analytical maneuvers include a literary critical examination of fiction responding to the neocolonial ties between the United States and India that were exposed after the 1984 Union Carbide gas leak in Bhopal (Jina Kim 2014). The workings of multinational corporations, which cheapen some lives in return for the comfort of others, force a reconsideration of the logic of disability activism and disability studies in the global North. Also notable is a study of how contemporary concepts of toxicity are transposed onto historically sedimented anxieties about a transnational Asia (M. Chen 2012). Fears about racialized contaminants arise out of the ambivalence that North Americans hold about the movement of bodies, objects, and capital alike across national borders. These are some of the possibilities that future work on disability may conjure in the field of Asian American studies.

DISABILITY   CYNTHIA WU

15

Discrimination

John S. W. Park

"Discrimination" comes from the Latin prefix "dis-," meaning "apart from" or "away from." Its root, "crimen," denoting "blame" or "judgment," gives us "crime" and all of its variants. Carrying negative and positive connotations, to discriminate is to come to a judgment about something or someone or to set it apart from something else with similar characteristics. To be "discriminating" suggests a finer taste and sensibility, the ability to distinguish good from bad, and the capacity to discern desirable from undesirable. It can indicate good judgment, a kind of refinement, and even snobbery. In the context of public law, "discrimination" most often refers to a formal declaration to treat two groups differently; such a collective decision can imply a majority's desire to elevate some and to denigrate others, even though they may otherwise share similar attributes. White supremacists in the United States have long insisted that racial discrimination is based on notions of "good taste" or "common sense" that distinguish "good people" (whites) from "other people" (nonwhites, beings who may not be fully human and thus not entitled to the same treatment as whites). While there are many forms of discrimination in the world—based on gender, age, sexual orientation, and class, among dozens of others—this essay focuses on the relationship between race-based discriminations (particularly in American constitutional law and in federal and state statutes) and their multifaceted impacts on Asian Americans and Asian immigrants.

The first clause of Article IV, Section 2, of the United States Constitution declares, "The Citizens of each State shall be entitled to all Privileges and Immunities of Citizens in the several States," and early litigants said that this clause forbade the states from "discriminations" against citizens of other states. In the Federalist Papers and elsewhere, some of the Constitution's framers claimed they had supported this article to prevent citizens in the more powerful states from discriminating against citizens of less powerful states, thus providing a legal basis for equality among all citizens of the United States. Nevertheless, discrimination against noncitizens, along with taking their property, was deemed less problematic. Although some Native Americans had converted to Christianity, exercised property rights, and even "passed into" American citizenship, those living as members of "sovereign tribes" were not counted in the census for purposes of apportioning seats in Congress.

As non-American citizens, these "Indians not taxed" and their sovereign tribes could not expect protection from the federal courts either, as they had no rights, privileges, or immunities under the constitution. They were, in the words of the United States Supreme Court, "domestic dependent nations" and "the relationship of the tribes to the United States [resembled] that of a 'ward to its guardian.'" In other cases, the court stressed that Congress and the president had "plenary power" over Native Americans and their tribes; such power could not be checked by the federal courts under the United States Constitution. As numerous state governments and then the federal government coordinated military efforts to remove Native Americans from their lands, the federal courts occasionally expressed sympathy, but otherwise did nothing (Deloria 1983). Similarly, African Americans were regarded as beyond constitutional protection. African slaves *were* property; even free blacks were not considered citizens in the same way as "free white persons." Under law, slave owners were entitled to recover their slaves with the assistance of state officials, even in states where slavery was unlawful. This understanding, reinforced through several constitutional provisions and subsequent federal statutes, envisioned formal, discriminatory treatment against black slaves; such treatment assumed that they were people governed by constitutional rules, but not protected under the Constitution (Higginbotham 1980; Morgan 2003).

By analogy, Asian immigrants were characterized as outside the nation when they arrived in large numbers by the mid-nineteenth century. In early California history, Asian immigrants were excluded from juries (1854) and barred from attaining naturalized citizenship (1879). Racial discrimination against the Chinese began in 1852, when California approved the Foreign Miners' Tax. While the tax carried no specific ethnic or racial designation, it was exclusively applied to Chinese immigrants. Over the next three decades, such discriminatory measures would increase as state legislators demanded state and federal action against the further migration of the Chinese. For example, the Page Act of 1875 prohibited the arrival of "lewd and debauched women"; in California, the rule was used against Chinese women. Seven years later, the U.S. Congress passed the Chinese Exclusion Act, which curtailed Chinese immigration by prohibiting Chinese laborers. In *Chae Chan Ping v. United States* (1889), the Supreme Court upheld such forms of racial discrimination and exclusion, averring: "These laborers are not citizens of the United States; they are aliens. That the government of the United States, through the action of the legislative department, can exclude aliens from its territory is a proposition which we do not think open to controversy." In other words, national majorities had the right to discriminate on the basis of race to keep out undesirable, "inassimilable"

immigrants (Wong and Chan 1998; John Park 2004; Erika Lee 2004).

Such racialized restrictions occurred *after* the passage of the Fourteenth Amendment, ratified in 1868, which promised constitutional protections to all "persons" as well as citizens: "No State shall make or enforce any law which shall abridge the privileges or immunities of citizens of the United States; nor shall any State deprive any person of life, liberty, or property, without due process of law; nor deny to any person within its jurisdiction the equal protection of the laws." In the aftermath of Reconstruction, however, white supremacists rejected political and social equality with African Americans. As newly emancipated slaves left the South, racial segregation became more pervasive and codified at the state level via Jim Crow laws. For about one hundred years after the Civil War, white American majorities legally discriminated against people of color, even though the federal government had to acknowledge that African Americans, Native Americans, Asian Americans, and other racial minorities were both "persons" and citizens of the United States (Woodward 1966).

Legalized racial segregation required novel justifications. In *Plessy v. Ferguson* (1896), the Supreme Court upheld that "separate but equal" accommodations and services for racial others were constitutional. Over the next six decades, white majorities supported segregation; in public school systems, for example, African American, Mexican American, Asian American, and Native American children were to be segregated (if such schools were established for them at all). For example, because they were deemed "yellow" and not white by the Supreme Court, Asian and Asian American children were to attend schools for "colored children" in Mississippi (*Gong Lum v. Rice* 1927). This systemic segregation against people of color was extended into other places and spaces, such as hospitals, military units, and labor unions. And, with regard to Asian immigrants and Asia Americans, such discriminations were applied to divergent ethnic groups. South Asian immigrants could not pass into American citizenship, Korean immigrants could not own land in states like California, nor could Filipino or Japanese immigrants get commercial fishing licenses or government jobs. Various state rules said that "Mongolians," "Orientals," and "Malays" could not marry "white" or "Caucasian" people (Chan 1991).

Throughout this period, if regular political power proved ineffective, whites used other methods to enforce segregation. At the turn of the twentieth century, membership in white supremacist organizations numbered in the hundreds of thousands as legislators, Supreme Court justices, police officers, and other officials joined groups like the Ku Klux Klan to secure white voting blocs. There was regional variety: James Phelan, the former mayor of San Francisco, promised to keep California free of Japanese immigrants when he ran for a United States Senate seat; in North Carolina, Furnifold Simmons claimed to be the "Chieftain of White Supremacy" and the "Great White Father" when he ran for his own seat. Both men won. During the first half of the twentieth century, legislators like these would block the passage of several antilynching bills in Congress.

White supremacy was so common that many Americans encouraged their representatives to seek alliances with the Nazi Party in Germany, as the racial attitudes of the Nazis were similar to their own. Before World War II, when Franklin Roosevelt complained that Adolf Hitler had no right to infringe upon the sovereignty of his neighbors—France, Czechoslovakia, Poland, Hungary—Hitler's reply was that the United States had no moral right to complain about such things, as white Americans had already done to Native Americans what the Nazis were hoping to try in Europe. Influenced by counterparts in the United States, Nazi scientists also endorsed eugenics—the selective breeding of "higher races" and the destruction or culling of "lower types," including people with mental and physical disabilities. Following British and American practices, Nazi officials used concentration camps to detain political prisoners, homosexuals, and other "undesirables." In the first half of the twentieth century, horrifying forms of race-based discrimination and apartheid were basic aspects of public law and policy in the "civilized" world. As Steven Casey (2001) and others have argued, American politicians had to persuade the American public that Nazis and other racists were indeed enemies and threats and not allies.

Even so, before the end of World War II, the Americans had evinced a self-consciousness and a sense of embarrassment about race-based discrimination as they tried to lead the struggle against fascism and communism. The Supreme Court insisted that Japanese American internment camps were not like Nazi concentration camps. The court likewise asserted that popular racial prejudices alone should never be used to justify racial discrimination, and that (from now on) American legislatures had to have "compelling state interests" and "narrowly tailored" methods whenever they used race-based discriminations. Such statements arose in *Korematsu v. United States* (1944), where the court rendered legal the indiscriminate internment of immigrants and American citizens of Japanese ancestry. Even though Fred Korematsu and Japanese Americans lost their fight against mass incarceration, the case marked a turning point in American public law, as the federal courts used it as a precedent to undo race-based discriminations in education, housing, voting, and other areas of public life (Klarman 2006).

As Mary Dudzuiak (2000) and other historians have noted, in the postwar world, U.S. domestic law changed in response to the Holocaust and within the context of

Cold War foreign policy. The Union of Soviet Socialist Republics joined with the People's Republic of China in a communist bloc to oppose the United States, Great Britain, Japan, and their allies. The communist world and the "free world" fought one another for the Third World—the so-called nonaligned nations—with each side trying to persuade these countries to follow its example and to reject the other side. In places like Vietnam and Korea, the communists quickly reminded everyone of past racism and anti-Asian discrimination in the United States (Borstelmann 2003). Communist sympathizers likewise stressed that Soviet and the Chinese Communist constitutions and laws promised policies and practices of equality that seemed more robust than the American versions. Although both communist states practiced one-party rule, and despite the fact that some communists enjoyed secret privileges that made them more equal than their comrades, their public rejections of race-based discrimination proved effective against a segregationist American adversary, a nation that retained racist laws. Racial segregation had the quality of absurdity, too; after the war, for example, a heroic Japanese American soldier was denied a proper burial in a cemetery in California, as the custom there was to reserve spots for whites only. It was hard to justify such a thing to his survivors, the Masuda family of Orange County, or to anyone for that matter (Takaki 1989).

Within this postwar context, and within twenty years of the landmark decision in *Brown v. Board of Education* (1954), the states had abolished formal segregation in their public institutions, and Congress had approved significant new civil rights legislation, including the Civil Rights Act of 1964, the Voting Rights Act of 1965, and the Fair Housing Act of 1968. Moreover, every president since Eisenhower was willing to use federal power to coerce white Americans into accepting racial integration. During the 1950s and 1960s, white resistance to racial integration was often violent, yet by 1970, in an amazing turn, formal race-based rules designed to discriminate and to disable people of color in the United States were either repealed or struck down. In law and policy at least, racial discriminations—those based on notions that some people were racially inferior or subhuman—were no longer legal.

Formal white supremacy has been illegal now for about four or five decades, or rather, for only four or five decades. Americans of all races have struggled with how or whether to "undo" the previous three and a half centuries of legalized white supremacy. President Lyndon Johnson used a popular metaphor to argue for "affirmative actions" to remedy past harms: "You do not take a man who for years has been hobbled by chains, liberate him, bring him to the starting line of a race, saying, 'You are free to compete with all the others,' and still justly believe you have been completely fair." Johnson, and his successors (Nixon, Ford, and Carter) approved federal laws and policies intended to expand opportunities for people of color once excluded from mainstream American institutions. Some of their appointees to the Supreme Court ruled that accounting for race to undo past harm was either "benign" or "remedial," and not at all like the accounting for race to further white supremacy (Spann 2000).

Other presidents and Supreme Court justices have not been so sure. In contrast, they advocated a "color-blind" approach to race-based discrimination. From this other perspective, government cannot be trusted to parse which racial discriminations are remedial and which are "invidious." Legally, "invidious" carries two broad meanings: it means "unjust" or "unfair," and it also means "likely to arouse resentment in others." For example, some white legislators, judges, and litigants have alleged that policies such as affirmative action are unfair to white people, and thus arouse their resentment. In the *Bakke* case (1978), the white plaintiff said that affirmative action policies at the UC Davis School of Medicine were unfair to white applicants, and about half of the United States Supreme Court agreed. This inspired other litigants—Hopwood, Ho, Gratz, Grutter, and Fisher. The persistent discomfort with any race-conscious law or policy also undergirded broader political changes, such as California's Proposition 209 in 1996. Proposition 209 amended the state's constitution to prohibit all of its institutions from considering race, sex, or ethnicity in decisions about public employment, public contracting, and public education.

Also, by the 1990s, in cases like *Ho v. San Francisco Unified School District*, many nonwhites, including Asian immigrants and Asian Americans, were challenging practices designed to increase the representation of "underrepresented minorities," a term that in some settings—like at elite colleges and universities—did not include Asians. As a result of this lawsuit, the school district was forced to abandon race-conscious policies that had limited the number of Asian students in order to increase the percentage of African American and Latino students within the city's most highly ranked schools.

In other disputes, progressive Asian Americans have warned against "negative action," which referred to policies that limited the number of Asian Americans at some colleges and universities. Too many Asian kids at Brown University would make Brown, well, less like "traditional" Brown, and some were suspicious that places like Brown had maintained a constant percentage of Asian and Asian American students even while their enrollments have grown tremendously at the major state universities. In the 1980s and 1990s, as Dana Takagi (1993) and others scholars had shown, administrators at many colleges and universities—including state institutions like UCLA and UC Berkeley—seemed obsessed with the number of Asians on their campuses, and some had favored changes in policy to limit their enrollment.

In other areas of public law, there were charges of "reverse discrimination," counterclaims of "unlawful discrimination," appeals for "colorblindness," and continuing diatribes against "affirmative action"—all of these conflicts suggested a nation and a law still obsessed with issues of race, identity, privilege, and discrimination. Although some have said that the early twenty-first century is "post-racial," claims of racial discrimination in a variety of contexts still exist and involve just about every racial group in America. Moreover, the civil rights revolution of the 1950s and 1960s did not undermine or undo lawful discriminations against noncitizens and nonmembers: it is still quite legal, and sometimes even required, to discriminate against noncitizens, including new immigrants of one kind or another. Many scholars and activists have questioned the morality of these discriminations, chiefly because they so resemble the distasteful discriminations that used to be so pervasive in American law. In the midst of so much racial tension, with recurring concerns about "profiling" and "unconscious bias," discrimination resembles a bad taste that never seems to go away.

16

Education

Shirley Hune

In the founding era of Asian American studies, the College Edition of *Webster's New World Dictionary of the American Language* provided four explanations of the term "education": (1) "the process of training and developing the knowledge, skill, mind, character, etc."; (2) "knowledge, ability, etc. thus developed"; (3) "formal schooling" or "a kind of stage of this," for example, higher education; and (4) "systemic study of the problems, methods, and theories of teaching and learning" (Guralnik and Friend 1968, 461). The first three features were given serious attention in the formation of Asian American studies, but only a few instructors took the fourth feature into account and experimented with teaching and learning methods. Does any of this matter in the ongoing development of Asian American studies?

What is the how, when, where, and why of "education" as a keyword in Asian American studies? Education is a foundational theme in the field. Constant reference is made to the origins of Asian American studies in the late 1960s and early 1970s as a protest movement in higher education that was part of a larger social movement to change the power structure and racialized culture of U.S. society, its institutions, and international relations. When a panethnic group of Asian American college students, community activists, and other supporters demanded ethnic studies programs, they sought also to increase access and equitable treatment for students of color and for those from low-income families,

to transform elitist, Western-focused, and biased curriculum (conventional knowledge), and to recover, reclaim, and advance a knowledge base that was more inclusive of the local and the global and incorporated multiple racial, ethnic, class, and other social experiences from their own viewpoints (Okihiro et al. 1988). Being able to attend college and complete a degree is not the same as being educated. Fundamentally, what kind of training, knowledge, ability development, or schooling were college students receiving when Asian American histories, cultures, and communities were omitted, disparaged, or distorted in the curriculum and Asian American students' scholarly interests were unsupported and even disdained?

The initiating demands for Asian American studies sought reforms in the hierarchical organization and practice of higher education. Advocates challenged traditional criteria for faculty hiring, retention, and advancement and called for more faculty of color. Many of them valued grassroots activities as well as practitioners and community activists as teachers. They promoted a mission of serving Asian American communities by linking theory and practice to address their needs and concerns, for example, using research to improve the lives of disadvantaged Asian Americans (Okihiro et al. 1988). Hence Asian American studies supporters proposed the recognition of community work in academe. This notion of broadening the definition of service as one of the criteria for tenure and promotion contributed to the greatest pushback from those who wanted to preserve the traditional rewards system of publications and grants. In addition, advocates sought a more democratic educational experience involving elements such as student-centered classrooms and critical pedagogy and having students serve on standing committees and search committees as part of the higher education decision-making process. In short, it came to be seen that an education that excluded Asian American studies was a disservice to the education of all students, not just Asian American students, and one that included Asian American studies was more democratic, participatory, and transformative of the status quo.

In the decades that followed, the founding focus of Asian American studies as a social justice and community-based agent in higher education continued to be widely acknowledged, but is seen today as severely weakened (Furumoto 2003). A few have called for reenvisioning U.S. campuses as community sites whereby Asian American studies can redefine its role as an educational tool for faculty who seek to combine academic and community interests (K. Chan 2000). Still others have deemed Asian American studies a largely ineffective project, notably in changing public understanding about race and of Asian American populations (*Journal of Asian American Studies* 2012). Nonetheless, new groups of students have emerged from time to time to stage protests and even hunger strikes demanding Asian American studies on campuses that lack such programs. Crises over faculty tenure cases also remind us of the fragility of faculty gains despite the continuing growth of Asian American studies across the nation and the high quality of the faculty and Ph.D. pool (Chen and Hune 2011). I return to the question of the core value of education within Asian American studies in the twenty-first century at the end of this essay.

Education also appears frequently as a topic in Asian American studies. As a multidisciplinary, interdisciplinary, and transnational field, education issues are covered in history, the social sciences, cultural studies, and other disciplines. In the space of this essay, I can provide only a few examples. A common theme has been the struggle of Asian Americans to be educated. In writings on the early history of Asian Americans, for example, scholars have documented how Chinese and Japanese immigrants from the mid-nineteenth through early twentieth centuries were first denied access to public schools and then attended racially segregated ones even after parents had petitioned school boards and the courts for the right of their American-born children to be educated with whites. Two landmark cases reached the U.S. Supreme Court but their decisions were sidestepped locally. After *Tape v. Hurley* in 1885, the San Francisco School Board created a separate school for Asians rather than allow Chinese American Mamie Tape to attend public school. Decades later, *Gong Lum v. Rice* in 1927 reaffirmed separate but equal schooling for Martha Lum in Mississippi based on the 1896 *Plessy v. Ferguson* Supreme Court decision by finding that Martha was not being denied an education because she could attend a "colored school." This unequal treatment reflected the dominant society's view of Asians as racially inferior and as aliens unsuitable for citizenship. As an alternative, many Chinese sent their children to mission schools organized by church groups in Chinatowns. Likewise, Japanese Americans developed mission and language schools for cultural preservation. Early on Asian American struggles for educational access and equality and to maintain their heritage were clearly proactive, intentional, multipronged, and predate the civil rights era and the founding of Asian American studies.

Contemporary analyses of Asian American education pursue similar themes. These include studies on language discrimination, parental and community involvement in schools, biases in college admissions, and public policy debates, for example, concerning affirmative action and undocumented students. Two studies on student access, in particular, position Asian Americans at the center of educational racial politics in the nation within the context of an outmoded black/white paradigm. In her analysis of the ways in which elite U.S. universities were limiting Asian American enrollment in the 1980s, Dana Takagi (1992) argued that these institutions were shifting admissions criteria from race to class, thus discounting the continuing prevalence of racism as a barrier for students of color. Here institutions used the model minority stereotype against Asian Americans to restrict their admissions rate. In another situation, Rowena Robles (2006) detailed how a lawsuit initiated by a few Chinese Americans, who promoted the model minority stereotype to enhance their acceptance rate against blacks and Latinos, resulted in the dismantling of affirmative action at a premier high school in California. Here Asian Americans were first agents for and then victims of educational policy change as it contributed to an unintended consequence that disadvantaged all students of color, including Asian Americans.

Many Asian American studies specialists in examining Asian immigrant adaptation have given attention to family and generational strains over educational goals. They also emphasize the opportunity of an American education as a motivating factor in immigration. Through the twentieth century and up to the present day, Asian Americans have continued to invest their own resources in education. For example, Japanese Americans organized their own schools in the internment camps during World War II. Asian American ethnic groups offer heritage language and cultural activities for their youth in after-school and weekend programs. Some parents, especially those with means, enroll their children in tutoring classes and cram schools to supplement their formal education and augment academic achievement, and in some cases, simply to keep their adolescents occupied (Zhou and Kim 2006). The research on stereotypes and related cultural identity and identity politics of Asian Americans is typically grounded in studies of Asian American youth and their academic and personal development and well-being. Likewise, transnational scholars often highlight colonial and postcolonial mentality and identity issues as part of the challenges encountered by some Asian Americans that can advance, hinder, or simply complicate their educational experiences as they negotiate their attachment to two or more homelands.

Despite the overarching framework of Asian American studies, education as a field, its theories, methodologies, research findings, and its own multidisciplinary and comparative lens, is largely missing from Asian American studies. Stated another way, education as a field is narrowly incorporated, some would say marginalized and neglected, within Asian American studies. Others have noted the limited presence of Asian American education scholars attending Association for Asian American Studies conferences, at a time of growing numbers of new doctorates and faculty in the education field. If we consider the two major journals of Asian American studies, *Amerasia Journal* and the *Journal of Asian American Studies*, research findings on Asian American education are sparse. An exception is *aapi nexus*, a journal devoted to Asian American and Pacific Islander policy, practice, and community. To date, it has produced four volumes on Asian American and Pacific Islander education (*aapi nexus* 2009a; *aapi nexus* 2009b; *aapi nexus* 2010; *aapi nexus* 2011).

Likewise, mainstream schools of education have given little attention to how ethnic studies perspectives and findings, and specifically those of Asian American studies, could enhance their research and praxis. This is evident in their general lack of consideration for Asian American and Pacific Islander faculty hires and the absence of Asian American studies materials in program offerings and academic and professional preparation. Moreover, in the public discourse on closing the achievement/opportunity gap for minority students, Asian American and Pacific Islander scholars who have raised their voices on behalf of the needs of their communities and student populations too often find their concerns ignored in the mainstream education field.

Not all disciplines participate or seek to participate in Asian American studies. Every field is preoccupied with its own professional organizations and scholarly arenas. Nonetheless as a multidisciplinary field, Asian American studies can be more inclusive and find more balance and opportunities for intellectual exchanges among scholars who conduct evidence-based, social action, and policy-focused research, and scholars who focus on the humanities, including cultural studies. In addressing the specific theme of education, I return to my earlier question: "Does any of this matter in the ongoing development of Asian American studies?"

It matters because Asian American scholars in education are making significant contributions to research and knowledge on Asian American and Pacific Islander communities and to the preparation of academics and practitioners, but their work generally is not made use of or necessarily recognized within the field of Asian American studies. They have played a critical role in demythologizing and problematizing the model minority stereotype, for example, by providing classroom and campus evidence of the multiple ways in which a racialized climate of inequality is harmful to Asian American students (S. Lee 1996; S. Lee 2005; Osajima 1993; Teranishi 2010). Many in education use qualitative research methods, notably ethnography and mixed methods, and comparative studies of groups and different contexts in order to incorporate the wide range of Asian American and Pacific Islander perspectives, voices, and experiences, such as their identity construction and development, understandings that are rendered invisible by the dominant culture's use of stereotypes and its overreliance on quantitative data (Museus 2009; Museus, Maramba, and Teranishi 2013).

Education specialists have examined intersections of family, language, the cultural competency of teachers, and other factors on Asian American K–12 success (Park, Goodwin, and Lee 2003; *Race Ethnicity and Education* 2006); analyzed the effects of class disparities on the achievements of specific Asian American groups (Lew 2006; V. Louie 2004); provided case studies of the challenges encountered by Asian American and Pacific Islander communities with lower levels of college attainment, such as Cambodians, Samoans, and Filipinos (see Chuuon and Hudley 2008; Hune and Yeo 2010; Maramba and Bonus 2013, respectively); and applied critical theory and praxis to combat racism in the classroom, promote student resistance to injustices, and enhance the leadership development of Asian American students (Osajima 2007; Poon 2013). Higher education institutions are being viewed as worksites to consider student incivility, gender, agency, and other influences on the status of Asian American and Pacific Islander faculty and administrators and their challenges (Chen and Hune 2011; Hune 2011). Finally, specialists are addressing policy challenges for Asian Americans and Pacific Islanders that include increasing both the input of their communities and the accountability of federal, state, and local agencies toward them (Kiang 2006; CARE 2010; CARE 2011; CARE 2013). These studies are only a few examples of recent work.

Two new initiatives, in particular, driven in large part by Asian American and Pacific Islander education specialists in conjunction with key Asian American and Pacific Islander legislators, research institutes, and community groups, are changing the landscape of Asian American and Pacific Islander education with implications for Asian American studies. One initiative is outreach and advocacy to state and federal legislators and agencies for the collection and reporting of disaggregated data on Asian Americans and Pacific Islanders to better serve their diversity as individuals and communities and to end their misrepresentation through being treated as a homogenous group. Disaggregated data will allow for more nuanced analyses of Asian American and Pacific Islanders' experiences in all aspects of their lives, including civil rights, employment, community development, and health as well as education, and improve appropriate allocation of resources and services to specific communities and subgroups (*aapi nexus* 2011; CARE 2013; Hune and Takeuchi 2008).

The second initiative is the federal government's creation of a new minority-serving institution program in 2007—the Asian American and Native American Pacific Islander–Serving Institution (AANAPISI) program. AANAPISI-designated campuses each serve a sizeable proportion of low-income Asian American and Pacific Islander students and they can compete for grants to improve college access and success programs. At present grant-funded AANAPISIs include a large number of community colleges, a sector generally absent from Asian American studies and that for more than a decade has consistently enrolled approximately 47 percent of all Asian American and Pacific Islander college students, many of whom are from low-income households and underserved communities. Both initiatives offer rich opportunities for Asian American studies to enlarge its umbrella and engage outside its current venues and frameworks through collaborative research and affiliations with other sectors of academe and disciplines, including education. Likewise, education specialists have much to gain from the approaches and findings of Asian American studies and other ethnic studies fields in conducting their work.

In closing, what will "education" as a keyword in Asian American studies look like in the next decades of the twenty-first century? Much has changed. The social movement and anti-imperialist context of the origination of Asian American studies has long been replaced by a more conservative, individualistic, and neoliberal political climate that is promoting anti-immigration policies and practices and race blind beliefs. Asian American communities are also different. There is a continuing flow of new groups of immigrants and refugees who are more likely to seek security and stability at first, not social change. In the twenty-first century, Asian Americans now engage in a broader terrain of political interests, economic opportunities, and social lives that contribute to a greater heterogeneity of locations and interactions as well as identities. National origin, gender, sexuality, religion, and generation foci, for example, and being multiracial, multiethnic, and/or transnational are other dynamics. Moreover, the majority of Asian Americans today are foreign born, their education and class differences have widened, and often their political gaze and interests are focused away from the U.S. and its continuing battles over race and global domination.

Most importantly, the arena in which Asian American studies operates has changed. Higher education in the U.S. has shifted from an era of expansion during a time of economic growth and broad support for public institutions to one where public higher education, which has provided opportunities for the poor, new immigrants, and people of color and houses many Asian American studies programs, is being diminished by the wealth of private colleges and universities, the growth of for-profit institutions, and the need to compete with reduced funding. We are in a new global information society of academic capitalism where knowledge is more a commodity for profit than a common good, a college degree is a credential for an entry-level job and not necessarily evidence of an education, and academic fields must demonstrate their worth in the entrepreneurial market place to obtain faculty positions (Slaughter and

Rhoades 2004). New technologies and models of education, for example, long-distance learning and MOOCs (mass open online courses), are challenging traditional teaching and learning. And, in the internationalization of higher education, undergraduate students from China and other nations are becoming the new source of diversity on U.S. campuses.

What then are the mission, role, and place of Asian American studies in this new context? There is no dispute about how Asian American studies has changed what we know, but where does Asian American studies fit in the new models of knowledge development and transmission and the competition for shrinking resources on campuses? What is the impact of an evolving U.S. higher education system that is increasingly entrepreneurial and whose institutions now compete in global rankings on a field such as Asian American studies? How is Asian American Studies making a difference in the education of students and preparing them for the twenty-first century, if any? What do students need to know today to be productive and contributing world citizens? Who will benefit from the knowledge production and skill development of faculty and students in Asian American studies? Is Asian American studies to be only a campus-based enterprise? In summary, how can Asian American studies remain relevant and meaningful as an educational endeavor today and for the near future?

17

Empire
Moon-Ho Jung

Empire never went away in U.S. history, but it has been making a comeback in recent years. Likening the United States of the twenty-first century to the British empire of the nineteenth century, right-wing scholars and pundits have enthusiastically extolled empire to justify and glorify colonial misdeeds of the past and the present. "In deploying American power, decisionmakers should be less apologetic, less hesitant, less humble," Max Boot declared in 2002 with no sense of irony. "America should not be afraid to fight 'the savage wars of peace' if necessary to enlarge the 'empire of liberty,'" he concluded. "It has done it before" (352). Indeed, it has. Along with Niall Ferguson and others, Boot's unabashed embrace of the word *empire* is refreshing—they saw no need for disavowal or subterfuge—but equating empire with "democracy, capitalism, and freedom" served only to underscore their longing for a bygone era, when white men like Rudyard Kipling and William McKinley could speak openly of empire's burdens and benefits (Boot 2002, 349; N. Ferguson 2003).

Empire likewise never went away in Asian American studies, but it deserves a greater comeback. I, of course, am not suggesting that we follow Boot's prescriptions. We, however, should embrace and grapple with the term *empire*, for it strikes at the heart of our field's founding mission. Asian American studies, as an intellectual and political project, emerged out of the struggles of student and community activists of the late 1960s. At least in most articulations, it was a radical project, committed to democratizing higher education, to producing new forms of knowledge, and to critiquing the U.S. empire, particularly its war in Southeast Asia. That critique of empire has often faded to the background over the past four decades, as the political urgency to struggle as and with Third World peoples competed with the seductive appeal to reclaim and proclaim our "American" roots. As a result, the field's practitioners have clarified *and* obscured empire's meanings and relevance to Asian American studies, in ways that disabled a vigorous rejection of "American power" that Boot and his ilk celebrate and promote.

The problem lies in part in the liberal genesis of scholarly work on Asian Americans, many decades before the 1960s. Following the tradition of Protestant missionaries who had defended the Chinese against the exclusion movement in the nineteenth century, Mary Roberts Coolidge, Robert Ezra Park, and other social scientists strove to demonstrate the inevitability and universality of immigration and assimilation. Although Park, for his part, at times acknowledged European expansion and conquest as the root causes of modern-day race relations, he simultaneously attributed the movements of goods and peoples to "a general tendency to redress the economic balance and to restore the equilibrium between population and food supply, labor and capital, in a world economy" (1950, 143). For Park and his students, Asian migrations and anti-Asian racism along the Pacific Coast of the United States in the 1910s and 1920s—the "Oriental Problem"—were not exceptional but emblematic of a universal race relations cycle of contact, competition, accommodation, and assimilation. If not a self-conscious apologist of empire, Park and his Chicago School nonetheless shifted attention away from the global forces wreaking havoc on different peoples of the world.

To many of Park's contemporaries on the left, there was no more pressing matter in the world than empire to frame a different understanding of migrations and social relations. In his influential treatise *Imperialism*, written in 1916 and originally published in 1917, V. I. Lenin theorized that imperialism was "the monopoly stage of capitalism," a stage marked by the global concentration and domination of "finance capital" and "the territorial division of the whole world among the greatest capitalist powers" (1939, 88–89). Purposely limiting his definition of imperialism to the economic realm, Lenin sought to identify a critical shift in capitalist development in the late nineteenth century, in which colonialism emerged as a central feature. "To the numerous 'old' motives of colonial policy," he argued, "finance capital has added the struggle for the sources of raw materials, for the export of capital, for 'spheres of influence,' . . . in fine, for economic territory in general" (1939, 124). Although Lenin did not address race or the United States at length, he notably observed "another special feature of imperialism" of particular significance to Asian American studies: "the decline in emigration from imperialist countries, and the increase in immigration into these countries from the backward countries where lower wages are paid" (1939, 106).

In terms of writings on Asian Americans, though, the Chicago School's fixation on "immigration," "assimilation," and "race prejudice" held sway through the 1960s (and beyond), generating waves of studies on generational and cultural conflicts and interpersonal relations (H. Yu 2001). Aiming to reconstitute the field fundamentally, an interdisciplinary corps of Marxists and self-trained Asian Americanists boldly charted a new direction for the field in the 1980s. Lucie Cheng, Edna Bonacich, and a cadre of UCLA graduate students drew on and applied a growing body of scholarship on world-systems and dependency—pioneered by Immanuel

Wallerstein, Andre Gunder Frank, Walter Rodney, and others in the 1970s—that had elaborated on Lenin's insights on imperialism. The motive forces behind Asian migrations to the United States, they argued, emanated not from discrete "push" and "pull" factors but from uneven world capitalist development. A system of migrant labor extended across the Pacific, *Labor Immigration under Capitalism* suggested, facilitated essentially by European and American imperialism in Asia and capital's demand for cheap labor in the U.S. West and Hawai'i (Bonacich and Cheng 1984). Driven by the politics of the Asian American movement, Cheng, Bonacich, et al. placed empire very much at the center of Asian American studies.

Around the same time, Ronald Takaki offered a sweeping history of the development of the United States into an independent republic and an industrial and imperial power over the course of the nineteenth century. Racial imaginings of American Indians, African Americans, Mexicans, and Asians, he argued, lay at the heart of republicanism, corporate capitalism, and imperial wars. White conceptions of self-control and self-regulation through metaphorical "iron cages," Takaki argued, rested on the political exclusion, economic superexploitation, and military conquest of nonwhites. As a result, he concluded, American workers "were denied the class consciousness, the feeling of community, and the power of collective action they needed in order to respond effectively to . . . the hegemony of a powerful capitalist bureaucracy" (1979, vii). Takaki not only drew historically obvious (but previously unseen) connections—between the enslavement of African Americans, the dispossession of American Indian and Mexican lands, America's ambitions in China and the Philippines, and Chinese migrations to the United States—but also highlighted how "white men in positions of influence and power," those previously cast as "pro-Asian" by Coolidge and others, shaped and profited from white supremacy and imperial expansion (1979, x).

If these studies challenged Asian Americanists to think beyond liberal narratives of the nation—indeed to explore how conceptions of the United States and "Americans" were rooted in race and empire—the field concomitantly has elided empire in U.S. history. When Takaki, for example, turned to Asian American history in the 1980s, first in *Pau Hana* (1983) and then in *Strangers from a Different Shore* (1989), the immigrant saga took center stage. Highlighting individual stories, he presented Asian Americans as quintessential Americans—immigrants "overblown with hope" but struggling to overcome racial oppression and generational and cultural divides to join a wider community of national belonging. Perhaps overwhelmed by his own hope for historical salvation, Takaki concluded: "The history of America is essentially the story of immigrants, and many of them, coming from a 'different shore' than their European brethren, had sailed east to this new world. . . . Their dreams and hopes unfurled here before the wind, all of them—from the first Chinese miners sailing through the Golden Gate to the last Vietnamese boat people flying into Los Angeles International Airport—have been making history in America" (1989, 491). Takaki was by no means alone.

To propose that the United States has been, at root, a "nation of immigrants," upon which Asian Americans could stake their equal claim, if not in the past then through interpretations of the past, feeds into a teleology that posits nation against empire. Like the original thirteen colonies, modern nations seemingly liberate themselves from tyrannical empires, across time and space. Although terms like Thomas Jefferson's "empire of liberty" and U.S. declarations and policies since, from the Monroe Doctrine to the Bush Doctrine, muddied such dichotomous formulations, the idea of individuals joining the nation—gaining the rights of immigration and naturalization, for instance—implies, in the least, their liberation from exclusion and oppression. And perhaps no word captures the essence of exclusion, of injustices of the past, more than *empire* (alongside *slavery*). In such usage, *empire* evokes its predominant meaning of "imperial rule or dignity," as in its lead definition in the *Oxford English Dictionary*: "Supreme and extensive political dominion; *esp.* that exercised by an 'emperor' . . . or by a sovereign state over its dependencies." The projection of Asian Americans as liberal citizen-subjects in the making appears to contradict that historical and cultural image of empire.

But there is another way to approach empire and Asian American studies, rooted in the *OED*'s secondary definition, which harkens back to its original usage in the English language more than seven centuries ago, "that which is subject to imperial rule." Based on that notion, we would focus not on trying to identify the specific qualities or discrete boundaries of distinct empires—an exercise which, in past and current political debates, has usually led to a most misleading question, "Is the United States an empire?"—but on studying the historical and cultural processes through which different peoples, including Asian Americans, have become subjects of imperial rule. It is a process that Arundhati Roy has explained eloquently over the past decade. Dismissing the notion that she speaks as an "Indian citizen," she has insisted that she is "a subject of the American empire" (2004, 42). And empire, for Roy, has meant "this obscene accumulation of power, this greatly increased distance between those who make the decisions and those who have to suffer them" (2003, 2). The contradiction is not between empire and nation; it is between empire and democracy.

It is that contradiction that Asian American studies is especially poised to expose and explain, but the field must embrace empire as an analytic and overcome nationalist impulses to reproduce a typical "American" story. Studies on World War II, for instance, generally have fixated on proving Japanese American "loyalty" to the United States, an understandable response to wartime vilification and incarceration. Takashi Fujitani has recently traced the deeper logic behind that framing by exploring empire across the Pacific. The total war regimes of Japan and the United States, he argues, marked a pivotal shift from "vulgar racism" to "polite racism." Even as both states continued to practice widespread violence on racial grounds, according to Fujitani, they both commonly also began disavowing racism, a shift that hinged on the production of liberal, national subjects. Japanese and U.S. states, in turn, projected onto Koreans and Japanese Americans the right to choose to serve the benevolent, inclusive nation (Japan and the United States), a putative choice that marked some as "loyal" citizens enlisted as soldiers, workers, and "comfort women" to advance empire and others as "disloyal" subjects targeted for renewed acts of state violence. Both "loyal" and "disloyal" subjects fell under the power of imperial rule (Fujitani 2011).

Asian Americans, however, have cultivated other ways of seeing and being that revealed the limitations and contradictions of nation and empire. When confronted with "loyalty" questionnaires in America's concentration camps, Fujitani notes, Japanese Americans raised a lot of their own questions. "If you were evacuated from your home and brought out to a concentration camp like this," an internee asked, "would you still feel loyal to U.S. . . . ?" "What have we got to fight for—especially now that we are in a camp like this?" asked another (2011, 167, 168). Perhaps not self-consciously, these responses nonetheless pointed to acts of resisting empire, its logic of discipline and punish. And as much as Asian Americanists should strive to uncover the intricate and violent processes of imperial rule, we must also shed light on its ruptures and limits. Racialized subjects of the U.S. empire, including Asian Americans, have always fought back. "Our strategy should be not only to confront empire," Roy advises for our current moment, "but to lay siege to it. . . . To shame it. To mock it. With our art, our music, our literature, our stubbornness, our joy, our brilliance, our sheer relentlessness: and our ability to tell our own stories. Stories that are different from the ones we're being brainwashed to believe" (2003, 3). That should define the mission of Asian American studies.

18

Enclave
Yoonmee Chang

"Enclave" when used in the context of Asian American studies is shorthand for "ethnic enclave." The enclave as such is, broadly, a geographically distinct cluster point for a racial or ethnic group. The enclave's political and economic structures become associated with ethnicity. In some cases, they can be accurately characterized as indigenous to, or at least historically embedded within, an ethnic group. In other cases, political and economic practices that look ethnicity based are adaptations with no inherent relationship to race and culture.

Vis-à-vis Asian America, places that are categorized as "enclaves" are known as Chinatown, Koreatown, Little Tokyo, Little Saigon, Manilatown, Little India, and so forth. Each of these enclaves has a distinct history as well as varying, ever-changing systems of social, cultural, political, and economic organization. Even within a monoethnic rubric, enclaves are heterogeneous. For instance, "Chinatown" is an umbrella term for many different spaces, the most iconic being in San Francisco and New York. But it also refers to lesser-known communities, such as in Philadelphia or Chicago, where geographical boundaries are blurrier and the majority Asian ethnic group might not be Chinese.

"Enclave" thereby refers to a variety of spaces that do not adhere to a single or stable model. Moreover, though enclaves could once be assumed to be urban, they are now increasingly suburban. The criteria for categorizing a space as an ethnic enclave have been under longstanding contention. What makes the enclave ethnic—the ethnicity of the residents or the ethnicity of the business community? Both? Why does this matter? Does the enclave take on its ethnic cast by population count or by social imprint and power? Why are these not always equivalent? (W. Li 2009; Sanders and Nee 1992; Zhou 1992; Peter Kwong 1996).

These questions are underwritten by an instructive, but false binary: the understanding of the enclave as a community, on the one hand, and as a ghetto, on the other. The enclave is defined as a community insofar as community denotes structures and practices of cooperation based on a sense of ethnic kinship. Race and culture are most saliently shared in the enclave, but so are political and economic interests. This characterization of the enclave suggests that it is a voluntary, self-segregated formation whose residents are empowered and cooperate for the community good (Zhou 1992; Jan Lin 1998). The linkage between "enclave" and "community" is at times so reflexive that the terms are used interchangeably.

The characterization of the enclave as a community is in direct opposition to earlier depictions of spaces like Chinatown as sites of impoverishment, filth, and intractable crime—in short, as ghettos. But it is worthwhile to ask what gets lost when this more negative construction of the enclave is minimized or erased. "Ghetto" has typically been used to denote spaces of racial-ethnic segregation in which residents are disempowered, due to unproductive, implicitly pathological structures of social, political, and economic organization. The damaged and damaging conditions of the ghetto are sometimes rightly identified as structural, results of formal laws and entrenched social practices; and other times are identified as cultural, the result of ghetto residents' behavioral inability to transcend, or cultural proclivity to create, their distressed conditions (Massey and Denton 1993' Wilson 1987). These conceptualizations of

"ghetto" imply that its residents are powerless victims or self-destructive deviants. "Ghetto" strips its residents of agency.

So it is easy to see why the term "ghetto" would be eschewed in favor of the agency-endowing "enclave." This substitution is strikingly specific to Asian Americans. A survey of the relevant interdisciplinary literature shows a mindful disavowal of "ghetto" in favor of "enclave" in studies of Asian American segregation (Y. Chang 2010). But "enclave" as a metonym or equivalent of "community" is not innocent. Its use performs a paradigm shift, in which racial-ethnic segregation is relieved of being a structural, social liability, and privatized as a cultural expression of a self-segregated community.

"Ghetto" is not so readily dispatched in regard to other racial-ethnic groups, namely African Americans. In this multiracial context, the use of "enclave" for Asian Americans put them in antagonistic relationship to blacks. As is well known, the model minority myth pits Asian Americans against African Americans, characterizing the former as hardworking, thrifty, and family and education oriented, in opposition to the malingering, sexually promiscuous criminality that stereotypes the latter. Like the model minority myth, "enclave" overstates and oversimplifies the socioeconomic success of Asian Americans. A central form of agency encoded in "enclave" is economic agency, namely the drawing upon racial-cultural bonds for economic advancement (Zhou 1992). But this arrangement has its winners and losers—business owners enrich themselves by exploiting workers under the banner of co-ethnic cooperation. Weighted toward such positive but unbalanced effects of cultural agency, "enclave" does not account well for the class divides within it (Peter Kwong 1996). In addition, "enclave" obscures the fact that Asian American segregation results from structural class inequity. Asian American segregation might result from voluntary interests, but also does so from de jure and de facto discrimination.

"Enclave" brings us to the unwieldy concepts of culture and class. I suggest that a major drawback of using "enclave" is that it privileges *cultural* agency, and thereby obscures racialized *class* inequity (Y. Chang 2010). This epistemological tension between culture and class is not only germane to defining the meaning of enclave, but is also a core problematic in Asian American studies overall. Overdetermined as the model minority, Asian Americans are cast as immune from, or at least easily transcending, poverty. This diverts attention from those who do not rise out of poverty, and enlists Asian Americans as testimony to American exceptionalism; Asian Americans are used as the metric of America's so-called classlessness. Though class inequality during the administration of President Barack Obama has strongly entered mainstream sociopolitical discourse, Americans' more recognizable exceptionalism has been their alacrity in avoiding the topic of class. Vis-à-vis Asian Americans, "enclave" feeds the obfuscation of class inequity. Certain usages of the term turn attention away to class configurations that are inequitable because they are, for that very reason, unpalatable.

19

Entrepreneur
Pawan Dhingra

Ethnic entrepreneurship supposedly symbolizes minority uplift based on principles of free choice, free markets, and limited government support. Within this neoliberal framework Asian American business owners have become yet another version of the "model minority," a population other minorities should emulate for their hard work and resourcefulness and whose achievements indicate a meritocratic United States. Ethnic niches, that is industry- or product-specific stores commonly associated with an ethnic group, have been heralded by politicians and minority communities themselves. So, more than simply an economic term, the entrepreneur (i.e., one who finds or creates opportunities and products, often through self-employment) is an ideological construct.

In truth, Asian Americans' entrepreneurship often results from their discriminatory treatment as unwanted foreigners within a capitalist system exploitative of minorities. Early Asian immigrants entered self-employment in response to the low wages and harsh conditions of paid labor and punitive immigration laws. By the late 1880s, Chinese Americans had subservient jobs as domestic servants, cooks, and gardeners due to forced residential segregation and job discrimination (Takaki 1989). In response they opened up restaurants, laundries, and other stores, labor considered too effeminate or cheap for whites to do. Japanese immigrants worked as farmhands, eventually earning enough to become independent farmers (Bonacich and Modell 1980). In cities such as Seattle, Los Angeles, and San Francisco, they also opened hotels, gardening services, grocery stores, and other establishments. These businesses were available for newcomers because they were labor intensive, did not require much capital to start, and relied on the entire family as unpaid laborers. By the late 1920s, Chinese and Japanese immigrants owned businesses at a higher rate than did white Americans (Bonacich and Modell 1980).

These groups had success at small business because of community support. They used rotating credit systems, that is informal, monitored networks among co-ethnics to borrow money (Light 1972). Still common among entrepreneurial communities, these systems compensate for the lack of formal loans available to immigrants without many assets who enter low-profit, high-risk industries. Also, owners employ unpaid family members and co-ethnics willing to accept low wages. In contrast, Filipino Americans' small business enterprise was limited, mostly in restaurants, barber shops, and pool halls near major Filipino settlements (Y. Espiritu 2003). As primarily bachelors who traveled during the Great Depression in search of farm jobs, there was little opportunity or community resources for Filipinos to start businesses. Yet, the usefulness of community resources does not mean that they should be uniformly applauded. Rotating credit and co-ethnic labor systems shift the burden of ensuring economic development from the state or entrepreneur to the community at large, while profits stay with the owner.

Even with community support, strong financial returns were not guaranteed. Racist retaliations threatened to stifle profits, such as ordinances in San Francisco that taxed Chinese laundries more than others and alien land laws barring Issei from owning land (Morrison Wong 2006). Many Chinese and Japanese American owners left their businesses once viable paid labor options arose.

With few exceptions (e.g., motels for Indian Americans [Dhingra 2012]) Asian American businesses did not grow in the 1940s through the 1960s, partly due to the internment of Japanese Americans and later due to the postwar economy that provided outside job opportunities. Following the Immigration and Naturalization Act of 1965, and later the arrival of Southeast Asian refugees, entrepreneurship today has increased. Among racialized groups, non-Hispanic whites recently have had the highest rates of self-employment, at 11.8 percent (between 2005 and 2007), almost 4 percent more than Latinos and over twice that of blacks (Poon, Tran, and Ong 2009). Vietnamese, Japanese, Indian, and Chinese Americans have self-employment rates similar to whites, while Korean Americans have a much higher rate, at 21.4 percent (Poon, Tran, and Ong 2009). Korean Americans started businesses because language barriers, nontransferrable educational degrees, and discrimination in hiring practices blocked white-collar job opportunities (P. Min 1996).

Once in business, immigrant entrepreneurs face multiple types of subjugation that further belie a model minority existence. Interracial tensions are common, especially for middleman minorities (Bonacich 1972). Middleman minorities purchase goods from big capital enterprises and sell them to poor, often minority residents in segregated, low-income neighborhoods. Due to racist development practices in U.S. inner cities, residents lack convenient access to large grocery stores and indoor shopping malls. Korean Americans filled that retail gap with small grocery, clothing, and liquor stores (P. Min 1996). Residents can resent the middleman minorities who, in order to make a profit, must charge more money for the same products sold in larger chain stores. Adding frustration are redlining policies that deny or overcharge minority residents for loans, coupled with the mistaken assumption that Korean Americans have received preferential treatment for loans. Cultural differences with merchants fuel tensions, such as language differences and Korean norms of not touching customers' hands or smiling at them. For their part, owners may arrive in the United States with racialized stereotypes of African Americans already in mind and not trust customers. While the state should take the lead in investing in cities, ethnic owners bear the brunt if seen as not investing private money. Boycotts, protests, and even violence have garnered much media attention, such as the Red Apple boycott in New York City in 1990 and the Los Angeles riots of 1992 (C. Kim 2000). Given that tensions simmer, owners and customers work to create smooth relations. For instance, owners hire African Americans to serve as intermediaries with customers, and customers frequent stores they consider more courteous (Jennifer Lee 2002).

Gender segregation further disrupts an idealized notion of small business. In the motel business, for instance, husbands run the "entrepreneurial" side of the business, engaging with the public and making decisions on business direction, upgrades, hiring, and so forth. Behind the scenes, wives engage in manual labor, such as ironing, cleaning, and monitoring other women (Dhingra 2012). Lacking a pay check and engaged in domestic work, women receive too little credit for their contributions. Women pursue their own, low-capital entrepreneurial niches, such as Korean American and Vietnamese American nail salons, due to a lack of opportunities in the workplace and as a hopeful way to juggle childcare and work responsibilities (M. Kang 2010). These popular businesses still are defined by race, for nail salon work suits dominant stereotypes of Asian women: subservient, attentive to detail, and with nimble fingers.

Owner-labor tensions also are endemic within immigrant small businesses. While employing other minorities is increasingly common, owners frequently employ co-ethnics, including those brought over through transnational ties and desperate for work. Working for co-ethnics offers some advantages, such as speaking one's native language on the job, flexible schedules, and access to training for one's own eventual small business (Portes and Zhou 1992). Cambodian immigrants in California have become prolific within donut shops because co-ethnics are hired for little or no pay until they can borrow enough money (again using some version of a rotating credit system) to buy a store (Ong 2003). At times they buy the store that they are working in, which allows the previous Cambodian American owner to buy a larger business. Yet, exploitation of workers is always at play. Owners can pay lower wages or less overtime to co-ethnics than to U.S.-born employees, especially if workers are undocumented. An extreme case of abuse was the prisonlike mistreatment of Thai immigrant garment workers in the El Monte sweatshop in Southern California, owned by a Thai American (Su and Martorell 2001). When possible, employees prefer working in mainstream businesses for the higher wages and better working conditions.

As families work long hours in businesses together, they might save enough to eventually turn a profit and attain a middle-class income. Yet what is less discussed are the rates of failure within immigrant businesses. Rather than file for bankruptcy, owners sell their businesses at a loss. Businesses' success and failure often depend on macro changes in the economy, putting owners and ethnic communities at risk of economic distress.

20

Environment

Robert T. Hayashi

Considering the term "environment" in relation to Asian American studies is like staring at one of those optical illusions full of dots that make up a face or figure that one at first cannot discern. In both instances, the modalities of viewing provide one a limited field of vision. In the case of the optical illusion, we rely on studying a static, one-dimensional image. When discussing the relation of Asian American studies to the term "environment," our perception is similarly restricted by the narrow meaning this term conveys since the mid-twentieth century—the natural world.

Until the late twentieth century, historians paid little attention to the environment, treating it as no more than the stage for human events, and while the fields of environmental history and environmental studies are now well established, they have traditionally failed to consider the experiences of Asian Americans who have seemed outside these lines of inquiry. Similarly, although Asian Americans have dramatically shaped the American environment, scholars in Asian American studies have eschewed the term, even as they have recorded the significant impact of Asians upon the American environment—notably their contributions to agricultural development (S. Chan 1989; Iwata, 1992; Matsumoto 1993). The role of Asian labor and Asian land use practices in shaping the American landscape—as farmers, railroad workers, and miners—is an important corrective to the historical tendency in environmental studies to overlook not only race, but labor. In addition,

sites of the Asian American experience—Chinatowns, relocation camps, immigration detention centers, temples, suburbs—have been richly detailed by scholars working in a range of disciplines. The related discovery and recovery of these places and of primary materials by scholars in Asian American studies have offered a heterogeneous chronicle of responses to and experiences of the American social and physical worlds. Yet, although scholars in Asian American studies routinely write about and teach such histories, their work remains mostly disconnected from the scholarship in environmental studies and related fields, and this has much to do with what the term "environment" has come to mean.

From the onset of European exploration of the Americas, the physical surroundings, the most expansive definition of environment, were replete with signs of indigenous habitation, and the environs—both natural and manmade—were repositories of cultural meaning. The physical removal and extirpation of indigenous peoples that accompanied European settlement erased much of this native presence in the environment, but does not fully explain the term's evolution from an "action of circumnavigating, encompassing, or surrounding something" to its present equivalence with only the natural world (*OED*). By writ, sonnet, and landscape painting, Euro-Americans converted native places into vacant spaces, *terra nullius*. They established a historical perspective with the European discovery of a primitive land as the starting point, and the English language charts this process. Divergent and already culturally rich places, including native ones, became the raw stuff of a process in making civilization, one that would later feed a national obsession with that base material: wilderness.

Whereas early European responses to the Americas were a mix of wonder and dread, the increasing industrialization of the nineteenth century catalyzed Americans' desire to protect natural resources. A growing middle class viewed the natural environment as a site of salubrious recreation and among urbanites there existed an ongoing concern for clean air and water. During the Progressive Era, a potent combination of wealthy industrialists and influential politicians helped establish laws to protect and conserve natural resources—men like Gifford Pinchot and Theodore Roosevelt, who instituted a tradition of government stewardship of nature as a protection of national heritage. As society shifted to give greater emphasis on preservation over conservation, a slew of landmark events—the founding of Earth Day, the passage of the Clean Water and Wilderness Acts—helped cement the equation of the environment with a new definition, that of "the natural world or physical surroundings" (*OED*).

At roughly the same time as these landmark moments in American environmental history, the term "Asian American" emerged from an intellectual revolution led by scholars exploring the social, political, and cultural worlds inhabited by Asian Americans—their environment. Yet deploying the now narrowed term "environment" to the study of this racial group long defined by its exclusion from American identity seemed akin to seeking out a face hidden in one of those patches of dots. The perspectives, experiences, and narratives of those who entered the continental United States from Africa, Canada, or Mexico, let alone Hawai'i or Asia, remained outside a metanarrative of exploration. Where did Asians, literally and figuratively excluded from American identity, fit within a national narrative of westward-moving pioneers settling a pristine land? What did they have to do with pristine nature and its protection?

The growing influence of place as a conceptual frame, first articulated in cultural geography, now offers a more expansive vehicle for analysis in several fields, including Asian American studies: one that circumvents the troubling limitations of environment. As a result, scholars of Asian America have been expanding both the lines of inquiry in their work and the geographic focus of the field, shifting attention to the American South, New England, Canada, South America, and beyond. The greater latitude provided by the term "place" complements the increasingly transnational character of research in Asian American studies, a field that has often used spatial metaphors to define its project: margins, displacements, and frontiers—as opposed to "the Frontier" (Okihiro 1994; Anderson and Lee 2005; Nomura, Sumida, Leong, and Endo, 1989). This emerging scholarship details the range of social, political, and material layers of meaning attached to American sites.

More recently, scholars in fields such as ecocriticism and environmental history have turned a critical lens on how the study of Asian Americans relates to dominant notions of the natural world (Hayashi 2007a; Hayashi 2007b; C. Chiang 2010; C. Chiang 2008). Scholars and activists working in environmental justice have articulated the interrelatedness of social and natural worlds as it relates to the experience of racial and ethnic minorities, including Asian Americans (Pellow and Park 2002; Shah 2011; Sze 2011; Sze 2007; UCLA Asian American Studies Center 2013). This work has helped deconstruct the received cultural legacy of the term "environment," revealing how notions of the natural world have functioned to racialize and disenfranchise Asians via the law and social practice.

Asian American studies thus holds the potential to reformulate the definition of environment, to echo the word's long obsolete definition of "encompassing, surrounding" (*OED*). Such work may provide a means both to encompass the slippery term "Asian American" and ground it in the material and cultural conditions of individual and collective experience, so that like those hidden faces, those whom it defines will readily emerge when we deploy the term "environment."

21

Ethnicity

Rick Bonus

Ethnicity appears prominently among Asian Americans and in Asian American studies as a basis for the group's and field's inaugural formation in the 1960s, when participants in the later period of the civil rights movement advocated for the coherence of several Asian-descent and historically affiliated populations into one coalition. Even though one may argue that "Asian American" itself is mostly thought of as a race-based designation, people with different ethnic origins comprise this category, thereby making ethnicity undisputedly a marker that is racialized in the same fashion as other ethnicities within certain racialized categories are collectively configured. Examples of ethnic groups within the classification Asian American include Japanese American, Filipino American, Chinese American, Vietnamese American, and South Asian American.

Ethnicity, in general, refers to a kind of group formation on the basis of one or several attributes that subjects of such a group may hold in common: religion, language, or any number of social, political, or cultural features and traits that they may possess, including, but not limited to, racial characteristics, geographical origin, and national identification. It is both a product and an ongoing process of determining who or what gets included and excluded in a group, making ethnicity, therefore, an endless construction of similarity and difference that marks and limits the boundaries of a community. Specific to Asian Americans, the major significance of ethnicity lies in its reference to the potentials and powers of political mobilization for a multiplicity of diverse groups whose affinities with each other were galvanized by the events surrounding the opposition to the Vietnam War and the struggles for Third World liberation, civil rights, and academic institutionalization (Wei 1993). As noted above, this malleable capacity of ethnic group formation, otherwise legible in the language and practice of panethnicity, was especially important in the founding moments of a movement for Asian American studies (Y. Espiritu 1992). The force and durability of such a capacity to organize by classification and to enable constructions of commonalities that move toward consensus is, nevertheless, situation-dependent, impermanent, and unstable. These are the reasons why ethnicity in Asian American studies continues to be a provocative subject of inquiry, debate, and discussion.

One primary focus in the study of ethnicity in Asian American studies constitutes the historicizing of ethnic categories within it to account for not only the processes by which a category is invented and naturalized within time and space, but to mark as well the particular motivations, expressions, and effects that constitute their formation and transformation. Ethnicity, in this way, is understood as having a genealogical trace, in opposition to the assumption that it is timeless, naturally occurring, and unchanging. To wit, ethnicity is understood not as having an a priori or self-evident manifestation. It is, rather, constructed or invented by individuals, collectives, and institutions (Sollors 1988). It is constituted by the workings of alliance building, imagined community formation, and deep or broad ascription (Anderson 1991). And, as in every homogenizing and instrumentalist-driven process, it is also fraught with opposition, deliberation, and practices of certain forms of violence. From the creation and endurance of stereotypes attached to an ethnic group, to the ways in which such stereotypes are resisted or replaced, and from the intricacies of political coalition building through identification of common interests to their downfall or subsequent contraction and expansion, studies of ethnicity bring to light deep and broad applications and limitations of group identity consciousness and calculation.

The question of ethnicity as it is defined in connection to origin, ancestry, parentage, or nationality looms large in ethnic studies. Because the U.S. Census has had a strong hand in determining a particular definition of Asian American as a category populated by those whose origins are from Asia and the Indian subcontinent, there is a resilient tendency to naturalize ethnicity as first and foremost a category that is putatively geographical and contingent upon birth. That is, one can quickly and easily presume one's ethnicity as primarily grounded on one's connection to a birthplace, giving it primordial status (the location of the beginning and perpetuation of one's existence) in the constitution of one's ethnic understanding. But there are several limitations to this particular bloodline formulation, notwithstanding its utility to policymakers, demographers, and community activists in acting upon patterns of socioeconomic phenomena occurring within and across origin-based classifications. What about those who are racially different from the majority of those within the same ethnic group? What about those who move to one or multiple locations after birth (or then go back and forth)? How do we deal with those who are socialized differently from or socialized in opposition to the dominant culture of that ethnicity? And how do we equitably account for sub-ethnic, language, and religious micro groups that are internally subsumed under a larger category of affinity?

Questions like these are oftentimes provoked and motivated by conditions of inequality. Consciousness of sameness may simply be derived from understandings of "what we hold in common" but that may be different from, though related to, practices of assigning value and imputing hierarchical arrangements within an ascribed category and in comparison with other groups outside of or larger than that category. In Asian American studies, these get played out in historical and contemporary forms of exclusion, disenfranchisement, and discrimination of Cambodian American women, for example, both as a marginalized population within the category Cambodian American and as a nondominant group under the category Asian American (Schlund-Vials 2012b). In cases like this, ethnicity gets to be understood, more than anything else, as a process of exercising and disputing power within and across intersecting, multiple, and heterogeneous identities and locations. How does one account for the qualitative difference in the experiences of non-Asians, women, nonheterosexuals, upper- and lower-class members, multiracials, non-Christians, and non-Muslim people subsumed under the specific ethnic categories within Asian America? What about those with limited schooling experience or restricted proficiency in the dominant languages? Why are their experiences different, and how are the oppressive conditions to which they are subjected propped up and resisted?

If identities within ethnicities are heterogeneous and intersecting, so are their attendant histories. In U.S. historiography, law, popular culture, and school curricula, there is a robust tendency to equate American ethnicity with U.S. immigration history, primarily associating American ethnic groups with their social standing as "Americans" in proximity to their adopted country and against their relationship to their original or former homeland (for example, Dinnerstein and Reimers 1999). Thus, each ethnic group's history is usually narrated as the travails of being and becoming Americans, a journey to assimilation (or not) in which tales of group membership are told according to the ways in which their distance to dominant culture is approximated across time and place, and their contributions and rates of acculturation are calculated, more often than not, to determine their worth in society. Thus, all ethnic groups in Asian America are fundamentally considered as immigrant groups, once figuratively denoted by their nominal assignation as "hyphenated Americans." And although this may not be in vogue now, with the hyphen commonly erased, each ethnic group in general continues to be named as the signifier that comes before the "American" sign. But this proposition becomes untenable to the degree that it is inaccurate when those who are native born (or already far removed from older immigrant generations) are assumed to be included in the ethnic category, and when certain populations' relationship to U.S. history cannot be registered within the tradition of an immigrant chronicle. Filipino laborers who were moving to many parts of the U.S. during the early part of the 20th century, for example, were colonized subjects and, therefore, migrants in technical terms, not immigrants (Bonus 2000). And the tendency to conflate refugee status with immigrant status does not do justice for many Southeast Asian and South Asian groups' differential incorporation into or resistance against U.S. society.

Persisting in the narration of ethnicity for Asian American people as a saga of immigration to a new nation is oftentimes a product, as much as it is productive, of a contributionist ideology and a U.S.-centric perspective. It misses out on the manners by which different populations are coerced to move elsewhere by labor recruiters, make individual and collective decisions to settle within and outside of the U.S., and create networks of political, economic, and social interactions that are not easily circumscribed by the physical boundaries of their multiple homelands. Many members of ethnic groups in Asian America are not only internal and multistep migrants; they are also transnational subjects of a global economy whose identification with and loyalty to one homeland that is the U.S. are multistranded, complex, and contradictory. Their stories of assimilation also constitute struggles of resisting assimilation (or practicing alternatives to it), their relationship to U.S. culture and society is not unidirectional, and their collective accounts of mobility and transformation—the so-called push and pull of immigrant struggle—are all embedded within the larger histories and changing configurations of colonization, globalization, and transnationalism.

Nevertheless, the force of ethnic identification is laden with dynamic practices of representation and recognition. Who gets to belong and who gets to be excluded? With what criteria and under what means of control, accommodation, and negotiation? Who will police its boundaries and who will refuse or resist its surveillance? In what ways? These are questions that point to both the power and perils of consensus building, including the mechanisms that aim to promote solidarity, community, and connectedness as they are utilized by governing states, institutions, groups, and individuals internal or external (or both) to the membership of the constructed label (Võ 2004). Social scientists, historians, and cultural analysts frequently refer to this process as ethnicization to highlight the invention, maintenance, and transformation of group identification. Struggles to keep alive social customs and traditions, or anything that enables members to bond with each other, whether in the form of linguistic preservation, borrowing, or replacement, or through creative expressions in art, music, literature, and drama to represent and change group consciousness, are all indications of the energy and seduction of ethnicity as an ongoing process of affinity creation and transformation. Hence, references to ethnic clothing, ethnic languages, and ethnic cultural centers, to name a few, are rife among ethnic groups within and outside Asian America.

Ethnicity, on the other hand, has also been used to discriminate against and circumscribe the existence and actions of specific groups. For example, the Page Act of 1875 and the Chinese Exclusion Acts beginning in 1882 targeted women and men by restricting their entry into the U.S. as juridically determined by their Chinese ethnic ancestry. Ethnocentric practices of dominating groups can amount to violent acts of devaluation, deracination, and atrocious forms of ethnic cleansing. Asian American history is replete with exclusionary laws, mandated quotas, and restrictive policies that controlled the entry and naturalization of Asian people as defined by their race, ethnicity, social status, sex, and sexuality. The Naturalization Act of 1790, the Gentlemen's Agreement of 1907–1908, and the Asiatic Barred Zone Act of 1917 are but a few examples. These promulgations have produced a cumulative effect of legitimizing the construction of ethnic groups imagined as Asian by race, and occurring in different intensities over time and space, as subjects who are undesirable, foreign (or forever immigrants), unassimilable, and exotic or mysterious (Ancheta 2006).

Currently, the vitality of ethnicity in Asian American studies is evidenced by the ongoing transformations of each heterogeneous group within its purview and their evolving relationships with each other, the larger Asian rubric, the rest of the U.S. population and community groups, and the interconnected societies and governments within and outside of the United States. The rise of the "model minority" status that became associated with the category "Asian" instantiated, among many, calls for the disaggregation of the "Asian American" classification (in view of its internal hierarchies) and even prompted many ethnic groups to seriously consider the dominance and marginalization of sub-ethnic

groups within their own ethnic label, as well as the removal of certain groups that are frequently thought to be part of Asian America. Criticisms regarding the inclusion or separation of Pacific Islander population groups in or from Asian/Pacific Islander combined designations, as well as questions regarding the fate of some Native American and Middle Eastern communities in relationship to the broadening or contraction of the meanings of "Asian" in state and society are but two of the most challenging areas of contestation and negotiation. And finally, coming from a more critical vein of ethnic studies are the breadth of alternative histories and epistemologies of ethnicity that radiate from the engaged political work of queers of color, Third World feminists, anti-imperialism activists, and transnational scholars (Manalansan 2003; Reddy 2011). These demonstrate the realities and complexities of ethnicity as it is constantly invented and transformed in the name of power.

22

Exclusion

Greg Robinson

Within the field of Asian American studies, exclusion is a leitmotif that brings together collective histories of immigration restriction, detention, mass confinement, and citizenship denial. It expresses the organized forces, based in both state and private action, that have marginalized Asian Americans, and against which they have had to struggle, first to be permitted to enter the United States at all, and then to become accepted within the larger society.

To understand Asian exclusion, it is necessary to look at the larger history of ethnic stratification in the United States. From the time of their first settlement, Euro-Americans determined that America was theirs by right, an ever-expanding "white man's country" that they did not mean to share with other inhabitants. Despite the vital role of African Americans and native peoples in building the common society, members of those groups were excluded by both law and custom from full citizenship in the nation. Instead, members of groups not deemed "white" were at different times enslaved, segregated, expelled, or massacred with impunity.

In defining the boundaries of whiteness, social and political elites initially drew on geographical origin, skin color, and religious faith as prime markers. As time passed, they increasingly deployed the artificial concept of "race" and referred to innate biological characteristics (largely borrowed or adapted from their European counterparts), a move that mostly acted to reinscribe and codify the same distinctions that had already been

drawn. The heterogamous nature of American life meant that drawing biological distinctions among its people was an even more logically absurd process there than elsewhere.

In the course of the 19th century, a complex racial regime was established. Jews and other non-Nordic European immigrants were at times subjected to hostility and unofficial bias as "lesser races," and ultimately restricted in their immigration. Members of liminal semi-European or non-European groups (Hispanics, Cape Verdeans, native Hawai'ians, Armenians) were arbitrarily characterized as white or subjected to inferior status. Only native peoples and those of African or Asian descent were subjected to legal exclusion, a status that remained predominant in the United States, with minor exceptions, until the late 20th century.

Yet within this exclusionary regime, Asian exclusion had a particular nature and operation, one that stemmed from both the timing of large-scale Asian immigration and the particular region of their settlement. Again, to understand this, we must look at the republic's first nationality law, enacted by Congress in 1790. It enshrined racial caste in the United States by restricting naturalization to "free white" immigrants. What was unclear from the start was whether that term meant "Caucasian" or simply "not black," a matter not resolved when Asians started to arrive. The first individuals of East Asian ancestry who came to antebellum America, including the (ethnic Chinese) "Siamese twins" Chang and Eng Bunker, the Chinese student Yung Wing, and the Japanese Joseph Heco, did not trouble the existing color line. All settled in the East, were received on equal terms, and were ultimately granted citizenship.

However, the arrival of masses of Chinese immigrants during and after the 1849 California Gold Rush, the first large group of East Asian ancestry in the United States, triggered widespread hostility in California. The

Gold Rush inspired the migration of waves of European and American prospectors hoping to make their fortunes. Having left their lives behind to come to the new U.S. possessions (war booty seized from Mexico), and traveling long distances overland or by sea around South America, they felt entitled to superior status and full benefits, and resented their hardworking Chinese counterparts. After attempting vainly to legislate against all aliens to eliminate the competition, the all-white legislatures seized on racial bias (mixed with bigotry over "heathen" religions) as a tool to discourage Chinese settlement, and enacted legal disabilities such as barring Chinese from testifying against whites in court. The clear purpose of the law was to make it impossible for Chinese prospectors to win in cases of contested claims. The precedent was thereby created for viewing Asians as "colored."

Following the Civil War, the "white or black" question was answered for Asians at a national level, but in contradictory terms. On the one hand, in early 1866 Congress passed a bill to protect the civil rights of the newly emancipated freedmen. Its first section provided that all those born in the United States, apart from untaxed Indians, were citizens with the right to "full and equal benefit of all laws." In his veto message of March 27, 1866, President Andrew Johnson objected, among other things, that the bill would grant birthright citizenship to ethnic Chinese as well as Gypsies, Indians, and African Americans. Following the message, there was extensive debate in Congress over whether these groups actually deserved citizenship. In voting to override Johnson's veto and enact the bill, Congress effectively determined native-born Chinese and other Asians admissible for citizenship on the coattails of blacks—a provision that the same lawmakers then made fundamental law by enshrining similar provisions in the 14th Amendment, adopted weeks later. The Supreme Court ultimately upheld the principle of birthright citizenship in the 1898 *Wong Kim Ark* case.

But there was a catch. Ensuring equal rights and (future) voting to a then-tiny number of American-born Asian infants was a small sacrifice for principle, more symbolic than real. Meaningful exclusion instead became concentrated at the level of the immigrants themselves—if they could be kept out, no citizens would be born. When Congress voted in 1870 a symbolic amendment to the original 1790 immigration act allowing "free Africans" to naturalize, Californian representatives blocked a proposal to abolish all the other racial restrictions (even if these bars had been erected as adjuncts to that of Africans), to avoid naturalizing Chinese aliens who could then vote. Instead, Asians would be fixed legally as foreigners, and even their U.S.-born descendants would share that image in the public consciousness.

Meanwhile, coalitions of nativist political leaders and labor unionists, many of them immigrants themselves, began organizing boycotts of Chinese-produced goods and calling for outright exclusion of Chinese laborers. It was not simply a question of undercutting competition—they saw agitating against the Chinese ("the indispensable enemy" in the piquant phrase of Alexander Saxton [1975]) as a tool for winning political power. Building on established stereotypes, they constructed a threat out of a combination of biological, cultural, and religious elements. The result was a violent exclusionist push by white settlers against the Chinese presence (and subsequently against other Asians, as they arrived). White terrorists in the West, abetted by local authorities, launched over a hundred anti-Chinese pogroms in the following years to drive out Chinese communities, with the goal of eliminating Chinese totally from the region. State and local lawmakers in California enacted racist legislation limiting Chinese employment, barring interracial marriage, and excluding (later segregating) ethnic Chinese public school students. To be sure, this color bar formed part of a larger nationwide, indeed international, movement of virulent white supremacist sentiment against all nonwhite groups. Yet the concentrated presence of Asians in the West, a frontier area newly "won" to white domination which featured an unbalanced gender ratio, stoked "yellow peril" fears among whites of an Asian takeover and aroused sexual jealousy and anxieties about masculinity, which contributed to its particularly violent character (Pfaelzer 2005).

Congress, incited by the Californians and their allies, meanwhile became a center of action. The legislative dimension of exclusion is well known. The first victory of nativist agitators was the 1875 Page Law. It barred entry into the country of "undesirable immigrants," including Asian women suspected of being prostitutes (a provision soon stretched to include nearly all Chinese women, who had the burden of proving their innocence). Seven years later, Congress enacted the first Chinese Exclusion Act. This legislation barred all "skilled and unskilled [Chinese] laborers and Chinese employed in mining" for ten years. In order to prevent the establishment of ethnic communities (and hence the birth of children with citizenship rights), Congress barred even established residents from bringing in wives. Subsequent laws—the Scott Act in 1888 and the Geary Act in 1892—extended the initial exclusion and added further restrictions. In 1898, following the U.S. annexation, exclusion was extended to Hawai'i. In 1904 the exclusion law was made permanent.

The exclusion of Chinese served as a template for nativists to agitate for the successive exclusion of other Asian immigrant groups: Koreans, East Indians, and Filipinos (who were not immigrants, strictly speaking, once the U.S. colonized the Philippines, but who were

nevertheless denied equal citizenship). Like the Chinese, existing residents were barred from bringing over their spouses.

The one partial exception was Japan. Following campaigns by West Coast nativists, President Theodore Roosevelt (who had his own racial prejudices) moved to cut off Japanese immigration in 1907–1908. Though the threat of war with the powerful Japanese empire staved off unilateral exclusion of Japanese immigrants until 1924, Washington and Tokyo worked out a so-called Gentleman's Agreement that achieved the same ends by informal means (by executive order, Roosevelt also excluded Japanese immigrants in Hawai'i from resettling on the mainland, thereby restricting half the nation's ethnic Japanese population to the territory). Japanese immigrants retained the right to bring over wives and children. The result was that sex ratios were more equal in Japanese than other Asian communities, though still majority male. Although the Cable Act (1922–1931) singled out American-born Japanese and other Asian women for loss of citizenship if they married Asian immigrant males, thereby restricting the marriage market, by the time of World War II the numbers of American-born children in the Japanese community largely surpassed that of the adult alien population.

Once exclusion was enacted, it defined Asian Americans—first Chinese, and by extension other Asians, who were popularly identified with Chinese—as officially undesirable. Immigration inspectors responsive to anti-Asian popular opinion, especially on the West Coast, followed their self-interest in interpreting their power to exclude as broadly as possible. Chinese and later other Asians who arrived at the Angel Island immigration station (including American residents returning from trips abroad) were routinely harassed by immigration officials. They were grilled thoroughly by interviewers, who presumed them to be untruthful.

Even those finally admitted were frequently forced to wait, sometimes for weeks or months, to obtain permission to enter or reenter the country. While initially courts stepped in to redress abusive rulings by immigration authorities, the federal government ultimately rejected judicial oversight under the doctrine of plenary powers.

As part of the exclusion law, those Chinese Americans already resident were subjected to a regime of surveillance. In order to establish their right to be in the U.S., unlike all other immigrants, they were forced to obtain passes ("certificates of residence," later renamed "certificates of identity") including descriptions and photographs, and find two white witnesses to vouch for them. Even established Asian American residents were denied due process against unfavorable deportation rulings. Similarly, because of the near-total exclusion of Asian women (apart from Japanese), ethnic communities were largely composed of aging bachelors, with relatively few nuclear family groups and U.S.-born children.

Exclusion pushed Chinese Americans into clandestinity and deception as a way of life. In order to be permitted entry, "paper son" immigrants posed as the children of existing Chinese American residents who granted or sold such sponsorship to outsiders. Alternatively, immigrants pretended to be American born, asserting that their birth records had been destroyed in the great San Francisco earthquake of 1906. Numerous Chinese traveled to Canada or Mexico and then were smuggled into the United States. In the end, a larger number of Chinese first entered the United States during the exclusion period, generally under false pretenses, than during the entire generation preceding it. The long-term result was that many Chinese Americans grew up uncertain of their true origins or families, and biological kin relationships were replaced by others (Erika Lee 2004).

Moreover, once the genie of anti-Asian racism loosed by the Chinese exclusion movement had been let out of the bottle, the marginalization of all Asians continued to spread. Even after the cutoff of Asian immigration—the ostensible goal of exclusion—had been achieved, the immigrants continued to face segregation and episodes of mob violence. White agitators organized pogroms against Japanese Americans in places such as Toledo, Oregon, in 1925 and Maricopa County, Arizona (future center of anti-Mexican agitation), in 1934. Filipino Americans were attacked by mobs in Watsonville, California, in 1930 and Hood River, Oregon, in 1932.

Legal discrimination expanded as well. Long after the Supreme Court's 1886 *Yick Wo v. Hopkins* decision formally barred laws with "disparate impact" on specific groups, Chinese operating restaurants and laundries continued to be handicapped by special legislation and licensing initiatives. The most significant example of anti-Asian legislation was alien land laws, enacted by California in 1913 and copied by nearly half the United States after World War I. These laws prevented "aliens ineligible to citizenship"—a transparent euphemism for Asian immigrants—from purchasing or owning agricultural land. As a result, Asian aliens (predominantly Japanese) were forced to rely on white associates to hold the land for them or place title in the names of their American-born Nisei children, who were citizens (Daniels 1962).

Asian American citizens were likewise targeted by legal discrimination. In a third of the states of the union, Asians were barred from marrying whites (Filipinos and East Indians were sometimes singled out separately for restriction). Chinese schoolchildren on the West Coast and in Mississippi were relegated to black schools, while California permitted local school districts to segregate "Mongolians" (i.e., Asians). Even in the supposed interracial paradise of Hawai'i, the establishment of "English standard schools" in the 1920s, open only to pupils whose English was acceptable to authorities, effectively excluded the mass of Asian Americans from equal educational opportunity (Asato 2005). West Coast Nisei, meanwhile, faced widespread Jim Crow exclusion in the shape of restrictive housing covenants—some 80% of Los Angeles housing was off-limits to nonwhites in 1940—plus exclusion from parks, swimming pools, and theaters.

One perverse shadow of Asian American exclusion by the outside society was forms of exclusion practiced among and between Asian groups. Masses of Nisei were exposed to their parents' prejudices against ethnic Koreans and Filipinos, while those descended from *burakumin* remained marginalized within Japanese populations (Geiger 2011). In both Chinese and Japanese communities, Christian ministers joined at times in movements to oppose and suppress Buddhism as a heathen and backward religion. Mixed-race couples, and especially their biracial offspring, occupied an uncertain position within Asian communities, and sometimes were shunned altogether (Spickard 2001).

This heritage of exclusion helped lead to the mass confinement of West Coast Japanese Americans during World War II. Although Japanese immigration was cut off after 1908 and completely halted in 1924, white nativists maintained a propaganda campaign against ethnic Japanese in California throughout the entire prewar period. Using the technique of the big lie, they repeatedly charged falsely that the Issei were agents of Tokyo, and Nisei were foreigners due to their (purely nominal and increasingly rare) status as dual citizens. In the months following the Japanese military attack on Pearl Harbor in December 1941, craven and careerist Army officials, supported by opportunistic political leaders, newspaper editors, and commercial group leaders, pressed for wholesale exclusion of the region's entire Japanese population. On February 19, 1942, President Franklin Roosevelt signed Executive Order 9066, which authorized the Army to set up an "excluded zone" that ultimately covered the entire Pacific Coast. Japanese Americans were taken from their homes without due process and forcibly transported, first to holding centers and then to a network of camps outside the Pacific Coast (G. Robinson 2001). Even after Japanese Americans obtained "leave clearance" and were paroled from camp, they remained barred from their home region. The exclusion would be progressively relaxed during 1943 and 1944 to accommodate certain groups, notably Nisei soldiers, but would not be lifted until after the U.S. Supreme Court's ruling in *Ex parte Endo* in December 1944. Despite the endemic anti-Asian prejudice and discriminatory legislation, a majority of Japanese Americans chose to return to the Pacific Coast in the years after the war (G. Robinson 2009).

Ironically, World War II also set into motion a dynamic that ended the legal exclusion of Asian Americans. Motivated by the desire to propitiate China, America's wartime ally, the Roosevelt administration campaigned successfully in Congress to remove the insult of total exclusion and replace it with the insult of near-total exclusion (China's annual immigration quota was set at 105). Yet, by the same act, immigrants of the "Chinese race" were finally declared eligible for naturalization. Three years later, East Indians and Filipinos were likewise rendered admissible in tiny numbers and authorized to naturalize, and in 1952 the McCarran-Walter Act ended absolute exclusion of immigrants from Japan and all other Asian countries. By that time, the U.S. Supreme Court had already struck down state laws directed against "aliens ineligible to citizenship," while California had repealed its school segregation laws and been forced to abandon its laws barring interracial marriage. In the succeeding years, the Japanese

American Citizens League helped lead movements for repeal of interracial marriage laws in other Western states. The Supreme Court's 1948 *Shelley v. Kraemer* decision, which struck down legal enforcement of restrictive covenants, led to an easing of housing discrimination against Asians.

Even a half-century after the end of state-sponsored discrimination, exclusion and its legacy remain vital factors in Asian American life. Integration into American society remains a challenge for many Asians, especially refugees and other new immigrants. Exclusion manifests itself in such areas as media stereotyping, the glass ceiling at the workplace, housing bias, and hate crimes on the street. Within Asian communities, various subgroups remain marginalized. Most notably, LGBT Asian Americans must often fight a dual burden of invisibility, and justify their presence within the larger community. We may hope that the success of Asian Americans in breaking through barriers of exclusion from mainstream American society will translate into further visibility and integration for gays and lesbians within Asian communities.

23

Family
Evelyn Nakano Glenn

In popular usage, the ideal family unit is a nuclear household consisting of a mother, father, and children residing together. However, the U.S. Census Bureau defines the family more broadly as "two or more people (one of whom is the householder) related by birth, marriage, or adoption residing in the same housing unit." In other contexts, "family" may refer to (all) those related by blood or marriage, regardless of whether or not they live under the same roof. Societies differ in how they reckon blood relationships. They may recognize kinship through only the male line (patrilineal), only the female line (matrilineal), or both male and female lines (bilateral). Moreover, the question of "what is family?" can be considered via its functions, namely, producing and reproducing persons as biological and social beings. These functions are accomplished through a gender and generational division of labor. Alternatively, family relations can be imagined; sociologists and anthropologists have used the term "fictive kin" to refer to those who are considered to be family members even if they are not formally related. As Alvin Gouldner (1960) observes, families also encompass "status obligations"—duties that are attached to one's kinship position in the family. For example, in many cultures, mothers are expected to care for young children; fathers to contribute economically; and children to obey parents. Importantly, status obligations have moral relevance. Others (both within the family and in the larger community) may judge whether a woman is a "good" or "bad" mother/daughter/wife/ etc. based on whether or not she performs her familial duties. Status obligations are also internalized in that members feel that they should perform them, and if they do not, they feel guilty.

This brief review highlights the socially constructed nature of the family and its malleability while pursuing a two-pronged inquiry into the Asian American family. On the one hand, given the socially constructed nature of the family, we can ask, what are the cultural, political, and economic factors that have influenced Asian American family formation? On the other hand, given the family's malleability, what strategies have Asian Americans pursued to maximize family survival and well-being? Integral to understanding the function of "family" within Asian American studies is an analysis of how successive histories of immigration prohibition, state segregation, and socioeconomic exclusion contributed to the development of particular family units in the United States.

In particular, Asian immigrants confronted laws and policies designed to prevent them from establishing conventional families. From 1850 to 1882, Chinese men were recruited to fill the demand for labor in agriculture, mining, and railroad construction in the American West. The few men of the merchant class who immigrated during this era were allowed to bring wives or concubines, but the vast majority of Chinese men lacked legal and economic means to do so. The Page Act of 1875 effectively barred Chinese women, while the Chinese Exclusion Act of 1882 cut off all legal entry for Chinese laborers. Unable to attain the ideal of a coresident family, the estimated half of Chinese immigrants who had left spouses in China developed "split household families" in which one member worked abroad and sent remittances while the rest of the household remained in the country of origin and engaged in reproductive labor

(Glenn 1983). Restrictive U.S. immigration policies and antimiscegenation statutes ensured that Chinese America remained a "bachelor" society. As Nayan Shah (2001) documents, the prevalence of homosociality and the paucity of families fueled white imaginings of Chinese as inassimilable aliens and Chinatowns as disease- and vice-ridden slums.

The next major wave of Asian labor migration (1890–1907) consisted of single young men from Japan. Unlike the Chinese, Issei men were eventually allowed to bring or send for spouses. Under the terms of the Gentlemen's Agreement of 1907, Japan halted the emigration of laborers and in exchange the U.S. issued passports to wives and children of Issei already in the United States. Thousands of Issei men took advantage of the opportunity to go to Japan to marry or to send for picture brides. The Issei population remained gender skewed, but by the time the Immigration Act of 1924 cut off all immigration from the Asian subcontinent, there was a significant presence of Japanese American families. These families were heavily concentrated in agricultural pursuits, particularly truck farming, plant nurseries, gardening, and produce marketing. Wives worked alongside husbands in field and shop, and children helped after school and during summers.

The Philippines became the next major source of Asian labor migrants (1924–1934) after the 1924 Immigration Act cut off immigration from other parts of Asia. As residents of a U.S. colony, Filipinos were deemed to be U.S. subjects and therefore eligible for entry. As with the Chinese and Japanese, Filipino migrants were overwhelmingly male and single; they were employed primarily as migratory laborers in farm fields and canneries. This migratory flow ended with the passage of the Tydings-McDuffie Act of 1934. Filipino men were more inclined than other Asians to transgress color lines by forming relationships with and even marrying white women and establishing mixed-race families. Yet formal and informal barriers to "miscegenation" ensured that the number of Filipino families remained small.

The situation for Chinese and Japanese families diverged with the outbreak of World War II. Japanese residing in the Pacific Coast states were forcibly removed and interned. In addition to destroying communities, internment place undue stress on family relations and sometimes broke up families. Among the impacts of the internment were the Issei generation's loss of authority due to their enemy alien status and lack of English-language fluency; the premature responsibility assumed by young Nisei who became mediators between the family and U.S. authorities; and family conflict generated by the federal government decision to separate out "disloyal" internees by administering loyalty tests. In the postwar years, family relations were haunted by the losses and traumas internees had suffered. The 1980s Redress Movement that sought an official apology and token payment for losses proved to be cathartic as family members finally openly talked about the internment. Meanwhile, opportunities for Chinese to form families expanded at long last. In 1943, in recognition of China's role as a U.S. ally, the U.S. Congress repealed the Chinese Exclusion Act and extended the right to become naturalized citizens to resident Chinese. The latter provision opened up non-quota slots to relatives of naturalized Chinese Americans. Special legislation at the end of the war allowed Chinese American service members to bring wives and fiancées. Augmented by a small number of Chinese professionals and intellectuals, the 1950s saw growing numbers of Chinese Americans who lived and worked outside the confines of Chinatowns. This period of pro-Chinese sentiment saw the publication of popular memoirs that portrayed Chinese American family life for mainstream American readers. Pardee Lowe's *Father and Glorious Descendent* (1943) and Jade Snow Wong's best-selling memoir, *Fifth Chinese Daughter* (1945), focused on cultural differences between immigrant parents and their children.

These developments were dwarfed by major changes that started with passage of the 1965 Immigration Act. This act removed national quotas and restrictions against immigrants from Asia, specified occupational preferences, and prioritized family reunification. In practice, three-quarters of visas for new immigrants were allotted to relatives of citizens and permanent resident aliens. In addition to large-scale immigration from China and Taiwan, sizable numbers came from Korea, the Philippines, and India. Compared to earlier immigrant cohorts, post-1965 immigrants were relatively well educated; indeed they had higher average years of schooling than the U.S. population as a whole.

The passage of refugee acts in 1975 and 1980 enabled the entry of large cohorts of Southeast Asians. Under the 1975 Indochina Migration and Refugee Assistance Act, the U.S. accepted 130,000 refugees from South Vietnam, Laos, and Cambodia. This cohort consisted of mostly skilled and educated asylees who had had close ties with the U.S. or South Vietnamese governments. Later, between 1981 and 2000, the U.S. accepted 531,310 Vietnamese who had fled Vietnam in small boats and found temporary sanctuary in asylum camps in Southeast Asia. Generally poorer and less educated than the first cohort, many of the "boat people" endured prolonged hardship, displacement, and separation before they could reconstitute families in America. Still, refugees from asylum camps were dispersed among many different nations for permanent settlement, so most Vietnamese refugees in the U.S. had relatives living in other countries. Given the loss of family members as a result of the war and during their escape, Vietnamese refugees value extended kin ties, so they make special efforts to maintain contact across national borders.

These post-1965 immigrants and refugees entered an economy undergoing transformation by globalization, deindustrialization, information technology, and neoliberal economic policies. By the late 20th century, the American labor market had become almost bimodal, with high demand for educated professionals in such fields as medicine, high technology, and engineering and for low-wage workers in domestic services, elderly care, janitorial, and food services. Civil rights struggles had weakened, if not dismantled, racial exclusion in employment. Consequently, Asian immigrants who had degrees from U.S. institutions or whose training was easily transferable could enter the market for skilled professionals. However, those lacking requisite education, language, or transferable skills were relegated to the low-wage sector or self-employment in small family businesses.

Educated Asian professional families are able to settle in suburban locations characterized by high performing public schools and excellent public services. For example, families of South Asian (primarily Indian) doctors, engineers, and high-tech professionals enjoy some of the highest family incomes of all Asian Americans and their high-achieving children are viewed as models of success. However, South Asian Americans are socioeconomically diverse and, like other Asian American families, are not without their problems. Margaret Abraham (2000), Shamita Das Dasgupta (2007), and other social scientists have exposed domestic violence as a social problem facing South Asian families. South Asian women activists have organized shelters and support services for survivors of abuse. Such "self-help" efforts reflect the high degree of organization of South Asian communities, which are knit together by cultural, political, and business organizations. The ethnic community encourages adherence to "traditional" cultural and religious beliefs, including the ideal of the patriarchal joint family system. Under this system, marriage is considered essential for both men and women, and parents are responsible for arranging appropriate marriages for their sons and daughters. Sons and daughters are afforded some power to accept or reject a match, but they also often recognize their parents' authority and plan to live with them until they marry.

At the other end of the spectrum, less advantaged families, especially refugee families, tend to be concentrated in economically disadvantaged communities plagued by failing schools, poor resources, and high crime rates. Among working-class and refugee Asian families, two incomes are needed to support the family. The growth of low-wage, female-intensive industries in services and some light manufacturing provide opportunities for women to find paying jobs fairly quickly. Immigrant men reportedly have a harder time, because their inability to speak English and their lack of U.S. credentials shut them out of jobs that are commensurate with their training and experience. Men may also be loath to take up "feminized" or devalued work. In this sense Asian women's "disadvantage" (being small, foreign, female) becomes an advantage, at least in the low-wage labor market. Regarding Vietnamese immigrant families, Nazli Kibria (1995) and Yến Lê Espiritu (1999) have each reported that gender relations may become more egalitarian, but also more conflicted as a result of shifts in men's and women's economic roles. As in other immigrant communities, a plethora of organizations supports ethnic cultural values, including the centrality of family, status obligation, and respect for parents and elders. Zhou and Bankston (2006) have found that youth who are more actively engaged in ethnic organizations are more likely to do well in school and less likely to become involved in alienated youth cultures.

The presumed role played by Asian American families and ethnic cultural values in children's school success raises the related issue of the model minority trope. The model minority image was first popularized in the 1960s when the focus was on explaining Asian American assimilation and success in contrast to the downward assimilation and lack of mobility of other racialized minorities. Explanations honed in on the supposed strengths of Japanese American and Chinese American families in contrast to the "pathologies" of single headed black families and authoritarian Latino families. By the 1990s and 2000s, the focus had shifted from lauding Asian Americans for their success to anxiety about their competitive advantage over native-born whites. The pot boiled over with the appearance of Amy Chua's 2011 best-selling quasi-humorous memoir, *Battle Hymn of the Tiger Mother*. Her account suggested that Asian American parents stressed high standards, achievement, and parental authority while white American parents were more concerned with nurturing individualism, self-esteem, and emotional well-being. The anxieties expressed in public debate reflected declining confidence in American exceptionalism and middle-class fears that America had become "too permissive," "too soft," "too complacent."

While it appears that Asian immigrant parents do indeed stress dedication and hard work, the reasons are not altogether cultural in origin. Vivian Louie (2004) points out that their orientation stems from historical and social circumstances. Parents have experienced restricted opportunity for higher education in their home countries, and they anticipate greater opportunity for education in the U.S., where there are more universities and less rigorous competition. They are also aware of U.S. racism and believe that their children have to try harder and do better than whites to overcome their disadvantage. For their part, children see their parents as having sacrificed much to give them a chance. They feel the sacrifice as a debt that must be repaid, which they can do by studying hard and succeeding.

Paradoxically, the post-1965 period also witnessed the reappearance of split household families. The economic and legal regime that enabled Asian immigrants to establish conventional families also facilitated the formation of transnational households. Family separation is perhaps most common among Filipinos, as adults migrate abroad to work. Unlike earlier cohorts, dominated by men, the majority of contemporary Filipino labor migrants are women, many of whom leave children and husbands behind in the Philippines. Most are relatively well educated, but were unable to earn enough as professionals or small business owners to pay for children's education and accumulate a nest egg. English speaking and skilled, they are in great demand as housekeepers, nannies, and care workers. Their remittances constitute a significant share of the Philippine economy. Some migrants plan to return eventually to the Philippines, but many hope to sponsor their children and other relatives to join them in the United States. In the meantime, female relatives take responsibility for childcare and housework in the country of origin. Parreñas (2005) and others have found that the domestic burden does not fall on fathers, thus preserving the gender division of labor and the ideal of "mother care."

Another type of transnational family arrangement is found among some affluent Taiwanese, Chinese from Hong Kong, and South Koreans. Under current immigration law, migrants who invest significant resources in the U.S. or Canada can gain entry and legal residence. However, male heads of household may find it advantageous to retain their businesses or occupations in Asia. At the same time, parents calculate that their children will have better futures with an American education. Thus, school- and college-age children are sent abroad for schooling to establish a beachhead in America. Mothers may live full time with junior high–and high school–age children, while fathers live and work in Asia. Alternately, children may be placed with relatives or friends or in boarding facilities run by co-ethnics, or they may live on their own with older siblings in charge, while the mother and father visit for varying periods of time.

Amid these developments, conceptions of family continue to be challenged by formations that deviate from the heteropatriarchal ideal. Even in earlier periods, some Asian Americans engaged in homosocial living arrangements, same-sex intimacy, interracial relationships, and transnational households to meet their needs and desires. In the current period, such practices as same-sex marriage, childrearing by same-sex couples, interracial marriages, and transnational and transracial adoption have become increasingly visible in the Asian American community. These historical and contemporary snapshots of gender, sexual, and generational dynamics capture only selected aspects of the panoply of issues and topics that can be considered under the rubric of family. They also reveal the flexibility of the family and the creativity of Asian Americans in fashioning their relationships and households to help them navigate their lives in America.

24

Film
Jigna Desai

Asian American studies has long engaged with how films constitute and contribute to the formation of public cultures (zones of cultural debate). More specifically, scholars have turned to films to examine public culture as a "space between domestic life and the projects of the nation-state—where different social groups . . . constitute their identities by their experience of mass-mediated forms in relation to the practices of everyday life" (Appadurai and Breckenridge 1995, 4–5). Film is recognized as a significant institution for establishing and maintaining a racial order within the American nation and empire. Asian American cultural criticism elaborates upon the significance of film and the cinematic apparatus to the interrelated formations of race, nation, and citizenship. In addition to legal rights and political participation, Asian American claims to social belonging and cultural representation as components of citizenship have flourished since the Asian American and Third World movements. Hence understanding, interrogating, and claiming political citizenship has been accompanied by attempts at seeking self-representation in film and video as a modality of cultural citizenship.

While some scholarship turns to Asian American filmmaking institutionalized under the rubric of Asian American cinema, nascent scholarship looked to a broader range of films that involve representations of Asia and Asian America. Focusing on questions of stereotypical and "negative" representations, the goals of this strand of Asian American film studies (Chong 2012; Klein 2003; Robert Lee 1999; Marchetti 1993; Palumbo-Liu 1999; Park 2010) are to interrogate film's historical and contemporary role in ideologies of racism, war, and imperialism. These analyses attend to what we might call racial formation and colonial discourse analysis by concentrating on how Asian Americans are visually framed within the American imaginary, identifying stereotypes and "negative" representations. Broadly, they show how the cultural apparatus of cinema constructs American identity and citizenship in relation to the figure of the Asian American as the racial Other. Scholarly essays and documentaries have created genealogies excavating the figure of the Asian/American in American cinema as the site of racialized and sexualized abjection, fear, anxiety, and desire. Harnessing the medium themselves, Asian Americans engage the power of film to articulate their own representations through analyses, reframings, and claiming a "voice"; documentaries like *Slanted Screen* (2006) and *Slaying the Dragon* (1988) argue that Hollywood has proliferated derogatory and discriminatory figures such as the Dragon Lady, Lotus Blosson, Fu Manchu, and "gook," sometimes using technologies such as yellowface. More recently, Asian American studies scholars, especially feminists, have insisted that we revisit these films and representations, questioning the blanket assertion that they are simply racist and sexist. Citing the agency of the actors in portraying these figures and the pleasure of Asian American viewers in watching these films, these scholars insist that performances by Asian American actors from Sessue Hayakawa and Bruce Lee to Anna May Wong and Nancy Kwan deserve to be considered more carefully.

Another strand of Asian American cultural criticism attends to Asian American filmmaking as a site of racialized storytelling and moving-image representation

(Desai 2004; Feng 2002; Hamamoto and Liu 2000; R. Leong 1991; Mimura 2009). While the social movements around race and civil rights in the 1970s created a transformation in political citizenship, cultural citizenship too was seen as necessary for transformation and enfranchisement. In response to the "negative representations" many artists, activists, and scholars called for the formation and development of Asian American filmmaking and cinema to correct invisibility and misrepresentations. For them, the response is two-pronged—we must be represented and we must represent ourselves, implicitly linking structure and representation in their claims to political and cultural citizenship. Accessing the means of production, Asian Americans filmmakers focused on various forms (documentary, storytelling, autoethnography, narrative features) to convey subjugated knowledges, alternative historiographies, and tell racialized and ethnic stories. Asserting the right of cultural difference and national belonging through filmic representation, Asian American filmmaking seeks to establish itself through the structures of independent cinema (e.g., *Better Luck Tomorrow* [2002] and *The Namesake* [2007]) and through nonprofits such as Women Make Movies (e.g., *The Grace Lee Project* [2005] and *Surname Viet Given Name Nam* [2005]). Independent Asian American filmmaking has flourished without the support of Hollywood, often assisted by the formation of Asian American nonprofit organizations, training workshops, independent programming, and festivals. In the name of community empowerment and self-representation, activist-artists have formed community and collective organizations that support film production, distribution, and exhibition, thereby producing and collating Asian American identities and audiences. Hence, Asian American cinema actively constitutes and shapes Asian American identities, communities, and culture.

Nevertheless, filmmaking, like literature, had to contend with the insistence that its purpose was to "correct" and replace racist and Orientalist representations of dominant cinema with "accurate" representations of Asian American communities. The demand for political and "positive" representations has been understood to be a manifestation of cultural nationalism and has been the site of feminist, queer, and postcolonial critique. Scholars point out that filmmakers have developed and deployed a variety of strategies and styles, such as documentary realism and experimental memoir, to respond to the politics of representation and assert alternative theoretical and methodological ways of understanding Asian American filmmaking. Asian American studies scholars too have sought a broader approach to media culture, race, and citizenship without eschewing the significance of representation (Davé et al. 2005; Desai 2004; M. Nguyen and T. Nguyen 2007; Nakamura 2007; Ono and Pham 2009; Shimizu 2007). They argue that all representations are made, manufactured, and mutable. Representation itself is neither positive nor negative, but is always produced through and in relation to power. Moreover, representation, like race, has very real effects within social hierarchies of power. The approach avoids pitting popular culture against authentic ethnic and alternative cultural production to look at how media, including digital technologies, film, and television, participate in the subjectification and administering of citizens within the nation. More wary about citizenship projects, some scholars also note that it is important to interrogate a compulsion to integrate and be recognized within dominant institutions such as media that promise access to citizenship for Asian American subjects who seek security in the very institutions that predicate their exclusion. Neoliberalism locates media and culture within the (supposedly accessible) domain of the marketplace that all good and proper citizens, including minoritized subjects, are responsible for accessing through their media acts. This form of privatized citizenship and corporatization of culture is characteristic of minoritized cultural citizenship within media capitalism. Hence, assertions of legibility and belonging within film and media are not only fundamental to claims of belonging, but film and media also marks and determines those who deserve access to citizenship.

25

Food

Anita Mannur

In *The Year of the Dragon* Asian American playwright Frank Chin narrates the story of Fred Eng, a Chinese American tour guide who makes his living by taking white American tourists through the crowded streets of San Francisco's Chinatown. Fred is continually frustrated by his job, which requires him to pander to Orientalist fantasies about Chinese Americans that lead to easy conflations of Chinatown with China, eliding the racial histories that mark Chinese Americans as Americans. To be heard, he must speak in terms that the mainstream understands. For Eng this means talking about food. "Food's our only common language," becomes his refrain through the play. He castigates his sister, a cookbook author, for inventing a "new literary form" that Chin names "food pornography." Sau-Ling Wong describes this as the deliberate self-promotion of one's ethnic heritage, particularly in the culinary realm, within a capitalist exploitative framework (1993, 58–62). For Chin, writing about food can only be pornographic—it exoticizes Asian cultures for an American audience eager to consume the palatable elements of multiculturalist difference (Mannur 2005).

Outside of the frame of the literary and theatrical, food is used in colloquial contexts to denigrate perceived forms of racial identification across the black-white binary. "Banana" and "coconut" reference white on the inside and yellow (East and Southeast Asian), brown (South Asian and Southeast Asian) on the outside. Rotten coconut, as Nitasha Sharma argues, referencing

brown on the outside, black on the inside connotes positive identification with whiteness. Among queer communities terms like "rice queen," "curry queen," and "sticky rice" serve as a shorthand to describe ethnic desires. Food is part of the everyday language of race in Asian America, but it is only within the last few years that critical discussions about food in Asian American studies have begun to take place. Indeed, Chin's dismissal of the place of the culinary in Asian American culture speaks to a marked discomfort that has surrounded discussions about food in Asian American studies. With the exception of Sau-Ling Wong's foundational essay and Jennifer Ho's *Consumption and Identity in Asian American Coming-of-Age Novels* (the first monograph to examine food in Asian American cultural productions) few Asian Americanists tackled the ubiquitous role of food within the mainstream imagining of Asian Americans with any seriousness before the 2000s. Why the discomfort with food in Asian American studies? In part one can associate this with the startling paradox in which Asian food finds itself in American culture. It is at once the most accessible, and, as I have argued elsewhere, the most "palatable" index of otherness. Food seemingly offers an instant and easy access to otherness.

From the early 19th century, Asian Americans have been inextricably linked with their foodways in popular discourse—literary, cultural, and political. Filipinos, Vietnamese, and Koreans are routinely depicted as indiscriminate consumers of disease-ridden animals, offal, and other unmentionables. Chinese Americans are unflatteringly portrayed as bucktoothed delivery boys, waiters, and cooks, and Indian Americans are depicted as individuals drawn to unpalatably fiery tastes.

Even as food structures the lives of Asian Americans, Asian American studies has only recently made the culinary turn, centering how food organizes the racial lives—discursive and material—of Americans of Asian descent. Historical studies of early Asian immigrant labor suggest that employment within restaurants, as tenant farmers, and migrant workers link Asian American livelihood to food. Whether it is the Chinese waiters, cooks, or busboys; Vietnamese shrimp boat operators in Texas; Hmong meatpackers in northern Minnesota; Filipino and Japanese laborers in the plantation economies of Hawai'i; Chinese laborers in Alaskan salmon canneries; or Bangladeshi and Punjabi seamen in Indian restaurants in New York City, Asian American laborers have played a pivotal role in agribusiness, food service, and the food and beverage industry. Wenying Xu puts it succinctly: "there is nothing natural or culturally predetermined about Asian Americans' vital relationship with food. Harsh circumstances made such work one of the few options available . . . they did what others wouldn't, and did it with pride and dignity" (2008, 12).

The willingness of Chinese workers to do "what others wouldn't" paradoxically fed into the anti-Chinese rhetoric of labor activist Samuel Gompers. In 1908, as president of the American Federation of Labor (AFL), Gompers published his well-known treatise on the problems affecting the American laboring classes of white men titled "Meat vs. Rice: American Manhood against Asiatic Coolieism." Endorsed by the Asiatic Exclusion League, Gompers's dictum anchors its anti-Asian xenophobia in terms of food, applying the language of "you are what you eat" to differentiate between white and Chinese immigrant labor. The oppositional placement of rice and meat suggests that food is more than a linguistic coding for ethnic difference. "Americans" are not just beef and bread eaters, any more than Asians are merely rice eaters (Mannur 2006, 1–5).

Yet such linguistic codings of Asianness are not exclusive to Gompers, nor has the passage of time dissipated the frequent appearance of such metaphors within cultural and literary discourse. John Kuo-Wei Tchen describes how Chinese immigrants were routinely imagined as rat eaters. Advertisements for rat poison were promoted with anti-Chinese sentiments, often depicting a purported Chinese predilection for vermin as the best way to eliminate rats (2001, 273). In one understanding of Asian American culinary practices what Asian immigrants have historically chosen to eat or been forced to eat has also served to characterize Asian Americans as abject, excessive, and alien.

In another critical reading of this, taking its cue from literary representations by authors like Maxine Hong Kingston, Bienvenido Santos, and other pioneering Asian American writers, this willingness to expand palatal preferences leads Sau-Ling Wong to describe Asian Americans as "big eaters." For immigrants to survive, it is often necessary for them to make do with what is available, whether it is in the form of accepting low-income jobs or eating the discarded parts of animals and leftovers. "Finicky palates," she argues, have no place in lives circumscribed by hard physical labor (1993, 26).

Asian American cuisines are often derided for appearing to be excessive. They are often seen as too different, too spicy, too sour, too pungent, too malodorous. Among the best-known examples of "excessive" eating in an Asian American context is dog eating. As Frank Wu and Robert Ku suggest, dog eating in the context of Asian American foodways is crucial because it emerges at the point where eating practices seem too different to engage critically (F. Wu 2002; Ku 2014). The taboo against dog eating is one site where principles concerning diversity conflict with practices of tolerating diversity. Tastes for what may otherwise be celebrated by the multiculturalist fetish for difference are condemned because of their aberrant excesses.

Excessiveness, as Martin Manalansan notes, racializes bodies through nonvisual senses. Smell is a powerful

FOOD   ANITA MANNUR

way in which Asian Americans experience racism. Food odors stigmatize the Asian American body, leaving behind a lingering trace of olfactory otherness. Through interviews with immigrants in Queens he describes the phenomenon of the "smelly immigrant" concerned about how to "contain the smell of kimchi to the domestic space" (2006a, 46). A telling interview with one individual reveals the anxiety about food smells remaining on the body: "I want people to smell Calvin Klein and not my wife's curries!" (2006a, 46). Food as a topic in Asian American studies, then, can move beyond the visual to examinations of how visceral responses to racial difference are often anchored in the realm of taste and smell.

The past few years have seen an upturn in Asian American critical studies of food. While critics are just beginning to formulate a critical vocabulary to think through the multiple significations of food, several Asian American writers have published novels explicitly about the topic. These include Linda Furiya's *Bento Box in the Heartland* (2006), SunHee Kim's *Trail of Crumbs* (2008), Don Lee's *Wrack and Roll* (2008), Amulya Malladi's *Serving Crazy with Curry* (2004), David Mas Masumoto's *Epitaph for a Peach* (1995), Bich Minh Nguyen's *Stealing Buddha's Dinner* (2007), Ruth Ozeki's *My Year of Meats* (1998) and *All Over Creation* (2003), Monique Truong's *Book of Salt* (2003) and *Bitter in the Mouth* (2010), and David Wong Louie's *The Barbarians Are Coming* (2000). These foodie novels do not shy away from the culinary but boldly position food as a lens through which to examine racialization and Asian American cultural and ethnic formation.

In more public circuits of popular culture, there is a new generation of Asian American celebrity chefs including Ming Tsai, Padma Lakshmi, and *Top Chef* winners—Vietnamese American Hung Huynh, Filipino American Paul Qui, and Korean American adoptee Kristen Kish—who join established chefs including Martin Yan, the long-time host of the pioneering cooking show *Yan Can Cook*, and *Iron Chef* Masaharu Morimoto to embody the public face of Asian American cooking in visual culture. The rise of the cosmopolitan Asian American chef signals a superficial form of acceptance. The nouvelle cuisine vogue of the late 1990s represented an important cultural moment in which Asian spices and ingredients were privileged in fusion cuisine, a kind of hybrid cooking that is at once reminiscent of model minority discourse—Asian ingredients assimilate quietly into the culinary scape of American cuisine creating a newer and better but "unobtrusive" blend of flavors—all the while subduing the brash excessiveness of what is unpalatable and inedible (Manalansan 2007; Mannur 2010; August 2012). The turn of the century has witnessed the explosion of new forms of fusion occupying new spaces in the U.S. landscape. Though food trucks have traditionally served immigrant working-class communities, the emergence of food trucks like Roy Choi's Kogi or Chi'lantro that serve Korean style tacos in L.A. and Austin suggest new ways of mapping comparative ethnic affinities—a form of minor to minor culinary transaction—that move beyond a white-Asian binary (O. Wang 2013; L. Siu 2013).

Embedded in interdisciplinary formations, food scholarship has expanded beyond an assimilation/exclusion narrative. No longer is the study of food banished as a form of producing academic scholarship lite divorced from the questions of race and class that have structured the field of Asian American studies. Instead food studies scholars are using food to establish new questions and critical methodologies for Asian American studies. As we move forward and develop ever more thoughtful ways to explore the myriad meanings of food, conversations about class, ethnicity, and race in an Asian American context will likely respond in kind.

26

Foreign

Karen Leong

A word already in use in Europe from at least the 14th century with multiple meanings related to the status of being outside, not familiar, or different (*OED*), "foreign" likewise has multiple meanings within the field of Asian American studies, including "not American," "outsider," "noncitizen," or "alien." The term is deeply embedded in U.S. racial formations specifically relating to Asian Americans, and as such often slips between connotations of nation, citizenship status, race, and cultural difference.

"Foreign" may more generally refer to that which is outside the borders of a nation. In the United States, the word "foreign" was written into the Articles of Confederation (ratified 1781) to indicate countries outside the states' established borders. While the Revolutionary War was still being fought, the United States established an Office of Foreign Affairs in 1780.

The word "foreign" in the United States also indicates the status of not having birthright or naturalized citizenship. Thus, the first Foreign Miners Tax enacted by the state of California in 1850 was directed at non–U.S. citizens, which included Europeans, Latinos, Kanaka Maoli (native Hawai'ians), and Asians, and charged them a monthly fee to mine for gold. An additional Foreign Miners Tax in 1852 focused on nonwhites who were ineligible for citizenship under the Naturalization Law of 1790, charging an additional $3 per month. With the first Chinese Exclusion Law in 1882, the United States named immigrants of Asians descent as "aliens not eligible for citizenship." The Alien Land Laws passed by several states beginning in 1913—primarily a response to the success of Japanese immigrant farmers—expanded the material consequences of involuntarily having to maintain a foreign status for immigrants from China, Korea, Japan, and India.

The definition of foreign was informed by United States' cultural definitions of what was different and nonnormative. Defining what is foreign more generally is part of the process by which a community establishes its social and cultural borders by naming what belongs and what does not. For example, anti-Asian nativist movements in beginning in the 1870s mobilized "native-born" Americans—angry over competing for employment with clearly inassimilable foreigners—against Asian immigrants. Nativism motivated mob violence against the occupants of Los Angeles's Chinatown in 1871, against Chinese miners at Rock Springs, Wyoming, in 1885, and against Punjabi lumber mill workers in Bellingham, Washington, in 1907. Lucy Salyer suggests that nativism contributed to Chinese exclusion and a more active federal role in regulating immigration (1995, 6).

The notion of who could qualify to become American thus was based in ideas of foreign status as defined by racial identity and cultural practices. The U.S. Supreme Court demonstrated this with its 1922 *Takao Ozawa v. United States* and 1923 *United States v. Bhaghat Singh Thind* decisions, both brought before the 9th Circuit Court of Appeals. Takao Ozawa, a Japanese-born man, argued for his right to become a naturalized citizen based on evidence of his cultural assimilation: he had lived in the United States for 20 years, he had attended UC Berkeley for three years, his children were all educated in American schools, and his family spoke English at home and attended Christian churches. Justice George Sutherland acknowledged in his decision that Ozawa "was well qualified by character and education for citizenship." However, based on his reading of the Naturalization Act of 1790 and the extension of naturalized citizenship to Africans in 1870, Sutherland concluded that "the intention was to confer the privilege of citizenship upon that class of persons whom the fathers knew as white, and to deny it to all who could not be so classified." Because Asians were not racially white, Ozawa was not qualified for citizenship (*Takao Ozawa v. United States*).

Following Ozawa's case, Bhaghat Singh Thind, a Punjabi man, sued for citizenship in 1923 based upon contemporary biological/geographic definitions of white racial identity. South Asians were classified not as Mongoloids but as Caucasoids. A World War I veteran, Thind argued that he should have the same access to U.S. citizenship as other white veterans who served in the U.S. military. Despite the fact that several Punjabis had received citizenship from several states, Justice George Ferguson rejected Thind's petition by dismissing scientific evidence of racial difference and privileging popular understandings of whiteness, stating, "The children of English, French, German, Italian, Scandinavian, and other European parentage quickly merge into the mass of our population and lose the distinctive hallmarks of their European origin. On the other hand, it cannot be doubted that the children born in this country of Hindu parents would retain indefinitely the clear evidence of their ancestry" (*United States v. Bhaghat Singh Thind*). Here, "foreign" identifies how people embody and display what is not normative to American society. According to Ferguson's interpretation, European immigrants were domesticated—or assimilated—into U.S. society and culture by virtue of not looking or acting foreign.

Social scientists from the 1930s through the 1960s also believed that the transition of Asian immigrants from foreign to assimilated Americans would be difficult. This was influenced by Robert Park's marginal man thesis, first articulated in relation to Jews as immigrants. Unable to fully discard his traditional culture, the Jewish immigrant would always be "living in two worlds, in both of which he is more or less a stranger," due to continual exclusion (Ng 1987, 55). Asian immigrants, likewise, were assumed to also face this instability of identity. Paul Siu's *The Chinese Laundryman: A Study in Social Isolation* posited that the Chinese laundrymen he studied were not strangers (a specific sociological definition authored by Georg Simmel in 1908) due to exclusion, but were a type of sojourner—"a stranger who spends many years of his lifetime in a foreign country without being assimilated by it" (quoted in P. Siu 1987, 299). Noting that racial discrimination contributed to this isolation, Siu's thesis nonetheless was cited by scholars to justify American anti-Chinese hostilities in early histories about Chinese Americans (Ng 1987, 54–58). As Franklin Ng notes, at issue was the attachment of sojourner status solely to Chinese immigrants when, based in the new immigration history of the 1980s, Siu's analysis actually could describe the reality for many immigrants to the United States, including those from Europe (1987, 66).

The influence of the sojourner theory may even have impacted political scientists' assumptions that the non-native-born status of Asian Americans discourages them from actively participating in electoral politics. Yet newer research suggests that foreign-born Asian Americans are actually the reason for the increased presence of Asian Americans as political candidates. In fact, their success often takes place in suburbs with a strong presence of Asian immigrants (J. Lai 2011, 7–8). This further complicates assumptions about what it means to be foreign and to become American.

A common phrase in Asian American studies that refers to the continued exclusion of Asian Americans—whether American-born or naturalized—as fully accepted members of the national community is "perpetual foreigner." Significantly, the development of Asian American studies as a valid field of research came out of the Asian American Movement, in which Asian American college students participated in the Third World Liberation Front with blacks and Latinos to demand curriculum reform that included the histories of nonwhite communities and their contributions to the United States; this movement also recognized how U.S. imperialism in foreign countries was linked to the marginalization of ethnic minorities in the United States (Maeda 2011). The use of the term "Third World" for the student movement and the proposed naming of the new college demanded by the students as the "Third World College" articulate the extent to which Asian Americans, along with other ethnic minority American students, felt like foreigners in their U.S. homeland.

This embodiment of the foreign has continued to define Asian Americans, and the consequences have not been insignificant. Mae Ngai defines this status of possessing U.S. citizenship yet being perceived as alien, "alien citizenship" (2003, 8). Japanese Americans were suspected of maintaining foreign loyalties to the emperor during World War II, which contributed to public demands for their imprisonment and relocation from the West Coast after Japan's attack on Pearl Harbor. Dr. Wen Ho Lee, a naturalized U.S. citizen who worked at Los Alamos, was held in solitary confinement for selling information about nuclear warheads to the Chinese government, while the federal government attempted to collect evidence. He was released in 2003 after a plea bargain in which he pled guilty to mishandling classified documents. The FBI justified focusing on Chinese Americans as potential spies because ethnic Americans with ties to their lands of ancestry often are targeted for recruitment by the intelligence services of those foreign countries (Hsien and Hwang 2000; Thomas Lee 2000).

After the terrorist attack on September 11, 2001, some Punjabi Sikhs and other Asians were targeted by some Americans who assumed that certain foreign styles of dress (turbans, for example) invariably indicated that a person was Muslim.

At the same time, greater attention to U.S. imperialism and the colonization of indigenous lands in the past two decades further complicates what is foreign and domestic for Asian Americans, and undermines a simply nationalist framework for Asian American studies (Chuh 2003, 136–39). From this perspective, the Chinese, Japanese, and Filipino laborers who migrated to Hawai'i, for example, can be understood as participants in and beneficiaries of U.S. settler colonialism that dispossessed Kanaka Maoli of their lands and contributed to the growth of the sugar plantations. Some scholars suggest that the hierarchy of race and wages that were used to separate and turn plantation workers from and against each other, with Asian workers disadvantaged in relation to European workers and advantaged in relation to the native Hawai'ians, complicates the role of Asian immigrants in a settler colonialism that primarily benefited white American plantation owners. Nonetheless, recruited by colonial business interests to Hawai'i and seeking themselves to acquire private property, most Asian immigrants supported Hawai'ian statehood and contributed to the erosion of native Hawai'ian sovereignty (Fujikane and Okamura 2008).

As the demography of Asian America today has shifted to a majority-non-U.S.-born population, the word "foreign" is now part of an internal debate within the field of Asian American studies. In its first three decades as a field of study, Asian American studies emphasized its distinction from Asian studies, seeking to demarcate a focus on U.S.-based racial formations for Asian immigrants and their struggles for civil rights within the U.S. polity. After the immigration reforms of 1965, however, and the rapid increase in immigrants from Asia, the focus in Asian American studies has expanded to include recognition of Asian American communities as part of larger Asian diasporas. Asian American studies increasingly has emphasized transnational Asian American communities that sustain ties and relations in both the United States, homelands, and other diasporic communities. In the early 1990s some scholars challenged the dominant East Asian orientation of Asian American studies, which overlooked the history and experiences of South Asians Americans and Filipino Americans, even though both communities historically have been part of Asian America from its very beginnings (Rondilla 2002, 58–59; Davé et. al. 2000).

Moreover, improved technology of travel and communication, the development of certain Asian economies, the globalization of labor, and the dominance of transnational economic structures have blurred what exactly is foreign and what is domestic in Asian American studies. While the nation-state still manifests its weight upon peoples' lives and choices, the increasingly rapid circulation of culture, ideas, social interactions, and capital across national boundaries challenges any bordered notion of what it means to be Asian American. This complex demography has presented a continued challenge and opportunity for Asian American studies as scholars seek to address both the U.S. and transnational contexts of Asian American experiences.

27

Fusion
Mari Matsuda

In physics, fusion is the collision of nuclei generating the power of the stars. The term "fusion" is used generally to mean "combination." In the surface realms of culture, "fusion" is pabulum jazz, celebrity chefs dabbling in "Pacific Rim" seasoning, or an Univision media venture. It is described in a brand launch as "fun, fresh, and even irreverent," as though "irreverent" is the outer edge of what one might do with fusion. Applied to Asian Americans, however, "fusion" retrieves the usage from physics. It is about the creation of radical change through the politics of coalition, wherein each part brings the strength of its identity, simultaneously creating new energy in actions around specific goals that will forever alter relationships of power. Professional activists might recognize this as the definition of organizing (Bobo, Kendall, and Max 2010). For critical race theorists, fusion's political potential is a reason to retain racialized identity, even as the racist structures that generated that identity are the target. Critical race theory has always done at least two things at once with regard to race: deconstruct it while working its politics. Yellow Power—a fusion of Asian Americans into a political force—is an attack on racist messages using a political construction of race.

Michael Omi and Howard Winant have dissected the concept of race generally, illuminating the regressive lumping and objectification that serve existing power structures (1994). The Asian American movement began in a moment of rising nationalist resistance to white supremacy, embodied in Black Power (Omatsu 1994). Note that urban Black, rural Black, immigrant Black, and AfroLatino were all present in the Black Power movement, and comprised a realm of difference united to reclaim Blackness as a source of both pride and political leverage. The Black Power political project included critiques of imperialism, colonialism, and militarism, an analysis attractive to Asian Americans in the Vietnam era. "Asian American"—which in the 1970s comprised significant contingents of Japanese, Chinese, Filipino, Korean Americans, and sometimes (problematically and not always unsuccessfully) Pacific Islanders—was a coalition designed to reclaim pride and power within a context of xenophobia, nativism, and racism in which Asians were called the "yellow peril" (Matsuda 2001). This fusion was both historically logical and culturally comfortable. Asian Americans as diasporic people faced common struggle, often in common loci: the plantation, the sweatshop, the cannery, the factory, the field. Because early immigration patterns had drawn more workingclass than elite Asian immigrants, there was a class bond among many Asian Americans, who took pride in the labor struggles of the generations before. Out of this shared class experience, it made sense to claim iconic historical moments, such as the World War II internment of Japanese Americans, as representative of the group experience. If the internment happened because of racist nativism and fear of economic competition it was not merely a Japanese American experience; it was an Asian American experience, reaching back to the massacre of Chinese miners in the century before, and forward to the urban "redevelopment" evictions of Filipino pensioners in Chinatowns.

Culturally, fusion made sense for Asian Americans, most of whom were raised with some sense that false pride would result in cosmic retribution, that the extended family was the unit of accountability (do not

shame your family), and that generosity at a potluck was a basic signifier of good character. More significant than a cultural home, however, was the movement built from it, which fought for access to basic material goods—housing, education, jobs, and political representation. Connection to the civil rights and antiwar movements, and the street battle to remake the academy to reflect "our history our way" (Umemoto 1989), required an analysis of race and political economy, and the creation of a shared utopian vision. Out of a visceral reaction to napalmed babies came a commitment to read, study, theorize, and name—of which this book is a manifestation. Thus fusion—a historical collision of oppression of Asians as Asians, the inspiration of Black nationalism, and a practice of group solidarity toward progressive ends—created the Asian American political formation (Iijima 1997). An alliance bent on changing power relationships requires some delineation. Fusion as used here is a progressive political practice, as distinguished from more politically ambiguous forms of hybridity. Forms of panAsian chic are a real part of life on Planet Asian America, but they are not the fusion referred to here.

Fusion among Asian subcultures is not the same as erasure. If a sentence begins with "All Asians . . ." a racist assumption often follows. The vast differences between a Hmong immigrant in Milwaukee and a seventh-generation Chinese American in Honolulu require care to avoid subsuming the experience of one into the dreaded melting pot. The more marginalized a particular group, the more important it is to retrieve its story and advocate from its particularity.

Hence, fusion is not appropriation, assimilation, essentialism, or multiculturalism. It does not make Asianness a cloak anyone can wear. It does not say the category Asian must be or do any one thing, and it does not reduce a movement for change into a mutual aid society.

Fusion is about power relationships and the choice to deploy an Asian American identity to confront history and change its course. Fusion among Asian subcultures is not the same as appropriation. Avoiding appropriation and commodification of our various cultures requires a distinction between honoring cultures and stealing them. For instance, it is good to love Okinawan *sanshin*. Selling it as "world music" without attribution and divorced from cultural context, however, is theft.

Fusion recognizes multiple oppressions. Asian American identity requires intersectional analysis (Crenshaw 1989). The majority of Asian Americans—including LGBT, immigrant, workingclass, and female Asian Americans—experience subordination on more than one axis; therefore intersectional analysis is required in Asian American political practice. It is just and it is strategic to understand the operation of multiple oppressions (Matsuda 2002, 393–98). The disjuncture between the heteronormative value system undergirding the mainstream early 21st century's robust marriage equality movement and the progressive possibilities at the forefront of a stillmarginal LGBT immigrant rights movement is one example of the problems lurking in unilateral approaches to oppression. Marriage equality, a supremely important goal, draws upon reactionary notions of liberal individualism and heteronormativity in ways that a truly inclusive gay rights struggle—one that included the undocumented—could not.

Fusion includes cultural exchange, pride, and identity, but it is not a cultural formation. The lovely home feeling of a riceeating tribe that values humility is a good thing, but it is not politics. Failure to go beyond drumming and grilling our way to racial identity allows forces of reaction to grow without opposition. Culture is not politics, but culture can and should act politically. The iconic example is the Asian American band Yellow Pearl (Chris Kando Iijima, Nobuko JoAnne Miyamoto, and William "Charlie" Chin), whose record *A Grain of Sand: Music for the Struggle by Asians in America* became the soundtrack of the Asian American Movement (Nakamura 2009).

Widely acknowledged as the first album of Asian American music, *A Grain of Sand* deliberately reached across Asian cultures, deployed history, and presented an explicit challenge to racism and imperialism. Yellow Pearl's explicit goal was to "serve the people," and the band's use of fused aesthetics (e.g., soul, jazz, and folk) mirrored the tactical deployment of a pan–Asian American identity; this identity was used as a united front against attacks on Asian Americans and Asians throughout the colonized world. As Yellow Pearl's cultural/social/political project illustrates, fusion is required for an effective response to imperialism/colonialism internationally and xenophobia/nativism domestically. Asian Americans as a fused political force is a strategic way to fight Asian-specific forms of subordination, including but not limited to exclusion from cultural production, racist stereotyping, Asianspecific impacts of immigration laws such as family reunification, bullying of Asian children, hate crimes against people who "look Asian," police harassment of people who "look like Asian gang members," hidden antiAsian quotas in hiring and college admissions, and the gaping absence of Asian American studies in most university curricula.

Fusion follows self-determination: no one is part of the movement who does not want to be, but we do not ignore our obligations and connections. Some Asian American subgroups are so large that they may come to seek power under their own identities. Others question why they are lumped with Asians to begin with. For indigenous Pacific Islanders, the historical and political issues of indigeneity are a more logical place of unity. Pacific Islanders are sometimes included with Asian Americans for purposes of advocacy and political access, invited to the White House, for example, at Asian American events. The delicate balance between sharing resources and access while a sister community builds its own political power, without erasing distinctions, requires care. The Asian Law Caucus, for example, represents Pacific Islanders in the Bay Area, bringing important public interest litigation when no one else will. This is invited by the Pacific Islander community. At the same time, that community should have its own legal resources and Asian Americans should support that goal. The harder and more important challenge is acknowledging the role of Asian immigration in furthering the subordination and colonization of native people while simultaneously appreciating our moments of solidarity, cultural blending, and mutual politics. This is a work in progress (Matsuda 2010).

Fusion always exists in coalition. Asian Americans are internally a coalition, and externally in a coalition. Asian Americans standing proudly beside native people, African Americans, Latino/as, workers, and antiwar demonstrators is definitional of the Asian American movement. This has meant conflict, misunderstanding, and reinscribed racism, because that is what coalition looks like (Matsuda 1991). The wonderful amalgamation that is Asian America makes no sense without a broader purpose of liberation. Meaning comes when real change happens. The point of fusion—of comparing and joining multiple experience—is to see oppression in structural terms and to end it through political practice, thus informed.

This quite didactic explication of fusion, derived from looking at the history of Asian American consciousness and political action, is subject to critique. It is arguably a historical artifact particular to a circa 1975 experience, the deployment of which makes less sense given contemporary immigration patterns and politics (Y. Espiritu 1992). For some new immigrants, the model minority myth is no myth. It is a check to cash. For others, rejection of fusion, categorization, and assimilation are acts of resistance. For some Asian activists, carving out a space separate from Blackness—as in "Beyond Black and White" (Matsuda 2002, 393–98)—is important for Asian identity. Finally, for postmodern theorists, categorization itself is problematic, and pointing out the possibility of performative identities with fluid boundaries and surprising incarnations is the ultimate antiracist move. It is increasingly common to describe a focus on ethnicity as in itself dehumanizing. The utopian side of postracialism is the premise that we are all equally human, and adopting Asian American fusion is seen as a barrier to realization of that equality. To these potentially antifusion positions, the challenge critical race theory suggests is the test of liberation: whatever stance Asian Americans choose should contribute toward the realization of the end of degradation and subordination of Asians in particular, and of all humans and all living and nonliving vital planetary things—mountain, river, air—in the grand utopian future.

28

Gender

Judy Tzu-Chun Wu

The term "gender" has multiple meanings and intellectual usages. Gender generally refers to the socially constructed nature of sex roles. The concept of gender challenges biologically essentialist understandings of maleness and femaleness, asserting instead that normative understandings of masculinity and femininity are socially defined ideas projected onto biological differences. Because women's studies scholars have had a vested interest in challenging naturalized and hierarchical differences between men and women, gender is sometimes used interchangeably with the category of woman. That is, studies of gender are at times primarily focused on women. However, scholars have also used gender to argue for the need to understand how masculinity and femininity are relationally defined as well as how gender hierarchies serve as a constitutive basis for power and underlie other forms of social inequalities (Scott 1986). Furthermore, the interpretation of gender as a form of performativity argues that there are no stable categories of sex differences (Butler 1990). Instead, gender is enacted through repeated and oftentimes unconscious patterns of behaviors or gender scripts that create a fiction of a cohesive and preexisting identity of manhood or womanhood. In addition, scholars of gender note that physiological differences do not necessarily divide neatly into two sexes, as some individuals are intersexed. Similarly, some societies recognize more than two genders, and some individuals are transgendered, i.e.,

they identify with a gender that is not normatively associated with their physical sex. Also, scholars of gender and sexuality have conceptually delineated these categories. Individuals who transgress gender norms are frequently perceived as transgressing sexual norms in their desires, behaviors, and identifications. However, gender and sexuality do not necessarily align in expected ways with one another.

Asian American studies scholars have utilized these multiple conceptions of gender to offer an intersectional analysis of Asian American racialization. As Sylvia Yanagisako (1995) has argued, the early scholarship in and teaching of Asian American studies tended to foreground immigrant, working-class, male subjects without an awareness of how this focus produced a masculinist Asian American nationalism. The gender wars between the writers Frank Chin and Maxine Hong Kingston that emerged in the mid-1970s could be understood as an attempt by Asian American men to assert their working-class and racialized experiences as the central basis for Asian American identity. Chin did so by critiquing Asian American women as feminist sellouts who cater to the Orientalist fantasies of white audiences. Asian American scholars have responded by producing creative and scholarly work that demonstrates how race, gender, sexuality, and class are mutually constitutive categories of difference and hierarchy. These intersectional formations shape the lives of Asian American women and men in the realms of economics, law, kinship, and sexuality, as well as cultural representations.

A race- and gender-stratified economy differentially positions men and women of Asian ancestry both in the U.S. and globally (Y. Espiritu 2008; Glenn 1988; Glenn 2004; Parreñas 2001). During the first wave of immigration in the late 19th and early 20th centuries, Asian laborers, an overwhelmingly male population, were deemed "cheap labor" by their American employers not only due to their racial otherness. Asian male laborers were less expensive partly because the costs of social reproduction were born by their female partners and extended-family members in Asia (Okihiro 1994). The small numbers of Asian women who migrated to the U.S. during the first wave and the larger numbers in subsequent waves of migration contributed in terms of their productive, reproductive, and sexual labor to maintain the overall Asian American community (Cheng Hirata 1979).

The American labor force during the second half of the 20th century and the beginning of the 21st century continues to be stratified in terms of race, gender, and immigration/citizenship status. On the one hand, Asian American men and women have greater access to the primary economy (i.e., stable jobs with benefits and higher pay and prestige) and even gain entry to the U.S. because of their professional skills, financial assets, and educational background (Choy 2003). On the other hand, the racial and gender glass ceiling continues to exist. Asian Americans also are heavily concentrated in the service industry and the secondary economy (M. Kang 2010). Asian American men and women with limited English skills and uncertain immigration or citizenship status are particularly vulnerable to economic exploitation, sometimes by their own family members and co-ethnics (Zhao 2010).

In these settings, gender matters as Asian American women are perceived to be particularly suited to certain forms of manufacturing or care work. In some cases, their economic exploitation allows for the financial survival of a business or company in an ultracompetitive and increasingly globalized economy. In addition, domestic care, paid or unpaid, continues to be regarded as female work. The reproductive work that some Asian American women perform for pay, such as domestic, childcare, elderly care, and health care work, allows other individuals (men as well as women, Asian as well as non-Asian American) to be relieved of their family responsibilities and to enter the paid work force (Boris and Parreñas 2010). Even when Asian women migrate as the primary breadwinners and are separated from their children and partners in Asia, these female-led split households elicit gendered recriminations and feelings of guilt as women are charged with "abandoning" their mothering responsibilities in order to financially sustain their families (Parreñas 2001; Parreñas 2005).

Race, gender, and sexuality shape the law as well as the workforce. Policies regarding immigration, naturalization, land ownership, taxation, and miscegenation combined to exclude, marginalize, and segregate Asian Americans from the U.S. polity (S. Chan 1991; Erika Lee 2004; Ngai 2005; Salyer 2005; Takaki 1989). Anti-immigrant sentiment in the late 19th and early 20th centuries tended to target Asian male laborers for exclusion and expulsion, but eventually almost all Asian immigrants, regardless of class, were designated aliens ineligible for citizenship. Filipinos were "nationals" rather than "aliens" due to American colonization of the Philippines, but they, too, were not full-fledged citizens.

In addition to these racialized exclusions, Asian American women faced additional legal challenges. Their sexuality or perceived sexuality became the basis for immigration exclusion or admission (S. Chan 1994; Gardner 2009; J. Gee 2003; Peffer 1999; Yung 1995). Also, following the principle of *femme covert*, Asian immigrants and even American-born Asian women were defined by their relationship to their husbands or fathers. The class and citizenship status of Asian American men largely defined the legal identities of Asian American women.

The gender makeup of the Asian American community has been transformed in the post–World War II period, particularly after the passage of the 1965

Immigration Act. Asian women are entering in equal and even greater numbers due to laws that privilege family reunification and certain categories of labor migration, as well as adoption and refugee migration.

However, gender and sexuality scholars point out that the principle of family reunification is defined via heteronormative understandings of kinship (Luibheid 2002; Luibheid and Cantu 2005). Heteronormativity assumes the naturalness of a gender binary as well as the belief that male-female marital and sexual unions are the normative units of kinship and should form the basis of social organization. As an indication of the heteronormative basis of immigration law, Asian women who enter through their marital relationship to American men continue to be legally dependent on their male partners for their immigration and citizenship status. These women consequently are vulnerable in cases of domestic violence, because state authority reinforces male power within the family.

In the era of neoliberalism and post-9/11, Asian American men and women face racialized as well as gendered suspicions about their eligibility for immigration entry and national belonging. Asian men, particularly South Asian, West Asian, and Muslim men, become likely terrorism suspects (Puar 2007). Asian women, in contrast, are perceived as likely welfare and immigration cheats through their capacity to give birth to anchor babies (L. Park 2011).

In addition to analyzing the gendered dimensions of the economy and the law, Asian American studies scholars also offer a critique of kinship and sexuality. A recurrent historical narrative of Asian America presents its transformation from an immigrant "bachelor" society to an American-centered family society (Nee and Nee 1986). This teleological conception of historical progress celebrates heternormative co-ethnic family formations. This narrative responds to what Jennifer Ting (1995) and Karen Leong (2001) describe as a perception of deviant heterosexuality among Asian Americans. Due to immigration exclusion as well as antimiscegenation laws, Asian American communities were disproportionately male and sustained an extensive and exploitative economy of prostitution. This lack of nuclear families among Asian Americans, along with their perceived gender deviance due to their dress, living arrangements, and occupations, contributed to their racialization and marginalization. As Nayan Shah (2001) points out, Asian Americans seeking civic inclusion to the U.S. polity understood that non-heteronormativity reinforced their racial exclusion. Consequently, the campaign for Asian American civil rights included the assertion of gender and sexual normativity.

Asian American historians have responded in various ways to the concerns about heterosexual deviancy. Evelyn Nakano Glenn (1983) and Madeline Hsu (2000) point to the existence of "split households" or transnational families in the late 19th and early 20th centuries with male producers in the U.S. and female reproducers in Asia. Nayan Shah extends this analysis to posit that Asian American men and women during the late 19th and early 20th centuries practiced a form of "queer domesticity." Male workers and female prostitutes sometimes shared housing with each other as well as with boarders, acquaintances, and occasionally children, not always born within wedlock. In other words, they resided in households that challenged the normative concept of an American family. In addition, the members of the predominantly male immigrant community at times formed erotic and sexual relationships with one another and with men of other racial backgrounds, a form of "stranger intimacy" (Shah 2012). Rather than regarding the disproportionate gender ratio as a form of racialized oppression, it is possible to understand the predominantly male homosocial environment of the U.S. West as an arena of sexual possibility and experimentation.

Women within Asian American communities also engaged in gender and romantic transgression. The heteronormative narrative from bachelor to family society equates the presence of Asian women with the formation of heterosexual families and the naturalness of intraracial sexuality and procreation. Margaret Chung's life illustrates instead how an Asian American woman could transgress gender and sexual expectations in her professional as well as her personal life. During the early 20th century, Chung became a physician, a male-dominated occupation. She also adopted a male nickname, "Mike," and partially cross-dressed; she was known as a woman, but she dressed like a man, wearing dark suits, rimmed glasses, and slicked-back hair. Chung chose not to marry and secretly engaged in erotic relationships with women, particularly white ethnic women. In addition, she adopted nearly a thousand offspring, mostly white American military personnel and politicians, during the Sino-Japanese War and World War II. Their family symbolized China-U.S. unity. Over the course of her life, Chung experimented with her gender presentation and roles, adopting more glamorous and highly feminine attire as she publicly became known as a mother of an interracial, adopted family (J. Wu 2005).

Scholars interested in studying more contemporary Asian American GLBTQ issues, individuals, and communities also offer complicated analyses of gender. Individuals who identify with nonnormative sexual identities or who are invested in challenging heteronormativity sometimes also adopt transgressive gender roles. And, at times, they also perform hyperfeminine or hypermasculine scripts. These studies also examine how GLBTQ individuals and social networks simultaneously claim Asian/American identity and foster alternative understandings of kinship, lineage, community, and diaspora (Eng and Hom 1998; Gopinath 2005; Leong 1995; Manalansan 2003).

In addition to uncovering these queer formations of Asian America, scholars also have paid increasing attention to interracial and adoptive families. Asian American women have one of the highest rates of interracial marriage, particularly with white men. These romantic pairings increased in the aftermath of World War II and the Cold War, which led to an increased American military presence in Asia and a proliferation of Hollywood cultural representations of Asian women (Marchetti 1993). Asian and Asian American women in interracial relationships helped to challenge and overturn antimiscegenation laws (Pascoe 2009). However, these interracial marriages were not purely symbols of a color blind America. Instead, scholars note how racialized, gendered, and classed understandings of Asian womanhood and white manhood channel sexual desire and marital partner choice toward particular types of bodies (Koshy 2004). As Ji-Yeon Yuh (2004) points out, Korean women during the U.S. occupation in South Korea may be looking for "Prince Charmings" among white American military personnel, but their partners may be seeking Asian "lotus blossoms."

The rise of Asian transnational adoption during and after the Cold War also reveals gender and racial hierarchies. Christina Klein (2003) argues that transnational adoption represented a domesticated version of American imperial ambitions in Asia. Adoption allowed (predominantly white) American families to embrace Asia. However, there were clear power differentials (among nations and within families) between those giving humanitarian aid and those receiving assistance. The hierarchy between white parents and Asian children also has a gender dimension. More Asian girls compared to boys are adopted by American families. These girls are viewed in the U.S. as unwanted in Asia, due to the presumed patriarchal and antifemale values of these Asian countries. In contrast, Asian girls are desired in American society for their presumed docility and adaptability.

Similar cultural, generational and gender dynamics also exist within same-race, co-ethnic families. One of the persistent tropes in Asian American literature focuses on intergenerational conflict, particularly between immigrant parents and their American-born children. Tensions regarding gender roles are a primary way in which these intergenerational and cross-cultural dynamics are represented and experienced. While immigrant parents are commonly depicted as seeking to reinstate gender norms from their home countries, their American-born children assert their desires to adopt the gender roles of their peers. The cultural war between the generations is often problematically caricatured and understood as an Orientalist binary between the gender conformity and hierarchy of Asian society versus the gender freedoms of American society.

The racialized and gendered dynamics of the economy, law, and family are profoundly shaped by cultural representations. These "controling images" or dominant representations of Asian Americans tend to accentuate nonnormative gender roles. Asian American men and women have been depicted as hypersexual as well as asexual (Y. Espiritu 2008; Robert Lee 1999; Okihiro 1994). During the late 19th and early 20th centuries, Asians men were characterized as sexual predators and economic competitors, i.e., yellow peril who were alien to and also threatened the United States. Throughout most of the 20th century, Asian and Asian American women were portrayed as prostitutes, geishas, and porn stars, alternately excluded and desired for their exotic sexual deviancy (Shimizu 2007). Since the mid-1960s, Asian Americans are frequently depicted as model minorities. This image celebrates Asian American heteronormative families for their stability, work ethic, and ability to transmit cultural capital. At the same time, this model minority image reinforces emasculating perceptions of Asian American men and docile images of Asian American women. The more recent furor over Tiger Moms revives a cultural anxiety among many Americans regarding Asian economic and resource competition. Not surprisingly, this racialized discourse, which emerges in an era of intense globalization, is expressed through a gendered debate. Asian American mothers are perceived as excessively focused on discipline and achievement, an excess that marks them as cultural and gender deviants, i.e., as not proper American mothers.

Applying a gender lens to Asian American racialization has generated complex and intersectional analyses of social oppression and social power. Early scholars have tended to focus on Asian American women's experiences and representations, although there is increasing attention to masculinity as well as sexuality. In addition to focusing on gendered and sexualized groups, identities, and constructs, the scholarship also reveals how gender hierarchies are embedded in the economy, the state, the family and in cultural representations. In contrast to earlier debates that pitted gender against race, Asian American studies scholars are increasingly invested in understanding how gender, race, sexuality, class, and other forms of social difference and hierarchy are mutually inflected and intertwined.

29

Generation
Andrea Louie

"Generation" is often defined as the time span between birth cohorts. Correspondingly, generational divisions may be spaced according to age differences between grandparents, their children, and their grandchildren. In this sense, the length of a "generation" is determined by the age mothers give birth to their children. However, "generation" also invokes shared experiences and identities that define birth cohorts. In the context of immigration, "generation" encompasses differences between the experiences and relationships of immigrants born abroad and those born in the country of settlement.

Economic, political, and legal factors shape immigration patterns and the experiences of various generations. These factors are necessarily the products of different historical contexts. In the case of minority immigrants and their children, racism, discrimination, and exclusion—along with other forms of adjustment and incorporation—shape generational identities. Limited economic and social niches circumscribed options for early generations of Asian immigrants in the United States. In addition, laws such as the Page Act (1875) restricted the entry of Chinese women and therefore the ability of the Chinese to form families in the United States. On the one hand, Chinese exclusion laws and the extension of these restrictions to other Asian immigrants (e.g., the 1924 Johnson-Reed Act) reflect the extent to which the experiences of early Asian immigrants were shaped by perceptions of labor competition and unassimilability. On the other hand, patterns of return migration make visible a continued investment in and connection to the homeland that may have been shaped in large part by such mainstream forms of exclusion, discrimination, and disenfranchisement in the United States.

Because of the way that they are shaped in relation to policy, politics, and a myriad of other factors, it is important to note that second-generation immigrant experiences vary according to group and time period. Processes of racialization and "othering" are key factors here, as Asian Americans frequently are targeted because of their "perpetual foreigner" status. Generational identities are also delimited by specific historical events. For instance, during World War II, in the case of Issei, Nisei, and Sansei (first, second, and third generation), Japanese Americans were categorized according to their generation standing. Issei, the immigrant generation, were denied naturalization rights and were therefore left in a precarious position when they were interned. Technically enemy aliens, Issei men, when forced to sign the Loyalty Oath, were left without protection from Japan. Alternatively, American-born Nisei were imprisoned in the camps despite their status as American citizens, and those of fighting age were impelled to fight for the U.S. in the war. Still, most Nisei soldiers fought for the U.S. willingly to prove their loyalty to their country of birth. Sansei, many of whom were born in the camps, were also clearly shaped by internment and its legacy. Another group that illustrates the numerous factors that shape generational identities is the Kibei, second-generation Japanese Americans (American born, or Nisei) who were sent to Japan as children to receive an education. This singular example highlights the great variation that exists in the experiences of a particular generation and destabilizes dominant teleological characterizations of assimilation over time and generation.

The passage of the Immigration and Naturalization Act (the Hart-Cellar Act) in 1965 abolished national quotas set back in 1924. The act also allowed for family reunification, enabling Asian Americans to sponsor additional relatives, and the Asian American population grew dramatically. As Pyong Gap Min notes, between 1965 and 2002, 8.3 million Asian Americans became permanent residents, comprising 34% of immigrants during this period (2006, 26). As a result of these new policies, multiple generations were able to immigrate at the same time, allowing for the formation of vibrant ethnic enclaves. Such simultaneous migration often placed great stress on families at they endeavored to adjust to U.S. life. Children, who often were able to learn English more quickly than their parents, occupied a translational position. It should be noted that the experiences of second-generation Asian Americans in the post-WWII era differs in important ways from those of second-generation immigrants post-1965 or post-9/11.

To be sure, the theme of generational or intergenerational conflict remains a common one that shapes scholarship about Asian Americans and the policies affecting them. Models of generational conflict as applied to Asian American families and communities often assume that conflict between generations is due to later generations assimilating to U.S. culture, and thus deviating from the ways of their elders. While different generations may adapt to U.S. culture in varying ways, with younger generations often more rapidly integrating themselves into a broader youth culture, it is also true that a number of discourses problematically frame Asian Americans as having strong cultural values. Such discourses operate in contrast to those concerning other groups such as African Americans, whose lack of culture is seen to lead to social problems (Ebron and Tsing 1995; Fong 2006). The emphasis on the richness of an oft-merged Asian and Asian American culture leads to the sense that Asian Americans are bound by traditional cultural beliefs. Thus, as younger generations adopt new cultural ways, priorities, and values, conflict with their more traditional elders arises out of incompatibility.

For example, younger generations may have ideas about educational priorities, marriage (who to marry and when), and career choices that diverge from parental and grandparental expectations. However, it also becomes clear that to fully understand intergenerational conflict, it is necessary to view it as more than a matter of contrasting cultural beliefs. Rather, a nuanced approach, which takes into account economic stresses, ethnoracial discrimination, and dominant assimilative discourses, recognizes a set of conditions that more broadly frame immigration and shape family dynamics. These issues have become particularly visible in the aftermath of the 1965 Immigration Act and the Vietnam War, responsible for the largest second generation in U.S. history. At the end of the Vietnam War in 1975, waves of Southeast Asian refugees from Vietnam, Laos, and Cambodia also made their way to the United States. Alongside the trauma of having left their homelands against their will, refugees faced resettlement obstacles. Notwithstanding the passage of refugee acts (in 1975 and 1980) intended to facilitate their resettlement, they nevertheless faced racism and discrimination. Many arrived during a time of economic recession, and were resented for the government assistance that they received.

The events of September 11, 2001, marked a dramatic shift in the ways that some first- and second-generation immigrants experienced cultural citizenship in the United States. As numerous scholars have noted, cultural citizenship extends beyond legal definitions of citizenship and speaks to broader issues of inclusion and belonging in relation to state power and empire (Maira 2009; Ong 2003; Rosaldo 1994). Whether Muslim or not, Arab Americans, South Asian Americans, and others perceived to look like the "enemy" have faced daily discrimination due to their perceived foreignness. While Junaid Rana (2011) notes that "Islamophobia" has deep roots and has been crafted through various means throughout Western/U.S. history, growing up post-9/11 has directly affected the ability of first-generation Muslim immigrants to gain legal citizenship. It has likewise impeded access to the homeland (for both first and second generations) and instantiated vexed senses of belonging to the United States (Maira 2010; Prashad 2009). Within a post-9/11 context, many second-generation immigrant Muslims of South Asian American descent struggle to create a sense of belonging and cultural citizenship. As Sunaina Maira (2009) notes, this has sometimes involved an emphasis on homeland ties, an interrogation of the promise on the U.S. as a multicultural society, or a critique of U.S. racial structures based on alliances with other people of color. Analogously, scholars such as Nitasha Sharma (2010) have examined the identification of second-generation South Asian Americans with African Americans.

A rich body of literature about second-generation Asian American issues exists, including Mia Tuan's work (1999) on the ethnic identities of later-generation Chinese and Japanese Americans, Nazli Kibria's (2003) research on second-generation Chinese and Korean Americans who grew up in Boston in the 1980s and 1990s, and Sucheng Chan's (2006) work on 1.5-generation Vietnamese Americans that focuses on personal narratives of their refugee experiences. Such works necessarily complicate characterizations of gradual assimilation over time to mainstream culture (Park and Burgess 1925). This model of assimilation is problematic in that it assumes a uniform mainstream culture, privileges conformity as a desired outcome, and stresses gradual and even mixing of cultural traditions *à la* the "melting pot."

While narratives of assimilation are prominent in folk and academic descriptions about processes of integration that occur over time, continued transnational relationships between migrants and the homeland (which extend beyond the first generation) prompt alternative readings of both assimilation and generation. These homeland ties, apparent in regular physical returns and involvement in homeland institutions, are evident in Peggy Levitt's (2009) research about transnationalism and second-generation Pakistani Muslims and Indian Gujaratis, who maintain ties rooted in religious beliefs and practices.

These transnational considerations foment broader questions about how and why the designation of generational cohorts is important in both academic and non-academic contexts, given that such labels are at times ambiguous. While the first immigrant generation is usually defined as the first members of a family to emigrate to another country and gain citizenship, this definition is complicated by scholarship on transnational migration. This work underscores that migration is seldom marked by a one-way, permanent movement to a new location, but rather is sustained by multistranded connections between locations that often extend beyond the first immigrant generation (Basch, Glick Schiller, and Blanc 1993). Second-generation immigrants may continue to be engaged in activities in the homeland, including long-term visits, the sending of remittances, or even finding a spouse (Waters and Levitt 2002). For example, it was common for immigrants to the U.S. in the late nineteenth and early twentieth centuries from varied backgrounds to return to their homelands after spending time living and working in the United States (Basch, Glick Schiller, and Blanc 1993; Hsu 2000). Such patterns continue today and complicate renderings of monolithic generational designations that focus on either initial migration to the United States, citizenship acquisition, or time away from the nation of origin (Rouse 1994; Smith 2005).

Correspondingly, the use of the generational designation "1.5" has become increasingly common in both folk and academic works to describe the distinct identities of those who immigrate as children (before adolescence). An in-between category, such a term illustrates the limitations of more traditional generational labels. Originally discussed by sociologists Alejandro Portes and Rubén Rumbaut (2001), the partitioning of generations in this way signals a post-1965 designation and is apparent in Asian American and Latino/a studies. Inclusive of immigrant families, the experiences of adult parents differed greatly from those of their children, who migrated at a young age. The term "1.5 generation" captures the particularities of having grown up for the majority of one's life in the U.S., but with strong ties to the homeland. Members of this generation are usually described as bicultural, often proficient in both English and their mother tongues. While technically immigrants, people in this category do not necessarily share the same perspectives as their first-generation immigrant parents, or their second-generation siblings or friends. Similarly, adoptees, particularly those from Asia adopted into non-Asian families, may technically be first generation, but may not share the language abilities or other orientations characteristic of this generation.

Second-generation South Asian Americans have formed a distinctive desi subculture (Maira 2002; Shankar 2008; Purkayastha 2005) that is characterized by a degree of identification with their culture of origin, but that is expressed in a manner that is a hybridized representation of this ethnic pride, usually distinct from the traditions of their parents. Maira's work on hip hop and bhangra youth culture, for example, emphasizes the ways that desis appropriate remixed versions of bhangra music that originated in clubs in Great Britain as the basis for their own youth culture. This youth culture is often global in scope, while at the same time allowing for local variations and expressions. For example, the fact that one can watch Hmong breakdancers from France on YouTube illustrates not only the global resettlement of Hmong refugees, but also the spread of a youth popular culture form that originated in the United States. Asian American youths have opened up new spaces of cultural production that can be shared over the internet in ways to which preceding generations did have not access. Older Hmong may engage in different uses of transnational media, such as in the watching of homeland videos made in Laos, Thailand, or even among their co-ethnic Miao in China (Schein 2008). This mode of participation is based less on self-expression and more in the desire of diasporic Hmong to maintain a connection to the imaginary of a homeland. As more elders migrate to the U.S. to be cared for by their adult children and sometimes to help out with grandchildren, new issues are raised regarding this new group of immigrants who are migrating at a much older age and are less able to negotiate U.S. daily life.

Second-generation Korean Americans also find themselves caught between the promise of American liberalism in the form of a U.S. university education, parental pressures and models of success, and structures of racism and discrimination. As Nancy Abelmann's (2009) work shows, many turn to evangelical Protestantism as a means to distinguish themselves from both their peers and their parents. Another interpretation of generation is also closely tied to changing economic conditions and how they shape the paths of particular generations. As Thuy Linh Nguyen Tu notes in *The Beautiful Generation* (2010), the specific experiences of second-generation children of Asian immigrants who made a living working in garment factories shaped their entry into the field of design.

It should also be noted that the field of Asian American studies itself has produced what can be seen as numerous generations of scholars and scholarship, defined not only by time period, but also key issues, political concerns, and theoretical perspectives that sometimes conflict with those of other generations. For many Asian Americans, a politicized identification as an Asian American also signifies a generational identity that is rooted in the U.S. but also characterized by continued (but changed) relationships with the homeland. As a panethnic (Y. Espiritu 1992) category, "Asian American" reflects an acknowledgement of shared experiences as people racialized as "Asian," a category that did not exist traditionally in Asia. While not confined solely to second- and later-generation immigrants, this form of identification is marked by an increased awareness of the experiences of racism and marginalization that forms the basis for new forms of community building, including the creation of a sense of historical memory for later generations based on the narration of these stories. Terese Monberg's work (2008) examines the role of alternative institutions such as FAHNS (Filipino American National Historical Society) and the work that the "Bridge Generation" (post-WWII second generation) plays in creating a sense of shared history through the retelling of stories of "Growing Up Brown." Cathy Schlund-Vials's (2012b) work on 1.5-generation Cambodian Americans illustrates the variability in the strength of ties to the homeland, depending on immigrants' age of arrival and place of residency. There are also numerous ways of being connected to the homeland, for example, through participation in transnational social justice movements such as the Cambodian American "memory work" discussed by Schlund-Vials or the Korean adoptee activism analyzed by Eleana Kim

(2010). Thus, in understanding the concept of generation, it is essential to consider both structural factors that shape immigration and economic adaption, as well as more subjective experiences that go into the choices that individuals within these generations make. Transnational flows have complicated the rendering of "generation," as well as the ways that immigrants and later generations maintain contact with the homeland in a variety of capacities, including economic, political, social, and cultural realms.

30

Genocide

Khatharya Um

Writing about genocide, Leo Kuper noted: "the word is new, the crime ancient" (1981, 9). While the annals of history are replete with mass killings and the deliberate, virtual decimation of communities, the term "genocide," which is derived from the Greek word *genos*, meaning "race" or "people," and the Latin word *cidere*, "to kill," was first articulated by Raphael Lemkin in 1944. In *Axis Rule in Occupied Europe* he defined genocide as "a coordinated plan of different actions aiming at the destruction of essential foundations of the life of national groups, with the aim of annihilating the groups themselves" (1944, 79). Later adopted in the 1948 United Nations Convention on the Prevention and Punishment of the Crime of Genocide (CPPCG), the definition was modified to include an intent to destroy "in whole or in part, a national, ethnical, racial, or religious group," involving either actual physical destruction or the creation of conditions that would ultimately undermine the viability of the group's continued existence, such as preventing reproduction or forcible transfer of children of one group to another (U.N. General Assembly 1948, 174). The CPPCG has since spawned new statutes and protocols to account for additional forms of mass atrocities and crimes not covered by the 1948 Convention, such as war crimes and crimes against humanity. Under the Rome Statute of the International Criminal Court adopted in 1998, genocide was recognized as one of four international crimes prosecutable in the international criminal court.

Since its initial articulation, "genocide" has engendered political, legal, and theoretical debates, centering largely on concerns over definitional and conceptual limitations that reflect its genealogy. That the term was born, at the dawn of the Cold War, of the push for accountability for Nazi crimes against Jews shaped the Convention definition of what constitutes "genocide." Despite the fact that Lemkin himself recognized other genocidal precedence, scholarship and public discourse have long privileged ethnically and racially motivated mass atrocities, and in particular the uniqueness and exceptionalism of the Jewish experience. Genocide studies thus were confined essentially to Jewish studies and outside the intellectual scope of ethnic and American studies. While the ratification of the CPPCG did provoke an immediate response from African Americans, genocide did not become part of the Asian American lexicon or politico-intellectual concerns until the 1960s with the strengthening of the civil rights movement in the U.S. and escalation of the war in Vietnam. It gained new centrality in the 1990s and 2000s following the resettlement of refugees from Southeast Asia, particularly from Cambodia, and subsequent emergence of scholars of Southeast Asian ancestry in academe.

From its genesis, the term "genocide" was highly politicized as evidenced by the limited categories covered under the Convention. In the face of political objections, principally by the then Soviet Union, mass killing of social and political groups was eliminated from the categories of genocidal acts. The conceptual omission of co-ethnic violence compelled Jean Lacouture (1977) to coin the term "auto-genocide" to characterize the Cambodian genocidal experience under the Khmer Rouge (1975–1979), where both perpetrators and victims were mostly Khmer, and where most of the atrocities were politically rather than racially, ethnically, or religiously motivated crimes committed against soldiers, government officials, and class "enemies" (Kiernan 1996).

The simultaneously restrictive and imprecise language adopted by the Convention further limits the usefulness of the CPPCG. An inadequate guideline for measuring "genocidal" scale of destruction, the phrase "in whole or in part" provokes a critical question about the genocidal process itself and the point at which extremism, in acts or ideology, makes external intervention imperative. Similarly, the emphasis on intentionality inhibits intervention and prosecution, and undermines accountability. Unlike the Nazis, most genocidal regimes do not leave copious records, making it difficult to prove intent. This challenge led the Yugoslavia and Rwanda war crime tribunals recently to decree that, in the absence of incontestable evidence, intentionality can be inferred from "the scale of atrocities committed" and the "systematic targeting" of victims on account of their "membership in a particular group" (Orentlicher 2007). In the Bosnian case, the court linked intent to knowledge of the impact of the act on the targeted group. Though significant, these judicial interventions remain insufficient in setting definitive guidelines for defining and responding to genocidal occurrences.

These legal and political constraints, including states' fear of being implicated in their own genocidal histories, undercut the efficacy of the Convention in preventing or arresting genocidal developments. In various historical instances, the international community has been reluctant to even evoke the term "genocide," let alone intervene to thwart or stop genocidal developments once they have begun. If interventionist acts have been rare, prosecution of perpetrators is even more so. It took forty-five years before the first international tribunal was established, here to adjudicate genocidal crimes committed in Yugoslavia, and it was almost half a century before the first conviction was handed down, in

this case for Jean-Paul Akayesu's role in the 1994 Rwandan genocide. In Cambodia, surviving Khmer Rouge leaders were finally brought to trial three decades after the collapse of the genocidal regime. Even then, the charge of genocide was applied only to atrocities committed in select instances, such as against ethnic minorities, though co-ethnic killings and brutalization accounted for the vastly greater part of the Khmer Rouge's crimes ("Cambodia Tribunal Monitor" 2011).

Almost from its inception, the limitations of CPPCG have compelled scholars and advocates to push for inclusion of other forms of state-sanctioned violence that engender multifaceted destruction of a group, and for recognition of other genocidal moments in history. In the U.S., the Civil Rights Congress advocated for the application of the term to discriminatory practices directed principally at African Americans but also other racial and linguistic minorities, with specific references to Puerto Rican and Asian Americans. In 1951, the Congress submitted a petition to the United Nations detailing the "record of mass slayings on the basis of race, of lives deliberately warped and distorted by the willful creation of conditions making for premature death, poverty and disease" committed or sanctioned by the U.S. government "with intent to destroy, in whole or in part, the 15,000,000 Negro people of the United States" (Civil Rights Congress 1951, 4). Genocide, the petition argued, was committed against blacks in the U.S. as the "consistent, conscious, unified policies of every branch of government" (1951, xiv).

Scholars and rights activists have since not only extended the argument to other racialized communities in the U.S., namely Native Americans and Latino Americans, but also highlighted other forms of genocide, such as economic and cultural genocide, that result from deliberate state actions directed at a group. Though the Convention had gestured to the notion of cultural genocide in its reference to the forcible removal of children, theorists such as Robert Blauner (1975) expanded the concept beyond the threat of physical extinction of a people to include language and educational policies and practices, religious conversion, and other acts that result in cultural invalidation and loss for marginalized communities, particularly in the United States.

In its petition, the Civil Rights Congress not only documented U.S. genocidal policies at home, but also pointed to the U.S. exportation of its racialized genocidal creed overseas. Arguing that the usage of jellied gasoline in Korea and the atom bomb in Japan manifested the same "contempt for human life in a colored skin" as in the "lynchers' faggot at home," they proclaimed these issues to be "the concern of mankind everywhere" (1951, 7). The transnational connections made between developments in Asia and the struggles in the U.S. were amplified for Asian American activists during the politically turbulent 1960s by the brutalizing U.S. military campaigns in Southeast Asia. With U.S. clandestine wars in Cambodia and Laos essentially shrouded from the American public, it was Vietnam that brought these issues home. The Mai Lai massacre and other widely publicized crimes committed by the U.S. military against civilian populations as well as high profiled court martial cases such as that of Lt. Calley underscored the connections between U.S. racist and imperialist policies. The Asian American struggle for visibility and selfhood thus came to resonate with the Vietnamese people's struggle for national liberation and self-determination. What was viewed as the integral link between antiracist resistance at home and antimilitarist stance against U.S. wars overseas came to define the Asian American movement of the 1960s.

The heightened transnational political consciousness that converged on Vietnam had a twofold impact. First, it engendered new and additional scholarship on the consequences of U.S. militarism and imperialism in other parts of Asia. This is especially evident in the literature on U.S.-Philippines but also on U.S.-Japan histories (Yoneyama 1999). Scholars such as Luzviminda Francisco, Howard Zinn, and Gabriel Kolko documented the atrocities committed by the U.S. during the Filipino-American War, that sanguinary encounter that Francisco (1973) referred to as "the first Vietnam." Others, such as E. San Juan Jr. (2005), the title of whose article exhibited a direct and deliberate link to the works of the Civil Rights Congress, and Dylan Rodríguez (2010), further argued that the policies and practices of the U.S. government, implemented with the deliberate intent to destroy Filipino sovereignty and cultural continuity, amounted to genocide. Second, it forced scholarly attention onto genocidal acts committed by other imperialist powers in Asia, such as during the Japanese occupation of China and Korea that catalyzed the early instances of Asian American diasporic activism. Combined, this analytic expansion decentered Asian American studies from its earlier U.S. focus, a shift made more emphatic by the emergence of the refugee communities from Vietnam, Laos, and Cambodia, whose experiences with political trauma and concomitant preoccupation with the "homeland" register a different tenor than that of many Asian immigrant communities.

The concept of genocide took on another and different significance in Asian American studies in the post-Vietnam era. Under the Khmer Rouge regime, Cambodia spiraled into one of the twentieth century's darkest moments; in less than four years, almost one-third of the population perished from starvation, disease, executions, and "disappearances" (Um 2012). Virtually no Cambodian is left untouched by loss in one form or another. While scholars and jurists debate the applicability of the term "genocide" to the Cambodian experience, most Cambodians and Cambodian Americans, over 50% of whom are refugee-survivors, have no doubt that what transpired was a holocaust. The legacies of this historical trauma are multidimensional and trans-generational. They are reflected in the demographics of the refugee community and in the relational dynamics within the family. They bleed through temporalities and inform the identity construction of the post-genocide generation (Um 2006; Ung 2012; Schlund-Vials 2012a) and the ambivalence that diasporas harbor toward the homeland (Um 2007).

The post-Vietnam and post-genocide resettlement of Southeast Asian refugees, as such, created new points of departure in Asian American studies. The nature and scale of the Cambodian experience reinvigorates the debate about the analytic importance of a geno-cide definition that is expansive but not diluted. The refugee presence, at once a product of the war in which the U.S. was implicated and a beneficiary of perceived American altruism, also complicates and destabilizes critical assumptions that have been the cornerstones of the movement's political agenda. Whereas previously Asian American movement could coalesce around an-tiracist and anti-imperialist agendas, left-wing dicta-torship disrupts the political imaginary. Some scholars and activists, particularly in the West, continue to em-phasize U.S. complicity in the genocidal destruction of Cambodia, both in radicalizing the Khmer Rouge and later in supporting them in the Third Indochina War. While many Cambodians do recall the devastation en-gendered by U.S. bombing campaigns and even hold America responsible for the tragedies that befell their country, the magnitude and self-implicating nature of the Khmer Rouge genocide overshadow all other suffer-ings in their preoccupation.

Similarly, postwar resettlement of Laotian refugees further exposed the U.S. "secret" war in Laos, where the tonnage of bombs dropped over the Plain of Jars between 1969 and 1972 exceeded the total tonnage dropped over both Europe and the Pacific during World War II (Fadiman 1997, 132), killing or wounding some 30% of the population and uprooting another 50% from their native villages (C. Robinson 1998, 13). As in Cambodia, while academic discourse may focus on the "genocidal" losses and dislocations engendered during the war, community discourse is equally, if not more, oriented toward mass atrocities committed by the com-munist regimes, both Laotian and Vietnamese, against Hmong resistance *after* the war (Hamilton-Merritt 2008). The framing of genocidal experiences beyond the context of U.S. imperialism to include persecution, subjugation, conquest, and imperialism at large moves the discourse of human rights in Asian American stud-ies toward new horizons.

The presence and increased visibility of Southeast Asian Americans, in essence, dislocates Asian American studies from its earlier political and intellectual moor-ings, shifting the field toward greater and new intel-lectual synergy with other fields of inquiry. Given the centrality of genocide to the Cambodian American identity and politics, memory, commemoration, and trauma engendered by politically induced rupture as well as by migration-related dislocations, previously kept in the domain of psychology, sociology, and geno-cide and cultural studies, have become important areas of inquiry in Asian American studies. The analytic at-tention placed on culture and race as mediating factors in post-trauma coping and healing also provides critical intervention against the eurocentricity of trauma stud-ies. Similarly, attention paid to the transnational activi-ties and activism of Southeast Asian diasporas locates immigrant agency and resilience in new contexts, en-gendering new possibilities for deepening connections between Asian American, diaspora, transnational, and area studies.

31

Globalization

Robyn Magalit Rodriguez

"Globalization" is a term used by academics, political figures, and activists to describe changes in economic, political, and cultural life due to accelerated flows of capital, goods, media, and people across borders (Appadurai 2000; D. Harvey 2007; Lowe and Lloyd 1997). Another term used to describe these changes is "transnationalism" (Basch et al. 1994; Ong 1999). "Transnationalism" is sometimes used to identify processes and practices engaged in by ordinary people or social movements, whereas "globalization" is used to identify processes and practices engaged in by more powerful world actors like governments or multinational corporations (Guarnizo and Smith 1998).

Globalization is often ascribed to social transformations since the 1970s due to deindustrialization (i.e., the relocation of factory production to Third World countries) in advanced capitalist countries like the United States. Many scholars note, however, that global interactions and interconnections predate the 1970s. Colonialism is an early form of globalization from this view. Most people who use the term agree, nevertheless, that there is something qualitatively different about the frequency and kinds of border crossings taking place today.

Globalization is appraised both positively and negatively. For critics, globalization is synonymous with neoliberalism, an economic philosophy that privileges the market and capitalist logics in regulating all aspects of social life. From a neoliberal perspective, the government is an inefficient and intrusive institution that should lessen its role in the provision of education, health, and other social goods. Critics of neoliberalism, however, argue that neoliberalism exacerbates inequality within and between countries. Other critics see globalization as symptomatic of the decline of sovereignty and think of the proliferation of capital, goods, media, and people from other countries as threatening to the nation-state. Alternatively, proponents of globalization see it as producing new forms of interconnectedness across national borders that decrease social distance between people and foster more cosmopolitan perspectives.

Globalization and transnationalism has given rise to more interdisciplinary approaches in Asian American studies (L. Lowe 1998; K. Scott Wong 2009). Notably, scholars based in Asia have become more engaged in Asian American studies (Huang and Bing 2008). Topics that have long been of central importance to Asian American studies are being studied in new ways. For example, while much immigration scholarship focused on how U.S. immigration law either prohibits or allows different Asian groups entry, a globalization approach incorporates more attention to the dynamics in Asian immigrants' countries of origin. Scholars have found that countries of origin actively produce and shape migration flows to the United States as "labor brokerage states" (Parreñas 2000; R. Rodriguez 2010; Guevarra 2010). Others have found that some even introduce "return migration" and other policies aimed at enticing their former emigrants to return "home" (L. Liu 2012; Ong 1999; Skrentny et al. 2007). A globalization approach reveals how migration between the United States and different Asian countries no longer takes place in only one direction.

Asian American studies scholars who take a globalization approach, moreover, track new and emergent social and cultural formations. They find that Asian Americans' families are increasingly spread across two (or more) countries. Transnational families are partly a consequence of the restrictiveness of U.S. immigration policy since 9/11. New "homeland security" laws have made the process of applying for family reunification, a mechanism that many Asian Americans have used since the 1965 Immigration Act to have their relatives join them, much more difficult. This creates a backlog that has petitioners in the U.S. waiting for decades before family members can join them (Hing 2006; Park and Park 2005). Even though it may be cheaper and more convenient to travel, border enforcement policies limits the kinds of travel people can participate in. The families of class-privileged "flexible citizens," however, can be transnational by choice (Ong 1999). Some opt to have their children raised and educated in the U.S. (with or without one of the parents living with them). "Parachute children" is a term used to describe this phenomenon (Zhou 1998; Orellana et al. 2001). Even if they are not "parachute children," members of the second generation often have transnational upbringings that involve direct or indirect exposure to their parents' countries of origin. Moreover, their definitions of who constitutes "family" are often quite expansive. Despite growing up in two-parent nuclear families in the U.S. they may think of "family" in transnational terms (Purkayastha 2010). Finally, they may even choose partners from Asia (Thai 2008).

The globalization of media facilitates Asian Americans', including the second generation's, familial and cultural ties to Asia. Film, television, fashion, music, and food from different Asian countries can be easily accessed in the United States (Liu and Lin 2009; K. Wang 2006). These cultural products, in fact, are actively marketed to Asian Americans. For example, "ethnic enclaves" or areas with high concentrations of Asian-owned businesses like "Chinatowns" that can be found throughout the U.S. are important hubs for the production, distribution, and consumption of Asian goods. Asian immigrants and their U.S.-born children work,

live, and frequent these kinds of spaces (Zhou 2004). At the same time, the Internet has become a key source of Asian popular culture and explains, for instance, the widespread popularity of K-pop (or Korean pop music) among Asian Americans more broadly as well as among Korean Americans (Shin 2009).

The transnationalism of many Asian Americans' lives has given rise to complex ethnic and racial identities and politics among both immigrants and their U.S.-born children. Asian Americans become naturalized U.S. citizens and participate in American political life, but they remain interested and participate as well in "homeland" politics (Lien 2008). Asian American panethnic collective identity, therefore, may seem less salient as a consequence of recent forms of transnationalism (Spickard 2007). Yet even panethnic movements, which trace their beginnings to the late 1960s, have always had transnational aspects (Fujino 2008). Meanwhile, second-generation Asian Americans' racial identities may actually be shaped not by their experiences in the U.S. but through travels to their parents' (or ancestors') erstwhile "homelands" (Yamashiro 2011). Indeed, Asian Americans may acquire some understanding of U.S. racial politics even before they ever get to American shores as they are exposed to U.S. global institutions like the military overseas (N. Kim 2008).

Though globalization is a late-twentieth-century phenomenon, scholars have been challenged to revisit historical scholarship that might have been overly U.S.-centric. Historians who study early Asian American migration, for example, have begun to broaden their analyses by paying closer attention to the context of Asia and drawing out parallels and connections between Asians in the Americas more broadly (i.e., Canada, Latin America, and the Caribbean), thereby taking a "hemispheric approach" (Hu-DeHart 2006; Erika Lee 2005; Lee and Shibusawa 2005; Ngai 2006).

32

Health

Grace J. Yoo

Health is defined as the absence of injury or illness. This definition incorporates multiple spheres of wellness including the physical, mental, spiritual, and social. To understand wellness of Asian Americans and within Asian American studies, the multiple dimensions of well-being, recovery, and healing need to be considered. Of utmost importance is to hear the voices of diverse Asian American communities in the process of comprehending the true meaning of wellness and health for Asian Americans. Although scholars in various disciplines have argued that race is not a valid biological or scientific concept, "race" and racialization continue to act as important social determinants of quality of life, health status, health care access, and quality of care for Asian Americans. In recent times, a growing number of public health scholars have documented and examined health issues that are critical in the Asian American community (Yoo, Le, and Oda 2013).

Historically, well-being has been studied by Asian American studies scholars in terms of how outsiders have depicted and viewed Asian immigrant bodies. Concerns regarding biological determinism and the negative uses of science against Asian Americans are founded in the history of public health science and public health policies. Influenced by the political and the social contexts of the time, public health science and policies were based on earlier racialized constructions of Asian bodies as carriers of smallpox, bubonic plague, and syphilis germs. These constructions were used to justify segregation and unfair and discriminatory treatment, as well as to exclude Chinese immigrants (Molina 2006; N. Shah 2001). Moreover, these constructions contributed to the notion of Asians as the "yellow peril," which constituted Asian bodies as a threat to the health and civilization of white Americans. Although Asian immigrants were constructed as inherently embodying these diseases, it was actually unsanitary conditions resulting from racist neglect of segregated areas that contributed to their spread among early Asian immigrant communities (Hom 2013). Barriers that Asian immigrants faced in their attempts to receive health care—including racial discrimination and harassment—only magnified these issues. Solutions for healthcare and well-being for many communities came from within. For example, in 1900, Chinese immigrants worked on the building of the San Francisco Chinese Hospital, one of the earliest mobilizing moments in the history of Chinese American communities (Hom 2013).

The San Francisco State strike of 1968–1969 and the eventual establishment of the College of Ethnic Studies were prompted in part by the need to continually voice concerns over community health and social problems—including gangs, crowded schools, housing shortages, and the displacement of the aged—that had gone long unrecognized in San Francisco's Chinatown, Japantown, and Manilatown (Collier and Gonzales 2009). Existing institutions—including higher education but also health care institutions—had ignored the histories and the wellness of Asian Americans. This need for a voice was in part due to the context of the post-1965 Immigration Act era, including the arrival of new immigrants who faced health issues compounded by anticommunist harassment in Chinatown, the pressures of redevelopment in San Francisco's Manilatown community, and the lingering effects of wartime incarceration and forced relocation of Japanese Americans. Through the passage of the 1964 War on Poverty Act and through the work of college-educated Asian Americans, the strike at San Francisco State College was intricately linked to the increasing agitation occurring within health and social services contexts in the San Francisco Bay Area. Asian American Movement activists were voicing inequities and the lack of availability of culturally and linguistically appropriate services in a variety of Asian American communities. Many of these activists would later go on to establish Asian American health and social service organizations and programs to addresses these inequities, including the Northeast Medical Services Center in San Francisco (1968), Charles B. Wang Community Health Center in New York City (1971), Asian Health Services in Oakland (1973), and Asian Community Health Clinic in Seattle (1973).

The actions of these activists, like those of Asian Americans who had done similar work for a hundred years before, filled a gap in healthcare for Asian Americans who were underserved by traditional healthcare institutions. Although services began to be developed, research data on the inequities that Asian Americans experienced were still nonexistent. Because of limited research, Asian Americans were easily stereotyped as the "healthy minority," a view similar to the "model minority"—in this case referring to a uniformly similar group with very few health problems. The healthy minority stereotype, like the model minority one, fails to account for socioeconomic disparities that impact health status and quality of life among diverse Asian Americans. These assumptions are also based on limited research within and across various Asian American subgroups.

The 1982 *Report of the Secretary's Task Force on Black and Minority Health* documented that Asian Americans were healthier than whites and other racial/ethnic groups. The report used aggregated data of Asian Americans and failed to examine subgroup differences. However, it also demonstrated to advocates and to health professionals the need for data collection and for an increase in research funding for the study of Asian Americans and health. In response to this need, two national organizations formed: the Asian American Health Forum and the Asian Pacific American Community of Health Organizations (Jang and Tran 2009). In 1988, the Asian Pacific Islander American Health Forum sponsored a national conference to address the health problems impacting Asian Americans and Pacific Islanders. This conference convened community leaders to discuss health issues and matters of access, research, and policy. Subsequently, *Confronting Critical Health Issues of Asian and Pacific Islander Americans*, edited by Nolan Zane, David Takeuchi, and Kathleen Young, was published in 1993 to discuss the pressing health issues in the Asian American community.

Medline and PubMed searches of published research on six major health disparity areas revealed that from 1986 to 2000 only 0.01% of articles included any Asian Americans in the study sample (Ghosh 2003). Moreover, the research that does exist shows that disparities between Asian American subgroups are significant. For example, in a 2008 study, compared to other Asian American subgroups, Vietnamese Americans were least likely to have a college education and most likely to be in only fair or poor health. Korean Americans were most likely to be uninsured, be current smokers, and be without a usual place for health care as compared to other Asian American subgroups. Additionally, Filipino Americans were most likely to be obese (Barnes, Adams, and Powell-Griner 2008). Adding complexity, gender differences by disease and by subgroup also exist. For example, prostate cancer is the most diagnosed cancer for Asian American men and breast cancer is the most diagnosed cancer for Asian American women. Also underscoring subgroup and gender differences, the incidence of lung cancer has been increasing among Asian/Pakistani American men and Korean American and Filipino American women, while colorectal cancer has been increasing among Kampuchean American, Korean American, and Laotian American men and women (Gomez et al. 2013).

A number of issues continue to be limiting factors in health and well-being research for Asian Americans. These include funding, the challenges of aggregating data in diverse populations, and methodological problems. Research on Asian Americans has been underfunded. More research is needed to elucidate the diversity of the health experiences among numerous diverse Asian American populations. In doing data collection with Asian American populations, methodological issues also need to be addressed, including conducting data collection in Asian languages and among less visible subgroups. There is also a need to oversample and conduct research in locations with high numbers of Asian Americans (Islam et al. 2010).

Responding to this need for better data, two studies have provided scholars the opportunity to explore health disparities among Asian Americans in a more comprehensive way. Conducted in 2002–2003, the National Latino and Asian American Study (NLAAS) was a national probability sample of 2,095 Asian Americans administered in Cantonese, English, Mandarin, Spanish, Tagalog, and Vietnamese. The survey oversampled Chinese, Vietnamese, and Filipinos and focused on social position, psychosocial factors, psychiatric disorders, and utilization of mental health services. Since its completion, it has been used by various researchers examining Asian American health issues, including those looking at the relationships between mental health utilization, racial discrimination, immigration, psychiatric

morbidity, body mass index, obesity, and substance-use disorders.

The second comprehensive data set is the California Health Interview Survey (CHIS), a California population-based survey study administered in Cantonese, English, Korean, Mandarin, Spanish, and Vietnamese. One of the largest health surveys in the United States, the CHIS is conducted on a continuous basis and provides data on Asian American subgroups. In 2009, the CHIS surveyed 47,614 adults, 3,379 adolescents, and 8,945 children. The Asian American sample consisted of 958 Koreans, 1,065 Chinese, 1,453 Vietnamese, 500 Filipinos, 428 Japanese, and 400 South Asians. Following the first survey in 2001, the CHIS has conducted ongoing telephone surveys with adults, adolescents, and parents of young children. Telephone survey topics have focused on health status; health behaviors including diet, nutrition, physical activity, and tobacco and alcohol use; chronic illnesses; insurance coverage; mental health services utilization and access; dental care; and neighborhoods and well-being. Through the use of the CHIS dataset, researchers have published peer-reviewed journal articles on an array of issues, examining subgroup differences among Asian Americans including limited English proficiency, racial discrimination, health care access, nutrition, risk behaviors, socioeconomic status, cancer screenings, and obesity. Because of these data sets, research is emerging that is providing a more complete picture of the health disparities impacting Asian Americans.

Scholars across various disciplines within Asian American studies are also recognizing the importance of documenting and giving voice to the responses to and meanings of well-being, illness, recovery, and healing among Asian Americans. Scholars Jennifer Ho and James Kyung-Jin Lee (2013) were leaders in initiating and editing an issue of *Amerasia Journal*—the premier journal in Asian American studies—on "The State of Illness and Disability in Asian America." This issue includes first-person accounts of living with breast cancer, autism, and caring at end of life. Moreover, this issue also explores poetry and the politics and the way disability and illness has traditionally been considered within Asian American communities. As co-editor James Lee states:

> Asian Americans are not more or less disabled or ill than any other peoples in the U.S. And yet the prevailing image of Asian American reticence, an ostensible silence around our wounded bodies, is affirmed over and over by the vociferous speech that gives our approach to woundedness a relentless, specific name: shame. (xvi)

The editors state that the silences and the lack of voices among Asian Americans on disability and illness ultimately lead to the shame and isolation that many feel.

Although biomedical approaches to healing have been particularly espoused by researchers, traditional and indigenous approaches to wellness have often been part of both old and new healthcare practices among Asian American communities. Almost half of Asian Americans still engage in such health practices. These traditional approaches include practices that are mind-body (e.g., meditation), biologically based (e.g., herbs), body based (e.g., acupuncture), and energy medicine (e.g. Qi Gong) (Mehta et al. 2007). These constructs and therapies for healing are also called complementary and alternative medicine (CAM). The first health care clinic created by Chinese immigrants in San Francisco was the Tung War Dispensary (1899), which included traditional Chinese medicine but quickly evolved into approaching wellness from a biomedical approach (Hom 2013). Now,

there is a movement among public health researchers who are exploring the role of CAM in conjunction with biomedical approaches to promote wellness. For example, San Francisco Bay Area research on Chinese Americans and tobacco cessation found relatively high rates of success when individuals used both acupuncture and nicotine replacement therapy (E. Chang et al. 2013).

Since the inception of the Third World Strike at San Francisco State College, the community, as a partner, has been central to the development of scholarship in the San Francisco State Asian American Studies Department (Asian American Studies Department 2009). In recent years, community-based participatory research (CBPR) methods have become nationally recognized by public health researchers as the best approach to bring viable presence and solutions to racial/ethnic minority communities. In dealing with the lack of visibility of the experience of Asian Americans and wellness, this methodological approach has allowed local community-based organizations in the Asian American community across the country a chance to partner with larger institutions. Moreover, it has been a mechanism to document key health issues through various needs assessments; it has also contributed to the creation of community-based interventions in various Asian American communities. CBPR, CHIS, and NLAAS all contribute to a voice that has been missing in years past. With these new forms of data and data collection methods, there is a chance for a more effective voice and the representation of a more comprehensive picture of wellness and Asian America.

33

Identity
Jennifer Ho

"Identity" is a term that simultaneously unites and divides Asian Americans. Those with Asian ancestry in the United States are united in this demographic label through the political reality of the history of racialization (exclusionary immigration and naturalization laws, restrictive marriage laws, mass xenophobic incarceration) that Asians in America have been subjected to (and continue to be subjected to) and by activist and academic beliefs in making visible the experiences and histories of Asian Americans within the larger U.S. society. Asian Americans are divided by the different types of identities that exceed this singular racial label—by differences of ethnicity, heritage, national origin, religion, race, class, immigration status, citizenship, able bodiness, sexuality, gender, region, education, language, age, and a host of other identitarian markers. Both the original (1976) and revised (1983) versions of Raymond Williams's *Keywords: A Vocabulary of Culture and Society* do not include the term "identity," which is telling for all the ways in which this word has evolved in meaning and importance in both popular discourse and academic scholarship. Where once a word like "identity" may have strictly been understood to describe psycho-social development, nowadays the word "identity" brings to mind phrases that have currency in our 21st-century lives: identity fraud (or theft), identity crisis, identity politics. We now apply adjectives to this term that reflect our understanding of the broadening of subjectivities in U.S. society: racial identity, ethnic identity, gender identity, sexual identity, religious identity, national identity, cultural identity, etc. As Carla Kaplan notes in her own entry on "identity" for *Keywords for American Cultural Studies*, "[o]ne of our most common terms, 'identity' is rarely defined" (2007, 123). Indeed, trying to define "identity" seems akin to nailing jelly on a wall. Yet this word is, perhaps, not just a keyword but *the* keyword that undergirds the field of Asian American studies.

The term's meaning, within an Asian American studies perspective, was born out of the modern civil rights movement of the 1960s and 1970s, a time when people were fighting for enfranchisement over and against a white supremacist society that took whiteness as a universal norm and that relegated all nonwhites to marginalized, second-class status. Asian American studies was galvanized by other identitarian movements—black civil rights, the American Indian movement, La Raza/Chicano pride, queer and women's rights movements. Recalling the work of scholar-activists from this period, Gary Okihiro observes that "like many of my generation involved in the struggle for ethnic studies and for a Third World identity, that insofar as Asians occupy the racial margins of 'nonwhite' with blacks, yellow is a shade of black, and black, of yellow" (1994, xii). What these causes all had in common was a desire to proclaim one's identity as valid and valued, different and distinct, from a universalizing normativity that made those who did not conform to a heterosexual, white, male identity as unequal "others" in U.S. society. As the second definition of "identity" in the *Oxford English Dictionary* states, "identity" is "a set of characteristics or a description that distinguishes a person or thing from others." An Asian American identity is distinguished from other racialized identities within the United States through the idea that as different as the ethnic groups that comprise Asian America are, they all share common goals. "Despite their distinctive histories and separate identities," writes Yến

Lê Espiritu, "these ethnic groups have united to protect and promote their collective interests" (1992, 2–3). Furthermore, the concept of an Asian American identity is rooted in U.S. soil; it is an identity that does not travel well, since the nature of aligning oneself with others of Asian descent has the most value within a U.S. context (S. Wong 1995). Claiming Asian American as a political and ideological identity and asserting the epistemological and pedagogical value of Asian Americans, Asian American studies affirms the culture, history, and set of experiences for Asian Americans as Asian Americans, recognizing the process of racialization in the United States that has created the conditions for a disparate group of people with ancestry in various Asian nations to be labeled, marked, and identified as Asian American.

The editors of the earliest assemblage of Asian American creative writing, *Aiiieeeee! An Anthology of Asian-American Writers* (and the first to use the phrase "Asian American" in the title of their book to consolidate an Asian American collective identity), begin their preface by stating: "Asian-Americans are not one people but several" (Chin et al. 1974, vii). While the communities they subsequently list include only Chinese Americans, Japanese Americans, and Filipino Americans (presumably these were the three Asian ethnic groups with the greatest numbers living in the United States at the time of their writing), their understanding of Asian Americans as multiple rather than singular is a truism within the field of Asian American studies, since the people found under the umbrella term "Asian American"—who can be identified as Asian American—include people from a multiplicity of nations, ethnicities, and regions: Viet Nam, the Philippines, Malaysia, Cambodia, Taiwan, Pakistan, Burma, Korea, India, Thailand, Syria, and the list goes on and on. The very vastness and diversity of people that comprise an Asian American identity is simultaneously one of Asian American studies' greatest strengths and most profound challenges, since there is little commonality that these disparate people share, except for the racial identity of being Asians in America. Which thus begs the question: Who is Asian American?

As noted above, the field of Asian American studies was founded on a desire to claim a political and ideological identity for people of Asian ancestry residing in the United States as Asian American in opposition to the manner in which Asians in America had become racialized and subject to the defining power of racist state apparatuses. However, there is no set agreement on who is Asian American, who identifies as Asian American, or what it means to claim an Asian American identity, particularly since the majority of people who would mark "Asian" on a census form do not self-identify as Asian American in their everyday lives but "instead link their identities to specific countries of origin" (Zhou 2007, 355), a fact confirmed by the controversial Pew Report "The Rise of Asian Americans," in which only 19% of the polled respondents identified themselves as Asian American (Taylor et al. 2012, 25). One could add that a term like "identity" has different valences and connotations for someone working in psychology or anthropology than for someone working in history or cultural studies. Central to this point are the contested meanings inherent in the term "identity" and the ways in which Asian Americans both surpass and are circumscribed by this term of common affiliation, as Lisa Lowe notes: "the profile of traits that characterize Asian American 'identity' is as much in flux as the orthodoxy of which constituencies make up and define Asian American 'culture'" (1996, 53). People of Asian ancestry in the U.S. are interpellated as Asian American by scholars wishing to study this particular demographic and by U.S. culture and society, yet how they are interpellated varies according to other factors (age, education, sex, socioeconomic status, etc.) contingent upon their subjectivities. For example, Southeast Asian Americans are often divergently interpellated from their East, South, and West Asian American peers, which suggests that there is a multiplicity to a term like "identity" that a singular racial label often belies (Schlund-Vials 2012b). Moreover, Asian Americans often refuse the hail of others who would seek to limit and stereotype them as Oriental, as alien, as model minorities. Therefore "identity," as a keyword in Asian American studies, exists as a set of contradictions, balances, and contestations that can often vacillate between opposite poles of meaning.

Indeed, embedded in the term "identity" is a series of binaries: self-other, choice-imposition, individual-society, sameness-difference, essential-mutable. How we understand the tensions within these binaries is crucial to understanding the pervasiveness and complexity of how the term "identity" informs the central intellectual questions raised within the field of Asian American studies. The tension of being unique, singular, and exceptional versus universal, collective, communal. The tension of similar experiences and histories versus the differences within experiences and histories. The tension of that which is inherent and immutable versus that which is changeable and variable. The tension of choosing which identities, forms of affiliation, and membership in various collectivities one wishes to demonstrate at any given time versus the ways in which others try to constrain that choice and impose ideas of their own onto one's sense of selfhood. Yet despite these various tensions found within the term "identity" and the impossibility of stability and fixity, it is, in Kandice Chuh's words, "the *undecidability* of identity" that "contributes to the construction of an Asian American studies geared specifically toward undermining racial essentialism" (2003, 14; emphasis in the original). The term "identity," with its inherent indeterminacy, allows for a generative ambiguity within Asian American studies, one that opposes concretized and totalizing definitions in favor of an Asian American epistemology that questions essentialist notions of singularity. One of the most significant contributions that the field of Asian American studies has produced is the examination of intersectionality—the ways in which scholars have recognized the multitude of identities inherent within the individuals that constitute the collectivity of Asian Americans and the ways that these various identities are not simply additive but comprise overlapping and sometimes contradictory statuses of oppression and privilege. Asian American studies scholars analyze queerness (Eng and Hom 1998; Manalansan 2003), gender (Y. Espiritu 1999; Y. Espiritu 2008; Eng 2001; Parreñas 2008), class (Prashad 2013; Y. Chang 2010), disability (C. Wu 2012), region (Joshi and Desai 2013; Bow 2010), multiraciality (Spickard 1997; Root 2001; Williams-León and Nakashima 2001a), and the intertwined nature of all these intersectionalities (and many others) within the context of various Asian American identities.

"Identity" continues to underpin so much of the work that Asian American studies scholars produce. The power of this keyword is evident when we recognize that people are both individual and unique entities but ones who share a collective social identity with others and who gain political enfranchisement through coalitional networks and group identification. Thus, the greatest strength of "identity" is also the greatest strength within the field of Asian American studies: the fluidity and flexibility of this keyword allows for an antiracist activism that guides the discipline of Asian American studies. Asian American studies was born in the crucible of social justice activism. It has grown, expanded, and changed along with the various constituencies that find themselves grouped under the umbrella of an Asian American political collectivity, but at its core Asian American studies remains committed to equality and an end to oppression for all people of all identities.

34

Immigration

Shelley Sang-Hee Lee

In Asian American studies and other academic fields, "immigration" describes a process of movement across national borders, long an important part of our understanding of U.S. social experience. The early twentieth century saw the emergence of immigration as a field of study, as scholars sought to explain large-scale movements and adaptations involved in the peopling of the United States. In recent decades, inquiries extended beyond people's journeys to and initial encounters in America to also examine issues of ethnicity, community, and processes of "becoming American." In legal discussion, immigration concerns a related yet different set of matters, specifically those involving citizenship and rights as defined by the state. While Asian American studies scholars have drawn on and engaged all of these approaches to immigration, they have also enriched the field through new paradigms and conceptual terrain that include diasporic and transnational perspectives.

The legal construction of immigration and the role of states in regulating it have informed scholarly and popular understandings of the term. In the United States an immigrant, by definition, is an individual who has been granted permission by a state to enter or remain in its borders for permanent settlement, and since 1875 immigration has been the purview of the federal government, under which it has become a process subject to thorough controls and regulation. A person who holds the status of immigrant, then, has passed through a regime of papers and examinations, met the United States'

criteria for admission and potential citizenship, and can claim a set of rights and a measure of national belonging. While immigration as an administrative process has long been understood as explaining how one enters the United States and becomes American, recent scholarship taking a critical approach has uncovered some of the ways that immigration policy has historically shaped an exclusionary ideal of citizenship that favors Europeans, men, the able-bodied, and heteronormativity (Ngai 2004a; Luibheid 2002; Canaday 2009).

Historical narratives about the place of immigration in U.S. history have also been influential. The historian Oscar Handlin, who viewed immigration as central to the American experience, described it as a process of rupture and discontinuity, in which people went from the old world to the new, from ethnic to American, and from static to dynamic lives (Handlin 1951). Being an immigrant was to be disoriented, although it was ultimately a temporary station en route to becoming American. Existing in tandem—and tension—with this image of immigration as disruptive was the idea that it was nonetheless a defining and proud aspect of American history and character, reflecting a multicultural orthodoxy that emerged after World War II. This was illustrated, for instance, in Americans' growing interest in their ethnic and immigrant origins, whereas earlier such things would be downplayed (Jacobson 2006). Although these understandings of the significance of immigration were deeply social and cultural, they remained tied to the state; for example, the celebrated Ellis Island in New York harbor was, after all, a federal immigration station, and the achievement of citizenship fundamentally underscored an individual's changed relationship to the U.S. state. While often presented as a universal experience, immigration as it was commonly understood through much of the twentieth century was anything but; it was Eurocentric, transatlantic, and ignored exceptions to the dominant experience, such as the forced migration of Africans across the Atlantic and the transpacific journeys of Asians who were processed at San Francisco's Angel Island, the less-storied counterpart to Ellis Island.

The late 1900s saw major shifts in the meanings of immigration. One of these was increased attention to individual agency, a development informed by the rise of the new social history. Rather than explain immigration in purely structural or macroeconomic terms, scholars such as John Bodnar argued for the centrality of immigrants' will and decision making in shaping their day-to-day lives (Bodnar 1987). Immigration, then, was not just about broad, large-scale economic and political developments triggering movements of people around the globe; it was also about the minds and inner lives of those individuals who undertook the journeys. This emphasis on agency has, furthermore, shed light on how immigration was marked by continuity as well as discontinuity, particularly with regard to ethnic traditions transplanted in the United States. Also having a transformative impact was the work of ethnic studies scholars who considered the experiences of nonwhite immigrants and subsequently redefined the paradigms of immigration. Historian George Sanchez, for instance, studied Mexicans in America, whose experiences sometimes resembled those of Europeans, but also departed markedly, as they crossed a land border that was unclearly demarcated, frequently traveled back and forth, and faced hostility in the United States (Sanchez 1993). With regard to Asians, Ronald Takaki and Sucheng Chan were among those who challenged entrenched assumptions about immigration, focusing on people who crossed the Pacific, faced persistent discrimination, and were eventually denied entry via exclusion laws. While still arguing for the centrality of immigration in American life and history, these scholars have changed the

terms of the discussion. They have not only expanded our view of immigration, but have also injected critical perspectives on its legal and social dimensions via attention to policy exclusion and racial and ethnic intolerance, highlighting the underlying white privilege that has informed understandings of immigration. More recent developments in immigration studies have moved even further from the kinds of universal, celebratory, U.S.-centric narratives described earlier. As scholars have confronted the limitations of understanding population movements according to Eurocentric, U.S.-focused, and unidirectional models and increasingly acknowledged the complexity and multidirectionality of migration, terms such as "transnationalism" and "diaspora" have come into greater use. Scholarship on the American borderlands, for instance, has highlighted the necessity for models and terminology that account for spaces in which state power is muted or contested and multidirectional movement is the norm. Recent studies on Asians have also shown how migration was frequently temporary, went back and forth, and encompassed destinations other than the United States. This includes historical scholarship about nineteenth-century working-class Chinese immigrants who maintained communities in the U.S. and China to contemporary middle- and upper-class "parachute kids" and "flexible citizens" whose translocal lives defy nationally discrete and bounded approaches to understanding the lives and identities of immigrants (Hsu 2000; Ong 1999; Zhou 1998; Y. Chen 2000).

To give a brief overview of Asian immigration to the United States, this has occurred in four overlapping stages structured by economic, social, and political factors as well as U.S. policies: pre-exclusion, exclusion, the postwar years, and post-exclusion. During pre-exclusion (mid-1800s through early 1900s), Asian immigration—from China, Japan, Korea, India, and the Philippines—stemmed from disruptions and opportunities attending the spread of global capitalism and imperialism. In China, the "opening" of the country after Britain's victory in the Opium War (1840–1842) was pivotal. After being forced to open ports to foreign commerce and other forms of Western domination, China endured depressions and civil conflict, which displaced people from their land and jobs and enlarged the overseas emigrant pool (Chan 1986; Hsu 2000). In Japan, although a modernization program followed the country's "opening" in 1854 by the United States, the toll of rapid transformation and relative underdevelopment was harsh, particularly for farmers (Ichioka 1988). Meanwhile, colonialism shaped emigration from Korea, India, and the Philippines. Long closed off from foreign powers, Korea endured a period of outside domination, dependency, and instability after Japan foisted upon it an unequal treaty in 1876 and then annexed it in 1910. In India, a British colony from 1857, one of the areas especially affected was the state of Punjab, where residents reeled from policies resulting in land shortages, underdevelopment, and high taxes as well as natural catastrophes (Jensen 1988). In the Philippines—a Spanish colony since the 1500s—the Spanish–American War of 1898 resulted in Spain's surrender of the territory to the United States, but that conflict led to a more prolonged one (the Philippine–American War) that brought great devastation, and in its aftermath, economic dependence and underdevelopment (Fujita-Rony 2003).

This first wave of Asian overseas migrants was diverse and geographically extensive—including Chinese and Indian coolies in near-slavery conditions, Japanese merchants, Filipino students, and Korean political exiles—but generally speaking, those who went to the United States and Hawai'i were driven by factors such as wages (in agriculture, fisheries, manufacturing, services, etc.), educational opportunities, and religious freedom,

and were predominantly sojourner male laborers. Chinese began arriving in large numbers in Hawai'i in the mid-1800s, before the islands became a U.S. territory in 1898. They started to go to North America following the discovery of gold in California in 1848, and after mining declined, they continued to immigrate, as development in the American West sustained labor needs in various industries. Japanese migration to Hawai'i emerged on the heels of Chinese recruitment (Azuma 2005, 27), and their numbers on the mainland underwent rapid growth between 1890 and 1910. With regard to Koreans, who came during the early twentieth century in much smaller numbers than the two aforementioned groups, the influence of American missionaries and officials with ties to Hawai'i planters was pivotal. Koreans had an even smaller presence on the mainland. The first group of Filipinos, who could travel to the U.S. and its territories without restriction under the status of nationals, arrived in Hawai'i in 1906 after shortages of other Asian laborers developed (Melendy 1977; M. Sharma 1984), and their mainland migration increased over the 1920s. Asian Indians primarily went to the mainland, where they found work in Canada and the United States. Across all groups, migrants found they could earn more in Hawai'i and the United States than they would as common laborers in their home countries, and with their earnings, they helped their families and villages. In turn, encouraging stories made it back home via letters and returnees and triggered "chain migrations."

While the dynamics of global capitalism and U.S. expansion inform much of our understanding of why Asians left their homes for the United States and Hawai'i, exclusion is a critical theme for understanding how they were received in America. An early indication of things to come was the Page Act of 1875. The first restrictive federal immigration legislation, it banned the entry of forced laborers, convicts, and women for the purpose of prostitution, but the latter provision was used to effectively exclude Asian (at this time mostly Chinese) women and constrain an already small female Asian population. From 1882 to 1934, with the rise of anti-Asian movements driven by economic and racial anxieties, a series of laws ended the first period of Asian immigration and began the era of exclusion. The anti-Chinese movement culminated with the passage of the 1882 Chinese Exclusion Act, which banned the immigration of Chinese laborers and proscribed foreign-born Chinese from naturalized citizenship. Japanese exclusion was enacted through diplomatic agreements and legislation. To save face internationally, Japan halted the emigration of laborers through the Gentlemen's Agreement of 1907–1908, although it continued to issue passports to laborers who had previously been in America as well as the parents, wives, and children of immigrants. Indian exclusion was driven by general anti-Asian sentiments as well as pressure from Canada and Great Britain, which were concerned about the anticolonial activities of Indians abroad. Informal exclusion was partially achieved by invoking existing bans such as those on persons likely to become public charges, and statutory exclusion was accomplished with the 1917 Immigration Act through an "Asiatic barred zone" targeting numerous countries, but tacitly intending to bar Indians. Although by the 1920s Asian immigration had been greatly reduced, the patchwork means by which this occurred bolstered calls for stricter measures. This came with the passage of the Johnson-Reed Act of 1924 through a provision barring the immigration of "aliens ineligible to citizenship," which covered all Asians except for Filipinos. This exception was addressed in 1934 with the Tydings-McDuffie Act, which reduced annual Philippine immigration to fifty and changed Filipinos' status from nationals to aliens.

The postwar period (1943–1965) saw key reforms that paralleled changing perceptions of Asia and Asian people during and after World War II. Proscriptions on Asian immigration and naturalization were repealed in 1943, 1946, and 1952, but because token quotas for Asian nations were small (one hundred for most), most new immigration occurred via non-quota categories for spouses, children, and others. Several Asian communities, however, were transformed. In 1940 the Korean population was about 1,700 on the mainland and 6,850 in Hawai'i, but over the 1950s to early 1960s, about 14,000 students, military brides, orphans, and professional workers entered (Melendy 1977). Asian Indians, numbering about 1,500 in 1946 added nearly 6,500 to its population between 1948 and 1965 (Takaki 1989). As before, classed, gendered, and heteronormative attitudes informing immigration policy structured migration in these years, but in different ways. Between 1947 and 1964, about 72,700 Asian women—mostly Japanese—entered the United States and for the first time, outnumbered men. Most were admitted as "war brides" under provisions in legislation passed during and after World War II (S. Chan 1991). Also entering in these years in large numbers were adoptees, students, and professionals. Between 1953 and 1963, 8,812 Asian children joined families in the United States via ad hoc measures or new refugee and immigration laws (Eleana Kim 2010; Oh 2012). The immigration of students and professionals was driven by U.S. demands for educated and technically skilled human labor, and policies facilitating their entry included reserving half of the quotas under the McCarran-Walter Act of 1952 for skilled immigrants (Hsu 2012). Asian governments also encouraged student and professional migration, with the idea that emigrants would return and apply their expertise to their home countries' development. For example, between 1956 and 1969, about 11,000 Filipina nurses entered the U.S. under the Exchange Visitor Program (EVP), which sought to draw international students and workers and foster better understandings of the United States abroad (Choy 2003).

The last phase of Asian immigration, post-exclusion (1965 to the present), saw comprehensive reform and an unprecedented volume of newcomers. Criticism of the system under the Johnson-Reed Act led to the passage of the Hart-Celler Act of 1965, which raised the immigration ceiling and allotted Eastern Hemisphere nations 20,000 annual visas distributed according to a system favoring "family reunification" and professional skills. Between 1966 and 2009, about 9.5 million Asians immigrated to the United States, with China, the Philippines, and India being the largest sending countries. Among the pre-Hart-Celler Asian sending nations, only Japan declined (S. Chan 1991). From 1960 to 2000, the Asian American population grew from less than 1 million to 10.9 million, an increase stemming largely from a multiplier effect in which immigrants used family preferences to bring relatives who subsequently sponsored other relatives, and so on. Additionally, once residents became citizens, they could bring close relatives (spouses, children under twenty-one, and parents) regardless of visa limits.

A final notable post-1965 immigration development, occurring via non-quota categories, was the arrival of refugees from communist nations in Southeast Asia (Vietnam, Cambodia, and Laos) after the Vietnam War. In 1975, the United States allotted 130,000 slots for the "first wave" of Vietnamese and Cambodian refugees, most of whom were educated, urban, and connected to the U.S. government. These refugees were resettled by organizations that matched them with sponsors who helped them secure jobs and necessities. A smaller group of Laotians paroled into the United States was also part of the first wave (Vang 2010). After these initial efforts,

refugees who continued to leave Cambodia, Laos, and Vietnam made up the much larger "second wave." One of the key policy responses to this development in the U.S. was the Refugee Act of 1980, which created a systematic process for reviewing and admitting refugees, and by 2000, about one million Southeast Asians had gained entry as refugees (Kelly 1986). Although by the early 1990s the refugee flow had largely ended, Southeast Asian migration has continued, mainly via family preference categories in the general immigration system or humanitarian parolee status. Southeast Asian newcomers tended to be young and arrived as family units. While their premigration socioeconomic backgrounds were diverse, downward mobility in America has been common. Among first-wave Vietnamese, for instance, about 38 percent had secondary school training and 20 percent had university training, but few were able to transfer their skills to the American economy (Kelly 1986). Professionals also faced licensing and other bureaucratic obstacles to resuming their former occupations. Unskilled and uneducated refugees faced especially challenging adjustments. In 1980, for instance, the majority of Hmong in America were illiterate, had few employable skills, and lived below the poverty line. Most Cambodians were also unemployed and lived in poverty (Chan 2004).

Immigration, as a material and administrative phenomenon, as well as a politicizing rallying point, continues to loom large in Asian America today. With regard to family-based immigrant visas—still the chief means by which Asians gain admission for permanent residency—Asian countries face four out of the five worst backlogs. Sibling sponsorship comes with the longest wait; people from China and India can wait as long as twelve years, and those from the Philippines up to twenty-three. Meanwhile, the nonimmigrant system, which admits people on a temporary basis—for purposes like education, tourism, and professional training—has increasingly become a channel for entry, although individuals entering with these visas must adjust their status if they wish to stay. This system, moreover, is also riddled with problems. H-1B visas for skilled workers, for example, are subject to caps and distributed on a first-come, first-served basis, and in high-demand years, the slots fill up within weeks. Such problems have given rise to an increase in the Asian undocumented population in the United States, which now numbers about 1.3 million. Asian Americans' concerns about immigration, thus, include backlog relief and fairer visa allotments as well as rights for the undocumented (Kieu 2013; Lim 2013; Ruiz and Wilson 2013). Given current characteristics of the Asian American population, in which most are foreign born (about three in four), and Asia is the largest sending region of immigrants to the United States, immigration will remain a highly important topic in terms of daily life and policy debates for the foreseeable future.

35

Incarceration
Lane Ryo Hirabayashi

Internment, like incarceration, is a bona fide keyword insofar as it is still practiced in the twenty-first-century United States. Internment entails the confinement of members of a politically suspect group without trial in an effort to isolate, contain, regulate, deprive, stigmatize, and dehumanize, sometimes reeducate, and possibly deport if not kill them. What most immediately distinguishes internment from incarceration per se is that at a technical as well as a legal level, "internment" refers specifically to government policies enacted against foreign nationals. While current research on populations of color in confinement—specifically African Americans, American Indians, Chicanos/as, and Puerto Ricans, among other groups—suggests that the terms "internment," "incarceration" (i.e., being jailed), and "imprisonment" actually bleed into one another, there are good reasons to be cautious about using these words as synonyms. As Aiko Herzig-Yoshinaga (2009) notes, terminology can be used to lie or clarify. Care is needed with the terms that we select so that they do not compromise our ability to capture clearly the distinctive dimensions of the processes through which persons are justly (i.e., punished, via a fair trial, for a crime) or falsely imprisoned and their experiences. For the purposes of this entry, I submit that the case of the selective internment, as well as the mass incarceration, of Japanese Americans during World War II provides a useful data set to illustrate the possible relationships, as well as the differences, between distinctive penal methodologies.

The arrests of Nikkei, or persons of Japanese descent, began immediately after Japan's attack at Pearl Harbor. Based on intelligence lists kept by the FBI, the Army, and the Navy, agents of the U.S. Justice Department swept down on the West Coast Japanese American communities, executing searches on and arrests of a little under two thousand Issei (first-generation immigrants) and Kibei (second-generation U.S. citizens raised in Japan) who were suspected of being disloyal to America. Those who were detained were largely men, and they were held without any specific charges, let alone actual trials. Besides their status as foreign nationals—the Issei were prohibited by law from naturalizing as U.S. citizens until 1952, and the Kibei were often dual citizens—three other features differentiated their imprisonment. First, they were imprisoned by the U.S. Justice Department in a federally controlled operation. Second, the fourth statute of the Geneva Conventions applied to these prisoners, and they could appeal to a foreign (i.e., the Spanish) consulate if and when they believed that their rights were being violated. Third, their longer-term disposition, as far as being eligible for repatriation back to Japan, was on a different footing than second-generation Jun Nisei, who were sometimes pressured to renounce their U.S. citizenship as part of the package to enable their deportation. Those prisoners who were eventually deemed to be loyal, or at least safe enough to be released before the war was over, were often sent to one of the ten War Relocation Authority camps described below. Others remained interned for the duration.

The subsequent removal in 1942 of over 110,000 Nikkei from Military Zone No. 1 in California, Washington, Oregon, and Arizona was initially orchestrated by the Western Defense Command and Fourth Army following the issuance by Franklin D. Roosevelt of Executive Order 9066, which empowered the Army to round up, remove, and confine persons of whole or part Japanese ancestry, whether they were U.S. citizens or not, supposedly in order to ensure national security. The Army's Wartime Civil Control Authority (WCCA) then supervised the removal of persons of Japanese ancestry from the West Coast into sixteen temporary camps and, within a year's time, moved everyone again to ten more permanent camps that were run by a civilian agency known as the War Relocation Authority (WRA).

Once a person was confined in a WRA camp, there were a number of different paths out. One was release. As early as 1942, if one could get clearance, find a job outside of the excluded areas, secure a sponsor, and would sign an oath promising exemplary, assimilatory behavior, one could garner release back into the larger society even while the war was still going on. Among those who left as early as 1942 were agricultural workers and students who sought to continue their studies at the college level. Another way out, for eligible young men, was to volunteer in 1943 for the Army, the only branch of the Armed Forces that would accept Japanese Americans. (Later on, in 1944, all Nisei men who were deemed fit were subject to the draft into the Army, only.) Concomitantly, Japanese Americans who were branded as resisters, or who wanted to be sent to Japan as expatriates, were subject to "segregation"—that is, they were sent to the WRA's Tule Lake camp, where so-called disloyals and "repatriates" were congregated after 1943. After the *Ex parte Endo* ruling in 1944, the WRA camps were closed down, one by one. When a camp was closed, everyone was first asked to leave, and then in some instances, forced to depart (Sakoda 1989). Tule Lake was finally shut down in 1946, although it is worth noting that a few enlisted men who earned prison sentences for their resistance to the government's actions against Japanese Americans remained in jail until then president Harry S. Truman pardoned them in December 1947 (Castelnuovo 2008).

Both the Army and the WRA utilized a deceptive set of descriptors in order to soften the reality of their actions. Avoiding any implication that the process entailed the massive violation of the constitutional rights of those subject to their agencies, the Army created special zones forbidden to Nikkei, paving the way for mass removal from West Coast military zones, and described mass incarceration as either "evacuation" (implying removal for an individual's own safety) or "relocation" (implying a temporary process revolving around removal from a given point of origin, followed in due time by release), assiduously avoiding the cold, hard fact that forced incarceration was an inherent stage in the process.

Two characteristics governed the initial use of terminology during and immediately after World War II. One, federal agencies like the WRA insisted on using a set of euphemisms such as "exclusion," "relocation," "evacuation," and the like throughout their public relations releases and publications. Two, the term "internment" was initially and exclusively applied to the arrest and imprisonment of Japanese nationals, including Kibei, in Justice Department–run camps like those at Crystal City, Texas, and Fort Lincoln, North Dakota. Thus, according to historian Roger Daniels, the term "internment" was *never* utilized by any responsible government or military official to characterize the confinement of Japanese Americans, almost two-thirds of whom were in fact U.S. citizens, held in the ten WRA camps during World War II.

In retrospect, the government had a clear interest in adapting euphemisms to describe mass incarceration. Descriptors like "evacuation" and "relocation" softened the presentation of the confinement process and promoted its supposedly provisional and transitory nature. These euphemisms also helped to disguise the economic losses entailed in forced removal as well as the fundamentally unconstitutional violations that forced confinement entailed. An oft-mentioned aspect of these euphemisms is that their use also allowed other citizens to believe that the camps in which Nikkei were interned were different, quantitatively and qualitatively, from the camps that were set up in various European countries by the Third Reich during the war. As Raymond Okamura noted (1982), both of the latter points allowed those implementing the order to feel that their actions were justified, even as the same euphemisms may have lulled Nikkei into accepting their supposed fate more passively.

Following the conformist decade of the 1950s, a more critical evaluation of the wartime camps followed the Third World strikes of the late 1960s at campuses on the West Coast such as San Francisco State, UC Berkeley, and UCLA, which resulted in the first and largest Asian American studies programs, including the first classes on Japanese American history and the Japanese American experience. In the 1970s, the first collective calls for redress/reparations were closely tied to Asian American studies programs that, not coincidentally, were proximate to the largest Japanese American communities on the coasts as well as in the Midwest.

Early on in the redress movement, the main point of controversy regarding the terminology about mass incarceration revolved around what word to use to describe the sites where the majority of Japanese Americans had been confined. We now know that the term "concentration camp" was used during the war years by a number of federal officials, including Roosevelt. Interestingly enough, three Euro-Americans were among the first authors to feature the term "concentration camp" in the title of their books: Bosworth (1967), Daniels (1972), and Bailey (1972). Concomitantly, community-based activists like Edison Uno (1974) and Raymond Okamura (1982) were important and influential advocates of accurate terminology. In standard usage, as Uno pointed out early on, a dictionary definition of "concentration camp" revolves around the confinement of political prisoners (also see Hirabayashi 1994; Daniels 2005; and Kashima 2003 on this point). The battle over the term "concentration camp" as an appropriate descriptor was largely played out in the 1970s and into the 1980s, and Japanese American community organizations won significant battles to have the WRA camps characterized as such on the plaques at Manzanar, in the Owens Valley northeast of Los Angeles, and at other WRA camp sites. It is widely understood, as well, that Japanese Americans have insisted on this wording without wanting to lessen the horrors that befell Jews, leftists, and homosexuals under Nazi rule (see Ishizuka 2006). While U.S.-style concentration camps were the end of Japanese Americans' journey of confinement, concentration camps were often a step on the path to execution for those whom the Nazis saw as less than human. In this context, it is worth remembering what the philosopher Hannah Arendt wrote about political imprisonment. As cited by the historian Richard Drinnon, Arendt acknowledged that imprisonment of political prisoners may vary in terms of purpose and intensity. Evoking Dante's *Inferno*, Arendt noted that while camps can be classified in terms of their perniciousness—"Hades" (e.g., prisons for holding enemies), "Purgatory" (e.g., forced labor camps), or "Hell" (e.g., death camps)—that does not alter the fact that all three types are still, in the end, concentration camps (Drinnon 1989, 6).

From the early contributions authored by historians and community activists, the campaign against government euphemisms was energized during the 1990s and 2000s by the ongoing critique of Aiko Herzig-Yoshinaga. Long a legend in the Japanese American community because of her seminal work on the U.S.

Commission on the Wartime Internment and Relocation of Civilians (CWRIC), created by President Jimmy Carter, Herzig-Yoshinaga and her husband, Jack Herzig, also provided a good deal of the research materials for the work of the Commission, as well as the class-action lawsuit of the National Council for Japanese American Redress (NCJAR) and the *coram nobis* cases of Fred Korematsu, Min Yasui, and Gordon Hirabayashi during the 1980s. As an integral part of her work on these campaigns, Herzig-Yoshinaga generated various iterations of a glossary, "Words Can Lie or Clarify," which offers a detailed analysis of U.S. government euphemisms and a list of alternative terms that more accurately reflect the realities of what happened during the 1940s (Herzig-Yoshinaga 2009).

There is now near-unanimity among Japanese Americans concerning the terminology around that history, and a lion's share of the credit for that has to go to Mako Nakagawa, a retired teacher, who began to champion the "Power of Words" campaign as a community-based movement out of the Seattle Japanese American Citizens League (JACL) chapter that she belonged to. Working painstakingly to express her stand in educational workshops, forums, and JACL chapter and regional gatherings, Nakagawa and her JACL colleagues, such as Stan Shikuma in Seattle and Stanley Kanzaki in New York, found that objections to euphemisms, including the term "internment," were more widespread than many had thought. Nakagawa and her supporters identified strong allies in a range of JACL chapters, most notably the one in Florin, near Sacramento, with activist Andy Noguchi, as well as in community-based organizations like Nikkei for Civil Rights and Reparations (NCRR), which sponsors Day of Remembrance observances and pilgrimages to various WRA camps. The Tule Lake Committee in particular has endorsed the Power of Words campaign because members such as Barbara

Takei want to ensure that what is "cast in bronze" about that camp is accurate.

Following up on Roger Daniels's point—that "internment" was never used as a synonym for mass incarceration by U.S. government officials during World War II—it is difficult to discern when, where, and why the word emerged in terms of that usage. Perusal of key texts indicates the following:

The publications of the U.S. Army and the War Relocation Authority are uniform in their consistent use of "exclusion," "relocation," and "evacuation/evacuee" and their cognates in order to describe what happened. Moreover, this basic terminological set is consistent through the government's publications. A good example of this can be seen in the language used in the original Evacuation Claims Act of 1948, up through the reconsideration of that same act in 1954 (see Amendment 1954). In point of fact, the word "internment" is used correctly in official intra-agency correspondence/reports/memos; in publications printed by the Government Printing Office for federal agencies such as the departments of State, Interior, Justice (including the FBI), and War, and the latter's many officials and divisions (secretary of war, general staff, Army commands, provost marshal general, etc.); and in bills debated and acts passed by Congress. These documents are found to describe accurately the wartime arrests to "intern" Issei (i.e., Japanese nationals) and their subsequent confinement in "internment camps" under the jurisdiction of the Justice Department.

Similarly, the basic terminology deployed by scholars in their book-length publications conforms to the federal government's usage. Books such as Leighton's *The Governing of Men* (1945), Thomas and Nishimoto's *The Spoilage* (1946), Grodzins's *Americans Betrayed* (1949), O'Brien's *The College Nisei* (1949), Broom and Riemer's *Removal and Return* (1949), and Eaton's *Beauty behind Barbed Wire* (1952), to cite a few prominent examples, reserve the term "internment" to describe the camps set up by the U.S. Department of Justice. The first book I know of that deviates from this pattern, slightly, is tenBroek et al.'s *Prejudice, War, and the Constitution* (1954). In that publication, the first words following "Internment" in the book's index is, "of alien enemies," which is as it should be. Nonetheless, as Aiko Herzig-Yoshinaga has noted, the general words "intern" and "internment" slip into the text as a synonym for the term "incarceration" on pages 123, 125, and 133, to cite three examples.

So, adding to Daniels's point that "internment" was not used by any responsible government agency during the war, my survey suggests that the word was not in use for the first decade after the war, either. In other words, there is little historical precedent from the 1940s or the 1950s that justifies the use of "internment" as a descriptor for the mass incarceration of the Nikkei. Since this usage as a synonym appears to be a post-1950 construct, I propose that it can now be discarded, as it is a misnomer, and thus another, more subtle, but nonetheless pernicious euphemism.

To wit: on July 7, 2012, the governing council of the JACL, the largest Japanese and Asian American civil rights organization in the U.S., voted unanimously (86 to 0) to reaffirm its 2010 endorsement of the *Power of Words Handbook*, as well as to redouble its efforts to ensure that the use of euphemistic terminology was curtailed. Thus, the JACL joined other influential community organizations that have championed this same position, including the Japanese American National Museum, Densho, and the Manzanar Committee. Although controversies and debates remain, the point here is that words *are* powerful and a broad sector of Japanese Americans have demanded an end to euphemistic terminology, including the use of the word "internment" as a descriptor for mass incarceration. Moreover, those of us who write about the Japanese experience in the Americas during World War II should give careful consideration to the social movement that led up to the unanimous endorsement of the *POW Handbook* at the Forty-Third JACL National Convention.

More generally, the debate over terminology—words, definitions, connotations, and such—is critically important because words convey meaning: thus, the terms that are selected necessarily shape descriptions and analyses alike in profound ways. The term "incarceration" denotes confinement in prison and, although no trials were held for the population on the U.S. mainland, "incarceration"—along with the more precise term "false imprisonment"—effectively captures how a wide range of Japanese Americans think and feel about what happened to themselves and/or their families. In the court of public opinion, Japanese American were found "guilty by reason of race." Concomitantly, it is necessary to eschew euphemisms such as "evacuation" and "relocation," and exercise more precision in using terms such as "internment" in critical, analytical, and scholarly work on the Japanese American experience.

To conclude, there are at least two general insights regarding these keywords that are worth reviewing here: first, that in Asian American and ethnic studies, terminology is not static but rather evolves in the context of racialization projects (Winant 1994). For me, personally and as a scholar, it has been a privilege to work in concert with the activists, organizations, and scholars who have all contributed to the Power of Words campaign. More than through my training, reading, or even archival or oral history work, it is in the context of the Asian American movement that I have found keys to understanding what Japanese descendants in the Americas, and what were then the territories of Alaska and Hawai'i, experienced during World War II.

Second, in order to keep the discussion about Japanese Americans' 1940s experience relevant, comparative research relating this history to the internment of Middle Eastern and Muslim detainees, and the incarceration of militant activists of color and prisoners of conscience, is imperative. Such work, however, can be effectively initiated only if and when the terminological foundations of comparison are soundly formulated.

36

Labor
Sucheng Chan

The word "labor" is a fraught one in Asian American history because it has distilled and encapsulated complicated and sometimes strident normative debates over the nature of Asian labor in the United States. How Asian labor has been used and treated by white employers and how that use has been denigrated, condemned, and opposed by white workers, their labor union leaders, politicians, and large segments of the public have been important issues not only in Asian American history but also in U.S. history more broadly. A central theme in the anti-Asian movements that persisted for almost a century was the allegation that "cheap" and "servile" Asian labor was a new form of slavery. Moreover, white workingmen, it was said, simply could not compete against people who could survive on so little sustenance and bodily comfort. Asian female labor was likewise castigated: immigrant Chinese prostitutes were accused of introducing venereal diseases and debasing and corrupting white American manhood while immigrant Japanese women who worked alongside their husbands on farms and in stores and boarding houses, especially if they did so on Sundays, were said to demean the ideals of domestic nurturance and moral uplift embodied in white American womanhood.

In the years during and after the Civil War, the accusations against "cheap" and "servile" Chinese labor had a special resonance once enslaved African Americans had been emancipated, at least on paper, even though in terms of lived experience most of the newly freed black men, women, and children continued to lead lives of destitution, particularly after Northern efforts at Reconstruction in the South were rolled back and Jim Crow laws sprang up all over the former Confederate states. Beyond the particular circumstances of the Civil War, however, the hostility against immigrant Asian workers can best be understood within the broader contours of and longer-term trends in U.S. history.

I argue here that labor has been a fulcrum upon which American exceptionalism, both in theory and in practice, has rested. Much has been written about the ways in which the U.S. nation-state differed and continues to differ from European and other Old World countries. The late political sociologist Seymour Martin Lipset identified succinctly the five characteristics—liberty, egalitarianism, individualism, populism, and laissez-faire—that form American exceptionalism's core. These, together, make the organizational patterns of the U.S. economy, polity, society, and cultural institutions unique (Lipset 1996). As I see it, all five phenomena are related to the kind of labor that is deemed most desirable: free labor. As men and women who can act as equal individuals and according to each person's interpretation of his or her best interests in a state of liberty, Americans, it is believed, can work with dignity in an economy built upon laissez-faire capitalism to earn living wages to support families whose members can aspire to individual and intergenerational upward mobility regardless of the circumstances of their birth. Should unfree labor be allowed into the country (after enslaved African Americans had been technically emancipated), the presence of such coerced or bound labor, which can take many forms—serfs, peons, Chinese "coolies," indentured servants (a vast majority of whom were of European origins during the seventeenth and eighteenth centuries), and contract laborers—would threaten the continued existence of free labor and free enterprise. Free labor took several centuries to evolve in the Anglo-American world (Bush 2000; Cooper, Holt, and Scott 2000; Foner 1970; Glickstein 1991; Guterl 2003; Hoefte 1998; Jordan and Walsh 2007; M. Jung 2006; Kolchin 1987; Northrup 1995; Saunders 1982; Steinfeld 1991; Steinfeld 2001). The controversy arising from the presence of allegedly unfree Asian labor was a small but integral part of the historically complex process through which free labor came into being and became synonymous with white labor.

In terms of politics, democratic activism in America has often taken the form of populism—an ideology focused on the well-being of ordinary people. It can flourish only when the nation is made up of free men and women cultivating free soil, working as free labor, and engaging in free enterprise who can participate in making decisions about the kind of society they want through exercising their right to vote—an equality based on the principle of one person, one vote.

To ensure the survival of such an idealized economic, political, social, and cultural system, articulators of anti-Asian sentiments have averred, threats to the system in the form of unfree labor must be excluded or deported should such slavelike persons manage to sneak into or be imported into the country. Furthermore, those who were or are allegedly incapable of embracing, participating in, and upholding democratic self-governance because of their cultural, ethnic, or racial origins must also be repelled from America's shores lest they introduce authoritarian ideas and practices such as socialism, communism, and fascism, on the one hand, and anti-statist thinking and behavior such as anarchism and syndicalism, on the other hand, that would sully the nation's chosen ideology and politics.

The tragedy of U.S. history is that in the process of trying to establish and preserve such an idealized society, racism, nativism, classism, sexism, and ideological demagoguery have been the weapons of choice against the nation's imagined enemies. Those branded as enemies or potential enemies have included peoples of color who supposedly can function only under the control of their masters yet who dare to demand the same treatment as white people; foreigners or aliens who bring in un-American ideologies yet dare to demand some of the same civil and human rights that citizens of European American ancestry enjoy; workers who, as free labor, dare to demand even better wages and working conditions, as well as more avenues for upward interclass mobility, than employers already grant them; women who dare to demand equal treatment as men; and political leaders who dare to criticize the flaws they see in American democracy and laissez-faire capitalism and to propose alternative models for structuring the nation-state. Asian workers in America engendered such vitriolic reactions because their presence exposed deep-seated contradictions in U.S. society—gaps between ideal and reality that exist because of that society's inability to live up to its ideals and to fully conceal, much less heal, its self-inflicted psychic wounds.

When Asian American studies emerged as a new field of academic inquiry and critique in the late 1960s and early 1970s, one of the first tasks that historians of Asian America undertook was to correct past and present caricatures and debasement of immigrant Asian and Asian American labor. They have tried to unearth, recuperate, and valorize the history of Asian American workers—pioneers from the Old World who helped build the New World of North, Central, and South America. However, until quite recently, Asian American scholars have largely been unaware of the irony that the would-be heroic image of Asian pioneering workers they have tried to craft contains a contradiction of its own: historically Asian workers have served as, albeit unwittingly, what I call colonial or imperial "accessories" to European conquest and colonization of the Americas. Europeans who settled and "developed" these two continents, as well as Australia, did so by fighting against, killing, removing, confining (usually on poor land incapable of producing rich harvests), and infecting (with Old World diseases to which New World peoples had no immunity) Native Americans, Native Hawai'ians, and Alaskan Eskimos in the United States; Inuit, First Nations, and Métis in Canada; and Aborigines and Torres Strait Islanders in Australia. Asian workers who contributed to efforts to turn supposedly "empty" frontiers well endowed with natural resources into white-dominated countries were implicated in a centuries-long historical process that dispossessed, subjugated, and caused the demise of huge masses of indigenous peoples. While fighting against oppression and creating new lives for themselves as ethnic minorities, Asian pioneers have unintentionally helped rob the land and resources of earlier inhabitants in not-so-empty continents. Asian American scholars who study Asians in Hawai'i and their relationship with Native Hawai'ians have led the way in highlighting this still-submerged and discomforting aspect of Asian American history, which they call "Asian settler colonialism" (Fujikane and Okamura 2008).

Were Asian workers indeed "cheap" and "servile" labor as their detractors charged? A review of the historical evidence offers a nuanced answer. Given the fact that the Chinese were the first group of Asians who migrated to Hawai'i and the continental United States in sizable numbers, much more has been written about the kinds of work they did than about the occupations of later-arriving Asian ethnic groups. The Chinese American occupational range was broad indeed. During the second half of the nineteenth century and the

first half of the twentieth, on the U.S. mainland Chinese mined for gold wherever it was found in the American and Canadian West; cultivated and harvested many different kinds of crops; fished for a wide variety of seafood; helped construct the western segments of five (and not just one) transcontinental railroads (four in the United States and one in Canada); built roads, bridges, tunnels, and other infrastructure; opened and ran stores that sold dry goods, groceries, and curios; owned and operated restaurants, hand laundries, boarding houses, gambling joints, and brothels; served as cooks and domestic servants in white households and rural work camps; manufactured woolen textiles, clothing, footwear, various household items, cigars, ethnic foods, and bricks; practiced skilled trades as brick masons, carpenters, plumbers, blacksmiths, and cane and rattan furniture weavers; and were expert repairers of all manner of broken things. A small number became well-off as labor contractors and middlemen. Professionals served as herbal doctors, photographers, letter writers, journalists, Chinese-language newspaper publishers, and interpreters in courts and immigration hearings (S. Chan 1986; C. Chiang 2008; P. Chiu 1967; S. Chung 2011; Cohen 1984; M. Jung 2006; J. Jung 2007; Peter Kwong 1979; H. Ling 2012, H. Liu 2005; Loewen 1971; Lydon 1985; Ngai 2010; P. Siu 1987; B. Wong 1997; Marie Wong 2004; R. Yu 1992). In Hawai'i, Chinese worked in sugar cane plantations, grew rice and vegetables, ran small businesses, worked as artisans, and offered various professional services (Char 1975; Dye 1997; Glick 1980).

The extraordinary mobility of immigrant Chinese workers, both geographically and occupationally, refutes the accusation that they embodied unfree labor, for mobility means freedom in the United States. As for being "cheap" labor, it is true that Chinese workers indeed received lower wages than their European American peers when they worked for European American employers, who valued them not just because they were "cheap" but also because they were industrious and reliable. Whereas white workingmen who opposed them attributed negative traits to Chinese workers, they were in fact feared because of their positive qualities that employers found attractive (S. Chan forthcoming).

Similarly, European Americans developed an intense antagonism toward immigrant Japanese workers because of their ability to survive economically and, in some instances, to thrive in the face of tremendous odds. In particular, they were so highly successful as tenant farmers, sharecroppers, and farm owner-operators that they dominated the production of dozens of labor-intensive fruits and vegetables not only in California but also in other states in the American and Canadian West (Iwata 1992; Matsumoto 1993). The Issei's occupational range was a bit narrower than that of the Chinese (Ichihashi 1969; Ichioka 1988). Relatively little hostile attention was directed against immigrant Japanese merchants and others plying urban trades. The attacks against those earning a living in agriculture, however, were sustained and vituperative. A dozen Western states passed antialien land laws to deprive them of the ability to earn a living as cultivators of the soil, laws that the Issei challenged strenuously and at great expense. Many land cases made their way to the U.S. Supreme Court. The Japanese lost almost all the cases in the high court, lower federal courts, state courts, and county courts. Only after World War II did public opinion increasingly turn in their favor, in no small part due to the heroic sacrifices that Nisei soldiers had made. More often than not, it was the general public, and not legislators, who voted down the discriminatory alien land laws when referenda related to them were put on the ballot (Castleman 1994; S. Chan 2014; Chuman 1976). In Hawai'i, Japanese contract laborers had become 70 percent of the labor force on the islands' sugar cane plantations by the time that the United States colonized (or euphemistically, "annexed") the islands in 1898. Congress passed an Organic Act in 1900 to make Hawai'ian laws conform to American laws—the latter had made imported contract labor illegal almost four decades earlier. Once they were no longer bound by contracts, Japanese plantation workers carried out increasingly larger and longer strikes (Beechert 1985; Okihiro 1991; Takaki 1983). Did they have a working class consciousness? Definitely, yes.

In both Hawai'i and the continental United States, immigrant Japanese were accused of something even more dire than being "cheap" labor: they were charged with "invading" U.S. territory in order to build Japanese colonies that would serve as beachheads for an expanding Japanese empire on islands in the Pacific Ocean and in the Americas (Duus 1999). Whereas Japan indeed had such expansionist goals, the Issei, in contrast, thought of themselves as frontiersmen who, like pioneers of European ancestry, were helping to tame the American and Canadian West (Azuma 2005).

Far less scholarly attention has been paid to Korean, South Asian, and Filipino labor in America for three reasons: they came in smaller numbers, arrived when frontier conditions were vanishing, and had a narrower occupational range. What all three groups actively engaged in was agriculture—Koreans and South Asians as tenant farmers (Cha 2010; Leonard 1992) and Filipinos as farm laborers on the mainland and in Hawai'i (Alcantara 1981; Takaki 1983). Chinese, Japanese, and Filipino workers all went on strike during the 1930s; Filipinos were the most militant and persistent in forming their own unions and going on strike to better their economic conditions in agriculture as well as in Alaska's canned salmon industry (Beechert 1985; De Witt 1978; De Witt 1980; Friday 1994; Kerkvliet 2002; Reinecke 1996). The historical record is thus very clear: immigrant Asian, particularly Filipino, labor was anything but "docile."

World War II was an important turning point in Asian American labor history. After war broke out, Chinese, Japanese, Filipino, and Korean Americans all signed up for military service. Even as their Issei parents were incarcerated, Nisei soldiers fought valiantly in the European theater and did critical work in military intelligence in the Pacific theater. Chinese Americans with college degrees, for the first time, were hired in defense industries and other economic sectors suffering from a manpower shortage because of the enormous number of Americans at the warfront. Having fought to defend democracy against fascism, second-generation Asian American veterans were no longer willing to continue putting up with the pervasive discrimination that their people had suffered. With the G.I. Bill, many veterans went to college and became professionals. By the 1960s, the economic profile of U.S.-born and college-educated Asian Americans had improved so significantly that journalists began to dub them a "model minority." But this was simply a contemporary attempt to use, once again, Asian Americans as "accessories" to pervasive European American domination. Asian Americans were contrasted with other minorities who were said to suffer deprivations because of their own lack of the character traits and behavior that lead to "success." An Asian American sociologist has sarcastically called Asian American professionals, especially those in the information technology sector, "high-tech coolies" to remind those Asian Americans who love their image as a "model minority" of the fact that European American men still control most of the levers of economic and political power in the late twentieth and early twenty-first centuries.

Just as the socioeconomic status of U.S.-born Asian Americans began to show notable improvement in the 1960s, the liberalization of U.S. immigration laws allowed Asian immigration to resume. The two principles guiding the new immigration were family reunification and the preferential treatment of aspiring immigrants with skills needed in the American economy. Among the first family members to arrive were the wives and children of Asian men who had lived in the United States for several generations but were unable to bring them to the United States due to the exclusion laws. Some of the post-1965 immigrants who come under the family reunification provision can find only low-paid manual and menial jobs that do not require proficiency in English or skills that can be acquired only through higher education. Men work in restaurants, factories, and as janitors in large commercial buildings; women work in sewing factories and as cleaners in hotels or other public venues. In contrast, most well-educated immigrants with professional skills and English proficiency find jobs commensurate with their education, though often at lower pay, or they establish their own businesses. A sizable Asian American middle class has been growing in the last several decades.

By 1980, census figures revealed a bimodal Asian American population clustered in two groups: a large number in well-paid, high-status positions and another large group in low-paid, low-status jobs. More and more scholarly studies now examine the former group, which includes both professionals and businesspeople (Xiang Bao 2007; Blendstrup 2007; S. Chang 2006; Chiswick 2011; W. Harvey 2008; Light and Bonacich 1988; P. Min 1996; P. Min 2008; K. Park 1997; Saxenian 1990; Varma 2006; Marie Wong 2004; Yoon 1997), but relatively little work has been done on the latter (Xiaolan Bao 2001; Chin 2005; M. Louie 2001; Mathews 2005). For this reason, the current picture of Asian American labor is a partial one. The corpus of writings on contemporary unionization efforts among Asian American workers and general studies of poverty among peoples of color, including lower-class Asian Americans, and what can be done to ameliorate their conditions is slim indeed. Why is this the case? Has the vision of some Asian American scholars been influenced by neoliberal ideology that sings the praises of unregulated, unfettered capitalism and small government but shows no concern for those workers whose toil for less than living wages is what enables corporations to make their enormous profits? Where has the materialist critique that underpinned Asian American studies in its early years gone?

37

Law

Neil Gotanda

The scope, significance, and depth of thinking on the law is difficult to overstate. Ancient religious traditions, the oldest forms of commerce and contract, the earliest recorded forms of government—all embrace notions of law. In modern society, legal thinking can be seen in virtually every aspect of our lives. Within Asian American studies, there is widespread acceptance and use of legal documents and legal categories. Yet little attention has been paid to studying as well as using these pervasive elements embedded in so many aspects of our discipline.

To begin such a study, three themes in modern jurisprudence are helpful to sort the ways that law is used and understood in Asian American studies. First we observe that government power in the form, for example, of federal laws on immigration, exclusion, and citizenship, and state laws on access to courts and land ownership, have directly affected and shaped Asian American communities in the United States. Focus on this dimension of law—direct orders of the state separated from their morality—can be seen as within the tradition of positive law (Bix 2013).

A different jurisprudential theme, liberal legalism addresses law and politics, and sees constitutional rights as limiting government. Liberal liberalism defines a broad domain of social, economic, and political activities (Kalman 1998). An examination of this domain helps in the interpretation of an early and sometimes continuing divide in Asian American studies. On one side are those disciplines—history, political science, sociology, legal studies—that are framed by legal categories and draw upon positive law materials. Eschewing legal categories and legal framing are the aesthetic disciplines—literature, poetry, art, cinema, music. Their exploration of the Asian American is not bounded by a legal or even naturalist frame. This distinction within Asian American studies is not simply a reflection of a traditional division of knowledge within the academy. The division is between those disciplines bounded by the legal and those disciplines that do not accept the normative limitations imposed by legal thought and categories.

A more recent school of legal thought—critical legal studies—helps describe a third usage of law found in the activist tradition of Asian American studies. Critical legal studies emphasizes the indeterminacy of the law and focuses on the role of social ideologies in shaping legal outcomes (Binder 2010). In Asian American studies, examination of the activist tradition has often focused upon courtroom dramas such as the cases of Vincent Chin and Wen Ho Lee. The study of the social function of such high-profile events, while based upon the trial of an individual, has gone beyond a focus upon the trial outcome, and emphasizes the ideological meaning of the trial for Asian American communities.

This essay will review these three dimensions to law and Asian American studies and conclude with a comment on the role of law in future directions for Asian American studies. The central role of government power can be seen by simply listing these enactments at both the federal and state levels. More than that of other non-White groups in America, Asian American history has been structured by direct governmental actions, especially at the federal level. Any historiography of Black and White in the U.S. could not be limited to statutes and court decisions. The scope of slavery, the Civil War, reconstruction, and the mass popular movements for Black liberation could not be captured by such a narrow methodology. Similarly, the deep history of Latinos, from pre-Columbian roots and the Spanish Conquest, through independence, the U.S.–Mexican War, the Spanish–American War, colonialism, and neocolonialism, is also beyond the scope of a description based on positive law.

Beyond the central role played by legal enactments, their documentation has also helped to shape Asian American studies. Stated simply: legal research is a readily accessible mode of historical investigation. From the beginnings of the colonial era, laws and their enactment were already subject to government-sponsored record keeping. By 1789, there were established practices of recording statutes, maintaining court records, and publishing judicial opinions. As government documents, they are more likely to be collected in archives and official histories. These practices, including the modern availability of commercial databases and digitized colonial records, have meant legal research may be less expensive than other forms of research. Our American system for the creation of knowledge is built on graduate school studies and academic positions where research resources may be limited. When, for economic as well as cultural reasons, legal records are chosen for source materials, that legal documentation has shaped the investigation and the perspectives possible for discussion. Positive law has, therefore helped frame the historical dimension of our field.

Beyond questions of history, as noted earlier, much of contemporary thought and action is framed by law, legal subjects, and legal relations. Besides immigration, citizenship, and family, the groups selected for examination in political, sociological, and economic analysis—racial, ethnic, voting blocs, income groups, residential location, employment—are often grounded in legal relations. Viewed in this fashion, legal thinking provides the structure and frame for questions to be posed and analyzed.

This grounding in the law can be seen as providing an important limitation to Asian American projects. The earliest narrative project of crafting an Asian American history established straightforward legal objectives as the conclusion for the histories. Securing entry and then reentry rights for Chinese was a statutory project (see, e.g., S. Chan 1991). Similarly, efforts to secure particular Asian Americans' civil rights—voting and access to courts as well as participation in civil society through employment, business, and education—implicitly adopted as an endpoint their full participation as American citizens (Ichioka 1988). As part of a story of resistance and struggle against racism and discrimination, civil rights and full citizenship have been crucial aspirational goals. But their legal character also defines the limits of those projects.

The citizenship category sought by Takao Ozawa would have allowed him participation in American civil society, but also reaffirmed the nonparticipation of noncitizens. The category of citizenship also ignored or even denied other freedoms outside of then permissible boundaries. Overcoming a racial barrier to naturalization ignores gender, marriage, or sexuality as they relate to citizenship. Laws by their nature are both inclusive and exclusive. By establishing categorical boundaries, there is the explicit establishment of norms that limit other human potentials.

If we view the history and literature divide of the early years of Asian American studies through a filter of legal thought, we can interpret some of the contours of the separation. Helpful in this regard is Lisa Lowe's influential 1996 crossover book, *Immigrant Acts: On Asian American Cultural Politics*. Lowe explicitly builds upon the same documentary materials as lawyers, historians, and political scientists and uses many of the same

legal categories—immigration, race, citizen, nation—in her investigation. By working with literature and using methodologies not restrained by the legal, Lowe can imagine goals for her project that go beyond liberal legalism. In examining the racialization of Asian Americans, she does not limit herself to ending "racial discrimination" with its implicit goal of assimilation to American society. Rather, she seeks to "open possibilities of cross-race and cross-national projects" (1996, 175). In her comment on American national culture, she notes that racism and barriers to Asian American citizenship have estranged Asian immigrants. The distance created by this estrangement makes possible an "alternative cultural site, a site of cultural forms that propose, enact and embody subjects and practices not contained by the narrative of American citizenship" (1996, 176).

One can see the differentiation of the legal and the aesthetic in the structure of *Asian American Studies: A Reader*, edited by Jean Yu-Wen Shen Wu, in the American studies program at Tufts, and Min Song, in the English Department at Boston College. Their book, published in 2000, was intended to be an introduction to the field of Asian American studies. Immediately after their introduction, they present a legal chronology to frame the history of Asian Americans. They title the first half of their readings "The Documented Past." These articles have a strong legal history flavor. The second half of their readings is titled "Social Issues and Literatures." Organized around topical concerns, the articles include more literary comment and end with four stories collected under "Representations and Identities." In their separation of the historical from the literary, there is the suggestion that the implicit legal framing of the historical is insufficient to address the issues facing Asian Americans and our aspirations for the future. That suggestion is explicit in their closing readings. Wu and Song state that the last section "gives space to experimental, exploratory and contemporary creative voices that are in the process of redefining what it means to write Asian American literature" (2000, xxiii).

A third dimension to the law can be seen in the familiar link in Asian American studies to social activism. One well-known example of such a campaign was the one that led to a series of trials around the 1982 murder of Vincent Chin in Detroit, Michigan. The incident and its political aftermath are regarded as an important moment in the politicization of Asian Americans identifying as Asian Americans. Chin was a 27-year-old Chinese American who was beaten to death by two white, unemployed auto workers. They apparently believed Chin to be Japanese and blamed him for their being out of work. In the subsequent state trial, they were convicted but sentenced to three years' probation and a small fine. Journalist Helen Zia and lawyer Liza Cheuk May Chan played important roles in developing broad Asian American support for pursuing the case. Publicity and community pressure led to a federal civil rights trial, appeals, and a civil lawsuit (Shelley Lee 2013).

In high-profile trials such as those growing out of the Vincent Chin case or the "espionage" trial of Wen Ho Lee, there is a different sense of the law from our earlier characterizations of positive law and normative jurisprudence. In cases such as these, the search for individual justice is important but not necessarily the sole or even the most important objective. To complement the trial outcome—the usual centerpiece of litigation or prosecution—the broader ideological implications for society and here, for Asian Americans, becomes an essential aspect of the case. This shift to the ideological suggests an alternative legal philosophy that better describes the law in political trials.

Critical legal studies (CLS) was a legal and political movement that began in the early 1970s as a radical extension of 1930s "legal realism." CLS emphasizes the indeterminacy of law. Rather than focusing upon "correct" outcomes, CLS argues that specific legal outcomes can be the product of social and ideological forces. The treatment of law by community activists in political trials should be seen as reflective of a CLS view of the law. In the Vincent Chin case, the atmosphere of indifference to anti-Asian violence, reinforced by local media and the state trial court, became an important theme of the publicity. Demands for "justice" in the face of the lenient sentence were aimed at the judicial system itself. Similarly, activist publicity around the trial of Wen Ho Lee emphasized that there was no actual evidence that he had committed espionage. Rather, his greatest offense was to be of Chinese ancestry at a moment when international tension between the United States and China was running high (Shelley Lee 2013).

These three different understandings of law—positive law, normative jurisprudence, and critical legal studies—offer important insights into Asian American studies. At the level of the subject matter for examination, and at the level of the methodologies of our disciplines, we can see law as formative and providing unintended direction. To transform this nonconscious framing of our work, the study of law needs greater attention on its own terms. This is especially true for legal studies at law schools where there continues deep resistance to "outsider jurisprudence," including feminist studies, queer theory, critical race theory, LatCrit studies, and Asian American jurisprudence. Within Asian American studies, there is the need for recognition that lawyering includes these academic investigations into the jurisprudential as a complement to the lawyering linked to community activism that has played such an important role for the field.

It is on the terrain of the aspirational that we can see the depth of the influence of the legal on Asian American studies. Law at its most abstract level can offer universal possibilities. But the visions of American liberal legalism are bounded by the terms of liberal democracy—individual human rights, democracy in government through voting, and restraints on arbitrary government power through the rule of law. Important as these are, their limits can be seen when compared with the aspirations of utopian socialism articulated in the Marxist and Maoist influences seen in the early years of Asian American studies. Beyond rights, utopian socialism envisioned universal human liberation. Economic want and existing social norms were to be superseded in a limitless and unbounded future. Today, these objectives sound dated and politically naïve. In their absence, we can aspire to international human rights enforced by the law of nations and an international court of justice. These are noble goals but not the older visions that fired the imagination.

Consider two trends within Asian American studies that have sought to transcend some of these limitations: the recognition of diasporic formations and the growth of Asian American religious studies. At the UC Berkeley Asian American Studies Program, scholars have sought to extend our ethnicity into a global diasporic frame. A transnational and diasporic network can offer a basis for far-reaching goals. Yet the foundational category of the Asian American is itself either a particularity within American society and part of a transnational formation. If the objectives crafted within Asian American studies focus upon an end to racial and ethnic discrimination, then the legal goal of universal citizen rights is genuinely important. Yet the limitations of the legal remain. International human rights offer full participation in civil society—an inherently partial vision of our human future.

Within Asian American studies, one of the few disciplines in which aspirations to the universal are part of the discipline is Asian American religious studies. Here,

we can see the potential for new directions alongside deeply troubling complexities. Like law, religion can offer a dimension of the universal. But unlike law, religion and the sacred are unbounded by the secular limitations of the legal. The comments of Pope Francis, speaking in a transnational context, hint at these possibilities. Similarly, the religious teachings of the Dalai Lama have illuminated spiritual dimensions beyond narrow ethnicity or human rights. Religion and the sacred can be open to all, not simply citizens.

Yet the diasporic religious vision can also be clouded by deep currents of violence. At worst, international religiously inspired violence has merged in Asian American stereotyping with a vicious new version of the Asian spy and saboteur—the Islamic terrorist (Leti Volpp 2002). While an example of American racial stereotyping, this terrorist stereotype can be extended to the scenarios of violence in Sri Lanka and other parts of South and Southeast Asia.

This conclusion is mixed. Law as a framing for the aspirational in Asian American studies retains an important place. Racism against Asian Americans in the forms of discrimination, violence, stereotyping, and international scapegoating can and should be addressed using legal norms and standards. At the same time, we should seek to develop new aspirational goals. Only by recognizing the limitations of legal norms and the law can we move beyond the legal to recognize new possibilities.

38

Media

Shilpa Davé

The word "media" is fundamentally about the power and control over the dissemination of information in mass culture. The intersections between Asian American studies and media explore Asian American cultural production and representation from the joint perspective of global culture and American cultural trends. The term "media" first appeared in the mid-nineteenth century, but the word takes its roots from the Greek language, where it is related to aspects of performance and literally means "voiced stop" (*OED*). The more common usage of "media," related to communicating with the masses, developed in the 1920s. "The media" was associated with reporters, journalists, and people working for organizations devoted to mass communication in print, radio, and film, and eventually television. While early media studies examined the types and influences of communications on the population that included the effects of advertising, consumerism, and audience response, contemporary discussion, research, and scholarship in Asian American studies address the types of messages created, consumed, propagated, and repeated about Asian Americans in American culture. In addition, scholars discuss how different mediums (digital, electronic, film, print, radio, and television) are used to communicate, influence, and challenge perceptions of Asian American identity and culture.

Historically, the media tends to elide Asian and Asian Americans into one group that emphasizes the foreign aspects of race and culture in comparison to a normative white middle-class American identity. Asians (and more specifically Chinese) were initially referred to as Orientals, a racial group that is defined in opposition to whiteness, and more generally as the opposite of the Occident or West (Robert Lee 1999). Edward Said's *Orientalism* (1978) revised traditional dichotomies between Eastern and Western definitions of culture, exposed the constructed nature of the East as an exotic foil to a Western norm, and provided an analytical tool with which to reexamine how imperialism and colonialism shape historical and cultural perceptions of Asians in American culture across multiple disciplines, including anthropology, history, literature, and media studies. The introduction of a cultural studies methodology to media studies in the 1980s and 1990s opened up new areas of research and analysis that utilized critical theories of ethnicity, nationality, colonialism, gender, race, and class, and paved the way for Asian American media studies.

While drawing from communications methodology, it is the melding of a cultural studies approach with comparative ethnic studies that forms the foundation for current discussions of Asian Americans and the media. In the field of communications, the study of mass media often focuses on the technological and production aspects of media. Critical theorists such as Marshall McLuhan (1963) argued that "the medium is the message," emphasizing that the format or delivery system of communications can trump the content, whereas others in the field such as Neil Postman (1985) worried that the format of television, for example, prevented complex discussions about issues and promoted entertainment that tended to oversimplify and present repeatable and superficial images. The roots and study of cultural theory were heavily influenced by two European schools of thought: the Frankfurt School (with key figures such as Theodor Adorno), in which studies of mass culture are examined with respect to class, labor, and economics, and the Birmingham School (led by theorists such as Stuart Hall 1973), which argues that popular culture is a part of interactive everyday culture that is constantly evolving and, significantly, is where consumers can act and make their own meanings in subcultures that are often resistant to mainstream productions. Asian American media studies combines aspects of both these approaches and also engages with topics of gender and sexuality.

Among the different types of media, "old" media refers to print, film, television, and radio that is primarily controlled by network and industry corporations but also includes independent productions, and "new" media refers to electronic means of communications beginning with technology from the 1960s that leads to more individual uses of media. In the twenty-first century, the term "social media" has emerged to describe the participatory culture of the masses in online communities and communication available via the Internet and accessible through new technological devices and innovations. Interactions occur on a variety of platforms including Facebook, Twitter, YouTube, online news sites, and blogs and range from dating to political protests to organizing social movements to corporate advertising and newsfeeds. The advent of digital media and multiple ways to access it has led to a "convergence culture" that allows for selective means to engage with media depending on interest (Jenkins 2006) and an evolving engagement with media, i.e., "spreadable media," (Jenkins, Ford, and Green 2013) that includes audience participation, corporate interests, individual innovations, and transnational flows.

While much of the research focuses on popular images and representations of Asian and Asian Americans in mass culture and Asian American responses to mainstream stereotypes, historically, the dominant representations and news of Asian Americans in mainstream media derive from U.S. immigration and naturalization laws and labor policies. These representations carry over into the contemporary culture of images that often exaggerate physical differences from a white American mainstream identity and dwell on alternative cultural values and behaviors that include accent and language, religion, food, and marriage practices (Robert Lee 1999; Davé, Nishime, and Oren 2005; Davé 2013; Nguyen and Tu 2007; Tu 2010). In the late nineteenth and early twentieth centuries, stereotypes were advanced by white or other ethnic actors in "yellow-face" or "brownface" roles in part because of interracial casting restrictions in Hollywood. Despite the easing of race-based censorship after World War II, yellowface and brownface performances continued, such as those by Mickey Rooney as Mr. Yunioshi in *Breakfast at Tiffany's* (1961), David Carradine as Cain in the television show *Kung Fu* (1972–1975), Jonathan Pryce as the multiracial Engineer in Broadway's *Miss Saigon* (1990), and Hank Azaria as the voice of Apu on the animated series *The Simpsons* (1990–).

Ongoing stereotypes that are repeated in popular culture depict Asians as a foreign and alien (and sometimes threatening) race, model minorities who assimilate into American culture, and transnational and global citizens associated with trade and world economics. The reappearance and revisions of stereotypes often are influenced by U.S. foreign policy or economic factors including wars, military engagements, and news related to competitions in manufacturing and technological innovation. The negative representation of the Chinese and other Asian American groups, sometimes called the "yellow peril" discourse, particularly references U.S. military and economic clashes with China, Japan, Korea, and Southeast Asia (Klein 2003; Ono and Pham

2008). According to this narrative, Asians threaten to take over or invade the U.S. either as an undifferentiated national group or as individuals dominating an area of expertise or industry. In opposition to the yellow peril discourse is the model minority discourse, which appears to be positive but instead is divisive, isolating Asian Americans from other U.S. racial minorities (i.e., African Americans and Latino/as) by defining them as hard-working or extremely smart overachievers. In this case they are framed as both a model of assimilation to American culture and a potential threat to both other minority and majority populations.

Historians have linked the origin of the yellow peril narrative in the U.S. to perceptions of the Chinese derived from nineteenth-century political cartoons and popular songs in which they were depicted as foreign, racially alien "coolie" labor that threatened white opportunities and/or white moral standards in the West; such depictions shored up support for anti-immigration legislation directed against the Chinese (the 1875 Page Act and 1882 Chinese Exclusion Act) (Robert Lee 1999). Chinese men were portrayed as desexualized, with buck teeth, slanted eyes, long ponytails (queues), and rice paddy hats, wearing long robes and speaking in accented, broken English. While men were represented as subservient, asexual, or villainous—such as the criminal mastermind Fu Manchu in the 1920s pulp fiction of Sax Rohmer—Asian American women were shown as hypersexualized. Their portrayals vacillate between unscrupulous, disloyal, and fallen "dragon ladies" and innocent, exotic "lotus blossoms" (D. Gee 1988; Elaine Kim 2011; Marchetti 1993; Shimizu 2007). These images have been resurrected and repeated in film, television, print, radio, and new media from Long Duk Dong in *Sixteen Candles* (1984) to Ling Woo in *Ally McBeal* (1997–2002), from the caricatures on Abercrombie and Fitch T-shirts (2002) to the "tiger mom" furor (2010) in print

and popular culture, and the Alexandra Wallace anti-Asian rant on YouTube (2011).

The model minority image appeared as a staple in media portrayals after the 1965 Immigration Act, when changes in U.S. policies resulted in the immigration of large numbers of professionals and students from China, Taiwan, Korea, the Philippines, and South Asia. The model minority stereotype in the media presents all Asians as immigrant success stories who assimilate into U.S. society but are not necessarily aligned with civil rights or activist movements in the United States. Instead, the characters or narratives promote mainstream middle-class values that do not often challenge gender or racial hierarchies. In general, many of the early representations of Chinese men and women carried over and were mapped onto other Asian groups such as Japanese, Koreans, Indians, South Asians, Filipino/as, and Southeast Asians despite the historical, cultural, and linguistic differences between these groups. Immigrants and natives from South Asia and the Philippines have been depicted as both model minorities and threats in the world labor market. After the attack on the World Trade Center and Pentagon, South Asians and South Asian Americans have also been associated with terrorism as well as labor and economic competitors with the United States.

In the twenty-first century, Asian American characters are sidekicks to white protagonists or part of racially diverse ensemble casts on several successful network programs. Asian Americans have also become the center of their own films and television shows following groundbreakers such as Margaret Cho in *All-American Girl* (1994–1995) and feature films such as *The Joy Luck Club* (1993). John Cho and Kal Penn have starred in three *Harold & Kumar* films (2004–2011) and actress Mindy Kaling produces her television vehicle, *The Mindy Project* (2012–). These narratives challenge the yellow peril discourse and the model minority narrative by creating characters whose "Asianness" does not define their identity but is part of their everyday existence. These narratives help to redefine how we think about Asian American identity and culture outside of the stereotypes we have been accustomed to seeing and lead to increasingly diverse representations of Asian Americans.

Although representations of Asian Americans are dominated by mainstream representations, there have been counters to these images in independent media. Independent media allows for the exploration of Asian American history and experience outside of the mainstream and opportunities to showcase the diversity of Asian American identities, identities that are evolving rather than fixed stereotypes (Feng 2002). "Old media" outlets produce bilingual and in-language newspapers for Asian American communities and U.S. radio stations from Washington, D.C., to Dallas, Chicago, and Los Angeles feature Korean, Vietnamese, Indian, Pakistani, and Chinese programming. VC (Visual Communications), a community-based funding organization for Asian American productions, and the Center for Asian American Media (formerly known as the National Asian American Telecommunication Association) are important distributors of documentaries and independent films that feature Asian American histories and experiences that challenge mainstream stereotypes (R. Leong 1992). Asian American film festivals on college campuses and in cities ranging from New York to Toronto to San Francisco and Seattle also provide vital outlets for Asian American filmmakers and stories. In Asian American studies and ethnic studies classrooms from primary and secondary schools to university and community settings, independent Asian American films are screened, including the Academy Award–nominated documentary *Who Killed Vincent Chin?* (1981); public television channels have aired documentaries such as *My America . . . or Honk If You Love Buddha* (1997) and *Daughter from Danang* (2002). The career of acclaimed Asian American film director Ang Lee started with independent productions such as *The Wedding Banquet* (1993). The celebrated director Mira Nair has focused on how migration and immigration influences South Asian community identity in the U.S. and abroad in such films as *Mississippi Masala* (1991), *Monsoon Wedding* (2001), and *The Namesake* (2006). Works such as these have inspired younger Asian American directors including Kayo Hatta, Justin Lin, and Eric Byler to make breakout films of their own.

The availability and widespread use of new forms of digital technologies and cross-media convergence have produced new ways of interacting with and consuming media. In addition, the reach of transnational media culture and growing production of global popular culture in Asia has influenced how we understand Asian American identity. Sharing between cultures grows as satellite television and YouTube can deliver Bollywood films, Korean serials, or Filipina beauty pageants right to our screen. In addition, popular television formats such as the Japanese cooking show *Iron Chef* have been revamped for American television and American shows such as *America's Next Top Model* have licenses across the globe, including programs such as *China's Next Top Model*, *India's Next Top Model*, and *Vietnam's Next Top Model*. Cross-media migrations such as Japanese anime influencing U.S. illustrators or joint-financed projects with Hollywood and Bollywood producers are also a result of converging media culture. These transnational interactions have created new opportunities for understanding how media works to produce, represent, and articulate Asian American identity beyond the narrative tropes of the immigrant, migrant, and native in the changing world of global communications and cross media exchange.

Scholars argue that new media offers a different kind of access for Asian Americans to organize and interact with each other as well as create alternative media representations of Asian Americans (Nakamura 2002). Asian Americans are a dominant presence online and use the Internet more than any other racial or ethnic group in the United States (Considine 2011). Additionally, Asian Americans are no longer only subjects of mainstream discussion and representation, they are also the producers and innovators in online narratives. Individuals, groups, small business, and advertisers are actively engaged in creating and producing blogs, commentaries, and YouTube videos that appeal to the Asian American consumer market. Asian American musicians can feature their music and entrepreneurs can market their products with increasing efficiency. The challenge is determining how online popularity influences and crosses over to mainstream narratives. Asian American studies research in social media questions how we interpret and utilize trends online and explores how online popularity influences mainstream depictions. Even with the advent of YouTube and the rapid growth in online productions, traditional media formats such as television, film, print, and radio remain influential and popular. The central questions and concerns in Asian American studies and media continue to revolve around popular trends and narratives, community engagement with culture, historical and social representations, and transnational cultural exchanges.

39

Memory
Viet Thanh Nguyen

Memory is fundamental to Asian American studies and cultures, even though as a keyword or term it has not been significant in the academic realm. Its importance holds true whether one speaks of Asian American culture as a self-identified panethnic whole, or Asian American cultures in their various ethnic parts. In either the panethnic or ethnic case, memory enables the formation of an Asian American "imagined community" (B. Anderson 1991). The Asian American panethnic community (Y. Espiritu 1992), the one that names itself as Asian American, is in particular an imagined community dependent on strategies of remembering and forgetting to forge a shared past. This shared past is a collective memory built from individual memories, and the search for that past is an active act of remembering. These two senses of memory—as a body of memories and as willful recollection—cannot be separated from each other. The dynamic interaction between the two constitutes "Asian American memory."

The beginning of Asian American memory can be located in 1968, when activists coined the term "Asian American." While Chinese American and Japanese American ethnic collective memories existed before 1968, a panethic Asian American collective memory did not, given that the term "Asian American" did not even exist. What the term signified was the assembling and recasting of fragmented ethnic histories and memories into a collective Asian American history and memory. This invention of a tradition (Hobsbawm

1992) could not have happened without both these preexisting memories and an active remembering of them under an Asian American rubric that could serve as a guide for further remembering. Under this new rubric, historians, literary critics, and writers began demonstrating that Asian Americans had existed in the United States in large numbers for more than a century and had produced a viable culture. This search for the shared past is not neutral, but is instead value driven, usually predicated on the need for resistance to domination and the call for a more just present and future. These values are hallmarks of Asian American collective memory, with one exemplary case for the 1960s generation being Japanese American internment, whose history would be recovered in subsequent decades. While American collective memory had silenced, erased, or distorted the history of internment, Asian American collective memory would foreground it and give Japanese Americans voice, to use a common trope in Asian American culture.

Central to the willful recollection that drives and forms Asian American collective memory is an ironic forgetting. Memory and forgetting are inseparable, and in order to remember their shared bonds as Asian Americans, Asian Americans also had to forget, to some degree, their differences. Chinese Americans, Japanese Americans, and Korean Americans, for example, had to forget the historical animosities between Chinese, Japanese, and Koreans, fueled by events such as the Japanese colonization of Korea and the Japanese invasion of China. These national feelings of resentment that many Asian populations felt toward each other in Asia, which Asian immigrants often carried to the United States, were impediments to imagining an Asian American community. In choosing both to remember bonds and also to forget differences, Asian Americans did not differ from other imagined communities, including those of the United

States and their nations of origin or ancestry. Where Asian Americans differed from these national communities was in what they chose to remember and forget, which was frequently at odds with American and Asian nationalisms. Most obviously, while many who live in Asia would not primarily see themselves as "Asian" or find "Asia" to be a unifying concept, Asian Americans accepted the existence of "Asia," even though that concept is European (Spivak 2008).

The most crucial antagonism, however, was between the memories of Asian Americans and the memories of other Americans. Since Asian immigrants began arriving in large numbers in the 19th century, other Americans had not seen them as part of an American imagined community. Americans excluded Asian immigrants from American memory, rendered symbolically, for example, in photographs of the completion of the Transcontinental Railroad that did not include any of the thousands of Chinese workers who were crucial in building it. Against this exclusion and erasure from dominant memory, Asian Americans engaged in practices of countermemory (Foucault 1977). Countermemory is oppositional memory, the memory of the subordinated and the marginalized, memory from below versus memory from above. Much of Asian American memory is an exercise of countermemory, one engaged in recovering what has been forgotten about and forgotten by Asian Americans.

Countermemorial work has been both individual and collective. The words and deeds of activists, historians, writers, and critics have been individual acts of memory and recollection that sought first to build collective memory and then to negotiate with it. Although some would argue that memory can only truly be individual, Asian American efforts to excavate, write, and rewrite the past are based on the supposition that collective memory does exist. According to

MEMORY VIET THANH NGUYEN

Maurice Halbwachs, the pioneering theorist of collective memory, we remember in groups, with preexisting social memories shaping what the individual recalls. Asian American cultural and political efforts show that through individual and collective efforts of countermemory, dominant collective memory can be changed and new social memories created for minorities. Suppressed minorities transmit memories orally, struggle politically to create movements that can be recalled later, write stories in minority languages as well as the majority language, and leave behind traces in archives. An activist countermemorial work begins from these memories, actions, stories, and archives.

The prototypical Asian American activist of memory was Frank Chin, who explored the legacy of the railroad for Chinese Americans as a writer, helped begin the redress and reparations movement for Japanese American survivors of the internment as an activist, and established a tradition of Asian American literature as a co-editor of the groundbreaking literary anthology *Aiiieeeeee!* (1974). Elaine Kim's *Asian American Literature* (1982) continued in establishing the history of an Asian American literature, which has been a key element of propagating Asian American memory. Literary critics like Chin and Kim looked for the Asian surnames of forgotten American writers, reread their out-of-print works, and discussed them under the rubric of Asian American literature. In this framework, anomalous writers who wrote about Chinese immigrant women at the turn of the century (Sui Sin Far), Japanese farmers in California (Toshio Mori), or Filipino union activists (Carlos Bulosan) became reclassified as forebears of an Asian American literary tradition. In a parallel fashion, Ronald Takaki wrote the first Asian American history by assembling the stories of disparate Asian ethnic communities who did not, for the most part, see themselves as Asian Americans. In so doing he reshaped how both Americans as a whole and Asian Americans in particular saw their past.

What is evident in the activist, historical, and literary examples is the present's interaction with the past and vice versa. This dynamic between present and past, between a contemporary worldview and the way it shapes a willful search for particular kinds of memories, is central to collective and countermemory. But as the search for the Asian American past has grown steadily over the last few decades, as evidenced by ever-increasing numbers of historical accounts, memoirs, museums, commemorative events, and fictions, one consequence has been the contestation of the relative homogeneity of the Asian American past, as imagined in the 1960s. James Young's notion of collected memories is useful here in discussing how any society is a collection of group memories, rather than a collective of one group's memory. Under the rubric of Asian American memory, for example, Vietnamese, Cambodian, and Laotian American collective memories exist alongside Chinese, Japanese, and Korean American collective memories. While these ethnic collective memories may be reconciled with an Asian American collective memory, they may also conflict with it and with each other, perhaps primarily around that aspect of Asian American collective memory as countermemory to dominant society. Thus, in a parallel fashion to how Asian American collective memory exists in a sometimes tense relationship with American collective memory, so too can the memories of particular Asian American groups lead to friction with Asian American collective memory. In the example above, Vietnamese, Cambodians, and Laotians have often expressed anticommunist and patriotic, prowar sentiments born from their memories of the Vietnam War (V. Nguyen 2013; Schlund-Vials 2012b). These memories exist in distinct conflict with the implicitly and explicitly Marxist inclinations of many Asian

American artists, scholars, writers, and activists who played important roles in shaping Asian American collective memory, most of whom were and are Chinese, Japanese, and Korean Americans.

Although these differences within Asian American collective memory and between Asian American collected memories can lead to conflicting versions of the past and present, they also generate a continual stream of stories about the past. The archives and histories of many individuals and groups remain to be explored and to be told, and the literary possibilities for writers are seemingly endless. The publishing industry has been happy to publish Asian American stories out of the belief that Asian immigrants and Asian Americans have interesting personal experiences due to the trauma of war, revolution, immigration, and Asian patriarchies. That expectation on the part of American readers, editors, critics, and agents is also an example of how the present shapes the past, as publishing demands influence mainstream Asian American literary production. The collective and collected literary memory of Asian Americans is therefore sometimes a countermemory to dominant expectations and sometimes simply a reinforcement of those expectations, oftentimes in the same text. The same can be said about one of the other key ways by which Asian Americans build collective memory, which is in the space of ethnic towns such as Chinatown, Little Saigon, Little India, Thaitown, Little Tokyo, J-Town, and so on. These urban spaces of ethnic entrepreneurship allow collective memory to flourish, shaped by past histories of racial discrimination. At the same time, they are also evidence of a racially stratified and divided capitalism that limits ethnic populations and exploits ethnic differences as commodities. In a similar fashion, ethnic memories are produced, exploited, and restrained in a capitalist economy where memory can be both countermemory and commodified memory.

Whether one speaks of collective and collected memories as being composed of texts or of spaces, what becomes visible is how Asian American memory has undergone tremendous growth since the 1960s. The so-called "memory boom," of which Asian American memory is a part, is at least partially an outcome of the failure of 20th-century grand narratives like capitalism, communism, and nationalism to remain persuasive (Olick et al. 2011). In their place come the micromemories of divided populations who fetishize their own victimization, trauma, regret, and identity, or so the argument against memory goes by those critics who stress the need to look to the future, or to return to grand narratives. What these critics overlook is that the countermemories of groups like Asian Americans are not reducible to identity, wound, and grievance, although those vulnerabilities exist and Asian Americans have not addressed them as significantly as they should. Instead, Asian American memory's genealogy can also be traced to the vast political movements of domestic resistance, civil rights struggle, anti-imperialist organizing, and armed revolutions against colonization that link American minorities to insurgent populations all over the world who rebelled against European domination in the 20th century. Asian American memories, while prone to co-optation and commodification by both dominant society and by Asian Americans themselves, also provide a record of these political and collective dreams for justice, equality, and freedom.

Nevertheless, all forms of looking back on the past in the name of constructing a shared set of memories inevitably overlook something as well, for forgetting is fundamental to remembering. For Asian American collective memory, overlooked populations have included those with mixed-race ancestries; those with surnames that do not sound Asian, including war brides and adoptees; those whose ideologies have not resonated with the dominant ideologies of contemporary Asian America, particularly those preferring accommodation with dominant power, or even service to power, rather than resistance to it; those who might be Asian by descent but who choose to affiliate with other communities and to form alliances other than with Asian Americans; in short, those who, if remembered, might trouble a contemporary consensus on Asian American collective memory. New memory projects initiated from within and without Asian American cultures and Asian American studies have begun to address some of these anomalous populations, expressing a dynamic with which Asian American collective memory is already familiar. In this dynamic, memories of the collective are not static, but subject to change in response to new challenges. These new challenges include demands for recognition by those who fit uneasily within the collective, as well as refusals to be a part of the collective from those who might appear Asian American but are not so in practice. Responding to these varied pressures, Asian American memory continues to change and to serve its crucial function of helping Asian America reimagine itself.

40

Militarism
Vernadette Vicuña Gonzalez

Militarism is a founding value of the United States: in defense of the right to own (and wrest away) property, later patriotically recast as "American interests," the turn to a state-funded military and the threat or implementation of armed aggression have been crucial. Arguably, militarism had its early iterations in the colonial era, before the United States of America was even a political entity. The ways European settlers executed a practice of land theft and the indigenous genocide that intensified during the period known as the Indian Wars influenced how U.S. militarism would be turned to Asia, Asians, and Asian Americans from the mid-1800s to the present. Militarism, or the valorization of military life and values, the prioritization of armed preparedness, and the legitimacy of armed force as an acceptable resolution for conflict, began its modern turn in the U.S. with Assistant Secretary of the Navy Theodore Roosevelt's ambitions to modernize the fleet and engage in imperial wars outside of North America, reached a high point with the emergence of the military-industrial complex in the post–World War II era, and has defined global relations today through a state of constant war, the most bloated military budget in history, and the matter-of-fact saturation of civilian life with military values.

Initial U.S.-Asia encounters in the mid- to late 1800s demonstrated an early American will to militarism in its governance of "America's lake." Commodore Matthew Perry's show of U.S. Navy steamboats bristling with guns at Edo (Tokyo) Bay in 1853 compelled a treaty that "opened" Japan to U.S. trade. Backed by the armed menace of his small armada, Perry's ability to insist on negotiations with Japan's highest officials confirmed the effectiveness of military superiority and the threat of its use as a bargaining strategy. Wanting to compete with European imperial powers for Asia's lucrative trade, the United States turned to other strategic sights in the region. It soon established a military outpost in the Kingdom of Hawai'i, negotiating a treaty in 1875 that would give the United States use of the harbor known as Pu'uloa (renamed Pearl Harbor). This foothold led the Navy to collude with American oligarchs who overthrew the queen of Hawai'i—an action that was later characterized by President Grover Cleveland as an act of war, and for which President William Clinton would apologize a century later. However, the needs of militarism in U.S. imperial foreign policy rendered the illegality of Hawai'i's overthrow moot: it was all swept under the rug with a congressional resolution—a procedural move that annexed Hawai'i and rendered it a coaling station for American warships on their way to the Philippines in the War of 1898. The war that featured Admiral George Dewey decimating the Spanish Navy in the Battle of Manila Bay with a modernized U.S. Navy (courtesy of Theodore Roosevelt) soon transmogrified a "splendid little war" into a colonial occupation of protracted violence.

These early armed encounters typified U.S. gendered racial attitudes toward Asia and Asians, which were exacerbated and made explicit in the crucible of war. A new war broke out on the islands once Filipinos, who had been involved in a revolutionary war against Spain, realized the United States' imperial intentions to take over where Spain left off. Extending past the 1902 official end date of the "insurrection," the Philippine–American War showcased brutal techniques that were

deemed more acceptable due to the racialization of Filipinos as savages (of which their turn to guerilla tactics was confirmation): the water cure and concentration camps were used as modes of individual torture and population control. Filipinos—the first "gooks"—were killed by the hundreds of thousands during the U.S. "pacification" campaign, which included atrocities such as the reduction of the island of Samar into a "howling wilderness" with the sanctioned killing of "everyone over the age of ten" (Go 2011, 58; Kramer 2006). Later conflicts such as the Vietnam War would feature the same kind of racialized violence and military strategy with regard to Asian life, rationalized by the supposed indifference to life in Asian culture ("the Oriental doesn't put the same high price on life as does a Westerner") or an acceptable calculus of collateral damage, as was the case with U.S. nuclear testing in the Pacific (Davis 1974). As Henry Kissinger infamously put it, "There are only 90,000 people out there. Who gives a damn?" (Dibblin 1990).

Asians settling in the United States—some of them "pushed" there by U.S. wars elsewhere—have had mixed encounters with U.S. militarism. On one hand, crises wrought by militarism have served to highlight the U.S. state's founding contradictions about citizenship and race. World War II is perhaps most cited as the watershed moment that best illustrates how race is deployed by militarism. With Japan's bombing of Pearl Harbor in 1941, the U.S. quickly moved to implement a premeditated plan of incarceration for Japanese and Japanese Americans living in the United States and Latin America. Executive Order 9066 placed over 100,000 people of Japanese descent, the majority of whom were naturalized Nisei, in "war relocation camps" (Higashide 2006). This racialization of Japanese Americans as enemy aliens was unique: German and Italian Americans were exempt. The targeting of Japanese also extended to

Japan; at the end of the war, the systematic firebombing of Tokyo and the nuclear devastation of Hiroshima and Nagasaki (the latter a fate that was evaded by Germany) were also partially attributable to a racialization of Japanese people that allowed for disproportionate response to be thinkable.

On the other hand, militarism has also yielded opportunities for belonging through martial service. The nationalist project of Asian American politics is at heart driven by a desire to belong to a settler legacy; "claiming" America and the rights attendant to citizenship forges alliances with a long-established imperial project. The heroism of Asian American men during wartime is often held up as evidence of their devotion to the United States and proof that Asians are deserving of citizenship. Eager to prove their allegiance to the United States, the members of the now-famous "Go for Broke" 442nd infantry unit voluntarily joined the segregated military in the European theater. Joe Ichiugi remembers that he "wanted to prove that [he] was a loyal American and wanted to fight for [his] country during a time of war" (American Veterans Center 2012). The 442nd went on to become the most decorated unit of the war. World War II also further cemented the United States' "special relationship" with Filipinos, who were then still under the administration of its colonial government. The outbreak of World War II and the loss of the Philippines to an invading Japan framed Filipino soldiers as brothers in arms. Already militarized during the United States colonialism of the Philippines, Filipino men who had been recruited into the colonial constabulary forces shifted skills that had been used to police their own people against an invading Japanese army. Both Japanese American and Filipino soldiering inspired postwar narratives of community pride and spurred significant Asian American campaigns to recognize their contributions with awards and veterans benefits. In these instances, while participation in war defined moments of sacrifice that could be used to lay claim to martial citizenship, it also meant forgoing a broader critique of a nationalist policy of militarism.

Asian women have had distinctly different experiences of U.S. militarism. While U.S. wars in Asia produced occasional opportunities for Asian women to migrate to the United States as war brides, these "benefits" did not extend to all women. By and large women bear the burden of militarism more heavily: war renders them vulnerable to sexual violence from soldiers, destroys their homes, puts their families at risk, and produces food shortages that inevitably affect women and children most intensely. For example, during World War II, women in Korea and the Philippines were forced into sexual servitude by the Japanese military as "comfort women" (Choi 1997). Today, in places where military occupation is the norm, such as Okinawa, Korea, and the Philippines, Asian women are pulled into arrangements of sexualized exploitation and economic dependence with the U.S. military, often with the consent of their own governments. Frequently shunned by their communities yet indispensable to the "needs" of troops posted abroad, these women occupy a fraught position as a kind of sexualized currency that cements fraternal relationships between states. They, and the mixed-race children they bear, are the collateral damage of U.S. militarisms in Asia and the Pacific. Compounding these sexual vulnerabilities, Asia and the Pacific, too, as regions, have been feminized by U.S. militarism, which has disempowered their state governments to act on behalf of their most exploited citizens vis-à-vis the U.S. military. In Korea, after the pyrrhic war that began and ended at the 38th parallel, the U.S. military policed the demilitarized zone for its South Korean ally and established camptowns where prostitution and the trafficking of women remain a central economy (Moon 1997; Höhn and Moon 2010).

Militarism has also generated a transnationally inflected critique. The resurgence of U.S. militarism during the Cold War, particularly during the Vietnam War, was a precipitating factor in the radicalization of Asian American activists during the civil rights era. The U.S. policy in Vietnam had made it clear that the United States was waging racial warfare abroad as well as at home. Asian American antiwar activism was distinct from the larger antiwar movement. Identifying with the "gooks" who were the targets of American military violence and responding to increasing anti-Asian hostility at home, Asian Americans linked U.S. Cold War interventions in Vietnam to a longer imperial project that began in Japan, the Philippines, and Korea. Student activists were galvanized into antiwar demonstrations that generated a more panethnic and transnational mode of solidarity and went beyond "bringing the boys home" to a critical anti-imperialist analysis of U.S. foreign policy. Groups like the Bay Area Asian Coalition Against the War organized to bring together students, churches, community groups, and others for a broad-based coalition that articulated opposition to the war and support for Southeast Asian resistance to U.S. aggression and unilateralism. At protest actions such as marches and teach-ins, signs urging an end to "genocide" and the "bombing of Asian people" were just the beginning of an evolving critique that supported Vietnamese sovereignty and vocalized a more trenchant stance against a global race war and a rising military-industrial complex (Liu et al. 2008). With growing attention to the distinct experiences of women under militarism, these critiques have become more nuanced; for example, feminists have pointed out the particularly gendered devastation visited on Asian women (and other women in occupied territories) by militarism's cultures of racialized

sexualization, from rape and sexual assault to the proliferation of a militarized sex trade (Manderson and Jolly 1997).

Today, wars, occupations, and weapons testing in Japan, Okinawa, Korea, Guam, and other sites mark militarism's reterritorialization of Asia and the Pacific as the new theaters of a global U.S. militarism. Asian Americans and Pacific Islanders (more recently including women) have come to be recruited disproportionally into the U.S. military, taking on the new burdens of violent imperial action in the Middle East (Camacho 2011). This global state of war has yielded Asian American resistance from within the ranks of the military. First Lieutenant Ehren Watada's refusal to serve in Iraq, and the arrest and torture of James Yee, the former captain and Muslim chaplain at Guantanamo Bay Prison, have rallied other Asian Americans to critique the United States's wartime ethics. Torn between serving in the military, the realization of the contradictions of militarism's claims to bring freedom, and the very real opportunities offered by the military in a time of economic austerity, these soldiers as well as militarized civilians illustrate the tensions of militarism's "multicultural" inclusions (M. Nguyen 2012). Testifying to the flexibility of racialization and shifting regional and national needs as defined by geopolitical power struggles, Asians, Asian Americans, and Pacific Islanders continue to engage in a complicated and fraught dance with U.S. militarism, its violent trajectories, and its conditional terms of "belonging."

41

Minority

Crystal Parikh

One day after the 2012 presidential election, Bill O'Reilly (2012), conservative commentator for the Fox News network, declared, "the white establishment is now the minority," to explain how the nation's first black president, Barak Obama, was able to win a second term in office. In response to O'Reilly's proclamation, *New York Times* op-ed columnist Charles Blow (2012) explained that, in fact, white Americans are projected to remain the majority racial population in the United States until 2043. Blow nonetheless acknowledged, "The browning of America is very real and unrelenting." Pondering the "meaning of minority," Blow also suggested that the imminent "seismic shift in American demography" required us to ask: "How should we consider a waning majority when their privilege of numbers gives way to what many other Americans have experienced as the minority plight?"

While as a demographic label, "minority" might refer to any of a range of social differences (e.g., religious or political affiliations), when used in popular, academic, media, and political discourses in the United States, the term almost uniformly refers to race and specifically nonwhite populations, unless explicitly qualified with an adjective indicating otherwise, as in the case of "sexual minorities." In 1945, Louis Wirth, a scholar from the highly influential "Chicago School" of sociology, defined "minority" as "a group of people who, because of their physical or cultural characteristics, are singled out from the others in the society in which they live for differential and unequal treatment and who therefore regard themselves as objects of collective discrimination" (1945, 347). Minority status thus "carries with it the exclusion from full participation in the life of the society" (1945, 347). Wirth concomitantly explained that the presence of minority groups in a society "implies the existence of a corresponding dominant group enjoying higher social status and greater privileges" (1945, 347). In this formulation, Wirth emphasized two features that have remained part of the conventional understanding of "minority" status in the United States up to the present day (including in the O'Reilly/Blow exchange). First, the term refers as significantly, if not more so, to dimensions of social and political belonging and power as it does to the size of a population. Second, it acknowledges that race ("physical characteristics") is a salient marker by which, again in Wirth's words, "the minority is treated and regards itself as a people apart" (1945, 348).

The commonsense usage of "minority" to refer to nonwhite racial groups reflects how deeply embedded notions of racial identity are in American cultural and social life and how pervasively they have structured access to legal, political, and economic power and privilege in this country. An enslaved African was counted in the nation's constitution as three-fifths of a human person until the passage of the Thirteenth and Fourteenth Amendments, in 1865 and 1868, respectively. Beyond this, well into the second half of the twentieth century, legalized as well as more informal practices of segregation meant full access to American sociocultural resources, economic mobility, and political rights depended upon one's being—or being able to pass as—white. Likewise, until 1952, resident aliens faced explicit racial criteria, namely, that lawmakers or judiciaries recognized one as "white," in order to naturalize as U.S. citizens. Whiteness itself has been a legally and politically contested moniker, so that it has been differently defined at various moments and locations in American history. Nevertheless, those who have been deemed white not only constituted the majority population, but enjoyed the lion's share of power and privilege over the past two and half centuries. As Wirth argued, "Since the racial stock from which we are descended is something over which we have perhaps least control and since racial marks are the most visible and permanent marks with which we are afflicted, racial minorities tend to be the most enduring minorities of all" (1945, 349).

Furthermore, racial discourses in the United States have been structured primarily as a binary between such empowered whiteness and its obverse, dispossessed and disenfranchised blackness. As a result, "minority" has primarily, although not always, been synonymous with African American social identity. Other racialized populations were occasionally lumped together with this largest group of "people of color," the descendants of enslaved Africans. But these other peoples were as likely to be represented as, in Mae Ngai's terms, "impossible subjects." That is, despite having a continuous social and cultural presence in the United States since the nineteenth century, Asians and Latino/as were represented as foreign absences or alien presences to be excluded altogether from national life. (The construct of the "dead Indian" accomplishes this absenting for yet another population, but also points to a very different history of colonial occupation, territorial displacement, and vexed and limited concessions of sovereignty that have defined the so-called "government to government" relations between a white majority and native peoples.)

However, after comprehensive overhauls in U.S. immigration law in 1952 and 1965, the nation underwent rapid and thoroughgoing changes in its racial makeup. In particular, for our purposes, the effective end of Asian exclusion brought a substantial number of new immigrants from East, Southeast, and South Asia, as well as from Pacific Island nations. While in 1960, African Americans comprised approximately 96% of the nonwhite population in the United States, by 2010, eighteen million Americans identified themselves as of Asian or Pacific Islander descent (5.6% of the total population), and over fifty million as Hispanic or Latino (16.3% of the total population). In the twenty-first century, "minority" has accordingly come to reference a larger and even more heterogeneous population, as reflected in Blow's observation regarding the "browning" of America.

This demographic expansion has profoundly complicated the meaning of "minority," especially in the context of the remarkable changes in U.S. culture and society during the postwar era. During and after the period of civil rights reforms, as entrenched racial hierarchy and white supremacy gave way to (neo)liberal conceptions of colorblindness and multiculturalism, the notion that one's racial identity determines one's social, economic, and political status came to appear less obvious to many Americans. Propounding the merits of a "post-racial" society, official and popular discourses suggest that adherence to *any* racial identity—whether that of whiteness or a minoritarian one—is at best misguided in an egalitarian society where access to material and social power is "colorblind." Indeed, this is a contemporary construction of the nation to which many racial minorities assent, and it is the critical foundation for the well-known representation of Asian Americans as *model* minorities." Beginning in the 1960s, this pervasive image posed Asian Americans as a minority population that readily overcomes the "problem" of its social and racial difference to enjoy remarkable educational, occupational, and financial mobility, high family or household incomes, and low rates of crime. As a stereotype, the "model minority" image means to commend Asian Americans, by attributing such success to the cultural values (e.g., family values or work ethic) and "natural" talents that characterize this group.

Various factual and conceptual problems plague the representation of Asian Americans as model minorities. For example, the model minority construct does not account for cost-of-living differentials in urban centers, where most Asian Americans tend to be concentrated, or for the fact that Asian Americans are often subject to occupational "ghettos" and paid lower wages than are commensurate with their educational qualifications. Nor does the model minority stereotype differentiate between different Asian ethnic groups, who have not all fared equally well with respect to normative measures of success. In truth, the economic status and material well-being of Asian Americans have been divided—a certain sector has enjoyed an advantage over those who continue to struggle culturally and economically.

Moreover, the model minority stereotype pits Asian Americans against other minority groups, who are deemed to be politically troublesome and socially undeserving of the rewards that Asian Americans enjoy. Yet the very designation of the model minority *as a minority* registers an ambivalent relationship, as it continues to mark out the racial difference of Asians in national culture from a normative majority (white) population, which retains for itself the privilege of designating those it considers worthy of the title "model." Even so, the remarkable resilience of the model minority image bespeaks the complex changes in the meaning of the term "minority" as a result of the demographic and social changes described above. Not only has the class status of different minority groups become increasingly diversified, but minorities exhibit tremendous ideological and political heterogeneity. Certainly, there was nothing monolithic about Asians in the United States prior to the 1960s. But the increasingly visible fissures have

made it extremely difficult to speak of any single, unified "minority" experience of Asian Americans, much less of a minority experience that is shared across different racial and ethnic constituencies.

For this reason, it might be especially exigent for us to also consider the "minor" as a *critical* position. In this case, a "minor" perspective might very well arise from the experience of being a member of a statistical minority. But it references, first and foremost, a specific *orientation* and *relationship* to that which is taken to be "natural" or "normal," regardless of how prevalent that normative ideal might actually be as a lived reality (e.g., middle-class nuclear families). In this case, to describe a subject, object, or practice as "minor"—for example, minor literature or minor discourse—is to concern oneself not with some inherent content that defines a particular race or ethnic group, such as language. Rather, it is to call critical attention to the way in which such a position, perspective, or practice is excluded from the norm, so as to account for how our normative ideals are themselves constructed as universal goods.

Thus, for example, Gilles Deleuze and Félix Guattari define a "minor literature" as "that which a minority constructs within a major language," rather than simply a literature that originates in a minor language (1986, 16). For these critics, a minor literature is characterized by "a high coefficient of deterritorialization" with respect to the major language and is inherently collective and political in character (1986, 16). In the name of the marginalized group, it challenges the very institutional structures and terms by which a community is set off as "minor." The "minor" is then no longer about a specific literature or tradition per se, but pertains to "the revolutionary conditions for every literature within the heart of what is called great (or established) literature" (1986, 18). Likewise, Abdul R. JanMohamed and David Lloyd describe a "theory of minority discourse" that is attentive to how "[c]ultures designated as minorities have certain shared experiences by virtue of their similar antagonistic relationship to the dominant culture, which seeks to marginalize them all" (1990, 1). As JanMohamed and Lloyd further contend, a theory of minority discourse does not simply celebrate the difference of particular groups in order to pluralize majoritarian culture without troubling it. Instead, such a theory should "provide a sustained critique of the historical conditions and formal qualities of the institutions that have continued to legitimize exclusion and marginalization in the name of universality," because "the universalizing humanist project has been highly selective, systematically valorizing certain texts and authors as *the* humanist tradition while ignoring or actively repressing alternative traditions and attitudes" (1990, 6). A minor critical perspective or cultural practice that recognizes and affirms itself as such allows us to see the way in which assimilation and integration is always an uneven and asymmetrical process.

To return to Wirth and his concern with "the *problem* of minority groups" (which is also the title of the well-known essay I have been citing), we find that the critical minor perspective is a significant departure from the terms he uses to address and approach the subject of minority groups. Wirth—and other postwar liberals like him—worried especially that the exclusion of minorities from full national belonging, in the United States and elsewhere, gave rise to conflict and a "rebellious attitude" that "weakens national loyalties and solidarity" (1945, 348, 368). From this perspective, the most salutary approach to the "problem" of minority groups was to achieve their dissolution, so that each individual could pursue his or her own voluntary affiliations and enjoy the "rights of man" to the fullest. As a result, Wirth was compelled to make a curious turn in his discussion of minority groups, as he wrote, "We are

less concerned . . . with racial minorities than ethnic minorities" (1945, 351). Wirth and other liberal scholars of race from the mid-twentieth century onward chose instead to highlight the example of ethnic Europeans, such as Italians and the Irish in the United States, as well as ethnic, linguistic, and religious minorities in Europe. Wirth certainly recognized that "the Negro in the United States has become the principal shock absorber of the antiminority sentiment of the dominant whites" (1945, 353). Nonetheless, he claimed in all earnestness that "the United States was in the forefront of the nations of the world in the treatment of minorities" despite "occasional relapses and despite the great contrast between the enlightened treatment we accorded our ethnic minorities and the backward policy we followed in the case of the Negro, the Indian, and the Oriental" (1945, 353, 370).

For liberal Americans like Wirth, the assimilation of European ethnics from the nineteenth century onward proved the hallmark of an exceptional nation, "a nation of immigrants." In this national self-image, the incorporation of European immigrants and their descendants as full citizens in a hybridized national culture (i.e., melting pot), served as a shining example for other nations. It was also to provide the model for assimilating those racial minorities in the United States who had unfortunately been treated otherwise. But a minor critical perspective illuminates the limits to such an idealized historical perspective on the integration of European ethnics. Unlike a normatively liberal approach that focuses *only* upon the relationship between the "problematic" minority group and the majority population, a critical minor perspective recognizes how the assimilability of European ethnics was defined over and against Asians, Latinos, and African Americans, whose persistent racialization served as a mark of presumed *in*assimilability to such liberal ideals. Moreover, a minority

the Summer of Love, and the rise of Black Power, the women's movement, and the counterculture (T. Anderson 1995).

During the 1960s, individual Americans of Asian ancestry participated in various segments of the movement, most notably its student, civil rights, Black Power, and antiwar components. As they protested for free speech, registered black voters in the South, and demonstrated against the Vietnam War, these individuals reflected upon their own position as racial minorities. Many began to see that as people of Asian ancestry in the United States, they suffered from racism that was similar to that experienced by black people in the U.S. and Vietnamese people in Asia. Furthermore, they came to believe that they should organize fellow Asians to address the discrimination and exploitation that their communities faced. Finally, they concluded that despite historical antipathy among Asians of different ethnicities in the U.S., all Asians shared a common relationship to U.S. racism. In 1968, Yuji Ichioka coined the term "Asian American" when he cofounded the germinal Asian American Political Alliance (AAPA) at the University of California, Berkeley. To recruit new members, AAPA contacted all Asian-surnamed members of a New Left organization called the Peace and Freedom Party. AAPA decried U.S. racism, called for solidarity among "Third World" people, and opposed the war in particular and U.S. imperialism more generally. In New York City, the Asian Americans for Action (AAA) was formed in 1969 by two Nisei women, Kazu Iijima and Minn Masuda, who were inspired by the Black Power movement and hoped to found a similar organization for their children. These two "little old ladies" contacted all the Asian individuals they saw at various antiwar demonstrations and invited them to meet with the group. Asian American organizations proliferated in the late 1960s and early 1970s. Members of AAPA and AAA were

united by a conviction that something was desperately wrong with an America that discriminated against and exploited nonwhite people within its borders and committed genocide against Asians abroad. Although these beliefs were generally in keeping with the ideologies of the New Left, Asian Americans also came to believe that the white-dominated mainstream movement did not take anti-Asian racism seriously and, hence, that it was important to organize specifically as Asian Americans. Thus, the Asian American movement emerged as an Asian-specific outgrowth of the New Left movement and also as a reaction against it (Maeda 2009).

Just as grouping the various aspects of the New Left, from pacifists to proponents of armed resistance, into a singular entity called "the movement" entailed papering over enormous differences of ideology and tactics, to speak of the "Asian American movement" required negotiating the tension between uniformity and variation. Prominent social movement theorist Sidney Tarrow defines social movements as "collective challenges, based on common purposes and social solidarities, in sustained interaction with elites, opponents, and authorities" (2011, 4). The collective solidarity signified by the term "Asian American" comprised Asians of various ethnicities within the U.S., which in the late 1960s meant primarily Chinese, Japanese, and Filipinos. Multiethnic groups like AAPA and AAA certainly contributed to the building of Asian American solidarity, but even single-ethnic organizations were considered to be part of the "Asian movement." For example, in the Third World Liberation Front strike at San Francisco State College, groups like Intercollegiate Chinese for Social Action (ICSA) and Pilipino American Collegiate Endeavor (PACE) were single ethnic but part of a multiethnic Asian American coalition, and more broadly, of a multiracial coalition including black, Latino, and American Indian students. The group Katipunan ng mga Demokratikong

Pilipino (KDP), with its roots in both Filipino American politics and Philippines radicalism, worked primarily on issues impacting Filipinos, such as fighting against the destruction of the International Hotel in San Francisco and opposing the imposition of martial law in the Philippines by President Ferdinand Marcos (Habal 2007). Groups like I Wor Kuen (IWK) and Wei Min She (WMS) emerged from Chinatowns in New York and San Francisco, and the Little Tokyo People's Rights Organization (LTPRO) came out of the Japanese American community in Los Angeles. Yet despite their tendencies toward ethnic-specific membership, KDP, IWK, WMS, and LT-PRO were important Asian American movement organizations because of their activism in Asian American communities and because they were aligned with the generally antiracist, anti-imperialist ideologies of the movement. In contrast to community-action/political organizations, arts and culture organizations tended to be thoroughly multiethnic. The East-West Players and Visual Communications in Los Angeles, Basement Workshop in New York City, Kearny Street Workshop and Asian American Theater Workshop in San Francisco, and Northwest Asian American Theater in Seattle all promoted cultural expressions by an ethnically diverse array of artists and writers, brought together multiethnic audiences, and promoted arts and literature in various Asian ethnic communities (Maeda 2012).

Although Tarrow's definition of a social movement relies on solidarity, no movement is unitary. Indeed, the Asian American movement featured tremendous variety in terms of geography, campaigns, and ideology. It spanned from New York and Philadelphia on the East Coast to college towns in the Midwest to Seattle, San Francisco, and Los Angeles on the West Coast to Honolulu and the Kalama Valley in Hawai'i. Participants sought to transform higher education through the establishment of ethnic studies, make Asian ghettoes better places to live and work by providing social services such as food, healthcare, and legal aid, opposed redevelopment that would displace poor residents, organized Asian American workers in sweatshops, restaurants, and service industries, and attempted to create a distinct Asian American culture. But despite sharing a basic urge toward justice and power, the Asian American movement was rife with contradictions. Even among groups fighting for the same goals, such as preserving the I-Hotel or organizing sweatshop workers, basic disagreements over ideology and tactics could become divisive. Given its diversity and flexibility, it makes more sense to speak of the "Asian American movement" (without capitalization) rather than the "Asian American Movement." Doing so sidesteps the problem of defining the Asian American movement precisely, in favor of understanding that a variety of loosely affiliated groups and individuals were united by a conviction that racism, class exploitation, and imperialism negatively impacted people of Asian ancestry in the United States, and acted on that conviction to transform society accordingly.

The Asian American movement changed dramatically during the 1970s, evoking the meaning of "movement" that suggests dynamism. Tracing the narrative of AAPA provides a useful way to understand the changes wrought more generally in the Asian American movement during the passage of over a decade. From its genesis in the New Left in 1968, AAPA went on to become a key Asian American organization. Its San Francisco chapter participated in the TWLF strike at SF State and its Berkeley chapter provided the major Asian American force in the TWLF strike at UC Berkeley. After the successful establishment of ethnic studies at Cal, some Berkeley AAPA members moved from campus to community—where they believed they could make the greatest difference—forming the Asian Community

Center (ACC) in San Francisco's Chinatown in 1970. ACC established "Serve the People" programs that provided free food and healthcare for the elderly, and operated a drop-in community center. In addition, ACC screened films from the People's Republic of China and opened Everybody's Bookstore; the films and bookstore provided a leftist perspective that was sorely missing from conservative-dominated Chinatown. Thus, ACC both sought to provide for the needs of the community and propagate a forward-looking ideology of solidarity and liberation. In 1971–1972, ACC transformed into Wei Min She ("Organization for the People"), a self-described anti-imperialist organization dedicated to eradicating the interlinked systems of class exploitation and racial oppression; members studied Lenin, Marx, Stalin, and Mao and dedicated themselves to protecting the rights of workers. Furthermore, WMS linked up with the Revolutionary Union (RU), a multiracial Marxist-Leninist organization, then subsequently merged along with the other components of the RU to form the Revolutionary Communist Party in 1975 (Asian Community Center Archive Group 2009). Over roughly a half decade, AAPA went from a student group to a cadre organization, and from flexible anti-imperialism to the disciplined ideology of Marxism–Leninism–Mao Zedong Thought. During the same period, IWK and KDP underwent similar transformations. Many groups within the Asian American movement eventually functioned within what authors have called the Third World Left or New Communist Movement (Pulido 2006; Elbaum 2002). Just as the groups that made up the Asian American movement evolved, over time individuals participants grew to understand themselves as subjects of systems of race, gender, and nation in new ways. Yuri Kochiyama and Richard Aoki entered the 1950s believing in the promise of American democracy, but over the course of the 1960s, grew to view race, class, and empire as integral to

the formation and maintenance of the nation (Fujino 2005; Fujino 2012).

As an outgrowth of the New Left, the Asian American movement called attention to the problem of racism facing Asians of all ethnicities in the U.S., opposed the exercise of U.S. military power against Asians across the Pacific, and sought solidarity with other racialized peoples both at home and abroad. During the late 1960s and 1970s, this movement brought into being the very category of "Asian American" and opened new possibilities for political activism and subjectivities from which to operate. The ideologies of the groups comprising the Asian American movement shifted over time, as did their priorities and strategies (Liu, Geron, and Lai 2008). During the 1970s, large-scale immigration from Asia enabled by the immigration reforms of 1965 transformed Asian America itself, making it more ethnically diverse, increasingly immigrant based, and more heterogeneous with regard to class than ever before. By 1980, Asian American activism had moved far from its origins in 1968, thus marking an inflection point in the Asian American movement. Many activists entered community-based nonprofits, unions, academia, or even electoral politics. But recognizing the social movement roots of the category of "Asian American" and marking its creation with the energetic word "movement" suggests that Asian Americans must persevere in their efforts to build a more just society. Today, despite the fact that progressives or radicals do not possess a monopoly on Asian American community politics (nor have they ever), issues such as immigration, the dismantling of the social safety net and affirmative action, LGBT rights, and ongoing racism continue to motivate Asian Americans toward movement.

43

Multiculturalism

James Kyung-Jin Lee

While what one might call the multicultural mode or inclination first entered the verbal imagination in the United States in 1935, the *OED* does not recognize its nominal usage until 1957; "multiculturalism" found its way and allied to multilingualism in the journal *Hispania*. But before the term entered the lexicon, and certainly before it became part of a popular if not normative understanding of how to negotiate cultural difference, it was quite the vexed notion. In 1784, J. Hector St. John de Crèvecoeur published *Letters from an American Farmer*, which includes the now famous chapter "What Is an American?" to which he answers in part, "Here individuals of all races are melted into a new race of man, whose labors and posterity will one day cause great changes in the world" (55). Crèvecoeur sought to demonstrate that an American was one who left aside past prejudices in favor of a presumably more egalitarian mode of relationship with one's compatriots. Yet even in this very early, proto-formulation of what would later be known as the "melting pot," this "new race of man" could not account for a major challenge: how to incorporate those who did not hail from Europe, most notably in Crèvecoeur's day Native Americans figured as uncivilized and blacks held in slavery, in both the North and South. By extension, then, "American" demanded a kind of cultural sameness to which nonwhite groups were required to enter in order to be marked as belonging to the United States. As the U.S. moved through its early republican phase, this

conundrum persisted: not only would we engage in civil war to answer the question of slavery, but the lead-up to and execution of the war foregrounded the question of how to belong to this "American crucible." Many Irish, cast as demonstrably nonwhite throughout their mass wave of immigration in the first half of the nineteenth century, refused in 1863 to participate in the Union effort—to help liberate African Americans from slavery—so committed were they to adhering to the mantle of whiteness via the ideology of white supremacy. The irony then to the "melting pot" is that on the one hand it was seen as the cultural and ideological antagonist to cultural and social segregation; the notion of the melting pot and its sociological successor, Robert Park's "assimilation" cycle, might be viewed as early expressions of and experiments in multiculturalism, as both subscribed to the idea—against prevailing and even dominant understandings of racial biologism— that peoples might indeed interact and change on the cultural level. On the other hand, that conformity to a singular cultural end product, "American," was a given was at best a compromise between virulent white supremacy on the one hand and what contemporary assimilationists would disparage as cultural relativism on the other. Until the later twentieth century, even the most charitable recognition of difference-in-equality presupposed a cultural, not to mention legal, desire for white belonging.

This assimilationist strain in what would become known as at least one, if not the principal, model of multiculturalism has its antecedents in Asian American practice, which exposes the muddiness of the term with regard to what kinds of social difference something called multiculturalism is meant to describe or produce. Put simply, it is not at all clear whether multiculturalism attends to what we might call ethnic difference or the most insidious differences based on race, the latter a production of the U.S./Western legacy of white supremacy that multiculturalism has done little more than to feebly mitigate. Or, as Avery Gordon and Christopher Newfield put it some two decades ago, "Is multiculturalism antiracist or oblivious to racism?" (1996, 3). This question is not at all put to rest, precisely because in the long fetch of U.S. history before the term came into household use, those marked as culturally different often worked within the constraints of racial hierarchy to win social recognition while leaving those structures intact. Two infamous Asian American examples capture this dilemma: in November 1922, a Japanese immigrant, Takao Ozawa, lost his Supreme Court appeal to be naturalized as a U.S. citizen; three months later, Bhagat Singh Thind, an Indian Sikh, was denied the right to be naturalized. In both cases, the plaintiffs argued that their capacity to become U.S. citizens had to do with their proximity to whiteness (the 1870 Naturalization Act enabled "white" persons and those of "African nativity" to become naturalized, the former under the stipulation of 1790 that "free white persons" were eligible for naturalized citizenship). Ozawa argued that his skin was paler than those of Southern and Eastern European origin who had won citizenship, and that his cultural upbringing and proximity to already white persons and culture made him eligible for citizenship. In contrast, Thind suggested that his "Aryan" ancestry put him in common with other "Caucasians," mobilizing linguistic and anthropological understandings of "Caucasoid" types as prototypes for white people. In the former case, the Supreme Court denied Ozawa on the basis of his non-Caucasian phenotype, while in the latter, it decided that despite his Caucasian "type" Thind was "clearly" not white in commonsense terms. The deleterious legal effect for Asian Americans was significant, as they would be unable to belong to this "race of men" for decades longer. Moreover, these two cases were crucial

in demonstrating how contestations over whiteness and white belonging remained the crux of cultural belonging in the United States. But it is equally important to note that these early Asian American assertions of legal and political rights were premised on the idea that racial proximity to whiteness, and not a challenge to the logic of whiteness itself; one might suggest that this approach continues to be a significant strain of how Asian Americans negotiate their place in the United States.

By the time race-based legal restrictions on citizenship eligibility were finally eliminated, this cultural logic remained intact, deeply imbedded in the U.S. psyche and, by extension, the Asian American one. Less than fifty years after these Supreme Court decisions, and only two decades after the internment of Japanese Americans during World War II, we see the emergence of the Asian American as "model minority," what we might call the predecessor to Asian American participation in multiculturalism. This 1960s conception and representation of Asian Americans as paragons of social mobility, in direct antagonism to calls by "Negroes and other minorities" ("Success Story of One Minority Group in the US," *U.S. News & World Report*, December 26, 1966) to work to abolish white supremacy, provided the space for Asian Americans to make claims on social belonging, this time with legal rights intact. This belatedly fulfilled Ozawa's and Thind's dreams for their descendants. The Asian American as model minority entered the popular consciousness at the very moment that the civil rights movement took on a decidedly radical turn; this well-known *U.S. News & World Report* article chronicling Chinese Americans' success came out a few months after Stokely Carmichael uttered the phrase "Black Power" as he assumed the leadership of the Student Nonviolent Coordinating Committee (SNCC) and just weeks after the formation of the Black Panther Party in Oakland. Two models or sociologies of multiculturalism were crystallizing in the 1960s: one that fulfilled Robert Park's model of assimilation, of which Asian Americans were becoming perfect expressions; another that spoke to an alternative ethic and politics that took seriously Du Bois's observation that racial difference resulted in a differential existential expression, and therefore differential political arrangement: "two souls, two thoughts, two unreconciled strivings; two warring ideals in one dark body, whose dogged strength alone keeps it from being torn asunder" (1903, 12).

Yet the differential consciousness that Du Bois prophesied in *Souls of Black Folk* captured the imagination of Asian Americans as well, so that in 1968 and 1969, Asian American students revolted alongside black, Chicano, Native American, and progressive whites to shut down classes at San Francisco State College, UC Berkeley, and other college campuses across the United States. Galvanized by the call to Black Power and the ethos of self-determination, and undergirded by the emergence of a Third Worldist worldview (inspired by the Bandung Conference of newly decolonized Asian and African countries in 1955), a concomitant if not unproblematically named Yellow Power movement sought to bring a radical politics of difference that refused the imperative of a kind of cultural incorporation that kept in place existing structures of power and relation. Whether protesting against American involvement in the war in Vietnam, working with working-class and elderly Asian Americans cramped in urban areas, counseling Asian American youth struggling with drug addiction, or fighting to include the histories, cultures, and literatures of Asian Americans in college classrooms, this radical movement proclaimed social and political transformation as the basis through which an alternative mode of identity could be forged. Over time, as the embers of such political fervor cooled, what remained were some long-standing community and cultural organizations,

and the establishment of the field of Asian American studies which has for almost half a century committed to produce research and pedagogical resources to help document and disseminate the specific contributions and insights that emerge from the differential experiences of the communities that make up "Asian America."

It should be noted, however, that the rise of Asian American studies coincides with the rise of a corporately driven embrace of "cultural diversity," to which what becomes known as multiculturalism is seen as synonymous. By the time Hazel Carby published a short article titled "Multi-Culture" in the Australian journal *Screen Education* in 1980, the emerging hegemony of cultural diversity as a way to understand and manage the swelling ranks of immigrant communities in the West, including the U.S. and the U.K., favored this idealization and celebration of ethnicity and culture. This ideology also facilitated the pathologization of other communities as well as a distancing from a racial analytic. "The paradigm of multiculturalism," Carby writes, "actually excludes the concept of dominant and subordinate cultures—either indigineous or migrant—and fails to recognize that the existence of racism relates to the possession and exercise of politico-economic control and authority and also to forms of resistance to the power of dominant social groups" (1980, 65). Such is the racial bargain that enabled Asian Americans to enter, however unevenly, social legibility or visibility in the U.S.; to be seen as part of the American "mosaic," to acknowledge the presence and participation of more than two races, one needed to displace the trenchant analysis of power that was endemic to a reading of the U.S. not as multicultural but as racially stratified. But the diffusion of analysis is only the beginning. For it is possible that the flourishing of Asian American life in a multicultural rubric has enabled the social disappearance of others, and nowhere is this more evident than in, on the one hand, the high visibility of Asian Americans on college and university campuses while, on the other, the black and Latino populations in U.S. prisons and jails have exploded. As Dylan Rodríguez points out, Asian American civic life thrives on the social death of black and brown life, "while the very articulation and material gravity of Asian Americanism sits on the precipice and precedent of the 1965 Immigration Act. . . . [W]e must contextualize this change in federal immigration law as a measure that further facilitated the effective expulsion of criminalized populations from US civil society" (2005, 257–58). Neither a multicultural analytic nor a multicultural policy can account for this phenomenon, that one minority group would enjoy such flourishing at the very moment that others suffer such penal costs, unless of course multiculturalism comes to be known as the very cultural logic that enables a coexistence of different communities or "cultures" while accepting or at best ignoring the political and economic subordination of other communities.

Perhaps the phenomenon that has done the most to both galvanize and haunt Asian American studies scholars over this vexed participation in multiculturalism—and it is hard to argue against the idea that Asian American studies itself has flourished as a field because of the general, wide acceptance of multiculturalism in academic discourse—is the manner in which the 1992 Los Angeles Uprisings (or Riots, as most Asian Americanists refer to the event) were and continue to be understood. The particular presence of Asian Americans in this late-twentieth-century civil crisis—often portrayed as the U.S.'s first multiracial or, fittingly, multicultural "riot"—demands an official understanding of the violence in this way: Asian Americans, specifically Korean immigrant merchants in Koreatown and sections of South Central Los Angeles, were betrayed by a racial state that left them subject to the violence of rioters and looters, abandoned so that the state via the police and National Guard could protect white spaces of the city such as Beverly Hills. In this "abandonment narrative," the armed defense of Koreatown and its businesses by their owners and other Korean immigrants was necessary and justified, the use of lethal force against black and brown looters a necessary evil, and perhaps even a social good. What undergirds and would protect Asian American social life then in this situation is the moral outrage that the state momentarily did not do its "job" of securing Asian American civic life against black rage, and the consequent moral defensibility of shooting black people. In this reading, it is an ethical impossibility for Asian American studies to imagine the case for letting Koreatown burn, which speaks to the political incommensurabilities that inhere when Asian American participation in U.S. social life via multiculturalism confronts blacks' (and others') deep social grievances over a racism that multiculturalism can neither address nor mitigate. A multiculturalist framework must in the final instance produce an ellipsis in defense of the racial innocence of the Asian American subject, even if this subject pulled the trigger and ended a black life, or as Neil Gotanda puts it, "The Korean 'model minority' is thus the measure of the African American 'monitored minority'" (Gordon and Newfield 1996, 240).

Thus we see the deep problematic of multiculturalism, a discourse that ostensibly allows for the incorporation of new "subjects," but subjects enabled consistently and persistently on antiblack grounds. This problematic emerged from the moment that Asian immigrants tried to make claims by disassociating themselves from persons of African nativity and has extended to recent examples of Asian Americans wondering why more black people were not arrested by police in 1992. Indeed, recent scholarship in African American studies has foregrounded this political and discursive antagonism between the coalitional, comparative approaches to race that might be viewed as a trenchant, robust multiculturalism and the view that such analysis still fails to acknowledge its antiblack animus. Jared Sexton, commenting on the multiculturalist trope which argues that scholarship necessarily must move "beyond black and white," critiques this vision of blackness as a temporal obstacle to progress: "What concerns me in the articulation of these various developments within the horizon of the multiracial—pointing toward both racial multiplicity and racial mixture—is their common point of reference, their common antagonism with a figure of blackness supposed to stand in the way of future progress, silencing the expression of much needed voices on the political and intellectual scene" (2008, 252). Multiculturalism can do little to provide analytical tools to point to the stark realities of difference and vulnerability in the United States. To wit: it is true but analytically brittle and historically impoverished to say that Trayvon Martin and Emmett Till were killed because they were nonwhite, but to understand that these two young men were murdered because they were black allows a historical reading of blackness that informs our understanding of these two acts of violence. Likewise, it is true that Vincent Chin died because he was not viewed as either white or American, but to embrace the history of anti-Asian sentiment provides a far more honed narrative understanding than the "person of color" rubric can offer. Asian Americans implicitly know this to be true; as Emi, Karen Tei Yamashita's Japanese American character in *Tropic of Orange*, puts it to her Chicano boyfriend as they dine in a sushi restaurant, "cultural diversity is bullshit," because it is no more than "a white guy wearing a Nirvana T-shirt and dreds. . . . It's just tea, raw fish, and credit cards" (1997, 128). When a white woman overhears Emi's diatribe and asserts that she loves Los Angeles because of its celebration of cultures, Emi notices that the woman holds her hair with chopsticks. Emi asks the sushi chef for two forks, holds them up to the white woman, and asks, "Would you consider using these in your hair? Or would you consider that . . . unsanitary?" (1997, 129). Cultural diversity as multiculturalism cannot account for the thick description of any social life that centrally involves contradiction, especially if those leading complicated, contradictory lives suffer from forces of our making. It prevents us from examining the possibility of communicability and sociality across the incommensurabilities that racism has wrought. In the end, cultural diversity reinforces the idea of the ever-emerging but also ever-elusive "race of man," an abstract notion of cultural difference that always demands the sameness produced by the silencing of stories of violence and exclusion. As such, an embrace of multiculturalism would be Asian America's ultimate undoing, as our allegiance to ignore the suffering of others inevitably prevents us from confronting the suffering within.

44

Multiracial

Rebecca Chiyoko King-O'Riain

According to the *Oxford English Dictionary*, "multiracial" means "made up of or relating to people of many races." Coming into common use in the mid-1920s, "multiracial" initially referred primarily to relationships that spanned across racial groups or collectives of monoracial people from different racial groups. But this word has shifted meaning in the United States, particularly over the last 80 years. In the contemporary era, "multiracial" began in the late 1980s and early 1990s to refer more specifically to people of mixed racial and ethnic descent as individuals, i.e., multiracial or mixed-race people and identities. Many, more specific terms, have been used to describe people of mixed Asian and Pacific Islander descent: "mixed race," "biracial," "hapa," "halfu," and "Amerasian."

"Hapa," which comes from the Hawai'ian term "hapa haole," meaning "half white/foreigner," is used in local parlance in Hawai'i to describe people who are part Asian. Because it is a native Hawai'ian word, its use has been criticized by Native Hawai'ians as a cultural appropriation by Asians in the islands. The word "hapa" found its way to the West Coast of the American mainland in the 1990s and was used by some to describe groups of people of mixed Asian descent often united by poor treatment or outright discrimination within Asian American and Pacific Islander (API) communities. On the mainland, "mixed race" also started to become popular and more politicized during the 1990s as a part of the multiracial movement. The term has also been criticized for reifying the concept of "race" (i.e., that you have to be part one race and part another, which takes for granted that races actually exist). Social scientists for the most part have taken the lead of activists themselves and refer to the multiracial movement as by and about mixed-race people.

"Biracial" comes out of the psychological literature and was traditionally used to discuss the identity development of people who are mixed with two distinct groups, but again, this has been criticized by multiracial activists as too "pathologizing" and not encompassing enough to deal with people who are mixed with more than two backgrounds. Within Japan, "halfu" was used to describe the mixed children of American servicemen and Japanese women in the post–World War II era. The term later spread to other parts of Asia in the wake of U.S. military occupations in Korea, Vietnam, and Okinawa. "Halfu" has become outdated and is rejected by many as emphasizing just "half" of one's identity. "Doubles" became a popular replacement in Japan in the 1990s, based on the claim that mixed people in Japan were not "half," but "double." "Amerasian" was used mainly in Vietnam, again to describe mixed children of U.S. servicemen and Vietnamese women. As such, it evoked faces that were reminders of war and occupation and has been rejected for focusing too much on national origins and not capturing the complexity of this mixed experience.

In 1967, the U.S. Supreme Court's decision in *Loving v. Virginia* found that laws that prohibited people from marrying across racial lines were illegal. Prior anti-miscegenation laws were based on the fear that mixed marriages challenged claims to white supremacy and threatened white racial purity. The assumption was that if racial groups mixed, the resulting mixed children would be "hybrid degenerates" with physical, mental, and/or social problems (Nakashima 1992). Others argued in response to scientific racist arguments against intermarriage that, in fact, mixed people would not be degenerate, but instead have "hybrid vigor." In truth, there had long been interracial sex at the highest levels of political life in the U.S., as in the case of Thomas Jefferson and Sally Hemmings, but much of this was never formally or legally recognized for fear of challenging white supremacy and power.

By 1994, the U.S. Census Bureau was under pressure from a multiracial movement to better represent the reality of the country's racial diversity, including the growing population of people who wanted to identify both personally and publicly as multiracial. Just a generation after the *Loving* decision, a critical mass of multiracial people sought to be heard and the Census Bureau was ready to listen. This was controversial, as the NAACP and the National Council of La Raza opposed multiracial activists' claims to the right to express their identities in the census. The worry was that if mixed-race people checked "multiracial" and not the communities of color that they felt they belonged to, that this would undermine the gains of the civil rights movements (particularly in voting districts, affirmative action, and the like). The Census Bureau took this under consideration and in response added the ability to check multiple racial/ethnic boxes on the census but did not proceed with listing a "multiracial" category. In the 2000 census, 6.8 million Americans (or 2.4% of the country's population) indicated they were two or more racial identities, making this population one of the fastest growing in the United States (Nagai 2010).

The term "multiracial" did not suit everyone. Specifically, many mixed-race and multiracial Asian Americans felt that they were not multiracial in the same ways that black/white mixed people were, or that mixed Asian/blacks faced more discrimination from the both larger society and the API community than Asian/whites did.

They also felt both excluded from and less accepted in Asian American communities—both in the past and at present—due to a lack of history of racial mixing in the U.S. and/or because of a history of mixing in Asia that was tangled up with resentments provoked by military occupation, colonization, and colorism.

Student and community groups of mixed Asian Americans began using terms such as "hapa," as in the San Francisco Bay Area's *Hapa Issues Forum*, published from 1992 to 2007. They reappropriated this term to give it a positive meaning and to move away from more derogatory terms often used to describe mixed-descent, part-Asian people linked with military occupation and war ("war baby," "Eurasian," "Amerasian"), illicit sexual relations ("ainoko," "love child"), and impurity ("halfu," "mixed blood").

A smaller percentage of Asian Americans identify as mixed than do Latinos, Native Americans, and the members of some Pacific Islander groups. And yet, in the 2000 census, Asian/white was one of the top three identities expressed. Even with continued migration from Asia, which could lead to a larger API marriage pool, intermarriage rates have stabilized somewhat and there is not a proportionately large mixed population. There are also cultural legacies around "racial purity" that make some Asian American suspicious of those that are less than 100% blood quantum Asian, whom they consider to be not "truly" Asian (Armstrong 1989). There is some evidence of shifting racial attitudes within Asian American communities, but there are still, for instance, racial eligibility rules in many Japanese American and Chinese American beauty pageants and basketball leagues, which state that if you are less than 25% Japanese or Chinese you are not Asian "enough" to participate (King-O'Riain 2006).

Asian American studies research initially focused on Asian pride and the development of Asian American communities within the United States. Within this narrative, interracial marriage was seen as assimilative and a threat to the sustenance of Asian American communities. Further, because the out-marriage rates in some, like the Japanese American community, was gendered (women were more likely than men to marry out with white partners), women came under particular political scrutiny in their marriage choices (Shinagawa and Pang 1996). As Asian American studies matured as a discipline, a more nuanced understanding of issues of multiraciality developed. One significant example of this was a special issue of *Amerasia Journal* edited by Velina Hasu Houston and Teresa Williams-León in 1997 entitled *No Passing Zone*, which made the case that multiracial Asian Americans were not all assimilated and trying to pass as white, but that their identities were as diverse as they were. It was a unique and important contribution both about, but more importantly researched and written by, multiracial Asian Americans themselves. A collection of essays covering a range of multiracial Asian American themes, edited by Williams-León and Cynthia L. Nakashima, followed in 2001, perhaps ironically titled *The Sum of Our Parts*.

By the mid-2000s, multiracial Asian Americans were well represented within both the Association for Asian American Studies and Asian American studies departments, with mixed-race courses and research projects widespread. However, some stereotypes of mixed marriages/relationships and particularly of mixed Asian American people persisted. Global ideas of beauty, flowing from the West to the East, impacted on popular looks via news anchors, media presenters, and music and acting icons. Some saw multiracial Asian Americans as exotic, "kinder, gentler," or more "palatable" Asian Americans. Others argued that it was white Western society that saw "lighter as being better"; Joanne

L. Rondilla and Paul Spickard tackled the issue of skin-tone discrimination and Asian Americans, including multiracials, in their book *Is Lighter Better?* in 2007.

Multiracial Asian Americans are now expanding their foci to ask how the multiracial experience is different in Asian nations or Asian and Pacific Islander communities that historically recognize racial mixing such as Filipinos, Samoans, and South and Southeast Asian groups. These analyses have opened up a discussion about the links between colonialism, sexualization, and racialization, and how they have played out on mixed-race bodies both in Asia and the United States.

Likewise, the presidency of Barack Obama has foregrounded the issue of multiraciality across the world in new ways. Obama, who is seen predominantly as African American, nevertheless has raised the visibility of multiracial people by openly claiming both his black father from Kenya and his white mother from Kansas. And he is equally proud that he grew up in Hawai'i, strongly influenced by Native Hawai'ian and Asian American cultures, while also recognizing influences from his Indonesian relatives and more recently discovered Irish ancestry. In many ways, Obama has faced the classic conundrum of mixed people. He was heralded by many as the first "black" president, while for others he was "not black enough" (Dickerson 2007) and for yet others, he was just a black man who was really "white" and had "neo-mulatto politics" (Bonilla-Silva 2008). Senate majority leader Harry Reid stated that he believed Barack Obama could become the country's first black president because he was light-skinned and had the advantage of "carrying no Negro dialect, unless he wanted to have one" (Zeleny 2010). Others essentially agreed that Obama opened up the definition of blackness and expanded it to represent a much broader and more diverse community (Logan 2008). As Kim DaCosta (2008) points out, what is interesting is not what Barack Obama "really" is, but that we ask this question at all and expect him to make political and identity choices based on a single race affiliation.

While the context and choices for multiracial people have shifted drastically in the last 20 years, the artistic expression and scholarly work on multiracial people and multiracial Asian American continues apace. Kip Fulbeck's photographic installation and book *Part Asian, 100% Hapa* (2006) was one of the most successful in the history of Asian American studies. Still others, such as Stephen Murphy Shigematsu (2012), have turned to Asia and personal biography to think about the types of hybridities and crossings that multiracial Asian Americans can take or, as Laura Kina has done, how that is expressed through art. Others feel that multiraciality is becoming ubiquitous, that everyone is jumping on the multiracial bandwagon because it is "cool" or "chic" to be multiracial (Spencer 2009), and that mixed-race people are just being commodified like Benetton poster models to sell ideas of racial colorblindness across Asia and the world (Matthews 2007).

"Multiracial," as a word, has come a long way, and while there may be positive views of multiraciality and mixed people now, it is probably best to recognize that not all multiracial people are symbols of racial harmony and the rainbow nation, and while it may link the East and West, even Hawai'i is not a multiracial paradise. Many people who identify as mixed or monoracial still face discrimination not based on what they have done or not done, but because of who people think they are and how they appear to others. Some multiracial people may be under constant social and political pressure to "choose one and only one" identity for fear of being called inauthentic or illegitimate members of the racial and ethnic groups to which they belong. In the end, "multiracial," as both word and concept, holds within it the hope of recognizing racial hybridity and multiple racial/ethnic backgrounds, ties, and connections, but at the same time it is clear that it is not, nor may it ever be, the cure-all for racism.

45

Nationalism

Richard S. Kim

"Nationalism" is a term fraught with multiple and complex meanings. The *OED* defines nationalism as "advocacy of or support for national independence or self-determination" that "usually refers to a specific ideology, esp. one expressed through political activism." This definition provides a useful starting point for examining nationalism as a keyword in Asian American studies. Indeed, nationalism has been central to the intellectual and political project of Asian American studies from its inception through its subsequent trajectory. Using nationalism as a keyword thus offers a productive means to chart a critical genealogy of Asian American studies that traces its key interventions, possibilities, and limits.

The field of Asian American studies emerged from the social movements of the late 1960s and early 1970s, including the student protests for ethnic studies courses at universities across the country. San Francisco State College was a particularly intense hotbed of campus activism. In 1968, the Third World Liberation Front (TWLF), a multiracial alliance of African American, Asian American, Latino, and Native American students at San Francisco State College, led a five-month student strike that resulted in the establishment of the first school of ethnic studies in the United States. A liberatory nationalist ideology underwrote TWLF protests for ethnic studies at San Francisco State. Influenced by the Black Power, antiwar, and Third World anticolonial liberation movements, the student activists of the TWLF demanded educational self-determination in institutional resources, representation, decision making, and power in their calls for an education relevant and accessible to their lives and communities. In doing so, they sought a redefinition of education by transforming how knowledge was produced and disseminated (Maeda 2012; Omatsu 1994; Umemoto 1989). The movement for ethnic studies reverberated throughout colleges and universities across the nation, creating institutional spaces for the development of the field of Asian American studies.

Established as a part of broader movements for social transformation in American society in the late 1960s, the intellectual project of Asian American studies is explicitly rooted in an orientation of protest and emancipation. In coining the term "Asian American" itself, student activists asserted a counterhegemonic subjectivity that rejected the racist, imperialist biases and stereotypes embedded in the term "Oriental." Animated by such decolonial, antiracist, and anti-Orientalist sentiments, Asian American studies centered its attentions on refuting Eurocentric representations of the forever-foreign and inassimilable Oriental that cast Asian Americans as perpetual outsiders to the U.S. nation-state. Much of the early scholarship in Asian American studies focused on claiming full and equal membership in the American nation through the recovery of a "buried past" that provided correctives to racist Eurocentric representations that ignored or distorted the experiences of Asians in the United States. These concerns for self-representation, self-definition, and self-empowerment were reflected in the titles and contents of foundational texts such as *Roots: An Asian American Reader* (1971) and *Counterpoint: Perspectives on Asian America* (1976). Guided by an analysis and critique of power and domination in American society, the scholarly, journalistic, and creative works compiled in these seminal texts underscored the centrality of race and racism in American life by documenting diverse histories of protest and resistance, radical nationalist politics, and community formation that attested to the richness and complexity of Asian American experiences.

The liberatory nationalist sensibilities that informed the academic orientation of Asian American studies extended to off-campus activism as well. The epistemological critique of Asian American studies was intertwined with the struggle for structural change and transformation in American society. Student and community activists viewed Asian American communities as primary arenas for social change. As such, community activism was central to the intellectual and political project of Asian American studies. Employing nationalist discourses of self-determination and service to the masses, activists called for community control over resources and institutions. Emphasizing grassroots political participatory models for social change, they established self-help programs around housing, legal rights, urban redevelopment, youth, health, schools, social services, and labor rights (Maeda 2009; Omatsu 1994; Umemoto 1989).

Cultural production also emerged as a principal arena for political struggle and the expression of the emancipatory possibilities of new identities as Asian Americans that refuted Orientalist stereotypes and affirmed an American belonging. The group of writers who edited the seminal *Aiiieeeee! An Anthology of Asian American Writers* (1974) exemplified these efforts. The Aiiieeeee! group stridently promoted a collective Asian American identity by seeking to identify and establish a distinct "Asian American cultural integrity" as an alternative presence in American culture. Viewing Asian Americans as an internally colonized racial minority in the United States, they articulated a counterhegemonic, antiassimilationist form of cultural nationalism as a resistive strategy against dominant society and culture that excluded and denigrated Asian Americans (J. Ling 1998). The discursive strategies of this cultural nationalism focused on the emasculation of Asian men's gender and sexuality and the imperative to reclaim and affirm an Asian American manhood.

This cultural nationalist position became a source of contentious debate in subsequent years. Feminist critics challenged the exclusivity of the cultural nationalist project, especially its preoccupation with recuperating Asian American manhood and valorizing the masculine attributes of an authentic Asian American subject that idealized heteropatriarchy and thereby suppressed gender and sexual heterogeneity (Cheung 1990; Elaine Kim 1990; S. Lim 1993; S. Wong 1992). Influenced by postcolonial studies, queer studies, and cultural studies, other scholars further assessed the homogenizing and essentializing tenets of cultural nationalism. David Eng, for instance, comments that the narrow and inflexible notions of Asian American identity emerging from the cultural nationalist project "focused on not merely defining but *prescribing* how a recognizable and recognizably legitimate Asian American *racial* subject should ideally be: male, heterosexual, working class, American born, and English speaking" (1997, 34). Reinscribing a compulsory gender and sexual normativity, cultural nationalism ironically mirrored the dominant ideology and discourses of the very racist regime it was rejecting. Proposing a model of "heterogeneity, hybridity, and multiplicity," Lisa Lowe (1991b) underscored the simultaneity of race, class, gender, and sexuality in the shaping of Asian American identities, past and present. Highlighting the processes of inclusion and exclusion inherent in nationalist projects, these critiques locating and theorizing heterogeneity and differences within Asian America complicated a nation-based discourse on racial ideology.

Changes in the academy and the post-1965 growth in Asian immigrant populations in the United States have also blurred the lines dividing Asian and Asian American that were fundamental to earlier nationalist conceptualizations of Asian American identities. Sau-ling Wong (1995) notes these dramatic changes ushered in a "denationalization" of Asian American studies that has "eased the cultural nationalist concerns" of claiming America. The concerns of a domestic identity politics that promoted an American belonging often led to a critical distancing from Asia. Even the term "Asian American" advanced a political solidarity that used "Asian" to modify the central subject of "American." Changes in the demographic makeup of Asian American communities since 1965 and the ascendency of the Pacific Rim in the global economy, however, have underscored the increasingly complex interconnections between Asia and Asian American that have destabilized the domestic emphases of Asian American studies.

The denationalization of Asian American studies has paralleled the larger transnational turn in the academy that has widened the scope of scholarly inquiry beyond the borders of the U.S. nation-state. Adopting a transnational frame of analysis, an emergent body of historical scholarship on Asian diasporic nationalisms by scholars in Asian American studies has been a particularly fruitful area of research. Often using non-English-language materials and non-U.S. archival research, these works have examined the complex and multiple ways in which Asian immigrants in the United States have mobilized to support and participate in the homeland politics of their respective countries of origin (Azuma 2005; A. Espiritu 2005; Jensen 1988; R. Kim 2011; M. Lai 1991; Ma 1990; Sohi 2014; R. Yu 1992). These transnational ties have not simply been nostalgic attachments to the homeland but have been deeply imbricated within global structures of inequality involving issues of colonialism, imperialism, empire, war, nation-state formation, and international relations. In explicating such complex global dynamics, these studies show that Asian nationalisms have been constitutively transnational in nature as Asian migrants are vitally located at key geopolitical interstices, affirming Oscar Campomanes's call for the "worlding" of Asian American studies by situating the "Asian American predicament as part of a 'world-historical process'" (1997, 534). Accordingly, these studies on diasporic nationalism have not only provided new questions and new perspectives but also opened new possibilities for scholars in Asian and Asian American studies to consider important connections between the two fields, which traditionally have been at odds over their differing intellectual and political imperatives.

At the same time, the internationalization of Asian American studies has not been mutually exclusive to the field's long-standing domestic imperative of claiming America. Some scholars have cautioned that the shift to transnational and diasporic perspectives threatens to elide race as a significant category of analysis in Asian American studies and thus diminish the presence and voice of Asian Americans in the context of U.S. race relations (D. Li 2000; S. Wong 1995). However, the emergent body of historical research on diasporic nationalism underscores the interconnections between the domestic and global by highlighting the international context of social and political formations of Asian immigrant communities in the United States that harks back to the international scope of the genesis of Asian American studies (Mazumdar 1991; L. Lowe 1998). Moreover, immigrants' involvement in the diasporic nationalisms of their homelands was rooted in the realities of racial discrimination they faced in America. Constituted as not belonging to American society, Asian immigrants were in many ways forced to live transnational lives, which led to new modes of organizing and new forms of political agency in the United States. Supporting their homelands provided a means for strengthening their positions in America. In doing so, immigrants often drew upon American political discourses in their diasporic nationalist activities. Asian immigrant nationalist politics thus involved a complex amalgamation of both transnational and domestic concerns.

The transnational call to think beyond the national borders of the U.S. nation-state has also brought critical attention to the nationalist discourse of American exceptionalism, including its settler-colonial underpinnings. This move has opened possibilities for putting Asian American studies into greater dialogue with Native and indigenous studies, particularly around issues of Native Hawai'ian nationalism and sovereignty. Candace Fujikane (2005), for instance, calls for the need of Asian American studies to foreground Native nationalisms and the colonial system of the U.S. nation-state. She notes that the identity politics of Asian American studies seek equal representation and access to a colonial system that Native peoples view as illegitimate and strive to dismantle. Native nationalism instead revolves around land, self-government, and international status as a sovereign nation. As such, Native struggles cannot be reduced to the rights-based framework of racial minorities, which serves only to reify the settler colonial structures of the U.S. nation-state (Kauanui 2008a; Trask 2008). Fujikane further observes that the antiessentialist critique of American nationalism and Asian American cultural nationalism in Asian American studies cannot be extended to Native nationalisms, which are incommensurably different. According to Fujikane, such critiques ultimately undermine Native nationalism's struggle for self-determination and reinscribe settler colonial claims.

In sum, nationalism has been central to the intellectual and political concerns of Asian American studies, shaping its overall development and trajectory. As a keyword, nationalism spotlights the intellectual richness and complexity of Asian American studies, manifested in its innovative interventions as well as productive tensions that have allowed the field to remain relevant and vital.

46

Orientalism

Sylvia Shin Huey Chong

Had the activists of the late 1960s christened themselves "Orientals" instead of "Asian Americans," we might be calling this volume "Keywords in Oriental American Studies." This alternate history is not so unlikely, for both terms expressed a similar desire for a pan-Asian coalition, and both were more inclusive than the skin-color-based calls for "yellow" or "brown" power. One of the first Asian American studies classes taught by Yuji Ichioka at UCLA in 1969 was entitled "Orientals in America," and the UCLA student group Sansei Concern initially changed its name to Oriental Concern in 1968 to accommodate more ethnic groups (Ichioka 2000, 33; Y. Espiritu 1992, 32–33). Like the reclamation of the word "queer" in the 1990s, the term "Oriental" had the potential to confront a history of exclusion, explusion, and discrimination by bringing together and politicizing precisely those groups it had deemed "other" in the past.

However, even before Edward Said's landmark work *Orientalism* (1978), activists felt that "Oriental" simply carried too much negative historical baggage for them to resignify. The "Orient" only existed as a figment of the European imagination, lumping together disparate peoples from Asia and Africa into an undifferentiated mass of colonial subjects, slaves, servants, and unwanted immigrants. "Orientals" were Suzie Wongs, Charlie Chans, and Fu Manchus—fictional stereotypes connoting exoticism, foreignness, passivity, and obsolesence—while "Asian Americans" were figures like

Yuri Kochiyama, Richard Aoki, Philip Vera Cruz, and Ling-Chi Wang—real people representing the heterogeneity of Asian American communities, causes, and activities. Thus, when Said described Orientalism as "a Western style for dominating, restructuring, and having authority over the Orient" (1978, 3), his term had great resonance with Asian Americans who were themselves contesting the domination and restructuring of Asians in America. As a critique of the racial ideology behind European colonialism, *Orientalism* appeared at the end of a massive era of decolonization that also fed into the energies of the Asian American movement—recall that the student strikes at UC Berkeley and San Francisco State that helped establish Asian American curricula were called for by the Third World Liberation Front, and that anti–Vietnam War protests also contributed to the consciousness raising of early Asian American activists. Thus, although Said never addressed the experiences of Asian Americans, or even the racial ideology of the U.S., he seemed to be speaking to the same concerns that birthed the Asian American movement.

Despite this resonance, Said's *Orientalism* remained somewhat peripheral to the development of Asian American studies as an academic discipline. Although *Orientalism* became a founding text of postcolonial studies, especially as a model for politicizing literary studies alongside broader investigations of the history and dynamics of imperial cultures, it has found less traction within Asian American studies, especially as Asian American literature focused on excavating an alternate canon and Asian American history delved into forgotten peoples and movements left out of narratives of the United States. Because Orientalism seems to name a racial ideology imposed from the outside (ostensibly the "West," or the "Occident"), studies of Orientalism focus more on issues of racist representation than those of ethnic self-expression and agency (Lye 2008, 96). Thus, when invoked, Orientalism in Asian American studies often stands as a synonym for "racism," especially those forms that focus on making-exotic or making-other. According to this usage, what is Orientalist about American racism is often its denial of Asian American assimilation or hybridity (another key term from postcolonial studies), casting Asians as "forever foreigners" indelibly marked with their racial origins elsewhere. This meaning has been compounded by the fact that some of the "Orientalists" Said targeted were scholars of Asia and Africa, often based in area studies departments like East Asian or Middle East and South Asian studies and employed to produce "useful" knowledge for guiding military or foreign policy in those regions. As Asian American studies found a home in the academy, it has often taken the opposite route, eschewing area studies and aligning either with American studies and English departments, or in coalitions with African American, Latino/a, and Native American studies under the umbrella of ethnic studies.

While these have been useful lines of argument, this collapse of Orientalism into xenophobic racism ignores the useful Foucauldian aspects of Said's original concept, which outlined a discursive realm that was both productive as well as repressive. In other words, Orientalism was powerful not simply as a way of dominating the Orient: it also created the Orient (and Orientals) as objects of knowledge and representation, whether in sympathy or with hostility. This was the key insight that allowed Said to link poetry with anthropology, fiction with science—these were not separate discourses, but related ideologies that constructed racial subjects both rhetorically and epistemologically. Henry Yu's work *Thinking Orientals* (2002) illustrates this more complex deployment of Orientalism within Asian American studies, combining an intellectual history of this particular racial ideology along with an account of how early Asian American sociologists used that ideology to make themselves and their communities legible as racial subjects.

Moreover, the impulse to refute the "foreignness" of Asian Americans also contradicts the transnational dimension of Asian American studies, which has recently become a larger line of inquiry. Scholars have defined the uniqueness of American Orientalism as the doubling or splitting of the Orient into both an inside, represented by the Asian American "foreigner-within" who becomes an integral part of the American racial order, and an outside, represented by those Asian nations whose military, economic, and diplomatic interactions with the U.S. loom large over the course of the long American Century (Ngai 2000; L. Lowe 1991; L. Lowe 1996; Palumbo-Liu 1999; Lye 2004). Thus, unlike the classic model of colonialism in which colony and metropole remain separated geographically and politically, Asian Americans in American Orientalism infiltrate the center of the empire. Furthermore, scholars focusing on Asian America as a transnational or diasporic configuration have challenged the assumption that Asian American immigrants always desire assimilation and sever ties to their countries of origin (Shukla 2003; Hsu 2000; Azuma 2005; Shibusawa 2006; Duong 2012). These scholars, often working with non-English-language archives and sources, do not start from the Americanness of Asian America as a way to refute American Orientalism. Instead, they maintain the otherness of these Asian American diasporas from the U.S. nation-state as a form of critical distance, but one that does not collapse into the romantic projections of Orientalist otherness.

Unlike its European counterpart, American Orientalism has drawn its vocabulary more from mass media and popular culture than from high art and literature, as is befitting the nation that gave birth to Kodak, Hollywood, Disney, and CNN. Accordingly, many of the investigations of American Orientalism have been based more in media and cultural studies than in literary studies, mirroring the way Said himself turned to analyzing mass media when understanding contemporary Orientalism in his *Covering Islam* (Said 1981; Robert Lee 1999; A. Lee 2001; Capino 2010; Shimizu 2007; Delmendo 2004; Davé, Nishime, and Oren 2005). Among these cultural studies approaches to American Orientalism has been a renewed interest in what I call "commodity Orientalism," or the history of trade in Orientalist consumer goods that has accompanied or even anticipated the movement of Oriental peoples into the United States (Tchen 1999; Yoshihara 2003; Josephine Lee 2010; Tu 2010). Uncannily echoing the complaints of Asian American students that "Orientals are rugs, not people" (Robert Lee 1999, ix), this line of work traces the association of rugs, tea, porcelain, and silk *with* people, but not just to dispute the objectification of Asian Americans. From the early American trade with China that made the fortune of John Astor in the early 19th century to the craze in "Japanese taste" around the time of the Russo-Japanese War (1904–1905), commodity Orientalism frames the movement of goods not only within a symbolic system but also a materialist economy that mirrors the circulation of laborers. At times, Asian American subjects may even twist commodity Orientalism to their advantage, marketing their goods or products as exotic in an act of "self-Orientalization." For example, Chinese American restaurateurs have been perfecting this art form for over a century, consciously shaping their menus and décor into a Orientalist fantasy for the enjoyment of their non-Chinese customers (Chow 2005; Hsu 2008).

Some recent versions of commodity Orientalism may involve intangible goods such as the popularity of yoga, Buddhism, or the martial arts, sometimes led by Asians or Asian Americans like D. T. Suzuki or Deepak Chopra, but more often enabling non-Asians to take on the role of Oriental master or teacher in these exchanges (Iwamura 2010). Here, an experience of "becoming-Oriental," rather than an object imbued with Oriental culture, is what is being commodified, enabling non-Asian consumers access to an idealized realm of spirituality, authenticity, or cultural otherness that some may view as a form of racial minstrelsy. Another variant known as techno-Orientalism has likewise transformed the process of assigning cultural and/or racial meaning to commodities. This term, coined within East Asian studies and anthropology (Morley and Robins 1995), refers to high-tech commodities that seem devoid of the "Oriental" cultural markers that accompanied the earlier rugs and teacups: Toyota vehicles, Sony Walkmen, Samsung cell phones, Nintendo gamesets, etc. While these products seem to be neutral, even culturally "universal" objects, they are nonetheless racialized as markers of Oriental technological advancement or economic domination. Techno-Orientalism accompanied the rise of Asian economic powers like Japan and South Korea, which aroused anxiety both in the sphere of international trade and also in domestic race relations, most tragically in the killing of Chinese American engineer Vincent Chin in Detroit, Michigan, in 1982 in the midst of a racial panic within the American auto industry. Asian Americanists have begun to take more interest in techno-Orientalism, examining its effects in the popularization of anime, K-pop, video games, and cyberpunk culture (Nakamura 2002; Nguyen and Tu 2007; Tu and Nelson 2001; Chun and Joyrich 2009; J. Park 2010).

Asian American studies has also taken the lead in investigations of America's imperial legacies at large. After all, Rudyard Kipling may have been known as a chronicler of the British empire, but his poem "The White Man's Burden" (1899) was about the American colonization of the Philippines. Here, Asian American studies does not simply replicate postcolonial studies, but produces an alternate history of American imperialism, as seen in the colonial occupations of the Philippines and Japan, neocolonial relations with Taiwan, South Korea, and Vietnam, and the continued colonization of Hawai'i, Guam, Saipan, and American Samoa (Rafael 2000; Jodi Kim 2010; Kauanui 2008b). In some of this work, Asian Americans are not always aligned with the colonized, but sometimes collaborate with or take on the role of imperialists, as in critiques of settler colonialism in Hawai'i or Asian American conservatives (Fujikane and Okamura 2008; Camacho and Shigematsu 2010; Prashad 2005) These critical, transnational investigations of American Orientalism not only reanimate the Third World internationalism of the Asian American movement, but also break new ground in critical ethnic studies by showing racialization as a complex and continuing process. One outgrowth of this new use of American Orientalism has been the linking of Arab, Middle Eastern, and Muslim Americans with Asian Americans, especially as the ongoing War on Terror intensifies the racialization of "brownness" across all of Asia and beyond (McAlister 2001; Volpp 2002; J. Kang 2002; Bayoumi 2009; Prashad 2008; Puar 2007; Rana 2011). Another development has been the investigation of Afro-Asian connections both internationally as well as within the U.S., connecting the larger realm of Said's Orient with post-Bandung national alignments as well as a politically productive African American Orientalism (Prashad 2001; Steen 2006; Mullen 2004; Deutsch 2001; Ongiri 2002). These two trends are an apt tribute to Said's original formulation of Orientalism, reuniting the black, brown, and yellow inhabitants of that imaginary geography into reinvigorated political coalitions, and allowing the Orient to write its own future.

47

Performance
Josephine Lee

"Performance" can mean the everyday accomplishment of a task or function, or acting in special contexts such as plays, music, or sports. The first meaning links "performance" to the fulfillment of social roles; in both cases, instances of "performance" reference and reiterate the conventions of meaning that define communities, societies, or nations ("as American as [eating] apple pie"). Scholars have adopted the term "performative" (derived from language philosopher J. L. Austin's "performative utterance" in *How to Do Things with Words* [1962]) to good effect in analyzing the everyday enactments that constitute aspects of identity such as gender, sexuality, class, and race (Butler 1988; Parker and Sedgwick 1995). These understandings of "performance" and its variants are tied to what Erving Goffman (1959) called the "presentation of self": how words and actions manifest human signification, relationship, status, and power.

The more specific case of theatrical performance is never far from these usages. Different attitudes toward theater, evidenced by those who applaud actors for their virtuosity or those who react with more puritanical suspicion, engage theater's basic tensions between actor and character, action and interpretation, and private motivation and public show. That Asian American studies and other studies of race and ethnicity frequently use "performance," as well as other stage terms such as "acting," "mask," "role," or "character," suggests similarly dramatic tensions in offstage life.

Many instances of Asian American "performance" bring up concerns about Asian American performance as a kind of "acting" that is artificial, excessive, or inappropriate. As Henry Yu's *Thinking Orientals* (2001) points out, in the first half of the twentieth century sociologists from the University of Chicago noted how Chinese and Japanese Americans successfully executed nuanced performances of American language and behavior; however, many felt that physical differences prevented them from being seen as fully American. In Robert Park's assessment, the successful assimilation of Japanese Americans was compromised by certain bodily attributes—facial features, skin color, or stature and build.

> The fact that the Japanese bears in his features a distinctive racial hallmark, that he wears, so to speak, a uniform, classifies him. He cannot become a mere individual, indistinguishable in the cosmopolitan mass of the populations, as is true, for example, of the Irish and, to a lesser extent, of some of the other immigrant races. The Japanese like the Negro is condemned to remain among us an abstract symbol, and a symbol not merely of his own race, but of the Orient and of the vague, ill-defined menace we sometimes refer to as the "yellow peril." (1914, 611)

The stigma of the racial "uniform" undoes the theory that racial performance is only a matter of cultural behavior. Race continues to be tied up with perceptions of intrinsic, even essential bodily difference. For Asian Americans, even the most successful demonstration of American culture or citizenship never affirms their identity as truly American; since they are also wearing a "racial uniform," their assimilation is seen as only artifice, a form of false acting that belies their true nature.

These assessments of Asian American performance were manifested in how Lieutenant General John De-Witt, commanding general of the Western Defense Command, justified the internment of Japanese Americans. DeWitt posited that "[t]he Japanese race is an enemy race" and "while many second and third generation Japanese born on United States soil, possessed of United States citizenship, have become 'Americanized,' the racial strains are undiluted." These "racial strains" made all Japanese Americans along the West Coast "potential enemies" whose very lack of military action could be interpreted as duplicitous behavior: "The very fact that no sabotage has taken place to date is a disturbing and confirming indication that such action will be taken" (Commission 1997, 7). Given these suspicions of Japanese American performance, even the pitch-perfect enactment of American activities such as playing baseball, saying the Pledge of Allegiance, or serving in the U.S. military—strikingly documented in internment camp photographs by Dorothea Lange, Ansel Adams, and others—could not render them trustworthy.

Fundamental assumptions that Asian Americans could never truly be American—that their "racial uniform" marked them as perpetually "Asian" and therefore foreign—cast doubts on acts of speech, action, labor, and loyalty. As scholarship on the tropes of "betrayal" (Bow 2001), "impersonation" (T. Chen 2005), or "spectacle" (Roxworthy 2008) details, the Asian American performance of what is seen as white American cultural identity has long been viewed as contradictory; no matter how skilled the Asian American actor, this performance is never taken for granted as fitting or felicitous. The fear of being targeted as "un-American" and singled out as the enemy might lead the Japanese American store owner to hang a sign declaring "I am an American" in his window; in the post-9/11 era, it might prompt turbaned Sikhs to wave the American flag. Yet

PERFORMANCE JOSEPHINE LEE

often these anxiously repetitive acts of American belonging only intensify the suspicion with which such performances are regarded. Even Asian Americans who inhabit the privileged spaces of the model minority in terms of professional or class status—such as Wen Ho Lee—receive severe reminders that their "American" performances may be questioned.

This racial typecasting is consistent with the long history of imagining an "Orient" as, to borrow from Edward Said, "a theatrical stage affixed to Europe." If the Orient was indeed the "stage on which the whole East is confined," then Asian Americans, like other "Orientals," became icons, "figures whose role it is to represent the larger whole from which they emanate" (1978, 63). What they represented, moreover, transformed Asia into the antithesis of the West: exotic, mysterious, uncivilized, and irrational. This history involved a host of familiar characterizations such as the despotic emperor or the hapless maiden that today are reincarnated in the continued popularity of Puccini's *Madame Butterfly* and the Asian villains of television, movies, and video games.

In the twentieth century, a fascination with imagining Asians as exotic and decorative gave way to more fearful representations of immigrants or of Japanese imperial power. In contrast to the "queer and quaint" orientals appearing in nineteenth-century works such as Gilbert and Sullivan's *The Mikado*, these more violent and degraded images of stage, film, television, and advertising imagined Japanese military power as well as Asian immigrant labor in the form of a "yellow peril" threatening American foreign interests, labor, and domesticity. These stereotypes exaggerated the "racial uniform" of the Asian body, fixating on racial signifiers such as skin color, eye shape, and teeth, and magnifying perceptions of physical difference with spectacular clothing, hair, and verbal and gestural mannerisms. The simplicity of these stereotypes heightened their power and obscured the complicated anxieties about cultural contact, modernity, capitalism, and gender and sexuality that undergirded them. Whether appearing in comedies such as Bret Harte and Mark Twain's stage adaptation of *Ah Sin* (1876) or melodramatic propaganda such as Henry Grimm's *The Chinese Must Go* (1879), these caricatures, most often played by white actors in yellowface, set the stage for the racial typecasting of Asian Americans as perpetual foreigners and unassimilable aliens.

Asian and Asian American performers in the United States took the stage amid these different modes of stereotyping. The 1834 display of the "Chinese Lady" Afong Moy in New York attracted attention for her "monstrous small" feet as well as for her "indigenous" dress. Later reports of a "Chinese Lady" (whether Moy or another woman is uncertain) advertised her as talking and counting in Chinese and eating with chopsticks, which "render[ed] the exhibition highly interesting to lovers of curiosities" (Tchen 2001, 104). Profitable enterprises such as Phineas T. Barnum's 1850 "Chinese Museum" featured a "Living Chinese Family" that included "Miss Pwan-Yekoo, the Chinese Belle," who fascinated white audiences: "She is so pretty, so arch, so lively, and so graceful, while her minute feet are wondrous!" (Tchen 2001, 118). This characteristic staging designated parts and actions of the Asian body as different and strange; it thus greatly limited the expressive potential of Asian American performance and undermined the Asian American performer. In both nineteenth-century (such as Chinese and Japanese acrobatic troupes or the conjoined twins Chang and Eng Bunker) and more contemporary performances (martial arts films that link feats of skill and strength with Asian bodies), Asian and Asian American bodies are displayed as curiosities in which exotic and extraordinary physical attributes define racial difference, even freakishness.

Richard Schechner's *Performance Studies* makes a distinction between "being," "doing," and "performing," where "being" is "existence itself," "doing" is "the activity of all that exists," and "performing" means "showing doing": "pointing to, underlining, and displaying doing" (2002, 22). Objectifying Asian bodies in displays at various fairs or exhibitions turns them into objects of interest simply for "being" rather than "performing"; what these performers do is framed as natural behavior rather than the achievement of acting or art. To counter this tendency, Asian American artists draw attention to the inner lives of performers as well as the contexts and constraints for performance. For instance, plays such as Philip Kan Gotanda's *Yankee Dawg You Die* (1988) and Sun Mee Chomet's *Asiamnesia* (2008) focus on the plight of Asian and Asian American actors working in a racist industry; each references a history of Asian Americans in theater and film as well as allows actors to display a full range of expressive abilities. Asian American solo performers such as Jude Narita, Dan Kwong, Denise Uyehara, and Zaraawar Mistry also push the limits of what it means for Asian Americans to perform multiple characterizations and styles of acting. Innovative opportunities for Asian American performance have also been provided by Asian American theater companies such as East West Players, the National Asian American Theatre Company, and Mu Performing Arts, as well as by new venues in theater, film, television, and the internet. Asian American studies is building a significant body of scholarship (Kondo 1997; Josephine Lee 1997; Shimakawa 2002; Esther Lee 2006; Yoshihara 2007; Gonzalves 2010; Y. Wong 2010; Srinivasan 2011; Burns 2012) that looks particularly at Asian Americans in theater, dance, music, and other performing arts, thus redefining Asian American performance in terms that are, if not epistemologically or politically radical, at the very least more expansive.

There are thus many examples of the complexities and possibilities of Asian American performance. These might indeed be traced through looking at a play such as David Henry Hwang's Tony Award–winning *M. Butterfly* (1988). *M. Butterfly* deftly deconstructs the connected ideologies of imperialism, racism, gender, and capitalism that inform stereotypes such as the exotic "butterfly," and stages its leading Asian character, Song Liling, as a consummate performer. But because the history of Asian American performance lies in large part in "embodied memory," the "ephemeral, nonreproducible knowledge" of what Diana Taylor calls the "repertoire" (2003, 20), I would like to note as my final example an instance of Asian American performance—glimpsed momentarily in the vast archives of Shakespearean performance—that moves beyond both script and expectation.

The title role of *Hamlet*, directed by Stephen Kanee for the 1978–1979 season of Minneapolis's Guthrie Theatre, was played by Randall Duk Kim. Kim, of course, is better known to Asian American performance scholars for his roles in the 1972 Off-Broadway production of Frank Chin's *Chickencoop Chinaman* and the 2002 Broadway cast of David Henry Hwang's repurposed *Flower Drum Song*, and to more general audiences for roles in films such as *The Matrix: Reloaded* and *Kung Fu Panda*. That Kim's now long-past Guthrie performance as Hamlet did not inspire a "colorblind" reaction is evidenced by a review by David George for *Shakespeare Quarterly*. George described a sense of incongruity, especially "in the bedroom scene when this Oriental Hamlet confronted his British-speaking mother" (1979, 219). But he does not peg Kim as a novelty act. Rather, George praised "the superior acting of Duk Kim and the peculiar odds against this was achieved," noting as problems in the production not Kim's "racial uniform" but rather the other, non-Asian actors: "There were a few actors against whom Duk Kim could play, but most of them gave him no chance" (1979, 220). In particular he praised Kim's "commanding diction" ("a pure, sculpted diction, entirely American") and "lithe movements"—such as "utterly natural relaxing and tensing"—and pronounced him "a deeply committed and reverent Shakespearean performer," quoting his previous *Hamlet* director Wallace Chappell's statement that Kim is "one of the best actors in the country doing Shakespeare, if not in the English-speaking world" (1979, 219–21). Kim's successes on the stage—including many leading roles at the American Place Theatre in Spring Green, Wisconsin, (which he, along with Anne Occhiogrosso and Chuck Bright, helped found) as well as one-man shows about Mark Twain, Edgar Allan Poe, and Walt Whitman—are unfortunately atypical for earlier generations of Asian American actors. Yet it is worth noting how his successful transformations into Hamlet's melancholy Dane and other characters insist on another distinctive idea of Asian American performance: as a dynamic and complex set of possibilities that might be brought to life in one person.

48

Politics
Janelle Wong

"Politics" is a term that is used broadly in Asian American studies. Scholars might refer to cultural politics or the politics of identity (Takagi 1994; Maira 2000; L. Lowe 1996), or they might refer to the political representation (J. Lai 2011; Lai and Geron 2006; W. Tam 1995) and participation of Asian Americans in civic, governmental, and institutional settings (Cain, Kiewiet, and Uhlaner 1991; Nakanishi 1991; Ong and Nakanishi 1996; Lien 1997; Janelle Wong et al. 2011). In part, the use of the term depends on the discipline, but for all, the term "politics" refers to processes or sites in which Asian American power is constructed, defined, negotiated, and deployed. That power may be in the form of and shaped by identity and culture, relations with dominant or marginalized groups, or civic and governmental influence.

In the emerging field of Asian American politics, politics is deeply associated with formal and informal political power, particularly though political participation and political representation. In the late 1960s, at the height of the civil rights movement and amid widespread demands for minority political empowerment, it was widely assumed that Asian Americans were too busy striving to achieve the American Dream to be concerned with political power. Instead, the group was praised as a model minority by some conservatives for having "survived adversity and advanced because of their emphasis on education and family values, their community cohesion, and other aspects of their cultural heritage" (Omatsu 2003, 158). A correlate of this characterization was a sharp contrast with Black Americans. Asian Americans flourished, the stereotype implied, by prioritizing educational and family values over political protest and explicit demands for policies designed to mitigate racial discrimination and inequality (c.f. C. Kim 2000). As the model minority stereotype embedded itself in the American conscious, it fostered the notion that, unlike other racially marginalized groups, Asian Americans' educational achievement and strong family values would ensure their success without political activism. The decades that followed were marked by unprecedented migration from Asia to the U.S., but along with the fact that they remained a relatively small, majority-foreign-born group with low rates of voting participation compared to other groups, the model minority stereotype served to reinforce the notion that Asian Americans were marginal to the U.S. political process.

Around the time of the 2012 presidential campaign, however, the image of Asian Americans in U.S. politics was beginning to change. Unlike in the past, Asian Americans were being recognized as a potential political force. In late October 2012, for example, *National Journal* ran a story with the headline "The Power of the Asian-American Vote Is Growing—And It's Up for Grabs" (Goldmacher 2012).

Until the passage of the 1965 Voting Rights Act, most members of racial minority groups in the United States, including Asian Americans, were systematically denied the right to vote. As a predominantly immigrant group in the United States, enforcement of a 1790 law permitting only "free white men" to naturalize and become citizens denied the franchise to most Asian Americans until after World War II. In 1943, Chinese immigrants received the right to naturalize, in part because of pressure from China, a WWII ally. It was not until the

passage of the 1952 Immigration and Naturalization Act (McCarren-Walter) that all Asian American groups were allowed to become naturalized citizens.

Despite a long history of limited voting rights and stereotypes that paint the group as apolitical, Asian Americans have sought to make their voices heard in U.S. politics outside of the ballot box. In 1886, during the era of Chinese exclusion, a Chinese petitioner brought a case all the way to the Supreme Court by challenging, under the 14th Amendment's equal protection clause, a law requiring wood laundry facilities in San Francisco to obtain special permits to operate. Don Nakanishi and James Lai note that this case, *Yick Wo v. Hopkins*, "demonstrates that early Asians in America were politically aware despite their lack of basic constitutional rights" (2003, 20). Citing Japanese American participation in farmworkers' strikes in Oxnard, California, in 1903 and the activism of Filipino American farmworkers in California's Central Valley in the 1930s, labor movement scholar Kent Wong suggests that "the strong tradition of Asian Pacific labor activism stands in sharp contrast to the widespread myths that Asians are docile, individualistic, and incapable of being organized, or organizing themselves (2003, 422).

Since the passage of the 1965 Voting Rights Act, voting requirements determined to be racially discriminatory have been outlawed, and Asian American voting participation has increased dramatically. Asian Americans continue to be underrepresented at the polls, however. The most recent data available on voter turnout show that 57% of adult citizen Asian Americans report turning out in the 2008 presidential election, compared to about 75% of White and Black adult citizens (File and Crissey 2012). According to government data, Asian American voting rates did not change significantly between the 2008 and 2012 presidential elections. Asian Americans made up about 6% of the U.S. population in 2012, but only about 3% of the national electorate.

The gap in voting participation persists for several reasons. Eligibility requirements prevent many Asian Americans from voting. The vast majority, 75%, of Asian American adults are foreign born, and of this group, about 40% are not yet citizens and ineligible to vote. In addition, Asian Americans tend to be younger than other major segments of the U.S. population. While 79% of non-Hispanic Whites are over the age of 18 and therefore of voting age, this is true of 76% of Asian Americans. But Asian Americans are underrepresented even among those that that are eligible to vote. One important explanation for this is that Asian Americans are not mobilized to participate in politics at the same levels as other groups (Janelle Wong 2006). This is especially true in national elections.

Like Latinos, Asian Americans are underrepresented in key battleground states. A little less than 20% of Asian Americans live in states considered competitive presidential battlegrounds. In contrast, more than 30% of non-Hispanic Whites and Blacks live in battleground states. The overall Asian American population is fast growing in swing states like Nevada, Virginia, and North Carolina, but the group still makes up a relatively small proportion of eligible voters in these states—less than 5% of the eligible voters in 2012. In presidential elections, then, Asian Americans are less likely to be mobilized to vote by campaigns seeking to sway voters in key swing states. And the data reflect this. Data from the 2008 Collaborative Multiracial Post-election Study show that in 2008, even among registered voters, Asian Americans were five percentage points less likely to be contacted and mobilized to vote than their White and Black counterparts (Frasure et al. 2008). Further, Asian Americans still face barriers to voting in terms of

Asian-language speakers' access to translated voting materials (Springer 2012).

Since the late 1990s, Asian Americans have increasingly identified with the Democratic Party. However, even in 2012, a large proportion of Asian Americans were not attached to any party. Fully 51% identified as independent or did not think in terms of political party identification (Ramakrishnan and Lee 2012). This is a higher proportion of nonparty identifiers than in the general population. As such, Asian Americans are "up for grabs" by the two major parties, but also seen as a moving target in terms of mobilization. Because political parties and their associated campaigns deploy their resources strategically to target the voters most likely to support their candidates, they tend to target high-propensity voters with a long history of support for their party. In recent national elections, campaigns have been reluctant to target Asian Americans for mobilization, given their relatively recent entrance into the voting population and uncertain party loyalties. In state and local contexts, though, Asian Americans may be seen as a more desirable constituency (c.f. J. Lai 2010).

Outside of voting, Asian Americans are most likely to participate in politics by working with others in their communities to solve a community problem (Lien et al. 2004; Janelle Wong et al. 2011; see also Võ 2004). On the whole they work on political campaigns, contact government officials, and take part in political protests at about the same or slightly lower rates than most other racial groups. In the 1990s, some observers were convinced that Asian Americans would attain political power though campaign giving. Don Nakanishi suggests that in key political circles, Asian Americans were viewed as "a veritable mountain of gold for Democratic and Republican prospectors in California and across the nation" (1991, 33).

In fact, campaign giving by Asian Americans has been a fraught topic over the past two decades. In 1996, a small group of Asian Americans was accused of raising illegal funds for the Democratic National Committee and the Clinton reelection campaign. At the heart of the scandal were several Asian Americans charged with raising money from illegal foreign sources in Asia. The role of Asian Americans in American politics was deeply scrutinized as the national media covered investigations by the U.S. Justice Department, House, and Senate. Two fundraisers, Johnny Huang and Charlie Trie, eventually pled guilty to felony violations of federal election law, but the effects of the investigation were far more wide reaching. In 1997, a coalition of Asian American advocacy organizations, including the National Asian Pacific American Legal Consortium, the Organization of Chinese Americans, the Asian Pacific American Labor Alliance, the Korean American Coalition, and ten other groups and individuals filed a complaint with the U.S Commission on Civil Rights and called for a hearing to expose discriminatory aspects of the government's investigation of the scandal. Federal investigators, members of Congress, and the media consistently represented Asian Americans as a whole, not just the accused fundraisers, as perpetual foreigners and a "Yellow Peril," or foreign threat to the United States (c.f. L. Wang 1998; Taeku Lee 2000). In 2012, Taiwanese American John Liu, the first Asian American elected to citywide office in New York City, was involved in a scandal when his campaign treasurer was arrested for raising funds using the names of fake donors. John Y. Park, an advocate for the New York City Asian American community, voiced his concern that the media's focus on Liu's potential improprieties would lead to extra scrutiny of all Asian American donors and have a negative impact on political participation among Asian Americans more generally: "I worry about John Liu. . . . But I am more worried about how this will hurt Asian-Americans' political involvement and scare off contributors" (D. Chen 2012, A-24)

Despite racialized media attention to Asian Americans and their campaign giving since the mid-1990s, data from throughout the 2000s suggest that Asian Americans donate to campaigns at levels proportional to their population, even in high-density localities (Adams and Ren 2006; see also Cho 2002). They are no more likely to contribute funds to campaigns than are white Americans (Janelle Wong et al. 2011, 23). Perhaps because there are relatively few Asian American candidates, Asian American donors are more likely to give funds to non–Asian American candidates, but they strongly support Asian Americans if they do seek office. Asian American candidates, however, receive most of their funds from co-ethnics or other Asian Americans (Adams and Ren 2006).

Ben Adams and Ping Ren (2006) speculate that lack of financial support from non–Asian Americans may account in part for the small number of Asian Americans who have run for elected office successfully. In fact, historically, Asian Americans have been underrepresented in elected office. Although the Asian American population grew tremendously from 1978 to 2000, the number of Asian Americans holding state office increased from just 63 to 73 and the number holding federal office increased from just five to seven over that period (J. Lai et al. 2001). James Lai identifies several additional challenges facing Asian Americans seeking to win elected office, including the lack of concentrated residential populations combined with single-district elections, the limited number of Asian Americans in the candidate pipeline, the need for stronger political networks, entrenched political interests that resist Asian American newcomers, and the lack of an ideological platform that will attract both Asian Americans and other groups (2011, 57).

Over time, however, Asian Americans' descriptive representation has increased at every level of elected office. According to the Asian Pacific American Institute for Congressional Studies (APAICS), the number of Asian American candidates for federal office has been rising fast in recent years. In 2008, there were eight Asian Americans running for congressional office. Four years later, there were 30 bids by Asian Americans for congressional office. A record number of Asian Americans were elected to Congress in 2012. Asian Americans are less geographically concentrated than Blacks and Latinos in the United States. As a result, there are few places in the United States outside of Hawai'i that include a majority of Asian Americans. Although most Blacks and Latinos are elected from districts where minority group members are in the majority, Asian Americans tend to be elected by a coalition of voters, of which Asian Americans may be a plurality, or more often, a minority, of the winning coalition. For example, in 2009, Representative Judy Chu was first elected to Congress in a special election to represent California's 27th Congressional District, which was just over 62% Latino, nearly 20% Asian American, and 15% non-Hispanic white.

Asian Americans are also running outside of traditional Asian American gateway cities like Los Angeles and New York. James Lai makes a compelling argument that "for the first time in American politics, Asian American candidates in suburbs in the continental United States are winning, sustaining, and building on Asian American elected representation" (2011, 228). This is in part due to the fact that more than 50% of Asian Americans live in the suburbs and that the group makes up a critical mass, either a majority or plurality, in many small and medium-sized cities in an increasing range of places (J. Lai 2011, 18).

Outside of Hawai'i, which is not only majority Asian American but also has a long history of Asian Americans holding office, including the first woman of color ever elected to Congress, Rep. Patsy Mink (a Democrat, elected in 1964), most Asian Americans seeking office must be able to gain the votes of non–Asian Americans to win state or federal office. In fact, this has long been the case. The first Asian American elected to Congress, Dalip Singh Saund, was elected from a mostly white district in Southern California in 1956. Saund, an Indian American, was an early Asian American activist. As the leader of several ethnic advocacy organizations in the United States, he pressed for passage of the Luce-Cellar Act of 1946, which allowed Filipino and Indian immigrants to naturalize. Although Saund was a proponent of Indian American causes, he was also very active in local community organizations, such as the Boy Scouts and March of Dimes. As a result of his activism in local and national Democratic Party politics and a strong local campaign that emphasized his advocacy on farming issues, he was elected to Congress in an overwhelmingly white district. Other factors associated with Asian American electoral success at every level of government include support from Asian American community-based organizations and Asian American ethnic media sources.

Today, more than 4,000 Asian Americans hold elected and major appointed office at the local, state, and federal level in at least 39 different states (Nakanishi 2011, 2). Further, members of both major political parties have appointed Asian Americans to prominent political posts in the recent past.

Although some assume that Asian Americans, as a predominantly immigrant group, may be preoccupied with politics in their countries of origin at the expense of U.S. politics, in actuality a very small proportion (less than 5%) of any Asian American national origin group participates in politics related to the country of origin (Janelle Wong et al. 2011). Further, research suggests that those who do participate in politics related to the country of origin are also the most likely to participate in politics in the United States (c.f. Janelle Wong 2006, ch. 8). In other words, political activists in one context are likely to be activists in other contexts as well.

Given the tremendous diversity that characterizes the Asian American community, an enduring question in the field of Asian American politics is whether or not Asian Americans constitute a meaningful political category. While members of this diverse group do share common identities, experiences, and attitudes, a coherent political agenda is still developing.

Panethnic identity is more common among younger and second-generation Asian Americans, but it is still emerging. Data from the 2008 National Asian American Survey, a study conducted in eight languages that includes more than 5,000 Asian Americans show that about 20% of Asian Americans identify with a pan-Asian label such as "Asian American" or "Asian" (Ramakrishnan et al. 2008). Although Asian Americans are classified by the census as a distinct racial group, some might be surprised to learn that, in 2008, only 55% of Asian Americans believed that they shared a "common race." Even fewer, 37%, claimed that Asian Americans shared common political interests. Asian Americans are more likely to believe they share a common culture (64%). In 2012, responses to these questions about Asian American commonality were similar. Shared identity or feelings of commonality are only a partial basis for group coherence then.

A fairly large chunk of Asian Americans, including more than 15% of Chinese, Indians, Koreans, and Filipinos, reported experiences with racially motivated discrimination in a 2012 Pew survey. A a whole, 19% of Asian Americans said they had personally experienced racial discrimination Yet few Asian Americans, only 13%, said they saw racial discrimination as a "major" problem (Taylor et al. 2012). Other surveys show that while nearly one in five Asian Americans reports having experienced racial discrimination, all racial groups, including Asian Americans, believe Asian Americans face the least amount of discrimination of any group. Although experience with racial discrimination could serve as common ground for Asian Americans, if few Asian Americans currently believe it is a major problem then it is unlikely to serve as the basis for mass political action.

The immigrant experience touches the lives of most Asian Americans, directly or indirectly. Not only are most Asian Americans immigrants, but 48% of Chinese, 46% of Koreans, and 60% of Vietnamese reported in the 2010 Current Population Survey that they speak English less than very well (Taylor et al. 2012). Even 18% of the mostly U.S.-born Japanese American group report speaking English less than very well. Across all national origins, including Japanese American, and regardless of nativity, a majority say that they continue to maintain communication with family and friends in the country of origin. Immigration, then, will likely continue to be an important political touchstone for Asian Americans.

Asian Americans share distinct policy attitudes according to the 2012 National Asian American Survey (Ramakrishnan and Lee 2012). For example, the majority of most Asian American national-origin groups, including Chinese, Vietnamese, Indians, and Korean Americans, express stronger support for the universal health care than does the general public. Fifty-five percent of Asian Americans support health care reform under the Affordable Care Act passed by Congress and signed into law by President Barack Obama in 2010, compared to just 38% of Americans generally. Fully 60% of Asian Americans favor protecting environment over economic growth, compared to 40% of Americans generally.

It should be clear, then, that Asian Americans converge to some extent around experiences and attitudes. Yet these experiences and attitudes are not absolutely consistent across all national origin groups or individuals. Shared experiences and attitudes alone will not hold the Asian American community together. Organizations, advocacy groups, and community leaders provide the institutional support necessary to cultivate a sense of common political destiny.

Asian Americans represent an emerging political group, but one that also has a long history of activism in the United States. Low levels of Asian American political participation are primarily a function of eligibility and mobilization, rather than attitudes. And Asian American elected representation is growing as the group moves into new geographic and ideological territory.

49

Postcolonialism
Allan Punzalan Isaac

Emerging from literary studies, postcolonial criticism initially examined how the experience of, negotiation with, and resistance to formal colonialism have shaped national cultures and literatures emerging from the former British empire (Ashcroft 1989). The consideration of subjects and subjectivity impacted by imperial incursions and fantasies, as explored in Edward Said's *Orientalism* (1978), has resonance for multiple populations from Asia with varied colonial legacies that have come to enter the political coalition called Asian America. The postcolonial signals the colonial legacy as part of the cultural heterogeneity and hybridity lived by ethnic groups such as South Asians from the different parts of the British empire and Filipinos emerging from Spanish, Japanese, and U.S. occupations, as well as Koreans and Southeast Asians who have undergone palpable, and oftentimes devastating, U.S. and European military interventions (Gopinath 2005; L. Lowe 1996; Shankar and Srikanth 1998; Schlund-Vials 2012b). As Asian Americanists extend the field of study to the Americas as a hemispheric unit, the postcolonial approach also makes visible the geography of colonialism and ways by which Asians have entered the Americas from other parts of Latin America and the Caribbean (M. Jung 2006; Yun 2008; Lee-Loy 2010; Khan 2004; López 2013; L. Lowe 2006). Decentering North America as the privileged site and voluntary immigration as the dominant trope for Asian American studies, the postcolonial maps the uneven flows of capital, goods, cultures, fantasies, and displacement of peoples across the continents. Thus, postcolonialism is intimately tied to concepts of diaspora, transnationalism, migration, and globalization.

The prefix "post" in postcolonialism does not necessarily mark the historical era after colonialism, but rather its aftermath and how formal colonialism and imperial state power are reconfigured and continue to structure lives and cultures. The approach acknowledges the legacies of ever-shifting borders to blur the divide between home(land) and abroad, foreign and domestic, and center and periphery. In the U.S. context, 1898 signified a dramatic shift in U.S. expansion beyond the continent by government annexation of Hawai'i and incorporation of former Spanish insular possessions such as Guam, the Philippines, and Puerto Rico. Pioneering scholarly collections that facilitated links among postcolonial, American, and Asian American studies include Amy Kaplan and Donald Pease's *Cultures of United States Imperialism* (1993), which opened avenues to connect diverse U.S. American imperial projects along the country's borders and among its overseas island possessions, and Vicente Rafael's *Discrepant Histories: Translocal Essays on Filipino Cultures* (1995), which collected early works of scholars like Oscar Campomanes, Martin Manalansan, and Michael Salman working at the nexus of Philippine, U.S. American, and Filipino American studies to navigate the shared borders of the U.S. and the Philippine archipelago.

Postcolonial theory wielded by Asian American literary critics has radically destabilized the nation-oriented politics that have historically anchored Asian American studies (Chuh 2003). Nguyen and Chen (2000) point to how postcolonial critique's attention to diasporic or homeland issues means that racial identity "is not necessarily a prime site of political and cultural mobilization" as in the early Asian American movement. The

entry of several Asian American ethnic groups shaped variously by colonialism including Indians, Pakistanis, Bangladeshis, Vietnamese, Hmong, Cambodians, Laotians, and Filipinos, among others, as well as Asian groups from the Caribbean, Hawai'i, and the Pacific Islands, has given rise to diverse histories of labor migration, refugeeism, and militarization. Some critics maintain that the postcolonial draws attention away from critical work on social and political inequality based on race, gender, class, and ethnicity in U.S. society. Sau-ling Wong has argued how "denationalized" (diasporic) and domestic Asian subjectivities in the U.S. are not logical evolutions of each other, but coexist as "modes rather than phases of Asian American subjectivity" (1995, 17). King-Kok Cheung in "Re-viewing Asian American Literary Studies" proposes that critics "assert and manifest the historical and cultural presence of Asians in North America and use our transnational consciousness to critique the polity, whether of an Asian country, Canada, the United States, or Asian America" (1997, 9).

Postcolonial criticism complicates voluntary migration as a dominant trope in Asian American and American studies to uncover varied racial histories and hierarchies when applied to U.S. imperial possessions. For example, the ambivalent "inclusion" of Filipinos into the U.S. polity as American "nationals" (like Puerto Ricans, Samoans, Guamanians, and U.S. Virgin Islanders at different historical junctures) reveals the contradictions in a political belonging founded on forced membership and social and political domination (A. Isaac 2006). The theoretical approaches issuing from postcolonial and ethnic studies together also raise the complicity of some Asian American political practices with U.S. imperial projects in relation to Native peoples across the Americas and the Pacific Islands. The Asian American movement has moved toward expanding civil rights for Asian-descent peoples, a double-edged political project that might in practice undermine the sovereignty of Native peoples (Fujikane and Okamura 2008; Najita 2006). Asian American postcolonial critique decouples national identity from the state, underscoring issues such as imperial interventions and forced incorporation of peoples and spaces by tracing the cultural, economic, and political continuities between older and more recent migrations and displacements, and by understanding how capital has shifted the terms of political and cultural domination (Choy 2003; Chuh 2003; Bascara 2006; See 2009).

Postcolonial critique's transnational consciousness and critique of imperial state power, while more pronounced with the changes in Asian American demographics since the 1960s and 1970s, arguably has roots in the early Asian American movement with its close alliance with other people of color in the U.S. and with Third World movements. Early cultural nationalism rejected the perpetual-foreigner condition to stake a claim to American belonging in historical, political, and cultural terms; at the same time, the movement's global politics vehemently opposed imperial wars in Southeast Asia and supported self-determination in the decolonizing Third World. The more recent examination of different colonial histories of Asian ethnic groups arriving on American shores emerges from this transnational historical awareness to complicate Asian American politics and culture. Articulating vexed political and cultural borders that map emergent postnational epistemologies, Asian American postcolonial criticism makes manifest reconfigurations and structures of imperial state power that reinstate the binary of the nation and its others (Chuh 2003).

50

Queer
Martin F. Manalansan IV

"Queer" has become a ubiquitous term in quotidian, scholarly, mass media, and political discourses to characterize and name things, relationships, situations, practices, and bodies from TV shows such as *Queer Eye for the Straight Guy* to academic endeavors such as queer studies. Its pervasiveness has resulted in messy contexts and situations as it is deployed in multiple and oftentimes contradictory ways. In its various uses, "queer" is and can be a vernacular word, a political idiom, and an academic field of study. The crux of the contentious nature of "queer" is whether the right question is "what is queer?" or "what does 'queer' do?" Is "queer" about ontology, identity, and being, or is it about processes, mechanics, and/or frameworks of analysis? "Queer" is necessarily about both aspects or dimensions.

In everyday usage, "queer" was and is still used as an umbrella term that designates identities, behaviors, and bodies as nonconforming to specific notions of the normal. In more scholarly deployments, "queer" has become a vantage, an approach, and a method that has been productively used to engage with virtually all kinds of phenomena from 17th-century romantic relationships to present-day human-animal relations. While "queer" has had a strong sexual connotation, it is no longer tethered to a monolithic notion of the sexual as it is applied intersectionally to other realms such as race, class, and gender. In other words, "queer" resists the easy partitioning or demarcation of discrete categories. For example, sexuality or, more specifically, the processes of sexualization (how things get sexualized) can occur coextensively if not jointly with operations of racialization, class formation, and gendering.

"Queer," as a word, has discrepant origins, meanings, and circuits of circulations. During its early use in the 17th century, it was a label for things, people, and situations that were considered renegade, wayward, strange, counterfeit, and/or perverted. By the beginning of the 20th century, with the consolidation of sexual orientation as a cultural identity marker, "queer" had become a derogatory stand-in for "homosexual" and gender insubordination.

The dramatic shift of "queer" as a concept and identity category from its rather denigrating semantic beginnings to a more vigilant and positive frame occurred during the 1980s. During this period, "queer" underwent a political and cultural "makeover." Gay and lesbian activists and organizations such as Queer Nation recuperated, appropriated, and resignified "queer" in a way that retained its nonnormative assignation and politically deployed it against the violent homophobia of the state and the private sector. By so doing, these social agents were responsible for the resurgence of a term that was seen as archaic and derogatory and transformed it into an idiom that engaged with and expressed the prevailing conditions of the times.

From a theoretical point of view, this lexical and structural transformation was aided and abetted by scholarly sources as well as events of the late 20th century. Michel Foucault was perhaps most influential in inspiring several of the crucial scholarly contributions. He vociferously articulated the cultural and historical dimensions of sexuality and was partly responsible for inciting scholarly attempts to denaturalize sexuality and gender.

Researchers in the social sciences, particularly anthropology, conducted cross-cultural mappings of "homosexual" phenomena through ethnographic studies of various practices, institutions, and bodies that exceeded the parameters of Western notions of sexual orientation. Activists, scholars, and the general public slowly came to realize the parochial and narrow cultural contexts of sexual orientation and identity categories such as gay and lesbian vis-à-vis those of the non-West. Operating in parallel realms, feminist theory and Third World and women-of-color feminism in particular were responsible for a trenchant critique of the universalization and naturalization of the category "woman" and provided situated understandings of racialized and minoritized women. Instead of a global womanhood, Third World and women-of-color feminism suggested multiple contexts and strategies for understanding women's issues. As such, their ideas complemented if not helped animate the thinking around "queer."

Gay and lesbian studies emerged in the 1980s as a product of the gay/lesbian and feminist activisms and early studies on homosexuality of the 1970s. There was consensus among scholars during this period regarding the detachment of sexuality and gender from their natural and biological roots and from their dependence on Euro-American categories and cultural mores. While visibility and rights-based activism were at the core of some of their activities, a significant number of scholars and activists realized, confronted, and engaged with the limitations of identity politics and the struggles for rights. They questioned: Rights for whom? Whose identity?

Part of the impetus for the transformation of "queer" came from activities (policy oriented, scholarly focused, and/or activist based) around the AIDS pandemic. The pandemic was not only a medical crisis but also a major semantic/semiotic one. Meanings of long-held categories such as homosexual, heterosexual, gay, and straight were put into question as policy makers, epidemiologists, AIDS prevention educators/ community outreach workers, and social workers were confronted with the discrepancy between behavior and available identity categories. People who were seen to be "practicing" homosexual acts or "exhibiting" homosexual behavior were not identifying accordingly. The discordance between identity and behavior was further complicated in the late 1980s by the population shift in the pandemic with the influx of AIDS cases who were nonwhite, nonmainstream, and mostly from immigrant and/or racialized communities. This shift created a muddled and confused atmosphere, dramatically troubling the terrains of sexual orientation and gender as designations such as gay, straight, male, or female often did not neatly adhere to either bodies or practices. This became a source of contention as political efforts around the pandemic, particularly service delivery and activism, were anchored around gay and lesbian political and social visibility and empowerment.

For example, AIDS service agencies found that in immigrant communities as well as communities of color, services and materials with the words "gay" and "lesbian" were met with resistance if not total rejection. While public health officials pointed to "traditional values" they deemed always already "premodern" and homophobic as the primary causes for these kinds of barriers to service delivery, more nuanced analyses by ethnographers, historians, and other humanistic scholars have demonstrated that gay and lesbian identity categories often do not translate and therefore AIDS service and prevention education work are not always effectively framed around such categories. By the 1990s, we see many of these agencies looking at non-Western "queer" categories such as *kathoey* (Thailand) and *bakla* (Philippines) not as antiquated forms of homosexuality but as possible gateways for sensitively and effectively imparting information about AIDS transmission

and for empowering and politicizing communities. In other words, "queer" not only became a fallback umbrella category for the "other" but was deployed to "mess up" and/or—to use a relatively archaic meaning of the term—"spoil" the seemingly cohesive categories of gay, lesbian, bisexual, and straight, thereby breaking down the monolithic understanding of the sexual that has been primarily anchored to sex-object-choice orientation.

Gaining momentum from the various legacies and historical contexts outlined above, the concept "queer" and its academic arm, queer theory/queer studies, "moved" the questions of sex and gender beyond the contexts of biological destiny and Western categories into more thorough engagements with cultural and historical exigencies. With this transformative makeover, "queer" was increasingly used to resist and refuse the coherence and stability of sex and gender and to argue for more capacious and open-ended understandings of these phenomena.

Nowhere are the processes, strategies, and vantage of "queer" more prevalent, productive, and paradigm shifting than in the field of Asian American studies. It is no wonder that there have been grumblings in some sectors about how the "queers" have "taken over the field." While it may be true that queer-identified scholars have emerged and that scholarship about LGBTQ Asian Americans has proliferated, it is shortsighted to see the value of "queer" as merely an identity add-on to "Asian" and "American," since that fails to grasp the substantive value of "queer" as a category of analysis that "does something" within this so-called "takeover" of Asian American studies.

The deployment of "queer" in this field is neither a mere additive measure nor an augmentation or supplement to that imagined totality called "Asian American." It is not just about mixing in the gay and lesbian factors, but rather aims to consider "queer" as pivotal to and constitutive of a critical understanding of Asian American experiences. "Queer" has remapped and reshaped the contours of Asian American experiences. It has been and is presently being used in Asian American studies scholarship as a theoretical, methodological, and conceptual scaffolding from which to conceptualize and engage with the historical, cultural, economic, and political exigencies, realities, and paradoxes that have beset Asian Americans. The queer approach in Asian American studies has also invigorated enduring fieldwide conversations about the erased/invisible, marginalized, and abject histories and communities of Asian America (Okihiro 1994).

From the mid-1990s to the present day, the queer approach has gained meaningful traction in Asian American studies through numerous publications (Bao and Yanagihara 2000; Eng and Hom 1998; R. Leong 1996). Far from merely encouraging an archeological excavation of Asian American gays and lesbians in the past, a queer approach enables a serious appreciation of the messy and wayward composition of such things as the law and the workings of the normal through popular culture, and a critical consideration of such issues as varied miscegenation, bachelor societies, failed masculinities, Orientalism, domesticity, and perpetual-foreigner status. For example, bachelor societies such as those of early Chinatowns and Filipino agricultural camps were seen as predominantly male-dominated sites, while a queer perspective renders these sites not so much as a haven for homosexual activity but rather as social stages for the performance of hegemonic understandings of race, gender, and sexuality. Chinese and Filipino men in the early 20th century were seen as failed masculinities or always already criminals, either sexual eunuchs (sexless and gender-insubordinate subjects) or sexual predators (hypermasculine and sexually aggressive subjects).

Such contradictory constructions of Chinese and Filipino men can be productively understood in terms of their queer and recalcitrant locations in the American nation-state at that time, with the Chinese ineligible for citizenship due to a long history of exclusion laws and the Filipinos not deemed or treated as citizens, though as American colonial subjects and American nationals they carried American passports. "Queer" operates as a frame that creatively brings together the practices and institutions of immigration law with the forces of race, class, and gender to help us properly and vitally understand the historical and cultural workings of state power.

While some have heralded the advent of a queer Asian American studies, it was far from becoming a ghettoized and discrete form of inquiry. In fact, the queer approach in the field has created crucial links and enabled new formulations and frameworks through conversations among Asian American scholars. Dana Takagi (1996), in her now canonical essay, called for the necessary braiding or intertwining of race and sexuality not only in the experiences of Asian American gays and lesbians but as a constitutive element of the history of Asians in the United States. She further demonstrated the links between an Asian American–focused gay and lesbian or queer studies and its connection to larger questions in the field through an engagement with the work of Lisa Lowe (1996), who has argued for a serious consideration of heterogeneity and the nonunitary nature of Asian American subjectivity. Both works raised a clarion call for capacious scholarly and political engagements that went beyond essential static identities or political trajectories that lead up to the nation-state as the final destination or telos.

This approach was demonstrated by works that reformulated the idea of Asian American immigration through the lenses of what Gayatri Gopinath (2004) called a "queer diasporic approach" or what David Eng

(2010) termed a "queer diaspora." By decentering the nation as the primary vehicle for the articulation of global migratory movement in general and Asian American immigration in particular, queer works have laid bare the racial and sexual undercurrents of gender formations (Gopinath 2004; Eng 2001), the inadequacies of gay liberation narratives and Western gay and lesbian categories (Manalansan 2003), the variable cultural expressions of desire, the sexist and racist foundations of the nation, and the virulence of state governmentality.

Various works have also helped elucidate the legal construction of the Asian migrant subject as always already deviant and showcase how legally framed racialized, heteropatriachal, and heteronormative expectations have authorized mainstream neoliberal agenda and structures that, in turn, have sequestered and given privilege to classed and racialized forms of kinship and intimacies, and fueled violences and social inequalities (Reddy 2011; Eng 2010; N. Shah 2012). In other words, the triumphant emergence of issues such as gay marriage, gays in the military, and gay-focused consumerism have given rise to an increased disregard for and the virulent erasure of race and class. Contemporary images of proper gay and lesbian citizens center on lifestyle choices, including where and how one lives, buys, and consumes products and services. "Queer," for example, has been used to denote a discerning "eye" and a range of elite, high-end consumptive practices. In *Queer Eye for the Straight Guy*, the gay man functions as the beacon and arbiter of good taste in the service of the heterosexual man, with the show's "queer" characters counseling hapless straight men in need of fashion makeovers. In other words, being queer or, more correctly, being gay has become less a matter of sex or even gender and more one of shopping and consuming. However, it is clear that not all gays and lesbians have the means to live fabulous, wealthy lives of Champagne, caviar, and Prada. Scholars have shown that the mainstreaming and normalization of these aforementioned "gay issues" have resulted in the domestication and tacit acceptance of various forms of social inequality, heteronormative ideals, and structural violence (Manalansan 2005).

At the same time, Asian American scholars have noted that the increased visibility of gay and lesbian issues has been used as evidence of an exceptional American modernity vis-à-vis a non-modern/non-Western sexually deviant "other" such as the figure of the terrorist in the post-9/11 world (Eng 2010; Puar 2007). To put it simply, the proliferation of American gay culture is used to portray the global South or, more specifically, the Middle East as backward, homophobic, and violent and therefore in need of rescue or a kind of "cultural" makeover. Asian American scholars have demonstrated how in a neoliberal America, colorblindness, cultural chauvinism/ethnocentricity, and gay images have gone hand in hand. In sum, Asian American queer scholars have revealed how increased rights and visibility for gay- and lesbian-identified subjects have led to potent yet veiled forms of racist, misogynist, and other phobic forms of structural violence and disparities (Hong and Ferguson 2011).

Critiques of a queer-focused approach in Asian American studies (and of queer studies in general) have pointed to its limitations in terms of its seemingly romanticized middle-class and hip antinormative stance. Many of the condemnations of the queer approach pivot around the ways in which such a stance has no durability or longevity. In other words, some critics say that there is no future for a queer approach to social justice causes or to critical ethnic studies. These reproaches do not take into account the astute critiques of temporality that queer studies scholars, particularly queers of color (R. Ferguson 2004), have put forward. Normality and, for that matter, queerness are moving targets. They

agenda (Maeda 2009; Pulido 2006; J. Wu 2013). While Asian American politics was connected to left critiques of capitalism and war in this formative period, the Asian American movement would not launch onto the national stage until the 1980s as a panethnic alliance in response to the brutal murder of Vincent Chin and subsequent antiracist organizing (Y. Espiritu 1992).

In the barest scholarly definition, race is a social construct. This fails, however, to describe the extent and power of race. Race is inextricably a concept of the modern episteme, intertwined in systems of imperialism, colonization, capitalism, and social structure that emerged out of the European Enlightenment (Goldberg 1993; Mills 1997; Silva 2007; Winant 2001). Tethered to race is the ideology of white supremacy that while appearing to be on the wane has transformed into an increasingly complex system of dispossession and violence. The inequality at the center of racism and white supremacy is based on the enduring power of race as a flexible and shifting category. In this essay I draw on the terms "racial formation," "racial capitalism," "racial liberalism," and "global racial system" to elaborate the dynamic range and durability of race.

As a construct that elaborates a social order, race has varied in meaning and usage over time. As some scholars would have it, racism predated the formal concept of race, which emerged in the contact of Spanish explorers and the New World. For example, in the period of classical antiquity, Greco-Roman prejudice against and social hatred of particular groups is described as "proto-racism" (B. Isaac 2006). Originating roughly in the sixteenth century, the concept of race imbued notions of difference that encompassed ideas of religious superiority and social hierarchy. Subsequently, the idea of race became an explanatory dogma that combined notions of physical difference, culture, and ancestry, leading to the predominance of scientific racism in the nineteenth

century. The word "race" draws its lineage from a history mired in campaigns of conquest and war that importantly included practices of religious conversion. The ascension of Christianity through colonization combined with the ideology of white supremacy developed in an epistemological and moral order in which race and religion became precepts of social hierarchy. With the expansion of scientific racism in Europe, race was systematized into taxonomies of inferiority and superiority, argued to be the basis of visible biological difference such as skin color and hair type, and justified by the belief in a divine right ordained to Christian civilization and the notions of moral development embedded in this worldview. It was not until the latter half of the twentieth century that this usage was debunked as a conventional belief and standard institutional practice of state racism.

In parsing this history in the United States, the influential concept of racial formation has provided an intellectual framework for a theory of race and racism that critiques a range of social relations, structures, and institutions. Michael Omi and Howard Winant define "racial formation as the sociohistorical process by which racial categories are created, inhabited, transformed, and destroyed" (1994, 55). Racial formation theorizes racism and antiracist social movements of opposition as an active social process. As a modern construct, race became a proxy for kinship systems that divide groups of people according to descent and geographic origin. Using the idioms of blood, skin color, and phenotypic difference, scientific racism was used to enforce social boundaries and regulations including legal statutes and spatial segregation. The system of race and racialization was embedded in social structures and hierarchies that depended on notions of culture and biology to fix cultural essences as naturalized traits. As a regulatory system, race defined acceptable social practices such as sexual couplings, marriageability, and the inheritance of property. In regard to sexual contact, fears of miscegenation resulted in rules for the maintenance of racial purity and categories of mixed race. The classification of mixed race emerged as both defiled and redemptive, creating passing zones in which racial privilege was accorded through the structures of white supremacy (Williams-León and Nakashima 2001). To pass as white, or as honorary white in the case of the myth of the model minority, is also one of the complications of racial hierarchies and collusion with privileges that are obtained through, for example, economic status and class mobility. Thus, racial performance is an important aspect of interpreting structures organized in relationship to whiteness, including social economies based in notions of beauty, desire, and sexual preference.

In the context of racism and the struggle against it, the story of race in the United States has been historically dominated by slavery and the ideology of white supremacy (Roediger 1991; Roediger 2008). Indeed, race is often coded as black in the American vernacular, complicating the analysis of race as it affects a broad range of communities of color and antiracist struggle. Antiracist analysis is further confounded by a masculinist narrative of recovery and a dependence on patriarchal narratives of redemption. Feminist-of-color and queer-of-color critiques have articulated important alternative strategies and tactics of antiracist organizing by emphasizing the moral structures of race (R. Ferguson 2012b). Indeed, the genocide of indigenous peoples of the Americas was made possible by an imperial morality that justified the conquest of lands through the practices of settler colonialism and the erasure of Native histories. In this system, race figured as a way to define property in the case of whiteness, and as a system of labor exploitation that defined U.S. modernity and capitalism (Harris 1995; Gilroy 1993). The American model of modernity developed according to a racial capitalism that distributed resources along lines of race, class, and gender that continued in political systems of authority and legitimated state practices of racism. This system enabled a ranking order at a global level, consented to by domestic systems of everyday racism, to provide a platform for U.S. imperial expansion through war, militarism, and violence. Because the abolitionist movement to end slavery emerged as part of the struggle of antiracism and emancipation that opposed the dictates of white supremacy, abolition continues as a model of antiracist struggle in the contemporary moment, particularly as it relates to the prison-industrial complex and the preponderance of black suffering (Michelle Alexander 2010; Gilmore 2007; D. Rodríguez 2006).

Race is thus an epistemological category of white supremacy that maintains structures of violence and dispossession, while its permanence is contested through the struggle to change and destroy such systems through antiracism and liberation struggles. According to the foundational analysis of Cedric Robinson (1983), racial capitalism imposed a simultaneous racism and antiracism that converged in a system of dominance, accumulation, and violence by mobilizing race in relationship to other forms of difference such as sexuality, gender, class, religion, and disability, among others (R. Ferguson 2012a; Melamed 2012; Reddy 2011). Racial capitalism, built upon hierarchy and social structures of dispossession, is quintessentially a system of accumulation that proffers an ethic of individual mobility while drawing on geographies of racial difference. Such divisions, fostered through the foundations of capitalism and ideas of social and material property, are the terrain from which gendered forms of racism and immigration led women-of-color feminist critiques to resist and transform exclusionary laws, labor discrimination, and sexism (L. Lowe 1996; Hong 2006). Despite the gains of civil rights and liberation movements, racism remains prevalent by virtue of the deeply embedded notion of race within U.S. social structures. With the advent of multiculturalism, "race" has been supplanted by supposedly neutral terms such as "minority," "ethnicity," and "culture." Yet the idea of race persists in the practices, logics, and rationales of racism and white supremacy. The continuation of the ideas of race into the present at times results in a paradoxical colorblind racism, or racism without racists, in which the ideology of culture and race are interchangeable (Bonilla-Silva 2010).

State systems of classification have often placed Asian Americans and other people of color in an ambiguous status. The categorization of citizens as "free white people" in the Naturalization Act of 1790 set the course for centuries of legislative struggle for civil rights. At the heart of the state sanction of racism was the use of census categories to deem certain groups eligible for full rights of citizenship while others were barred. Throughout the nineteenth century Asian immigrants, particularly Chinese and South Asians, were excluded from citizenship through classifications that deemed them nonwhite. Racial capitalism as a concept articulated through practices of war and migration helps to explain the racialization of Asians in the United States. Based in the popular racism of the second half of the nineteenth century, the specter of a yellow peril exemplified in the legal control of Chinese migrants was the result of labor unrest that was sanctioned by state racism and immigration policy. The U.S. government established a range of legal regulations and policies derived from conjectures about nationality, gender, and race that circulated in popular culture—first in the Page Act of 1875, which specifically banned Chinese women from immigration ostensibly to control prostitution, and more broadly in the Chinese Exclusion Act of 1882 that targeted laborers. By 1898, the legacy of a frontier mentality and manifest destiny that led to the military conquest of Native Americans and their genocidal extermination expanded across the Pacific as the U.S. consolidated its imperial legacy in gaining control over Hawai'i, Samoa, Guam, and the Philippines, as well as Cuba and Puerto Rico. The placement of Japanese and Japanese Americans in internment camps during World War II, justified by the Alien Enemies Act of 1798, drew upon a racialization process in which the demands of war and militarism demonized already racialized domestic populations as enemies of the state.

It was not until the mid-twentieth century that prohibitions on immigration and naturalization were finally overturned through the 1952 McCarren-Walter Act. To the present day, the taxonomic rationales of the census continue to place Asian Americans in a bipolar race continuum of either black or white. South Asian Americans were once nonwhite, then white, and now through legislative battles are classified as Asian American, whereas Arab Americans are classified as white. Contemporary Asian Americans represent a wide range of class and income categories, placing some in wealthy and prosperous middle-class groups, while others such as Cambodians, Laotians, and Vietnamese face high rates of poverty and limited access to resources (Lui et al. 2006). With these latter groups, poverty and marginalization is the product of how Asian Americans are racialized as model minorities that are high achieving while histories of war and displacement as refugees created systematic forms of disenfranchisement.

After World War II, the policy of containment known as the Truman Doctrine that solidified the Cold War with the Soviet Union came at a moment of shifting domestic race relations and the rise of racial liberalism. As Truman began a process of limited endorsement of a civil rights agenda to placate African Americans, the dictates of Cold War ideology defined a large part of the world as potential enemies, including domestic populations. Asian Americans, predominantly Japanese Americans who had just been subjected to a state policy of internment, were deemed foreign and outside of U.S. nationalism, and pitted against other communities of color. Following the Truman presidency, the use of covert actions to implement U.S. imperial goals without direct military involvement expanded under the Eisenhower administration. In 1953, a U.S.-backed coup in Iran reversed a national project to control oil reserves, and the strategy rapidly spread to other parts of the world, notably Asia and Latin America (Abrahamian 2013). As this program of covert international intervention expanded in the following years, the civil rights struggle reached fruition in a shift of race relations. Patterns of immigration also began to change dramatically through state selection after 1965, creating new Asian immigrant populations throughout the United States. Such demographic changes were the devices of a racial liberalism that offered limited civil rights to some racialized groups while antagonizing others, and, notably, at the cusp of new waves of immigration that fundamentally changed the social and economic makeup of the country. By the late 1960s, Asian Americans were mythologized as a model minority by the media, scholars, and a state apparatus that used the language of social mobility and work ethic as a racial wedge while ignoring the histories of racial oppression and differential patterns of migration created by U.S. policies and statutes. Racial liberalism emerged as a direct response to the black freedom movement that refuted white supremacy as a normative and public practice expressed in Jim Crow segregation (Singh 2004; Singh 2012). Alternatively, black radicalism linked to the internationalism of decolonizing social movements called for the end of global white supremacy beyond the United States (R. Bush 2009; Daulatzai 2012). Radical ideologies of

liberation were subsumed within multiracial and pan-ethnic solidarity movements which resolved to forge an alternative system to that of racial capitalism and global white supremacy (Y. Espiritu 1992; Pulido 2007; J. Wu 2013).

Drawing on the patterns and legacies of war, migration, and the formation of diaspora communities, Asian Americans have been collapsed into the U.S. racial formation through a mixture of racial policy and foreign policy. Racializing Asian Americans followed a pattern of connecting frames of war to domestic enemies beginning in World War II with the Japanese, and later in the Korean and Vietnam wars. Southeast Asians were cast through representations of war and colonialism that circulated through the racialization of refugee and mixed-race populations in the United States (Chong 2011). Similarly, a history of crisis developed around U.S. involvement in the Arab and Muslim world, with diplomatic and military entanglements in, for example, Iran, Egypt and the Suez Canal, Lebanon, and the Israeli occupation of Palestine. The contemporary global War on Terror, defined by the twenty-first-century wars in Iraq and Afghanistan, extends this history, which links foreign policy to domestic immigrant communities. After 9/11, South Asians, Arabs, and Muslims were targeted for surveillance, detention, and deportation (Cainkar 2009; Maira 2009). An array of Asian Americans were affected by those policies, particularly Cambodian Americans, who faced deportations based on selective enforcement (Hing 2006). The construction of enemy terrorists configured Arabs, South Asians, and Muslims alongside other Asian Americans and communities of color as racialized figures through the broad mandates of the Patriot Act and the U.S. War on Terror campaign.

Although the history of race in the United States is largely dependent on skin color and phenotypic difference, the twenty-first century has brought forth the often hidden relationship of religion to racism, particularly in terms of the figure of the Muslim in the U.S. racial formation and the role of the War on Terror in this racialization. The threat of terrorism and the racialized Muslim are the latest entrants in a long genealogy of how race and religion have been imagined in Asian American populations. For example, the mid-nineteenth-century idea of the heathen Chinese migrant, which mobilized the racialization of a yellow peril in opposition to an American nationalism described as white and Christian, in the latter half of the twentieth century translated into godless-communist threats from across Asia. Other stereotypes of race and racialization based on presumptions about religion and geographic origin include the so-called Hindoo, encompassing Muslims, Hindus, and Sikhs, and the misnomer of Mohammedan, applied to people from South Asia to West Asia and North Africa. United States foreign policy and military involvement across the globe, particularly in Asia, the Pacific, and the Middle East, has historically been framed through notions of the Orient and what Edward Said refers to as Orientalism as a way of knowing and dominating parts of the world to further a U.S. imperial agenda (Said 1978; Said 1994). The deployment of race in relationship to the spread of globalization is part of a centuries-old global racial system (Winant 2001; Winant 2002; Clarke and Thomas 2006; Mullings 2005; Mullings 2008). When racial capitalism is imagined beyond the confines of the U.S. nation-state, race must also be understood as circulating at global levels alongside racism and white supremacy. The global racial system frames histories of domination and exploitation such that slavery, genocide, war, and labor migration can be analyzed through the rhetoric and mobilization of racial discourse at the regional, hemispheric, and even planetary level. In other words, if war is the means of achieving imperial interests, race is the historical category from which to justify and achieve colonial conquest.

The figure of the racialized Muslim is at the forefront of some important interventions of critical and intersectional analysis. From gender and sexuality critiques (Naber 2012; Razack 2007; Reddy 2011; Puar 2007) to labor and political formations (Daulatzai 2012; Rana 2011), the figure of the Muslim represents important challenges in terms of the flexibility of the race concept, and in how race is collapsed into the categories of religion, gender and sexuality, violence, imperialism, and white supremacy. Islam and the figure of the Muslim have emerged as the new global racial system of the twenty-first century. And yet this system is not new in the theory of racism, in which egalitarian principles of democracy are wedded to imperial morals of apartheid based in an older system of racism (Winant 2002, 18).

Empire and white supremacy are at the heart of U.S. histories of race. With the expansion of technologies of war and militarism, race is a concept in which state violence and conquest are justified. Perhaps the greatest challenge of race is imagining the struggle against white supremacy. As race continues to confound, and racism proliferates, opposing global apartheid and the consequences of the global color line depend not only on a black and white opposition, but a vast array of communities of color to take part in the world struggle for an alternative that goes beyond racism, war, capitalism, and white supremacy.

52

Refugee

Yến Lê Espiritu

In the devastating aftermath of Hurricane Katrina in 2005, reporters, politicians, and media commentators used the term "refugee" to describe the tens of thousands of storm victims, many of whom were poor African Americans, who were uprooted from their homes and forced to flee in search of refuge. Almost immediately, prominent African American leaders, including Jesse Jackson and Al Sharpton, charged that the use of "refugee" to refer to Katrina survivors was "racially biased," contending that the term implies second-class citizens—or even non-Americans (Sommers et al. 2006, 40–41). For these critics, "refugeeness" connotes "otherness," summoning the image of "people in a Third World country" who "carried the scraps of their lives in plastic trash bags," wore "donated clothes," and slept "on the floor of overpopulated shelters" (Masquelier 2006, 737). In this context, calling U.S.-born African Americans "refugees" was tantamount to stripping them of their citizenship—"their right to be part of the national order of things" (Masquelier 2006, 737). As the Katrina controversy makes clear, the term "refugee" triggers associations to highly charged images of Third World poverty, foreignness, and statelessness, which are intimately related to core issues of personal and national identity. These associations reflect the transnationally circulated representations of refugees as incapacitated objects of rescue, fleeing impoverished, war-torn, or corrupt states—a "problem" for asylum and resettlement countries.

Liisa Malkki (1995) has argued that the construction of refugees as out-of-place victims reflects nationalism's fiction of an unproblematic link between territory and identity and an idealized relationship between the state and its citizens. Viewing state borders as geographical givens, the "there's no place like home" mantra implies that only those fleeing tyrannical governments would forsake their state's protection to embark on a perilous path as refugees. According to Randy Lippert, in the early Cold War, "refugeeness became a moral-political tactic," demarcating the difference between the supposedly uncivilized East and civilized West, and fostering "cohesion of the Western Alliance nations" (1999, 305). This "moral-political tactic" was the impetus behind the production of the "refugee" as a sociolegal object of knowledge and management at the onset of the Cold War (Malkki 1995). In 1951, prodded by the United States, whose paradigmatic refugee was the Eastern European and Soviet escapee, the United Nations officially defined "refugee" as a person who harbors "a well-founded fear of being persecuted for reasons of race, religion, nationality, membership of a particular social group or political opinion" (U.N. General Assembly 1951). This definition privileged sufferers of political oppression above victims of natural disaster; it also sharply distinguished political refugees fleeing persecution from economic migrants moving in search of a better life, even when it is impossible to disentangle the political from the economic (Carruthers 2005, 921).

For the most part, state interests have determined whether, when, and where displaced persons receive asylum in the West. With the beginning of the Cold War, the term "refugee" became interchangeable with "defector," as the "provision of asylum became a foreign policy tool" awarded by Western countries primarily to those who fled or refused to be repatriated to Communist countries (Gibney and Hansen 2005, 25). In 1948, following the admission of more than 250,000 displaced Europeans, the U.S. Congress enacted the country's first refugee legislation, which provided for the admission of an additional 400,000 European refugees. Reflecting the anticommunist imperative of the time, subsequent refugee laws granted admission primarily to persons "escaping" from Communist governments, largely from Hungary, Poland, Yugoslavia, North Korea, and China, and in the 1960s from Cuba (Office of Refugee Resettlement n.d.). In the face of the massive exodus of refugees from Southeast Asia beginning in the late 1970s, and continuing outflows from the Soviet Union and Cuba, the U.S. Congress passed the Refugee Act of 1980, which adopted the 1951 United Nations definition of "refugee" and established a uniform procedure for the admission and resettlement of refugees of special concern to the United States. While the purported goal of the 1980 act was to eliminate the "previous geographic and ideological restrictions on granting of refugee status," the actual admissions proposals for fiscal year 1980 continued to prioritize refugees who had "close ties to the United States," whose resettlement would further U.S. foreign policy objectives, and for whom the "United States has stood uniquely as a symbol of freedom from oppression" (Palmieri 1980, 701).

According to Ambassador Victor H. Palmieri, U.S. coordinator for refugee affairs, refugees from Southeast Asia were the main beneficiaries of the Refugee Act of 1980. To tackle what Palmieri characterized as "a human tragedy of staggering dimensions," the United States proposed to admit a total of 168,000 refugees from "Indochina" in fiscal year 1980, in comparison to the proposed 33,00 from the Soviet Union and 19,500 from Cuba (1980, 701–2). Palmieri concluded that these refugee admissions constituted a "major commitment by [the U.S.] government and by the American people" to help "these persecuted and uprooted persons begin new lives in our country" (1980, 702). Palmieri's portrayal of Southeast Asian refugees as desperate individuals fleeing political persecution and/or economic depression invokes racialized images of the "refugees" as grief-stricken objects of rescue, which completely discounts the aggressive roles that the U.S. government, military, and corporations played in generating this exodus in the first place. This "willed forgetfulness of the American imaginary . . . write[s] out the specificities of forced migration and the legacy of the American/Vietnam War," enabling Americans to remake themselves from military aggressors into magnanimous rescuers (Palumbo-Liu 1999, 235).

Social scientists also participated in turning Southeast Asian refugees into "an object of sociological inquiry and psychiatric correction" (Ngô, Nguyen, and Lam 2012, 677). Soon after Vietnamese refugees arrived in the United States in 1975, the federal government, in collaboration with social scientists, initiated a series of needs assessment surveys to generate knowledge on what was widely touted as a "refugee resettlement crisis." Viewing the newly arrived refugees as coming from "a society so markedly different from that of America," government officials and scholars alike regarded the accumulation of data on Vietnamese economic and sociocultural adaptation as essential to "protect[ing] the interests of the American public" (Dunning 1989, 55). Casting Vietnamese as objects of rescue, this literature portrays the refugees as "incapacitated by grief and therefore in need of care"—a care that is purportedly best provided in and by the United States (DuBois 1993, 4–5). Other substantial data sets on Southeast Asian refugee adaptation followed: from the Bureau of Social Science Research Survey; the Institute for Social Research Survey; the NICHD-funded survey; and other government records, including the 1980 census (Haines 1989). Constituting the primary data sources on Southeast

Asians from the mid-1970s and throughout the 1980s, these large-scale surveys, which cumulatively produce Southeast Asian refugees in the United States as a *problem* to be solved, delimit and conceptually underpin future studies of these communities in the United States. As a consequence, it is as *refugees*—the purported desperate seekers of U.S. asylum—and not as migrants, transmigrants, diasporics, or exiles, that Southeast Asians have become most intelligible in U.S. policies and the public imagination.

In order to challenge this "desperate refugee" narrative, scholars in Asian American studies would need to imbue the term "refugee" with social and political critiques—to conceptualize "the refugee" not as an object of investigation, but rather as a *paradigm* "whose function [is] to establish and make intelligible a wider set of problems" (Agamben 2002). We could begin by considering how the refugee, who inhabits a condition of statelessness, radically calls into question the established principles of the nation-state and the idealized goal of inclusion and recognition within it. As Giorgio Agamben explains, refugees disturb the organization of the modern nation-state because their condition of statelessness is fundamentally opposed to the notion of rooted citizens, thus calling into question the "original fiction of modern sovereignty" (1998, 142). As a consequence, nations tend to externalize refugees ideologically; thus refugees in general come to constitute objects of state suspicion and threats to security since they represent an aberration of categories in the national order of things. In other words, refugees are a "problem" not because they are pathetic but because they make visible "a transgression of the social contract between a state and its citizen" (R. Liu 2002, 9). As someone "out of place"—that is, without the protection of the state—a refugee is an anomaly whose status needs to be brought back into place by either naturalization or repatriation.

Robyn Liu warns that the desire to provide a durable solution to the "refugee problem"—"to create or restore the bond between a person as a citizen and a state as her legal protector"—ends up affirming the status of the nation-state as the ultimate protector and provider of human welfare (2002, 9). In the same way, Nevzat Soguk maintains that humanitarian interventions on behalf of refugees—represented as "citizens gone aberrant"—"enforce intergovernmental regimentation that reinscribes the statist hierarchy of citizen-nation-state" (1999, 194). As Viet Thanh Nguyen succinctly states, a benign "immigrant studies affirm[s] the nation-states the immigrant comes from and settles into," and a critical "refugee studies brings into question the viability of the nation-state" (2012, 930).

As subjects of U.S. war and imperialism, the presence of Southeast Asians in the United States calls for an alternate genealogy for Asian American studies—one that begins with the history of U.S. military, economic, and political intervention in Asia (Schlund-Vials 2012a). A critical refugee study of Southeast Asians would turn "our attention to issues of war, race and violence and not so much to questions of identity, assimilation, and the recuperation of history" (V. Nguyen 2012, 930). The perceived marginalization of Southeast Asian issues in Asian American studies has less to do with deliberate exclusion than with the field's initial focus on the racialization and internal colonization of Asians within the United States. To situate Southeast Asians within the context of U.S. war in Southeast Asia would return Asian American studies to the "Third World frame" that Asian American activists adopted at the height of the Vietnam War—one that links the U.S. modern racial state to the U.S. modern empire. As Lisa Lowe suggests, racialized immigration from Southeast Asia to the United States exposes the myth of voluntary immigration and "obliges us to rethink the history of the United States as a history of empire" (1998, 76). In short, a meaningful inclusion of Southeast Asian issues into Asian American studies' curriculum and research agenda would spawn new questions about "the international within the national," which would have enormous ramifications for the objects and methods of the field (L. Lowe 1998).

Finally, critical refugee studies need to take seriously the range of Southeast Asian perspectives on the before and after of the wars in Southeast Asia. Like other communities in exile, Southeast Asians in the United States feel keenly the urgency to forge unified histories, identities, and memories. Against such moral weight of "the community," we need to ask what happens to events that cannot be narrated. What lies just underneath the surface? Which memories are erased, forgotten, or postponed and archived for future release? Where and how then do these "nonevents" fit into the narration of history (McGranahan 2005, 580)? As Khatharya Um writes, "straddling the interstice between the need to speak and the inability to express, silence is, for many refugees, a self-imposed and an externally compelled strategy of survival" (2012, 842). How would refugees, not as an object of investigation, but as a site of social critique, articulate the heretofore unspeakable? How do we as scholars pay attention to what has been rendered ghostly, and to write into being the seething presence of the things that appear to be not there (Gordon 1997, 7–8)? To take seriously evolving Southeast Asian perspectives of the war is to remember Southeast Asia as a historical site, Southeast Asian people as genuine subjects, and the wars in Southeast Asia as having an integrity that is internal to the history and politics of these countries.

53

Religion
David Kyuman Kim

Religion is a synthetic concept for Asian American studies. It represents much of what animates and vexes Asian American studies as a discipline and Asian Americans in their everyday lives, especially in light of the dynamic flux and flow of the alchemy of identity. Deploying religion as a keyword in Asian American studies demands making accounts of generic sociological data such as religious affiliation, the racializing cunning of Orientalism, the American cultural preferential option for Christianity, and the tenacious presence of white supremacy. Situating religion in a racial discourse about Asian America will inevitably reveal racist associations with the "Oriental" religions of Buddhism, Hinduism, and other "exotic," non-Western traditions in the conversation. These are companion traditions to Christianity in the grand narrative known as the "world religions." And yet, these notably Asian religions are decidedly "other" to the Christian moral and theological norms that have shaped the mythology of American exceptionalism.

Religion refers to structures, beliefs, values, and practices of living, making, and finding meaning. There are overlapping yet critical differences in how religion serves as a keyword for Asian Americans and for Asian American studies. As a keyword for Asian American studies, religion indicates horizons of beliefs, practices, values, communities, histories, traditions, worldviews, identities, and ways of making and finding meaning for Asian Americans. While Asian Americans practice and identify with Buddhism, Islam, Hinduism, Christianity, Shamanism, Confucianism, Jainism, Sikhism, and a host of other "world religions" (let alone the huge variety of sects within each of these traditions), leaving the matter of religion to this sort of typology inadequately reflects the complex functions that religion plays in the lives of Asian Americans. After all, what can be said about the fantastically diverse constellation of traditions and practices called "religion" among Asian Americans? Indeed, much needs to be undone in the scholastic affair of naming the religions of Asian America as a sufficient methodological conceit.

The root of the word "religion" derives from the ancient Latin "religare," meaning "to bind" and "to bind again." It makes sense to ask, in considering the centrality of religion for Asian American studies, what binds and rebinds Asian Americans? Toward this end, consider the ways in which religion and race configure the social imaginary of Asian America. As Charles Taylor frames it, social imaginaries are mutually constitutive spheres such as the public sphere, market economy, and civil society that form horizons of meaning for modern life. A social imaginary refers to "the ways people imagine their social existence, how they fit together with others, how things go on between them and their fellows, the expectations that are normally met, and the deeper normative notions and images that underlie these expectations. . . . [A social] imaginary is that common understanding that makes possible common practices and a widely shared sense of legitimacy" (2003, 23). Religion generates social imaginaries for Asian America. It mediates the particular and the general, such as the ordinary experience of being a racialized subject in the American empire. Religion is a social imaginary that provides frameworks of interpretation for making sense of Asian American experience. It marks the convergence of spheres of life and ways of being in the world.

While traditions such as Buddhism, Hinduism, and the like render coherence for Asian American identity, there are negative binding forces at work as well (D. Kim 2003). The specter of Orientalism haunts the discourse about religion in Asian American studies. The vibrancy and visibility of Asian American religious communities intensifies with the massive influx of immigrants from Asia after the passage of the 1965 Immigration Act. Not surprisingly, much of the scholarship on Asian American religions of the last thirty years has focused on immigration, underscoring the centrality of "the new immigrant church"—where the "church" is a stand-in for temples, gurdwaras, mosques, and non-Christian religious communities. In part, the impetus of this research was a demonstration that Asian American immigrants are bellwethers for an underrecognized and underacknowledged religious diversity/pluralism (Eck 2002; R. B. Williams 1988; Min and Kim 2002; Carnes and Yang 2004). Religious diversity/pluralism is a kissing cousin to the politics of representation. The argument has purchase in the context of a Protestant Eurocentrism and the predominance of white supremacist norms about what "American religion" looks like. Will Herberg is the straw man here. Herberg (1960) articulated the dominant yet wildly inaccurate conceit that America is a nation whose religious stories are readily captured in the mythic triptych "Protestant Catholic Jew." And yet even when positioning Asian Americans as a corrective to Herberg's anemic pluralism, one still finds misrecognition and a presentist view at play. It is not simply that religion appears magically among Asian American communities after 1965. Religion has been an integral part of the Asian American experience from the beginning of Asian American history (Takaki 1989; Iwamura and Spickard 2003; D. Yoo 1999).

Again, the specter of Orientalism and white supremacy appropriately pervade analyses of Asian American religions, particularly when giving due credence to histories of Asian migration that reveal the transnational forces of "the church," Western missionizing, and U.S. foreign policy that sought to establish American-style secularism in shaping Asian American peoples. Think of the complex genealogy of missions and the massive conversion of "heathen" Chinese in Asia and the proleptic racist legacy of these movements in the migration histories of overseas Chinese in the United States. The subsequent structural effects of these forces culminated in the Chinese Exclusion Act. Further, the entanglement of religion and racism helped to animate the social and legislative actions of hatred against "Hindoos," Japanese, and Filipinos that were patterned after the anti-Chinese movements of the turn of the twentieth century (Robert Lee 1999, 108). Surely, the American wars, imperial and otherwise, in the Philippines, Japan, Korea, and Vietnam have shaped Asian American lives, through the inducement of migrations and the creation of refugees (Prashad 2007, 176). Religion was party to all of these transnational migrations: from the oppositional role of Catholics to American colonization in the Philippines and later to martial rule during the Marcos era; to the resurgence of cultural Confucianism among Chinese and Korean immigrants; to the dispersion and reconfiguring of Buddhism by and among Japanese, Thai, and Vietnamese transnationals; to the racialization of South Asians through Islam in post-9/11 America.

It would be a mistake to conclude that these conditions render Asian American religious identities utterly irredeemable. Asian American studies has been adroit in adapting the core insight of the postcolony, namely, that one can never fully exorcise the imperial even after the fall of empire (Mbembe 2001). Religions for Asian American life cannot nor should they exist apart from Orientalism and white supremacy and the overdetermining effects of a Western modernity shaped by Protestantism. Instead, these communities are much better served by gaining a fulsome appreciation for how the horizons of meaning of Orientalism, white supremacy, and the centripetal force of Protestant Christianity shape and racialize Buddhism, Christianity, Hinduism, Sikhism, Confucianism, Islam, *and* secularism. This is not to say that Asian American Christians feel diminished by their fellow white Buddhists or Christians and the like (Suh 2004). Instead, it is to note that ethnic hierarchies, racial logic, Orientalism, and other characteristics of white supremacy that Asian American studies has vigilantly subjected to critique since its inception operate for Asian American religionists whether they detect it or not. While the lived experience of multiracial Asian American religious communities may disavow its presence in their common and collective spiritual lives, the persistence of white supremacy demands otherwise. Desires for forms of living religion apart from the dehumanizing effects of anti-Asian racism and the constitutive power of race is understandable but unrealizable if not utopian in its aspirations. Longing to be free of the toxic effects of white supremacy in one's spiritual life makes sense. And yet arguing that Asian American psychic, spiritual, *and* public life can somehow exist apart from these effects is to insist on a state of false consciousness that is thoroughly at odds with the core practices of critical thought that have been the hallmark of Asian American studies.

Asian American religions highlight a paradox of the American social imaginary. Asian American religions simultaneously function as synthetic stereotypes of Orientalist cultures, inheritances, and racist claims of foreignness, while they also represent archetypes for wooly narratives and celebrations of American pluralism. Which is to say, Asian American religions ably represent the other and the assimilated celebrants of American multiculturalism. As noted by the recent, large-scale study of Asian Americans and religion conducted by the Pew Research Center for Religion and Public Life, despite constituting just under 6% of the American population, Asian Americans have had a disproportionate impact on the valorization of religious diversity in the United States. As the Pew report argues, "[Asian Americans] have been largely responsible for the growth of non-Abrahamic faiths in the United States, particularly Buddhism and Hinduism. Counted together, Buddhists and Hindus today account for about the same share of the U.S. public as Jews (roughly 2%). At the same time, most Asian Americans belong to the country's two largest religious groups: Christians and people who say they have no particular religious affiliation" (Pew Forum on Religion and Public Life 2012).

Alarmingly, such celebrations of Asian Americans as agents of religious pluralism produce a new variant on the model minority myth. In this context, analysts swap out educational and economic excellence for the civic virtues of multiculturalism, diversity, and pluralism as signs of the exceptionalism demonstrated by Asian American public life. For example, as socially conservative, ethnically coherent, and situatable in an American mythology of felicitous pluralism, the Asian American evangelical resonates with the narrative of Asian America as a model minority in the public sphere (Busto 1996). Just as the model minority myth has overshadowed the suffering and oppression of the vast majority of Asian Americans in the spheres of the economy, culture, and education with its persistent message that Asian Americans are unlike other racial and ethnic minorities insofar as they affirm a bootstrap mythology of American success, the exceptionalist narrative about Asian American Christians as prototypes of minority religious flourishing has obscured and skewed what counts as "acceptable" religion. Overinflating the value of "statistical significance" based on demography––and

subsequently undervaluing and not accounting for minorities among minorities like Asian American Muslims and Sikhs––is more than simply methodologically irresponsible; it unwittingly obscures violence and discrimination.

Even as a pluralist narrative about religion in the U.S. celebrates Asian Americans for serving as banners for the multicultural creed, it is critical to see that there is a dark side to this sort of notoriety. Setting aside the specious designation of certain ethnicities as stewards of particular religious traditions ("The Japanese are Buddhists, the Chinese are Confucians, the Indians Hindus. Right?!"), there is an existential problematic that arises in this racialization of Asian American religion. Must Asian Americans cultivate a possessive investment in "our" traditions? How do we contend with the hybridity of these traditions when deep in the mix we find Orientalist remnants such as the fetishization of Asian American faces practicing Buddhism or Hinduism? How might Asian American studies dispatch a constructive critique of this anxiety of authenticity without dismissing the traditions as unviable and irretrievable?

The constitution of Asian American identity through religion, race, and the American imperium has found its most clarifying instantiation in the aftermath of the 9/11 terrorist attacks. In a climate of opinion in which "Islam" has been transformed from "mere" religion to a symbol of terrorism directed against all things American domestically and abroad, the brown-skinned peoples of Asian descent and those who appear to be vaguely "Arab" have become targets of racism and violence. In a post-9/11 world, religion has intensified the racialization of Asian America. The culture of the American war on terror has intensified the American white supremacist taste for racial reductionism, where the counterpoise to secularized Protestant cultures and peoples is a terrorizing "Islam." And the racializing logic here is to compact and condense through appearance and ignorance. Asian American Sikhs have been targeted for violence because of a cartoonish presumption that turbans and beards are markers of "Muslim terrorists." The shooting at a Sikh temple and the alarm over the rising visibility of Asian American Muslims in American public life are exceptions that are proving a white supremacist rule. We also have witnessed the limits and limitations of American multiculturalism in the moral and political indignation over the would-be "mosque" designated for construction in the area near the Ground Zero site in Manhattan. Never mind that the proposed Muslim cultural center found its inspiration in the civic-minded model of the YMCA––the "Young Men's *Christian* Association." Here it was clear that an American supremacist anxiety had trumped the civic virtues of multiculturalism and pluralism. Seemingly "the one" to which "the many" should defer is increasingly intolerant of the brown and the non-Christian. E pluribus unum, perhaps.

Indeed, the continuing racialization of Asian American religions continues to emerge as a difference that celebratory pieties of toleration and diversity find difficult to absorb, let alone cultivate as markers of a vision of collective unity. It is *this* context that demands Asian American religious communities to engage in the reclamation project of Asian American religious traditions––projects in which Asian American claims to Buddhism, Christianity, Hinduism, Sikhism, Islam, Zoroastrianism, and other *Asian* religions will flourish only through a full and comprehensive racial consciousness. The religions of Asian America necessarily find shade and purpose, specter and meaning in the face of white supremacy and race. Asian America must set aside the wish to live and practice its religious traditions apart from these forces of power. The private and public are porous rather than fully separable. Seeking escape from stereotype by insisting on an alternative authentic archetype is politically naïve and, potentially, an act of bad faith. Seeking recognition for Asian American religions free from the overdetermination of white supremacy and anti-Asian racism is a laudable but ultimately self-defeating enterprise. Socially and politically engaged Asian American Buddhism, Christianity, Hinduism, Sikhism, Zoroastrianism, and Islam do not represent compromises of these traditions but rather are necessary and vital reinvigorations.

54

Resistance
Monisha Das Gupta

Resistance has a different valence in physics, biology, the social sciences, and the humanities, but each usage alludes to withstanding or opposing a force, power, or pathogen. The online *Dictionary of Critical Theory* (Buchanan 2012) helpfully steers us away from the desire to fix the definition of resistance, and, instead, encourages us to treat the concept as a "problematic" or a "theoretical starting point that is at once perplexing and productive." Many scholars in the humanities and social sciences have been deeply influenced by one such starting point: philosopher Michel Foucault's formulation, "Where there is power, there is resistance, and yet, or rather consequently, this resistance is never in a position of exteriority in relation to power" (1990, 95). The strategic, fluid, relational, and always-open-to-contest understanding of power enabled the idea that knowledge is a power effect exposed to destabilizations. Asian American studies itself was born as a site of resistance to the erasure of the histories and experiences of Asian Americans in university curricula. In the 1960s and 1970s, documenting, contextualizing, and analyzing the forging of this racialized group, developing material in which Asian American students could see their lives reflected, and connecting the issues that working-class Asian Americans faced in their communities to what was being taught at the university animated the demands to institutionalize the interdiscipline (Umemoto 2000).

While these motivations fueled all branches of ethnic studies, Asian American studies faced a unique challenge in claiming Asian Americans as people who were agents of social change that was aimed at dismantling structures of oppression. The dominant and persistent representations of Asian Americans as compliant and passive make it difficult to associate resistance with Asian Americans. The emergence and refinement of the model minority image of Asian Americans since the Cold War cast them as socioeconomically successful immigrants who reaffirm the foundational U.S. ideologies of the free market, equal opportunity, upward mobility, and individualism. Popular discourse represents Asian Americans as inherently conservative—averse to confrontation and social tumult. The model minority myth of Asian American success negates the need for and existence of Asian American resistance. Furthermore, most narratives about the social movements of the 1960s and 1970s continue to use the black-white framework and obliterate Asian American contributions to the fight against U.S. racism, imperialism, capitalism, and gender inequality during this period (Maeda 2009). Within this framing, resistance and Asian America become antithetical.

To bring the word "resistance" together with Asian America, then, is to engage in a counterhegemonic exercise. Resistance, in the traditional sense, has been associated with mass mobilizations, militancy, and organized struggles against racialized subordination such as those led by Asian migrants in the first half of the twentieth century on the plantations in Hawai'i, the fields in California and Washington, the canneries in the Northwest, and in internment camps. In the latter half of the twentieth century, the nonviolent struggles against the war in Viet Nam, U.S. military occupation in the Pacific (Hawai'i, Okinawa, South Korea, and the Philippines, for example), and the Marcos dictatorship in the Philippines form the iconic images of public protest. These events are valorized instances of resistance because they make Asian Americans vocal and visible.

The murder of Chinese American Vincent Chin, beaten to death by two white autoworkers in Detroit in 1982, and the violence unleashed against South Asian immigrants in Jersey City in 1987 led to a new wave of organizing that started to identify and address the multiple manifestations of anti-Asian violence. Feminist, queer, labor, and youth organizations as well as media watch groups proliferated. They got institutionalized as nonprofits in ways that could not have been anticipated in the 1960s and 1970s. A new generation of Asian Americans heatedly debated the merits of oppositional politics that focused on ethnic pride and identity, and those based on issues and cross-racial alliance building (Aguilar-San Juan 1994a). The participation of Asian Americans in popular culture, and the implications of funded organizing raised the fear of cooptation, and further unsettled the meaning of resistance (Davé, Nishime, and Oren 2005; S. Shah 1997).

While social movements overlap with resistance, they do not exhaust the sites and forms of Asian American activism. Drawing out the double meaning of her book, *Immigrant Acts*, Lisa Lowe reminds us that the title not only refers to law but also "names the *agency* of Asian immigrants and Asian Americans: the *acts* of labor, resistance, memory, and survival as well as the politicized cultural work that emerges from dislocation and disidentification" (1996, 9). Lowe points to the small forms of resistance, and to culture as a site of resistance. Her work confronts Asian American studies' ambivalence about the resistive qualities of culture. Even though cultural work—music, art, literature, and poetry—formed an intrinsic part of the Asian American movement (Maeda 2009), certain formulations of the project of Asian American studies continue to suspect the efficacy of cultural resistance.

Attention to the mundane and nondramatic forms of resistance, which spring up at the filaments of power far from the state and the economy, reveals a multiplicity of sites where Asian Americans continue to express themselves or destabilize the relation of power that dehumanized them. The poetry etched on the walls of the immigration station in Angel Island, the artful ways in which Chinese and Japanese women survived the interrogation at that station, the contestations in courtrooms to the unequal treatment of Asian Americans, and the leisure activities of Filipino men in dance halls and boxing rings provide a few examples of everyday forms and sites of resistance in the late nineteenth and early twentieth centuries. In the Asian American movement, literature, poetry, and music channeled resistance as do Asian American rap, hip hop, spoken word, and political comedy today (see, for example, O. Wang 2007). The electronic mediation of cultural expression and organizing in cyberspace, as well as the entanglement of creative work with both corporate and nonprofit sites of consumption, have posed theoretical and practical challenges to imagining resistance. Post-9/11, the shutting down of public spaces of protest has meant that dissent within surveilled and profiled communities has become hard to identify. As Sunaina Maira (2009) has argued in the case of South Asian and Muslim immigrant youth, the lack of vocal, collective, and public expressions of dissent should not be mistaken as silence or submission. Instead, she asks scholars and activists to consider a range of responses that depart from explicit and organized protest, and can lie on the continuum between complicity and resistance.

Since the 1990s, Asian American struggles have matured to engage with the differences in class, gender and sexual privilege, and political ideologies within Asian

American communities (A. Chung 2007; Das Gupta 2006; Manalansan 2003; Mathew and Prashad 2000; Omatsu 2008; Parreñas 2001). These struggles have given rise to sophisticated analyses of the workings of power. Several Asian American groups have organized against labor exploitation, domestic violence, and homophobia within their communities, and corrosive political ideologies like Hindu fundamentalism. Such issue-based organizing has required activists to confront and address the various forms of privilege that certain Asian Americans enjoy and exercise to exploit, marginalize, and violate the rights of co-ethnics.

The Vietnamese American community is ideologically divided as a result of selective U.S. refugee policies. Vietnamese refugees who came to the United States in the 1970s harbor anticommunist sentiments as do those who, in later years, escaped the abusive conditions of re-education camps. This hostility of Vietnamese refugees toward communism, a reality that unsettled the leftist antiwar Asian American activists, who stood in solidarity with the communist-led efforts to unify Viet Nam and fight U.S. imperialism (Maeda 2009), continues to haunt the crafting of progressive politics in the Vietnamese American communities. Vietnamese American activists have had to wrestle with the anticommunist legacy of the diaspora and the trauma of the war and displacement while articulating a critique of U.S. capitalism, imperialism, and heteropatriarchy (Duong and Pelaud 2012).

The intersectional approach to power relations has complicated the earlier movement's narrative of racial oppression as the defining and unifying experience for Asian Americans. It has opened up possibilities of forming coalitions with other marginalized groups on the basis of common issues. The approach has also tackled progressive social movements that routinely ignore the specific needs of Asian Americans and other people of color. Neither racialization nor a commitment to social justice guarantees a critical consciousness. Thus, an anti-oppression framework that takes on these conflicts might be more robust than that offered by "resistance."

The new century, which has seen an escalation of violence against Asian Americans and the coming of age of the second generation of post-1965 migrants, prompts a reexamination of the antagonistic relationship between resistance, conceived as anti-institutional, and electoral politics that restricts political action to existing systems. Both models have been used to mobilize Asian Americans, though the strategies are usually seen as irreconcilable. Conventionally, scholars and activists have promoted electoral politics as the most effective path to empowerment for Asian Americans, while others, concerned about cooptation, have favored protest politics, and community-based organizing. In fact, community-based ethnic organizations are often the entry point into the electoral process (Diaz 2012). In the twenty-first century, certain kinds of Asian American political participation have leveraged the legislative process to creatively push for measures that protect Asian Americans against workplace discrimination, exploitation in low-wage service jobs, and hate crimes directed at the community. The work of undocumented youth to access higher education, stop deportations, and fight back against immigration enforcement; the state-by-state lobbying by domestic workers to pass a bill of rights; and the sustained legislative campaign to have the Federal Bureau of Investigation recognize the violence committed against Sikhs as a hate crime are but a few recent examples of the ways in which activists have successfully combined protest politics with advocacy to change public policy.

The "Asian American" in Asian American resistance is an equally troubled category because of the disjuncture between the methodological nationalism (Wimmer and Schiller 2003) of the disciplines from which Asian American scholarship has emerged, and the transnational configuration of many Asian American struggles. Historically, we can think of the North America–based independence movements of South Asians, Koreans, and Filipinos against British, Japanese, and U.S. colonization. The protests against the Viet Nam war that linked domestic racism against Asian Americans to the brutalization of Vietnamese people, and the tenacious Filipino American resistance to the U.S.-backed Marcos dictatorship were transnational in their reach. A transnational consciousness—amplified by the current U.S. imperial ventures and the global dimensions of economic inequality—informs contemporary Asian American cultural and political resistance (see Sharma 2010).

Yet a strand of thought in Asian American studies places Asian migrants squarely within U.S. frames of reference, and signifies them as settlers (see Danico and Ng 2004 on the debate over whether Asian Americans are sojourners or settlers). From this perspective, that Asian Americans stayed put and built communities, instead of being driven out by racist policies and treatment, testifies to their resistance. The framework of settlement-as-resistance occludes the very workings of U.S. imperialism that Yến Espiritu (2003) has argued is fundamental to the transnational turn in Asian American studies. Settling, when conceptualized as resistance, erases indigenous presence, and naturalizes the United States' authority over the land that is being settled. Candace Fujikane (2008) has made this case in the context of Hawai'i. Transnationalizing Asian American resistance requires much more than movement politics that link issues and organizing across national boundaries. To gain clarity about how the United States built its empire, transnationalism as a framework provokes Asian American studies to go further than understanding that U.S. imperialism established the transnational patterns of Asian migration to the United States. It requires tracing the transpacific incarnations of U.S. imperialism back to the colonization of native America, and the appropriation of indigenous land. This conceptual shift implies contending with settling as a means of colonization rather than resistance.

55

Riot

Edward J. W. Park

The term "riot" occupies a central yet complicated place within Asian American studies. In its historical usage, the term signifies the critical importance of collective acts of violence that terrorized Asian immigrants and forced them to evacuate and retreat from various geographic regions and areas of social life. Anti-Asian race riots began soon after the first significant population of Chinese immigrants arrived in California, beginning with the 1849 California Gold Rush and lasting through the Great Depression, when Filipino farmworkers were targeted and attacked in various farming communities. Today, in Asian American studies, the term is most closely associated with the politics of naming the civil disturbance that occurred in Los Angeles from April 29 to May 4, 1992. Along with competing terms such as "rebellion," "uprising," and "civil unrest," the use of the term "riot" continues to cause controversy and reflects the complex location of Asian Americans in contemporary U.S. racial politics.

Anti-Asian race riots were pervasive throughout the American West from the 1870s to the 1930s. Riots as organized collective acts of violence were aimed at all major Asian American ethnic groups that arrived during this time. Riots took place in all types of places where Asian immigrants lived and worked, including major cities, small towns, and remote agricultural and mining communities. Much of the violence stemmed directly from economic competition between whites and Asians over natural resources, jobs, and other economic opportunities. However, not all anti-Asian race riots can be reduced to economic causes alone. The racially charged perception that Asian immigrants brought crime, vice, and disease along with the prevailing sense that Asians were unwilling and unable to assimilate fueled mob violence.

In 1854, the California Supreme Court overturned the conviction of George W. Hall, who was found guilty and sentenced to death for the murder of Ling Sing, a Chinese miner, based on the testimony of three Chinese men. The court based its decision by extending Section 14 of the California Criminal Procedure, which prohibited "blacks" and "Indians" from testifying against whites, to include the Chinese. Coming at a crucial, early stage of Asian American history, the *People v. Hall* decision provided the legal cover for whites to physically attack Asians with impunity. While various state laws were changed (California's in 1872) to comply with the Equal Protection Clause of the 14th Amendment of the U.S. Constitution, the de facto impunity for violence against Asian Americans continued. This was especially true in the West Coast and the interior West, where courts routinely rejected Asian testimony against whites. In addition, the U.S. government passed laws from the 1882 Chinese Exclusion Act to the 1917 Barred Zone Act that prevented the immigration of Asian laborers. Combined with a set of laws and court cases that declared all Asians ineligible for naturalized citizenship, this formal exclusion from the nation and its body politic added a veil of legitimacy and even tacit approval to the hostile treatment of Asian Americans, who appeared to have neither permanent nor equal claim to the nation. Within this context, anti-Asian race riots—along with government policies of discrimination in areas of residential segregation, land ownership, and employment—became one of many tools to manage, remove, and contain the presence of Asian Americans until World War II.

The Chinese experience with race riots would set the tone for the treatment of other Asian ethnic groups. From 1870 to 1890 alone, there were 153 anti-Chinese riots in the United States. Most widely known are the Los Angeles Riot of 1871, Rock Springs (Wyoming) Riot of 1885, San Francisco Riot of 1887, Tacoma Anti-Chinese Riot of 1885, and Seattle Anti-Chinese Riot of 1886. These riots demonstrate the complexity of causes, motivations, and consequences of collective acts of violence.

The first major anti-Asian race riot was the Los Angeles Riot of 1871, which expelled the Chinese population from the city and burned Chinatown to the ground. The riot was precipitated by the death of a white rancher who was caught in the crossfire of a gunfight between two Chinese factions. A mob of 500 attacked, robbed, and lynched Chinese residents to send an unequivocal message that the Chinese were unwanted in the city. The destruction of Chinatown would be followed by the steady decline and eventual demolition of the Mexican Sonoratown in an effort to Americanize Los Angeles and transform it from a Mexican outpost to the "Iowa on the Pacific" (Hise 2004). The Rock Springs Riot of 1885 demonstrated that the racial divide—cynically manipulated by employers yet zealously supported by white workers—left no room for the Chinese in the formation of working-class solidarity. The San Francisco Riot of 1887 translated the brutal hostility against the Chinese into a political movement led by the California Workingmen's Party. Anti-Chinese sentiment consolidated white workers who were themselves riven with differences of immigrant status and ethnicity; the slogan "Chinese must go!" effectively dramatized the assertion that whatever separated white workers was trivial in light of the "yellow peril" (Pfaelzer 2008).

In the Tacoma Anti-Chinese Riot of 1885, a mob of 500 whites forcibly marched 200 Chinese to the train station in the rain and left them waiting overnight without any shelter, resulting in the deaths of two from exposure. The Seattle Anti-Chinese Riot of 1886 followed the "Tacoma Method" and attempted to physically remove all Chinese from the city. Despite court orders and federal troops, hundreds of Chinese residents were shipped out of the city by steamers and railroad cars; this led to the collapse of the Chinese community, leaving behind only domestic workers who had the protection of their white employers. Despite the brutality of these acts—officials at the time counted 18 deaths in Los Angeles and 28 deaths in Rock Springs (scholars since then have judged the actual numbers to be many folds higher)—the perpetrators of the violence escaped punishment. Those found guilty in Los Angeles were set free on technicalities and those who were arrested in Rock Springs were released when the grand jury refused to bring charges against them. The defendants in the Rock Springs Riots received a heroes' welcome on their return. In both Tacoma and Seattle, some of the perpetrators were tried, but none were convicted as all-white juries either declined to bring criminal charges or acquitted them (Hildebrand 1977).

This logic of using collective violence to eliminate the very presence of Chinese was extended to other Asian groups that arrived to fill the economic vacuum created by the 1882 Chinese Exclusion Act. In 1907, the Bellingham Anti-Hindu Riot resulted in 200 Asian Indians, mostly Sikhs working in lumber mills, forcibly being removed from the northwestern part of Washington State. Korean American farmworkers were met by armed mobs in Hemet and Upland, two farming communities in Southern California, in 1913; Japanese farmworkers were literally driven out of Turlock, California, in trucks in 1921 and told never to come back unless they wanted to be lynched (Daniels 1977).

As American nationals, Filipinos were not subject to the anti-Asian immigration laws and they arrived in significant numbers from the early 1900s. High unemployment and intense labor competition brought on by the Great Depression resulted in anti-Filipino race riots that began in Exeter, California, in 1929 and crisscrossed the agricultural heartland of Central California, including in Watsonville, Stockton, and Reedley, in 1930. In addition to labor market competition, the widespread presence of taxi-dance halls catering to Filipino farmworkers became a source of popular outrage spurred on by public officials and newspapers. The resulting race riots involved thousands of participants who used guns and dynamite to terrorize Filipinos and destroy their labor camps. The most notable riot was in Watsonville, where the death of Fermin Tobera galvanized the Filipino farmworkers to double their efforts to establish labor unions and safeguard their civil rights (DeWitt 1976). Yet the anti-Filipino riots also helped California politicians to successfully lobby for Filipino exclusion and removal, resulting in the passage of the Tydings-McDuffie Act of 1934, which reclassified Filipinos as aliens subject to immigration restriction, and the passage of the Repatriation Act of 1935, which encouraged Filipinos to return to the Philippines (Cordova 1983).

Within this context, anti-Asian race riots were part of a broader strategy of institutional racism in which collective violence both expressed popular sentiment and demanded government intervention to deal with the Asian problem in a decisive way. Prior to World War II, these efforts succeeded with the passage of federal, state, and local laws that prevented immigration, withheld mainstream economic opportunities (for instance, by state laws that prohibited landownership), and imposed severe residential segregation, as the vast majority of Asian Americans retreated to a handful of overcrowded and impoverished ethnic communities (S. Chan 1991).

In contemporary Asian American studies, the term "riot" has taken on a different usage. On April 29, 1992, a mostly white jury in Simi Valley, California, acquitted all four Los Angeles Police Department (LAPD) officers charged with assault with a deadly weapon and excessive use of force against Rodney King, an African American who had been arrested after a high-speed car chase. The four police officers—Stacy Koon, Laurence Powell, Timothy Wind, and Theodore Briseno—brutalized King for one minute and 19 seconds with Tasers and batons before restraining and handcuffing him. An amateur videographer videotaped the incident from his apartment, and the footage was repeatedly broadcast by the media, resulting in widespread outrage and condemnation. As city leaders held a press conference to condemn the verdict, a spontaneous protest that began at the intersection of Florence and Normandie avenues in South Central Los Angeles quickly spread into the adjacent neighborhoods of Pico-Union, West Adams, and Koreatown. Woefully unprepared, the LAPD drew defensive parameters that protected affluent communities and commercial centers such as Hancock Park, the Financial District, and the Wilshire Corridor, but allowed looting and violence to continue unchecked within the poor and working-class sections of central Los Angeles. The most devastating civil unrest in modern U.S. history ended when order was finally restored by the California National Guard after five long days on May 4 (E. Park 1999).

The politics surrounding what to call the 1992 Los Angeles civil disturbance revealed cleavages not just within Asian American studies and communities but also within the broader U.S. society. Even as the event was unfolding, some activists and scholars emphasized the political and protest dimensions of the event. These activists and scholars saw it as a "rebellion" and an "uprising" that was the result of decades of economic exploitation, social injustice, and unfulfilled promise in the inner city. Los Angeles congresswoman Maxine Waters defended her use of the term "rebellion" by making the connection between what she saw as acts of rage to decades of crushing unemployment, widespread poverty, rampant police abuse, and government neglect. This position, however, was drowned out by the dominant media and other political leaders who labeled the event a "riot" and focused their attention on the looting, violence, and destruction, which lead to 53 deaths and over $1 billion in damage. Mayor Tom Bradley, the most important African American political leader in the city, minced no words as he characterized the event as a criminal riot that was separate and distinct from any legitimate political protest.

In this debate, Korean Americans were deeply implicated as one of the causes of the rebellion and the primary victims of the riot. Six months prior to the Rodney King beating trial, Los Angles had been captivated by the trial of Soon Ja Du, a Korean American convenience store owner who shot and killed Latasha Harlins, a 15-year-old African American girl whom she accused of shoplifting a bottle of orange juice. The trial came at the height of the decade-long Korean-black conflict in which African American activists charged Korean American business owners with exploiting and abusing African American residents. The light sentence given to Du after the jury found her guilty of voluntary manslaughter—five years of probation, 400 hours of community service, and a $500 fine—heightened tensions and has been cited by numerous scholars and activists as one of the causes of the civil disturbance (P. Min 1996). At the same time, the disproportionate damage to Korean American–owned businesses (including 175 of the 200 liquor stores destroyed during the civil

disturbance) and the decision on the part of the LAPD to allow looting to go unchecked in Koreatown for five days while protecting other, more affluent parts of the city led Korean Americans to claim they were victimized by both the mob and the authorities. Their sense of victimization extended into the rebuilding process, when African American political leaders successfully led the opposition to rebuilding the liquor stores and left many Korean Americans without a livelihood (E. Park 1999).

Against this backdrop, some segments of the Korean American community took great offense at calling the event anything other than the "riots" because terms such as "uprising" and "rebellion" seemed to give political cover to what they viewed as senseless violence. Kapson Yim Lee, the longtime editor of the English edition of *Korea Times*, went a step further, asserting that Korean Americans who avoided the term "riot" were attempting to ingratiate themselves to African American politicians. In Los Angeles, this placed a great deal of pressure on Korean American and Asian American activists and community-based organizations that were engaged in coalition work, particularly during the rebuilding process. Using the term "riot" would offend and alienate African Americans and other progressives who desperately wanted to retrieve political and protest intent and meaning from the event, but using the term "uprising" or "rebellion" would often stop all conversation within the Korean American community. Organizations such as KIWA (Korean Immigrant Workers Advocates, now Koreatown Immigrant Workers Advocates) decided to use the term "civil unrest" as a gesture of compromise, but this invited more anger from others who felt the term avoided any moral judgment (K. Lee 1997). Other organizations such as KYCC (Korean Youth and Community Center, now Koreatown Youth and Community Center) that were more dependent on Korean American funding sources adopted "riot" after great pressure from members of their board of directors and Korean American organizations including churches, victim's associations, and the ethnic media.

Likewise, the politics of what to call the event in Los Angeles represented a significant challenge for the field of Asian American studies and scholars working in the discipline. Much of the scholarship on the civil disturbance used these competing terms in the titles of books and journal articles to signal their political sympathies, but with nuances that make facile generalizations difficult. Over time, the Korean term for the event—"Sa-I-Gu" (literally 4–2–9, which refers to April 29, 1992, the first day of the event)—has become more widely used within Korean American and Asian American community circles. Within Asian American studies, the use of the term "Sa-I-Gu" has also become more common and has allowed the field to center the Korean American experience and subjectivity in the discourse surrounding the event. But, clearly, this is not a settled issue within Asian American studies and multiple labels are still used. Finally, this is a dilemma not for Korean Americans and Asian Americans alone; the African American newspaper *Los Angeles Sentinel* ran an editorial on April 26, 2012, that commemorated the 20th anniversary of the civil disturbance and used six different terms for the event: "rebellion," "uprising," "revolt," "riot," "civil unrest," and "urban insurrection" (Simmonds and Bihm 2012). Much like U.S. race relations and the place of Asian Americans in it, the term "riot" has undergone significant transformation, but what that change means is still up for debate.

56

Sexuality
Martin Joseph Ponce

In contemporary usage, "sexuality" refers to sexual orientation or the direction of an individual's desire. It is closely entwined with but also separable from biological sex (male, female, intersex) and gender expression (masculinity, femininity, transgender). The categories of heterosexuality, homosexuality, and bisexuality are based on a binary sex/gender system and are defined by an individual's object choice. Prior to this modern sense of sexuality as denoting erotic preferences and tastes, however, engaging in certain sexual acts did not necessarily entail definite sexual identities. It is not until the nineteenth and twentieth centuries through the work of sexologists, psychoanalysts, and state administrators that sexuality was gradually differentiated from sex and took on the psychological and emotional valences that it currently possesses, drawing into its orbit connotations of desire and attraction, fantasy and pleasure (Canaday 2009; Davidson 2001; Oosterhuis 2000).

Challenging notions of sexuality as a transhistorical, transcultural, immutable category of identity, many cultural studies researchers today consider sexuality to be a highly volatile nexus of power and knowledge whose meanings, uses, and values shift across time and place. Michel Foucault's account in *The History of Sexuality, Volume 1*, of the ways that institutions like the Church, political economy, medicine, psychiatry, criminology, and education generated "a steady proliferation of discourses concerned with sex" from the eighteenth century forward has been particularly influential (1990, 18). Work in this vein has elucidated the formal and informal systems of power that constitute sexuality as a domain of human experience subject to surveillance by authorities and that privilege certain sexual practices as normal and productive, while deeming others unnatural, sinful, criminal, and/or pathological in specific historical and social contexts. Queer theory's critique of fixed sexual identities and social normativities geared toward the social reproduction and advancement of capital, nation, and empire has impacted a range of interdisciplinary fields, including Asian American studies.

Though the convergence of queer theory and Asian American studies took place in the mid-1990s, sexuality has been central to Asian American studies since the field's emergence in the late 1960s and 1970s. Jennifer Ting (1998) has shown how the Asian American movement's press frequently invoked issues related to sexuality such as bourgeois marriage and the nuclear family, interracial relationships, and physical desirability and self-esteem. Although the bulk of these writings naturalized and valorized same-race heterosexuality, there were a number of self-identified lesbian and gay activists involved in the social movements of the 1970s. Recording conflicts between their commitments to racial and sexual communities and agendas, these writers and activists called for frameworks capable of analyzing the ways that race, sexuality, and gender intersect to produce interlocking forms of oppression and complex identities (Cornell 1996; Mangaoang 1996; Ordona 2003; Tsang 2000; Tsang 2001; Wat 2002).

The prominence of sexuality in Asian American studies is perhaps due to the fact that it has so often marked racial and ethnic difference as such. From the mid-nineteenth century to the present, sexuality and its entanglements with gender has been one of the primary modalities, to paraphrase Stuart Hall (1996, 55), through which Asian racialization in the United States has been lived and represented. Institutions like the law and immigration bureaus, cultural forms like political cartoons, literature, and film, and academic disciplines like sociology and anthropology assigned Asian groups "racial" characteristics relating to their bodies, habits, and dispositions by linking them with "sexual" traits and proclivities (Y. Espiritu 2008; Elaine Kim 1982; Robert Lee 1999; L. Lowe 1996; Marchetti 1994; P. Siu 1987). Foucault's notion of administrative "biopower," defined as the "diverse techniques for achieving the subjugation of bodies and the control of populations" (1990, 140) provides a means for examining Asian racialization as a sexualized and gendered process. The Page Law of 1875, for instance, cited race, gender, and sexuality in barring "women for the purposes of prostitution" from "China, Japan, or any Oriental country" (L. Kang 2002). The anti-Chinese movement that led to the Exclusion Act of 1882 not only vilified Chinese women as transmitters of venereal diseases and as prostitutes who corrupted white men and boys, but also cast suspicion on Chinese men's sexual practices and gender embodiment due to their hair and clothing styles and their "feminized" work as laundrymen and domestic help (Eng 2001; Erika Lee 2004). During this period, detainees at Angel Island were stripped and inspected for "Oriental diseases" and women were interrogated about their sexual pasts (Lee and Yung 2010, 77).

The gender imbalance produced by the U.S. immigration system (in tandem with Asian patriarchal conventions discouraging women from working abroad) contributed to the sexualization and differentiation of Asian American males in the early twentieth century. San Francisco's Chinatown, as Nayan Shah has shown, was perceived as a "bachelor society" brimming with dissolute, sexually perverse, opium-smoking men who cohabitated in "queer domestic arrangements" and posed a health hazard as syphilitics and lepers (2001, 78). Whereas Chinese men were read as either unmanly or coercively threatening, unattached Filipino and South Asian men were seen as hypersexual seducers, especially during moments of economic contraction and labor competition. Images of roving single men eager to court susceptible white women, eugenicist anxieties about the degenerate hybrid progeny spawned from such unions, and surveillance of same-sex interracial liaisons between Sikh men and white adolescents provoked state intervention and vigilante violence—the latter most notoriously against "Hindus" in Bellingham, Washington, in 1907, and against Filipinos in Watsonville, California, in 1930 (Baldoz 2010; Y. Espiritu 2003; Shah 2011). White supremacist beliefs regarding the purity of white women and the white race, coupled with business incentives to ensure a mobile family-free labor force, also led to the passing of antimiscegenation laws from the 1860s to the 1930s (Koshy 2004; Pascoe 2009). The Cable Act of 1922 stripped women of their U.S. citizenship if they married "aliens ineligible for citizenship," that is, Asian men (Volpp 2005).

The biopolitics of sexuality governing the legality and desirability of marriage, family, and other social relationships takes on added significance when construed in a transnational context shaped by U.S. imperialism, wars in Asia, and the uneven political economies of the global capitalist system. In contrast with attempts to ban Chinese women immigrants, the Gentlemen's Agreement of 1908 forbade Japanese laborers from immigrating but allowed Japanese men in the United States to send for their wives and children, leading to the "picture bride" practice of securing wives in Japan. (Following annexation in 1910, Korean men and women also participated in this practice). The War Brides Act of 1945 and its amendments enabled non-Asian and later Asian American G.I.s to bring their Asian wives and children to the United States as non-quota dependents. The family reunification provision inscribed in more recent immigration laws has, under the guise of uniting family members, facilitated the migration of service-oriented laborers necessary for capitalist accumulation while simultaneously shifting responsibility for the welfare of new immigrants from the state to the family, thereby exacerbating queer noncitizens' vulnerability to homophobic persecution (Reddy 2011). Finally, the explosion of international labor migration since the 1970s has rendered the transnational family, in which one or both parents work abroad and sends remittances home, a site of emotional and material tension within families as well as between workers, their host countries, and their homeland governments (Fajardo 2011; Manalansan 2008; Parreñas 2001; Parreñas 2005; R. Rodriguez 2010).

Postcolonial and diasporic frameworks further illuminate the ways in which sexuality is constitutive of international relations and globally connected communities. As Neferti Tadiar (2003) elucidates, the language of family and romance has been used to euphemize (neo)colonial domination and to characterize literal and metaphoric "sexual economies," such as the "Pacific marriage" between the U.S. and Japan in the post–World War II era or the "prostitution economies" of subordinate countries whose natural resources, labor, and bodies are extracted, exploited, and circulated on the global market. The Japanese military's conscription of thousands of females, many of them colonized Koreans, to work as "comfort women" during World War II also reveals the imbrication of imperialism and institutionalized sexual violence (Soh 2008; Yoshiaki 2000). The postwar formation of U.S. military camptowns near bases in South Korea, the Philippines, Thailand, and Okinawa and the regulation of military prostitution in those areas similarly exposes the sexual politics of empire building (Moon 1997; Sturdevant and Stoltzfus 1992; Yuh 2002). The mixed-race children produced from these conditions, often stigmatized in South Korea and Viet Nam for their associations with war and prostitution, prompted state and religious organizations to address the needs of orphans through transnational adoption programs, even as adult adoptees themselves have developed alternative forms of kinship beyond the (transracial) nuclear family and the nation-state (Eng 2010; Eleana Kim 2010; Jodi Kim 2009). The United States' involvement in Asia, the "domestication" of Asian female sexuality, and internet and "mail-order bride" practices have rendered Asian women desirable mates for non–Asian American men (Constable 2003).

From another angle, scholarship in queer diaspora studies has examined how sexuality is not only regulated by U.S. institutions and discourses but also by homeland political movements that seek to enforce culturally "authentic" codes of behavior on their compatriots abroad. These frameworks illuminate the ways that (queer) diasporic subjects navigate the competing claims on their allegiances, negotiate ethnic and mainstream gender and sexual norms, remake domestic relationships, and create alternative public cultures and expressive practices (Gopinath 2005; Manalansan 2003; Ponce 2012). Queer diasporic critique has also unraveled the temporal logics underwriting the bifurcated meanings of sexuality in "developed" and "developing" nations. Jasbir Puar's (2007) term "homonationalism" denotes how the United States's supposed progressive tolerance toward upstanding (white) gays and lesbians depends on demonizing other, especially Muslim, Arab, and South Asian, societies as morally backward and un-modern for both harboring "monstrous" sexual deviants prone to terrorism and refusing to accept non-heterosexuals in their midst. This spatio-temporal critique extends into the international arena the trope of

cross-generational Asian Americanization in which the new generation establishes itself against the immigrant generation's views of extramarital or queer sexual relations as lamentable signs of Western decadence (Y. Espiritu 2003; Maira 2002).

Whether as an instrument of U.S. biopower that has generated what Judy Wu calls Asian Americans' "compulsory sexual deviance" (2003, 60) or as the locus of homeland anxieties and familial discipline, sexuality remains a principal domain of Asian Americanist critique, activism, and rearticulation. The protests against the 1991 New York production of *Miss Saigon*, the controversy surrounding Lois-Ann Yamanaka's novel *Blu's Hanging* in 1998, and the furor incited by *Details* magazine's satire "Gay or Asian?" in 2004 represent a few recent examples of sexuality's contentious place in Asian American social life (Yoshikawa 1994; Fujikane 2000; Masequesmay and Metzger 2009, respectively). Debunking sexualized Asian images disseminated in Hollywood film and other mainstream media—the dragon lady, lotus blossom, lascivious Chinaman, Filipino rapist, effeminate houseboy, asexual nerd—remains a venerable undertaking. At the same time, feminists and queer theorists have cautioned against reinscribing heteronormative ideals regarding "proper" gender roles, sexual desires, and respectable domesticity (Cheung 1990; Eng and Hom 1998; Elaine Kim 1990). Celine Parreñas Shimizu (2007) and Nguyen Tan Hoang (2014), for example, have approached female "hypersexuality" and gay male "bottomhood" as categories to be analyzed and reevaluated, not merely condemned as inherently degrading.

Recent scholarship has implicitly heeded Dana Y. Takagi's challenge to "rethink identity politics" in both racial and sexual terms (1996, 32). Opening up sexuality beyond rigid classifications and prescriptive moralisms has led to reconsiderations of inter- and intraracial, cross-sex and same-sex relationships through affective registers of intimacy, longing, friendship, material sustenance, and "queer sociality" (Ponce 2011; Shah 2011; Sueyoshi 2012; J. Wu 2005). Such approaches may provide alternatives to the identitarian codifications that subtend what David Eng calls "queer liberalism," the dominant form of U.S. sexual politics aimed at petitioning the state for recognition through marriage and military service equality, antidiscrimination laws, and the right to privacy (2010, 4). Framed within the racial history of state intervention in sexual matters, this style of politics should give us pause. Thus, while analyzing sexuality in its manifold guises—as the sign of racial difference, of vitality or degeneration, of racial commitment or betrayal, of liberty or repression, of asymmetrical power relations—the contemporary moment also demands that Asian American studies continue to trace historical and emerging lines of affinity and attachment—enduring and ephemeral, sexual and otherwise—that are informed but not coopted by the biopolitical and neoliberal logics of state and diasporic nationalisms.

57

Terrorism
Rajini Srikanth

"Terrorism" comes from the Latin word *terrorem*, meaning "great fear, dread." The *Oxford English Dictionary* (1971) marks 1795 as the first time the word was used, in the phrase "reign of terrorism," to refer to the "government by intimidation as directed and carried out by the party in power in France during the Revolution of 1789–94." The reference is to Maximilian Robespierre, a member of the Jacobin political club that overthrew the French monarchy; Robespierre terrorized opponents who, in his view, undermined the objectives of the revolution (Mayer 2000; Žižek 2011).

Terrorism seeks the following outcomes: "regime change, territorial change, policy change, social control, and status quo maintenance" (Kydd and Walter 2006, 52). Types of terrorism include "state-sponsored terrorism, religious terrorism, suicide terrorism, transnational terrorism, and homegrown terrorism" (Mahan and Griset 2008, xiii).

The earliest Asian American victims of terrorism were Chinese immigrants who were targeted by anti-Chinese groups between 1850 (when news of gold brought Chinese to California) and the early 1900s. The perpetrators of this terrorism included white miners in the gold fields of California, trade union members, railroad workers, and Irish and German immigrants who felt that the presence of Chinese laborers undermined their own opportunities for work (Pfaelzer 2007; S. Chan 1991; Takaki 1989). Cities such as Tacoma, Washington, and Eureka, California, were "purged" of their Chinese inhabitants by angry white residents, and Chinatowns were burned to the ground. In 1907, lumber-mill workers from India were driven out from Bellingham, Washington, by 500 white men who terrorized them. Japanese, Korean, and Filipino laborers were also "terrorized" in the early years of the 20th century (Berlet and Lyons 2000). On the global stage, the Philippine–American War (1899–1902) led to excesses, including water torture, by the U.S. military against the anti-imperial resistance fighters in the Philippines. A "scorched earth" policy destroyed the resistance fighters' food supply, and civilians, too, were not spared (Schumacher 2006). Mark Twain (1901) wrote a scathing condemnation of the self-righteous cruelty of the advocates of U.S. imperialism in the Philippines.

The internment by the United States government of 120,000 Americans of Japanese ancestry (two-thirds of whom were American citizens) might well be considered an act of state-sponsored terrorism. In the days and months following the bombing of Pearl Harbor by Japanese planes on December 7, 1941, there was intense anti-Japanese feeling among the general population. This sentiment was stoked by the U.S. government, which proclaimed that anyone of Japanese descent could not be trusted, and then proceeded to buttress that claim by removing and confining in concentration camps, through presidential order, the Japanese Americans living on the West Coast (G. Robinson 2009). In 1988, the U.S. government apologized for and made reparations to surviving internees for this state-initiated racist action.

Nonetheless, there is debate over whether the word "terrorism" can be applied to violent actions by governments on citizens of their own or other nations. Some scholars argue that terrorism is, by definition, the actions of non-state actors or subnational groups to "obtain a political, religious or ideological objective through the intimidation of a huge audience" (Enders and Sandler 2002, 145–46). The International Commission of Jurists states that "in principle, anyone can commit terrorist acts: it is important, therefore, to focus on the act itself and not the actor" (International Commission of Jurists 2009, 3).

The violence of decolonization struggles has sometimes been equated with terrorism (Lawrence 2010; Prochaska 2003). Others make a distinction between armed struggle and guerilla warfare, on the one hand, and terrorism, on the other (Burgorgue-Larsen and Úbeda de Torres 2011; Enders and Sandler 2006; Elbaum 2002). The Cuban Revolution (1953–1958), the Algerian Revolution (1950s and early 1960s), the Kenyan Mau Mau resistance to British colonial rule (1950s), the Sandinista revolution in Nicaragua (1978–1990), and the African National Congress's 30-year armed struggle against the apartheid government of South Africa are seen as emancipatory or revolutionary movements that employed violence against oppressive regimes.

Violent resistance to democratic governments is, by contrast, usually labeled as terrorism, because the democratic process theoretically should allow for the expression of dissatisfaction and anger through nonviolent means (Robison, Crenshaw, and Jenkins 2006). Thus, when non-state actors in democracies take up arms, they are perceived as unreasonably choosing to reject the available paths of engagement in order to terrorize the nation (Nadarajah and Sriskandaraj 2005).

Some examples of terrorism within the last 100 years include the actions of the anticzarists in the years leading up to and during the Russian Revolution of 1917 (Mayer 2001), the violence against intellectuals and the bourgeoisie during the Cultural Revolution in China (1966–1976) (Dutton 2008; MacFarquhar and

Schoenhals 2009; Žižek 2011), and the brutal crushing of opposition and dissent by the dictatorships of Argentina's Jorge Videla (1976–1983) and Chile's Augusto Pinochet (1973–1990). Non-state terrorist actors in the 20th century include the Zionist group Irgun in British-controlled Palestine (Beinin 2003), the Basque separatist group ETA in Spain, the Irish Republican Army in Northern Ireland, the left-wing Red Army Faction in Germany, the left-wing and anti-NATO Red Brigades in Italy, the ethnic nationalist Sri Lankan Tamil Tigers (LTTE) (DeVotta 2011), the Palestinian groups Hamas and the Popular Front for the Liberation of Palestine, Aum Shinrikyo in Japan, the Maoists in India, and al-Qaeda and its various affiliates in different parts of the world. In all these cases, there is deep dissatisfaction with the existing social and political order. The state is seen as normalizing oppression and presenting a narrative that ignores the just claims and demands of the groups that challenge the state.

Within the United States, the Ku Klux Klan terrorized African Americans (Cunningham 2008) in the late 19th and first half of the 20th centuries, and the radical left-wing Weather Underground Organization conducted numerous antigovernment attacks protesting the bombing campaigns in Southeast Asia in the 1970s (Alimi 2011). However, the word "terrorism" forcefully entered public consciousness with the 1993 bombing of the World Trade Center and the 1995 bombing of the Oklahoma federal building. These two attacks spurred Congress to pass the 1996 Anti-Terrorism and Effective Death Penalty Act (AEDPA), which introduced sanctions leading to deportation of noncitizens convicted of felonies, regardless of whether they were committed when the person was a minor and regardless of any time served. For instance, young men of Cambodian descent in their 20s were deported to Cambodia (a country they left when they were children) because of felonies

committed when they were adolescents growing up in tough urban neighborhoods in the United States (Grabias 2006; Kwan 2013).

The attacks on the United States of September 11, 2001, dramatically escalated the public's and the state's attention to terrorism and led to then president George W. Bush declaring a "global war on terror." He vowed to seek out terrorists anywhere in the world and pursue them relentlessly. In 2009, shortly after President Barack Obama took office, the ICJ insisted that the new administration "repudiate" Bush's phrase, because it had allowed his administration to violate international human rights laws by, for example, setting up the detention facility in Guantànamo Bay, Cuba, in early 2002 (International Commission of Jurists 2009). The international outrage over Guantànamo arose from the imprisonment and torture of over 700 Muslim men, who were picked up in Afghanistan (following the United States' bombing offensive there in October 2001) and charged, on insubstantial evidence, with involvement in al-Qaeda. There has been a concerted effort by lawyers (a significant number of them from the private bar working pro bono) and international human rights organizations to obtain the release of these detainees. Since 2004, approximately 600 of them have been released to their home countries or other countries that have agreed to or been coerced to take them (Srikanth 2012).

Since September 11, 2001, the global conversation on terrorism has been dominated by the United States (Hamid 2007). On October 26, 2001, Congress passed a set of greatly strengthened antiterrorism measures providing the government with increased powers to require special registration (from September 2002 to May 2003) of individuals from 23 Muslim-majority countries as well as Eritrea and North Korea in order to monitor the activities of individuals and groups, prevent the flow of monies and other material help to organizations deemed to be supporting terrorism, and facilitate the sharing of information between local law enforcement and the Federal Bureau of Investigation (Cainkar 2002). These expanded powers were authorized under what is known as the Uniting and Strengthening America by Providing Appropriate Tools Required to Intercept and Obstruct Terrorism (USA Patriot) Act. Many noncitizens from Pakistan, Bangladesh, and Middle Eastern and Southeast Asian nations were deported for minor immigration violations, dismembering families as a result (Chen and Yoo 2010). Asian American law professor Viet Dinh, who served as U.S. assistant attorney general for legal policy from 2001 to 2003 in the Bush administration's Department of Justice under John Ashcroft, had a central role in crafting the USA Patriot Act (Ashcroft and Dinh 2011).

John Yoo (2011), another visible Asian American in the Bush administration, was one of the principal authors of the "torture memos," the now infamous communications from the Office of Legal Counsel (OLC) to the president providing justification for the use of torture, which was euphemistically labeled "advanced interrogation techniques." Yoo has been heavily criticized by many of his legal colleagues for his misuse of rhetoric and manipulation of the law, and the international community has soundly condemned the use of torture by the United States (Cole 2009).

The aggressive deployment of the state's surveillance and apprehension apparatus has had a profound impact on Asian American communities. In the days immediately following the attacks of September 11, 2001, entire communities were terrorized by the state; men of Middle Eastern descent, South Asian men including Sikhs, and Muslim men in particular were targeted for detention and harsh treatment. Raids in the middle of the night led to men being taken to the Passaic County Jail or the Metropolitan Detention Center in Brooklyn where they were interrogated, degraded, and tortured (Mathur 2006). More than 1,100 men were rounded up and held in detention immediately after 9/11, and they were incarcerated for an average of 80 days (Bayoumi 2008). Though Section 102 of the USA Patriot Act explicitly calls for the protection of the "civil rights and civil liberties" of "Arab Americans, Muslim Americans, and Americans from South Asia" and for the "condemn[ation]" of "any acts of violence or discrimination" against these groups, the reality on the ground is very different (New York City Profiling Collaborative et al. 2012).

Veena Dubal, director from 2009 to 2011 of the National Civil Rights and Security Center of the Asian Law Caucus and defense attorney for many Muslim men under surveillance and deportation orders for supposed terrorist activities, remarks on the pernicious reach of surveillance mechanisms: men are wrongfully accused, deemed to be terrorists or abetting terrorists, stripped of their civil liberties, undermined in their professions and occupations, and left with mere shells of their former lives and selves. According to Dubal (2011), the FBI has "compiled files" on tens of thousands of "potentially . . . innocent Americans." The Obama administration's controversial use of drones against suspected terrorists in Yemen and Pakistan is a more recent counterterrorism strategy. The violation of these nations' sovereignty and the loss of civilian lives are deemed by critics to constitute acts of state terrorism (*New York Times* 2013).

Finally, there are indirect forms of assault on Muslims and those of Arab descent through perspectives disseminated in social studies textbooks. Analysis of these textbooks (Saleem and Thomas 2011), focusing on three states (Texas, California, and Florida) that comprise 33% of the market, reveals that terrorism is consistently linked to Arabs and Muslims, and Islam is portrayed as fostering terrorism. Students of Arab descent and Muslim faith feel targeted and demonized by these depictions; interviews of these students show that they reject what is conveyed in the texts and disconnect from the lessons that draw on these readings. The politics of "terrorism" used to indiscriminately target Arab Americans and Muslim Americans leads to the alienation of young people in these communities and risks making them feel like unwelcome guests in their own country (Aslan 2010).

58

Transnationalism
Lan P. Duong

"Transnationalism" is a term used in many disciplines: the social sciences, anthropology, sociology, international law, economics, feminist studies, and cultural studies. A prominent keyword in these fields, it is nonetheless a contested term. Although there have always been the transnational phenomena of migration and movement, transnationalism—as it is commonly used today—expresses a contemporary condition, one that is vitally associated with a post-Fordist economy, finance capital, and flexible accumulation. This is especially marked in the ways that globalized corporations, large-scale flows of capital and information, and migratory workforces have become more dominant within late capitalist modernity. In this context, transnationalism refers to a profoundly felt interconnectivity between people and places. It gestures toward the ways in which people, ideas, and goods traverse regions or nation-states, the interconnections of which have been intensified by twenty-first-century modes of telecommunications and transportation that enable the hyperswift crisscrossing of both commodities and capital. Arising from these processes, studies of the transnational tend to decentralize the nation-state as an analytic framework within which to study the modes of culture, history, and people that are formed and re-formed transnationally.

Particularly within the social sciences, transnationalism encapsulates recent migration patterns that highlight the multiple arrivals and leave taking of migrants who are moving and resettling for a variety of reasons. As a result of such traffic, transnational migrants may have various alliances to different countries simultaneously in a dynamic of the "here" and "there" that is a part of the transnational condition. Such subjects may also develop a conglomeration of (filial, affective, economic, and organizational) networks as a consequence. For many scholars, a transnational paradigm recognizes the intricate mapping of social experience across axes of time and space and allows for a broader understanding of the ways in which cultures and identities circulate both nationally and transnationally.

However, it is precisely because of transnationalism's elasticity in explaining such an expansive range of phenomena that some researchers have also attempted to critique the ways that transnational modes of analysis fail to capture the complexities of state powers and their relation to the transnational subject (Waldinger and Fitzgerald 2004). With an uncritical notion of transnationalism and a lack of proper historicization of the transnational, moreover, its usage may lead to celebrations of mobility, hybridity, and cosmopolitanism. In the wake of the term's popular currency, scholars have further qualified "transnationalism" as it contrasts to and may be coupled with other terms, such as "diaspora," "globalization," and "feminism."

In looking at the ways that transnationalism differs from diaspora, Jana Braziel and Anita Mannur (2003) underscore the affective qualities of being a diasporan. They explain that the diasporic experience describes people and communities that have been displaced, with migrations that tend to be more forced than voluntary. Transnationalism, in contrast, alludes to a more abstract discourse that underscores the circulation of people as well as information, goods, and capital across national territories. For Braziel and Mannur, diaspora enables a rethinking of what it means to deterritorialize, draw

the bounds of community, and define the terms of citizenship.

Others have delineated how transnationalism works in contradistinction to globalization. As Françoise Lionnet and Shu-mei Shih (2005) argue, the transnational and the global are spatially different; globalization assumes a universal core from which everything spreads outward, while transnationalism locates particular sites of exchange and hybridity. Moving away from the binaries of local and global, the transnational is thus constitutive of the center and periphery, across multiple spatialities and temporalities. For these authors, this quality of transnationalism opens a critical and productive space for analyses of a "minor transnationalism," which looks at the resistant mode of minorities across different texts and contexts within a comparative frame.

Another way in which transnationalism has been qualified is through the lens of feminism. Inderpal Grewal and Caren Kaplan (1994) distinguish earlier feminisms like global and international feminism from a formulation of transnational feminism that does not align all women together. Transnational feminists contend that feminist scholars must always consider the crucial differences of class, privilege, location, and ethnicity that exist between women against the context of multinational corporate agendas and those of the nation-state's. Transnational feminist scholars critique the dominant tenets of a Western feminism that disavow the subjectivity and agency of marginalized women, contesting at the same time the terms of a Western postmodernism that would elide the narratives and experiences of those in the global South.

Within Asian American studies, the "transnational turn" has also been the subject of many articles (R. Leong 1989; Hune 1989; Mazumdar 1991; Collet and Lien 2009). A transnational emphasis in this field has been shaped by factors such as post-1965 immigration patterns and an upsurge of scholars who analyze communities, cultures, and politics within transnational frameworks. In earlier strands of the debate, some Asian Americanists have decried this move to "denationalize" Asian American studies, which displaces the U.S. as a site of critique for the problems of classism, sexism, and heterosexism that take root within U.S. borders (S. Wong 1995). Other scholars are also critical of this direction in the discipline because of the ways that it dislodges questions of race and coalition building in the formation of Asian American communities (D. Li 2000).

However, for another group of critics, the notion that "Asians on the rim" constitutes a swathe of subjects whose trajectories necessarily interweave with a multitude of different types of histories is an important consideration. As Arif Dirlik (1996) notes, this consideration, however, must also be deeply attentive to the local in order to oppose the global, most especially in the guise of global capitalism. Responding to these debates, scholars argue that a progressive political project can indeed be achieved through the lens of transnationalism as a way to critique U.S.-centrism and the kinds of nationalisms that occur at home and abroad, within both the local and global (C. Lee 2005). Moreover, rather than an either/or approach to national and transnational concerns, Asian American scholars are encouraged to use a multipronged approach in tracing the lives and livelihoods of Asians in the Americas and other parts of the world (J. Okamura 2003).

Debates about transnationalism show the recent investment that scholars have in a mode of analysis that goes beyond the logics and reach of the nation-state. Nonetheless, for transnationalism to remain a critical term, it must also be allied with a hyperawareness of its alignments with global capitalism and appropriations of minority politics and identities. Further, transnationalism, as a process, concept, and methodology, must always be defined in relation to a historically specific context of cross-border processes and thus tend to the imbalanced relations of power as well as systems of knowledge that often undergird transnational movement. In this way, transnationalism can be used as an effective critique of local and global forms of power, serving as "a strategic research site" that tracks cultural productions, community formations, social movements, and political change within multiple contexts (Faist 2010).

59

Trauma

Cathy J. Schlund-Vials

According to the *Oxford English Dictionary*, "trauma" (noun) refers to "a wound or external bodily injury in general; also the condition caused by this." Shifting from the physical to the psychological, "trauma" analogously denotes "a psychic injury, esp. one caused by emotional shock the memory of which is repressed and remains unhealed." In adjectival form, "traumatic" signifies the following: "of, pertaining to, or caused by a psychic wound or emotional shock, esp. leading to or causing behavioral disturbance." Within recent memory, these "psychic wounds" and "emotional shocks" are inextricably linked to war and state-authorized mass violence. As Cathy Caruth avers in "Unclaimed Experience: Trauma and the Possibility of History," "The experience of the solider faced with sudden and massive death around him, for example, who suffers this sight in a numbed state, only to relive it later on in repeated nightmares, is a central and recurring image of trauma in our century" (1996, 10). Haunted by "repeated nightmares" of "sudden and massive death," Caruth's didactic vignette encompasses a now-familiar psychological narrative of a priori violence, presentist (non) response, and unreconciled aftermath.

Despite the generalized nature of Caruth's soldier account, the contemporary currency of the term is historically fixed to a specific wartime referent: the American War in Viet Nam (1959–1975). While accounts of post-traumatic stress disorder (PTSD) circulated in the aftermaths of World War I (1914–1918), World War II (1941–1945), and the Korean War (1950–1953), it was not until 1980 that PTSD was included in the *Diagnostic and Statistical Manual* of the American Psychiatric Association. Hence, the term's etymology by way of U.S. foreign policy (with the exception of the "Great War") brings to light its militarized connection to the Pacific, East Asia, and Southeast Asia. As important, integral to the American psychological history of PTSD is the figure of the returning war veteran, pathologically cast in the role of traumatized migrant. Given the implied focus on migration and the concomitant evaluation of internationalized affect, PTSD as transnational diagnosis is both relevant and legible to Asian American studies, a field that consistently considers traumatic histories and politics abroad alongside distressing policies and practices at home. For instance, the compulsory incarceration of Japanese Americans during World War II disturbingly (albeit divergently) coexists with the August 1945 atomic bombings of Hiroshima and Nagasaki. The present-day plight of Southeast Asian refugees and Southeast Asian Americans is troublingly rooted to the expansive violence of the American War in Viet Nam. At the turn of the twenty-first century, South Asian Americans and Arab Americans emerge as traumatized victims of conflict-driven xenophobia and anti-Islamic hate crimes as per the racialized tenets of the so-named "War on Terror."

Alternatively, while Caruth's abovementioned assertion focuses its analytical attention on the *individual* survivor, the now-established field of trauma studies is equally concerned with *collective* (and collected) memory, particularly with regard to genocide survivors. From Germany to Rwanda, from Bangladesh to Bosnia, and from East Timor to Cambodia, the systematic extermination of millions foregrounds Holocaust survivor Elie Wiesel's (1999) evocative assertion that the legacy of the twentieth century was "so much violence, so much indifference." As Asian American studies scholars have argued, Asian bodies, without the benefit of international tribunal or war crimes court, have repeatedly been the traumatized recipients of "so much violence, so much indifference" vis-à-vis U.S. foreign policy (D. Rodríguez 2010; Jodi Kim 2010; Schlund-Vials 2012b). To be sure, such state-authorized violence is by no means limited to the Asian American experience, nor is it the explicit domain of international human rights. Indeed, what connects fields as diverse as Native American, Latino/a, and African American studies is a vexed and often ignored history of racialized (and gendered) violence. Such painful narratives are harrowingly evident in all-too-familiar histories of state-sponsored land removal, racially motivated massacres, and constitutionally sanctioned enslavement. Incontrovertibly, the traumatic memory of U.S. racism ignited the mid-century civil rights movement; it was analogously at the forefront of *Brown v. Board of Education* (1954), wherein the majority opinion accessed the psychological cost of white supremacy as the basis for dismantling Jim Crow segregation.

Notwithstanding its contemporary resonance as a post-conflict, post-genocide modifier in the twentieth and twenty-first centuries, trauma's etymologically Greek origins and pervasive usages underscore a more expansive genealogy. Reintroduced to the medical lexicon by seventeenth-century Dutch physician Steven Blankaart, "trauma" was initially synonymous with physical injuries caused by an external force (*OED*). More than two hundred years later, "trauma" would assume a more interior register vis-à-vis Sigmund Freud's clinical work at the turn of the twentieth century. As an incontrovertibly *embodied* term, "trauma" is concomitantly Janus faced, encapsulating past, present, and future frames. This tripartite construction is at the forefront of Freud's "Remembering, Repeating and Working Through," wherein the Austrian psychoanalyst recapitulates a specifically trauma-driven process. Methodologically predicated on so-termed "intrusive recollection," Freud observes that a patient's feelings of fear and anxiety are evident "not as a memory but as an action; he repeats without, of course, knowing that he is repeating" (1976, 271).

Inadvertently (yet nevertheless productively), Freud's characterization of trauma through unacknowledged repetition on one level resonates with Raymond Williams's original "keywords" project from 1976, which sought to map the multivalent registers of a term through multiple social and cultural states. Expressly, Williams's attempt to trace the prevalence of an idiom through multiple iterations and understandings echoes the process of diagnosing the source and present-day impacts of trauma. On another level, Freud's evaluation of traumatic recurrence coheres with the troubling events that undergird the formation and continuation of Asian American studies, which (to reiterate and expand) unswervingly considers the racialized recurrence of exclusion, imperialism, and citizenship. From dominant-held notions of perpetual foreignhood to mainstream acts of model minoritization, from state-sanctioned immigration prohibition to federally authorized militarized invasion, Asian American scholars (in the humanities and social sciences) assume the role of social, political, and cultural psychoanalysts who identify the failure of U.S. exceptionalism via the traumatic experiences of Asian immigrants, migrants, and refugees.

On the one hand, at stake in Asian American studies is an evaluation of the United States as an amnesic patient that rehearses, restages, and replays acts of racial violence by way of contemporary foreign policy and present-day domestic practice. Diagnosis involves a simultaneous consideration of the nation-state comprised of the psychological and corporal. Whereas the nation represents an imagined formation (in which certain bodies are socially and culturally deemed acceptable while others are cast as inassimilable), the state is defined by certain material "acts" (e.g., naturalization law and immigration policy). Accordingly, the very title of Lisa Lowe's foundational work—*Immigrant Acts: On Asian American Cultural Politics* (1996)—highlights this critical yet vexed relationship between Asian American studies, migration, legislation, and action.

On the other hand, this assessment of field politics and practices attends to a converse connection to and association with trauma. If the United States as pathologized nation-state is a de facto first premise in Asian American studies, then the Asian/American body is both symptomatic of this condition and the primary victim of it. Drawing on Williams's oft-quoted, emotionally driven axiom, this relationship between external cause and interior consequence—which syncretically involves traumatic forgetting and painful remembering—substantively "structures the feelings" that circumscribe the field of Asian American studies. These affective turns, which take emotive shape in vehement calls for sociopolitical recognition, vociferous pronouncements about equal representation, and determined criticisms of systemic oppression, collapse the temporal bounds of long-standing anti-Asian American racialization (Y. Espiritu 1992; Omi and Winant 1994; Okihiro 1994; V. Nguyen 2002; Chuh 2003; M. Chiang 2009). Continuing in an affective vein, if integral to the very idea of "nation" is, as Ernest Renan averred, not a common language or culture but instead a shared sense of grief, then Asian America is ostensibly unified vis-à-vis a panethnic history of inequality, exploitation, and disenfranchisement. This reading of the field through "aggrieved" frames coincides with the notion of a legible "Asian Americanist critique." Indeed, as Lowe surmises and summarizes, at the forefront of such an appraisal is a cyclical "tireless reckoning" of the past in the present.

Set adjacent this historicized and historical sense of indefatigable critique, one of the field's founding precepts—recovery—potently reverberates with a medicalized reading of Asian American studies. Rooted in reclaiming what has previously been forgotten (via state-sanctioned directive, dominant practice, and hegemonic omission), recovery signals a distinct and identifiable preoccupation with history and memory (Yoneyama 1999; Eng 2001; A. Cheng 2001; J. Chang 2012). Historically situated alongside Freud's prescription of "intrusive recollection," the field's recovery work was ignited in the 1960s and early 1970s by the civil rights movement, anti-imperial "Third World liberation" movements, and the antiwar movement (Wei 1993; Louie and Omatsu 2001; Prashad 2002; Võ 2006; Fujino 2005; Fujino 2012). Accordingly, the initial aim of such recuperative labor was the formation of a largely under-mined, interdisciplinary Asian American archive. Correspondingly, historians actively rescued lost histories of nineteenth-century railroad workers, spectral paper sons, and plantation laborers (Takaki 1979; S. Chan 1991). Authors and literary critics unabashedly salvaged forgotten works by Sui Sin Far, Carlos Bulosan, and John Okada (Chin et al. 1974; Chin et al. 1979; Elaine Kim 1982; Lim and Ling 1992; San Juan 1995). Last, but certainly not least, social scientists militated against the amnesic registers of the "model minority myth" via analyses of immigration, economic disparity, and racial formation (Omi and Winant 1994).

In sum, from West Coast race riots to World War II incarceration, from the Spanish–American War to the American War in Viet Nam, and from economically driven migration to involuntary exile, the sites that constitute the Asian American studies archive reflect and refract the field's traumatic contours (Robert Lee

1999; Võ and Bonus 2002; G. Robinson 2009; A. Isaac 2006; Pelaud 2010). "Tirelessly" committed to exposing the intimate relationship between domestic law (e.g., de jure discrimination and immigrant exclusion) and foreign policy (vis-à-vis "over there" wars in the Philippines, the Pacific Rim, Korea, Southeast Asia, and the Middle East), Asian American studies scholars, to reiterate Freud's trauma-driven delineation, assume the role of "intrusive recollectors." Following suit, Asian American studies as an interdisciplinary field destabilizes dominant characterizations of wholesale U.S. democratic virtue via a constant reiteration of the past, cohering with what Anne Cheng (2001) highlights is a racially inflected movement from "grief to grievance." At the same time, the multiple "Asias" in "Asian America" (Rachel Lee 1999) make necessary an unflagging attention to what Lisa Lowe (1996) argues is unique to a field marked by a previously discussed cultural, political, and social "heterogeneity, hybridity, and multiplicity." Therefore, to map the traumatic development of Asian American studies is to correspondingly consider the periodic amnesias with regard to geography (e.g., Southeast Asian American studies), complex colonialism (e.g., South Asian American studies), comparative/hemispheric ethnic studies, and identity (particularly with regard to queer studies, disability studies, and gender/sexuality studies).

60

War

K. Scott Wong

War is a fundamental component of the human experience; indeed, across cultures, some of the earliest examples of oral and written traditions deal with warfare. Chris Hedges asserts, "war forms its own culture . . . it is peddled by mythmakers—historians, war correspondents, filmmakers, novelists, and the state—all of whom endow it with qualities it often does possess: excitement, exoticism, power, chances to rise above our small stations in life. . . . It dominates culture, distorts memory, corrupts language, and infects everything around it" (2002, 3). Taking the concept of war in the conventional sense, an armed conflict between two or more factions, it is obvious that war has played a central role in Asian American history. Wars of aggression, conquest, imperialism, colonialism, and civil conflict have all contributed to the presence of Asians in the United States. Wars of other kinds, however, also figure prominently in Asian American history: race wars, culture wars, gender wars, and trade wars, to name just a few.

One could argue that the European conquest of the "New World" was the first step of the process of creating Asian America, when one considers that it was Asia that Columbus and those who followed in his wake were seeking. Once Europeans realized that this land mass was not Asia, they sought the Northwest Passage, a water route around North America to the Pacific, and after the British American colonies were established, there developed a brisk Asia trade from the East Coast, based primarily in Boston, New York, and Philadelphia. Asians and Pacific Islanders would eventually sail on European and American ships across the Pacific Ocean because of these trade and whaling routes. Thus Asians and Asian commercial goods were present when the American republic was founded after a war of independence from the British crown (Tchen 1999).

The wars waged in Asia would be responsible for bringing the largest numbers of Asian immigrants to these shores. The earliest major conflict to consider is the first Opium War (1839–1842) between China and Great Britain, which was the result of a trade imbalance between the two countries. The British bought a number of goods from the Chinese (tea, spices, porcelain products, silks, etc.), but the Chinese wanted little but silver from the British. Therefore, the cash flow out of Great Britain into China far exceeded that returning to the crown. The British searched desperately for a product that the Chinese would purchase in enough quantity to alleviate the trade imbalance. The British hit upon opium, which they imported from their primary Asian colony, India. Before too long, the Chinese found themselves with a serious opium addiction problem among all social classes and an outflow of money that favored the British. In an attempt to halt the opium trade, the Chinese seized a shipment of British opium and destroyed it, which prompted the British to declare war on China. The British victory resulted in the opening of more Chinese port cities to foreign trade, including from the United States (Haddad 2013).

Another Chinese defeat at the hands of the British in 1860 served to further erode Chinese sovereignty and control over emigration. With more ports open to foreign trade one cannot underestimate the importance of the increased ability of the Chinese to emigrate and their exposure to information and ideas from the West. When news of the discovery of gold in California reached southern China in 1849, the American trade ships already in Chinese port cities were prepared to carry Chinese emigrants to California to join the Gold Rush. Christian proselytization in the Chinese interior, which was allowed after the British victory in 1860, was the catalyst for the Taiping Rebellion, which pitted Christian-inspired Chinese rebels against the central government, resulting in a civil war that lasted over a decade and cost approximately ten million deaths. The destruction of farmland and villages led to countless peasants having to seek new livelihoods, often through emigration. Other internal conflicts also forced Chinese to emigrate. Friction between the Cantonese and Hakka (Kejia) ethnic groups in southern China led to frequent skirmishes and hostage taking. Some hostages were sold into the infamous coolie trade that took Chinese to Cuba and Peru on the foreign ships which were by then a permanent presence in Chinese ports.

Fearing a war with the United States, Japan opened its ports to foreign traders soon after Commodore Matthew Perry sailed into Edo Bay with his Black Ships in 1853. Impressed with Western might, Japanese officials embarked on a program of modernization that led to the Meiji Restoration of 1868. This restored the emperor to power and brought about a series of reforms that increased industrialization, created new land tenure and taxation arrangements, and mandated other actions that produced a labor surplus. As a consequence, many Japanese laborers emigrated to Hawai'i and the Americas in search of better livelihoods. The drive toward modernization also contributed to increased Japanese militarism, which led to the first Sino-Japanese War of 1894–1895 and the Russo-Japanese War of 1904, all of which contributed to Japan's full annexation of Korea by 1910. A brief period of Korean emigration to Hawai'i and the United States followed, but the Japanese soon made emigration illegal.

American imperialism in the wake of the Spanish–American War led to the Philippine–American War of 1898–1902. The American victory over the Filipino resistance allowed the U.S. to formally colonize the Philippine Islands, thus giving Filipinos the legal status of "American nationals," which enabled them to emigrate to Hawaiʻi and the U.S. mainland somewhat more easily than other Asians. British imperialism, backed by military force, radically transformed the economy in parts of India, most notably in the late nineteenth century in the Punjab, which created a surplus of laborers, many of whom emigrated to Canada and the United States. Thus, a combination of wars of imperialism, colonialism, and conquest, instigated by forces both outside of and within Asia, created a variety of circumstances that gave rise to Asian immigration to the United States and its territories, often in the form of recruited labor migration.

While the aforementioned military conflicts had a major effect on Asian emigration to the Americas, the vast and long-lasting wars of the mid-twentieth century had the greatest impact on Asians in both their homelands and the United States. World War II had grave consequences not only for the people in Asia, but for Asian Americans as well, while the wars in Viet Nam, Laos, and Cambodia would contribute to a substantial influx of immigrants from Southeast Asia to the United States. The most obvious impact of World War II in Asia (referred to by the Chinese as the "War of Resistance" and the Japanese as the "Pacific War") was the immense loss of life, the destruction of the countryside and the urban infrastructure, and the use of two atomic bombs against Japan, ushering in the nuclear age and the Cold War. Among Asians in the United States, the impact of World War II was most keenly felt by the Japanese nationals and Japanese Americans living on the West Coast. Because of their suspected loyalties to Japan, over 110,000 people of Japanese descent, 70 percent of whom were American citizens by birth, were incarcerated in a network of camps throughout America's West, Southwest, and Arkansas. The injustice of this mass incarceration of Japanese Americans would have a profound impact on their postwar lives and provoke a later generation of Asian American activists to initiate a redress and reparations movement to gain compensation for the war-time losses incurred by Japanese Americans.

While the war had horrendous consequences for the Japanese American community, other Asian Americans benefitted from it, especially Chinese Americans. In part due to China's alliance with the United States against Japan, the social and cultural status of Chinese Americans improved in the eyes of many Americans. The Chinese Exclusion Act was repealed in 1943 and occupational opportunities opened up to Chinese Americans that had previously been denied to them. Finally able to leave the Chinatown economy, many Chinese Americans found work in the defense industries, offices, factories, and other venues that eventually allowed them to enter the American middle class. After the war, Chinese women were allowed to enter the country in greater numbers, many of them joining their husbands after years of separation, and Chinese Americans began raising families at a rate similar to that of other Americans.

Many American military personnel who participated in the postwar occupation of Japan became romantically involved with Japanese women, some of whom eventually emigrated to the United States as "war brides," many becoming parents to a postwar generation of mixed-race Asian Americans. Not long after World War II, the United States would enter the conflict in Korea, leading to an increased American military presence in East Asia. This situation gave rise to American-Korean unions, which led to another group of "military brides" who likewise mothered a generation of new Asian Americans. The Korean War also resulted in a large number of orphaned Korean children, children left parentless by the war or abandoned by their American military fathers. These children, in the late 1950s, became the first group of Asian children to be adopted in large numbers by mostly white Americans (Yuh 2002; Eleana Kim 2010).

America's involvement in the war in Viet Nam brought similar changes to the Asian American population. Not only did the war cause great physical damage to Viet Nam, it caused an enormous loss of human life and set in motion a series of refugee flows from Viet Nam, Cambodia, and Laos, primarily to the United States. The intensive bombing of Southeast Asia by the American military (more than in all previous wars combined) left the countryside, the urban infrastructure, and the economy of the region in shambles. Vast areas of farmland were rendered unusable because of toxic chemicals, tainted water supplies, unexploded ordnance, and remaining landmines. This situation, coupled with the rise of brutal political regimes, led to starvation, genocide, and civil war, contributing to an exodus of refugees from 1975 through the 1990s (M. Young 1991; Wilcox and Chomsky 2011; Martini 2013).

Those who fled Southeast Asia in the wake of the communist victories in their homelands often encountered hostility in the United States. The war had created a great rift in American society and many Americans viewed the new arrivals as the same enemy they had fought in Viet Nam, as a drain on social welfare programs, and as simply another group of foreign Asians who did not fit their vision of what was "American." This hostility surfaced in ways that were reminiscent of earlier anti-Asian actions: disputes over fishing territories and religious practices, efforts to establish English-only policies in schools and businesses, and violent hate crimes. Still, immigrants from Southeast Asia persevered

to create new communities in America, while acknowledging and remembering their past struggles (Freeman 1989; S. Chan 2003; K. Yang 2008; Tran 2010).

It should also be noted that Asian Americans have had a long and sometimes contentious history with the American military. During World War II, soldiers drafted out of the internment camps formed the all–Japanese American 442nd Regimental Combat Team and the 100th Battalion, which fought bravely across Europe, becoming the most highly decorated combat units for their size in American military history. In contrast, other Japanese American citizens decided to refuse the draft or decided against serving in the military unless their constitutional rights were restored. Many of these men, some of them called "No-No Boys," served time in federal prisons as draft resisters (Okada 1976; Muller 2001). At the same time, about twelve hundred Chinese Americans served in all–Chinese American units stationed in southwestern China in the 14th Air Service Group (K. Scott Wong 2005). While race-segregated units no longer exist in the American military, there are stories of Asian American soldiers being singled out by their commanding officers during the war in Viet Nam as examples of what the "enemy looks like" (Kiang 1991; Whelchel 1999).

Military conflicts have thus had a profound impact on the course of Asian American history. They have shaped the contours of immigration flows to the United States and have played important roles in determining the geographical, ethnic, class, and gender demographics of Asian American populations and communities. Once here in the United States, Asian Americans have also figured very prominently in "culture wars" or "race wars" that have affected how Asian Americans have been perceived, received, and treated in American law, society, and culture. Anti-Asian attitudes across more than a century and a half reveal that "culture" and "race" are inextricably linked in many Americans' ideologies and worldviews. In an American form of Orientalism, Americans positioned Asians and Asian immigrants as "the Other," a race apart that could never become "Americanized." Since Americans initially had the most contact with Chinese in China and the Chinese were the first Asians to arrive in the United States in substantial numbers, the Chinese were the first to encounter widespread anti-Asian sentiments, and Asian immigrants who followed were often subjected to such prejudices.

When the Chinese first entered the United States in recognizable numbers, in the 1850s, one could say that they arrived at the worst possible time for them to receive anything but a hostile reception. Arriving in California to participate in the Gold Rush, they represented a number of traits that were anathema to white American sensibilities: they were nonwhite, non-Christian, spoke a very different language, wore strange clothes, and ate odd food, with sticks no less! Furthermore, they came to find gold, the precious metal that Americans had claimed as their own, since it was found in "American" soil. As more Chinese arrived and took on other occupations (railroad labor, shoe making, agricultural work, restaurants and laundry operations, etc.) they were seen as labor competitors. And because many came owing money to creditors who lent them money for their passage to America and were often unable to change residences until their debts were repaid, they were viewed as "slaves," while others were confused with the "coolies" sent to Cuba and Peru, and some were hired to break strikes by white workers. These circumstances, combined with the debates over slavery, race, and labor that were occupying many American politicians and labor leaders, led many to call for the exclusion of Chinese laborers (Salyer 1995; Gyory 1998; Lee 2004).

Using South Asian, especially Sikh, immigrants as a model, Joan Jensen employed sociologist Otto Dalke's analysis of the typology of violence that leads to riots or other forms of "wars" against a group of people. Members of the targeted group usually have a history of being victims of violence, are regarded as undesirable competitors, and have some trait or characteristic that can serve as a focal point for negative rhetoric and behavior. At the same time, established authorities usually support the violence or do very little to prevent it, there is often an organization or association dedicated to promoting the violence or the spreading of propaganda against the minority group, and there is some form of media outlet that supports these sentiments and actions. Finally, the upper and middle classes either stand by or encourage these measures (Jensen 1988, 42). In the pre–World War II era, all Asian immigrants fell victim to anti-Asian activities along this model, which resulted in physical violence; detention; internment; incarceration; and residential, educational, and occupational segregation, as well as prohibitions on family members' immigration and the denial of the right to become naturalized citizens.

Issues surrounding labor, race, and culture were also tied to American concerns about Asians and gender. Aspiring female Chinese immigrants felt the brunt of such American anxieties regarding the presumed sexual proclivities of Asian women. In 1875, Congress passed the Page Act, which prohibited the immigration of Asian contract laborers, felons, and prostitutes. By then, the belief had developed that Chinese women were naturally inclined toward prostitution, and that they were especially dangerous because they corrupted the morals of young American males. Later, in 1882, the first Chinese Exclusion Act specified that Chinese laborers could not bring their wives. Furthermore, a number of Western states passed antimiscegenation laws prohibiting marriages between "Mongolians" and whites. These actions served to retard the growth of Chinese American families, which, in turn, kept the number of Chinese American citizens lower than that of other immigrant groups. While other Asian women did not face as severe immigration restrictions, once here, they often suffered from the kinds of sexualized gender assumptions (S. Chan 1994; Peffer 1999).

In the post–World War II era, which saw the repeal of the Chinese Exclusion Acts, the increase of female immigration, and the passage of the Immigration Act of 1965, which did away with immigration quotas based on national origins, there have been another set of armed conflicts and resultant "culture wars" that in many ways mirror those of the past. After World War II, the main threat that Asians posed to America was no longer seen in terms of culture, language, religion, or gender issues, but rather, the spread of communism. When the Chinese Communists came to power in 1949, Chinese Americans were caught up in the Cold War, with Chinatowns coming under surveillance due to the fear of domestic Communist activity, and the internal splits between those who supported the Communists and the Nationalists. This tension would be exacerbated in the mid-1950s because of the Korean War, and then in the Sixties, with the war in Viet Nam. Communism became the latest contagion that Asian Americans might use against America, and the signs of this looming invasion of the American body politic were similar to those discerned in the past: anti-Christian values, anticapitalist ideologies, deception, dishonesty, and skewed gender roles.

The postwar era also witnessed the revival of Asia as a major economic and military power, and many Americans have viewed this development in warlike terms. As was the case in the nineteenth century, when Britain had a severe trade imbalance with China, the United States has battled with Japan and, more recently, with China in similar "trade wars." Due to the effects of modernization, globalization, the spread of capitalism, and the resulting practice of outsourcing jobs to foreign countries, Asian countries have dominated the manufacturing sector in the decades following World War II. In the 1980s, Japan's growing economic strength, especially its success in automobile manufacturing, prompted a harsh rhetorical reaction by some Americans which, along with the attendant decline of the U.S. automobile industry, played an important role in the murder of Vincent Chin in Detroit in 1982. Today, many Americans perceive China as our main economic rival and, again, this economic competition is seen in combative terms.

The events of September 11, 2001, have had a grave impact on Asian Americans, especially Muslim Americans and those mistaken for Muslims, Sikh men in particular, because of their turbans. The "War on Terror" has led to domestic detentions, deportations, and murders, and the steady harassment of these groups' members. Attacks on Islam in general, based mainly on deep misunderstandings of the religion and its adherents, have also become frequent (Davis et al. 2011). Thus war, whether in the form of armed conflict or societal clashes revolving around cultural, racial, or gender assumptions, has had a long and often corrosive impact on Asian American history. Wars of mass violence have brought Asians to these shores and other kinds of wars have haunted them well after their arrival here. However, these wars have not been completely one-sided. Throughout their history, Asian Americans have resisted their opponents. They have fought back against violence, taken their grievances to court, devised ways to circumvent exclusion laws, and contended for their civil rights whenever possible. It is the struggle of these conflicts that has given the Asian American community the strength to endure.

61

Yellow

Robert Ji-Song Ku

Per a basic dictionary definition, yellow is a component of light, the most luminous of the primary colors, occurring in the spectrum between green and orange, with a wavelength between 570 and 590 nanometers. Part of growing up in the United States is to eventually begin associating a handful of basic colors with racial categories and, along with them, prescriptive notions of race. Together with the cognate colors white, black, red, and brown, yellow has come to signify a major racial category in the United States.

The etymology of "yellow," in its simplest color sense, begins with the Old English *geolu*, which corresponds to the Old Saxon *gelo*, Low German *gel*, Middle Dutch *geluw*, and Indo-European *ghelwo*. The earliest written form occurs around AD 700 in what is among the first Anglo-Saxon alphabetical glossaries, the *Epinal Glossary*. The word appears in the Old English text *Beowulf*, when Wiglaf is about to join Beowulf to battle the dragon: "*hond rond gefeng, / geolwe linde*" (he seized the hand-round [shield], the yellow linden-wood). As an adjective applied to the human complexion, prior to indicating Asian people, "yellow" described the aged or diseased. In 1817, for example, Lord Byron wrote in his long poem *Beppo*, "No, I never Saw a man grown so yellow! How's your liver?" As a colloquialism in the United States, at least as far back as the mid-nineteenth century, "yellow" has meant cowardly, as when P. T. Barnum referred to someone's heart being yellow in his 1857 memoir, *Struggles and Triumphs*. At one point, "yellow-belly" sat beside "chicken" and "scaredy-cat" as among the most commonly used American euphemisms for "coward."

The practice of referring to a *race* of people as "yellow" in the United States occurred as early as 1834, when American newspapers, such as the New York *Sun*, began to use the term to describe people believed to have naturally occurring yellow skin, the "Asiatics" in particular. A few decades later, the most respected scientists in Europe and the United States would begin to promulgate the theory that the human species were organized into three primary races that were identifiable by color: Caucasoid by white, Negroid by black, and Mongoloid by yellow. Although highly disputed as meaningful typological categories since they were first introduced, these terms have endured and are employed by some anthropologists even today. The people thought to belong to the Mongoloid race by one scientist or another over the years have included not only East and Southeast Asians but also Polynesians and Native Americans. In addition to yellow complexion, physical traits attributed to Mongoloids included the epicanthic fold of the eyelids (aka "Mongoloid eyes") (Jacobson 2000; Painter 2010).

The eugenics movement, whose founding is generally attributed to the English scientist Francis Galton (1822–1911), relied on dubious scientific formulations, such as the Mongoloid concept, to justify its mission to scientifically improve the heritable characteristics of human beings. The influence of eugenics is evident in works such as Lothrop Stoddard's *The Rising Tide of Color against White World Supremacy* (1920), in which the author warns of the threat nonwhites pose to white civilizations. Stoddard made special note of the threat posed by Asians, especially as immigrants to the United States (Jacobson 2000; Painter 2010). The idea that the yellow race would bring the ruination of the white race began as soon as Chinese laborers began to arrive in California during the mid-nineteenth century. The perceived threat to whites' employment and way of life would soon produce a specialized term: "yellow peril." A series of exclusion acts, severely limiting the immigration of Asians, were instituted, including the Page Act (1875), the Chinese Exclusion Act (1882), and the immigration acts of 1917 and 1924. Concurrent with the notion that the yellow body represented economic competition against white labor was the suspicion that the yellow body was a source of pollution and disease, which was used as justification for antimiscegenation and other discriminatory laws (Saxton 1975; Robert Lee 1999).

As with all processes of racial categorization, the precise referents of color-based racial categories in the United States have been fluid, overlapping, and inconsistent over the decades, if not centuries. Historically, white has equated to Americans of European ancestry (but not always, as in the initial reception of the Irish and Jews), black to African (specifically sub-Saharan), and red to Native American or other indigenous. Brown has referred to Latinos (or Hispanics) as well as to Filipinos. Recently, and particularly after 9/11, brown has come to indiscriminately evoke people of South Asian, Arab, Muslim, and so-called Middle Eastern backgrounds. (The notion of "flying while brown," a modification of "walking while black," has gained new currency during the U.S.-led War on Terror.) Thus, a century after the fear of yellow bodies preoccupied a racially anxious America, the fear of the brown body has become the preeminent racial anxiety in the post-9/11 era (Prashad 2000; Bayoumi 2009; Rana 2011).

"Yellow," meanwhile, has been popularly used to identify people primarily of East Asian (specifically, Chinese, Japanese, and Korean) backgrounds, simply because they constituted the largest Asian populations in the United States. Secondarily, due to the Vietnam War, the term also began to be applied to people of Southeast Asian heritage (principally Vietnamese but also Cambodian and Laotian). This is in keeping with the legacy of U.S. military conflicts elsewhere in Asia, such as in Japan and Korea, where Asian bodies were regarded as "yellow hordes" antagonistic to American objectives (Chong 2012). It is likely that many other Asian American groups, such as Thai Americans, Burmese Americans, Tibetan Americans, Hmong Americans, and Mien Americans, might popularly be regarded as yellow if they were to occupy a more prominent place in the American racial imagination.

While white and black have garnered both positive and negative, as well as neutral, connotations over the decades, red and brown have mostly been perceived as pejorative, especially in recent times. To wit, when William Taft coined the term "little brown brother" to refer to Filipinos at the start of the twentieth century, there was little public outcry. However, when George H. W. Bush affectionately called his Mexican American grandchildren "little brown ones" in the late 1980s, he was widely criticized. Also, the controversy over sports teams using the term "red" to refer to Native American identity has led to both the renaming of mascots (as with the St. John's Redmen becoming the Red Storm) and the steadfast defense of the practice (as in the case of the Washington Redskins).

"Yellow," meanwhile, has almost entirely been used as an offensive epithet. As a signifier of race in the United States, yellow has historically been positioned between white and black. During the Jim Crow era, when laws segregated white America from black America, many Asian Americans wondered where they belonged (Okihiro 1994). In this, yellow shares secondary status with brown and red in the powerful white-black binary that has come to dominate racial discourse in the United States.

As with "yellow peril," the word "yellow" has been notably paired with other words to refer to social, cultural, and political phenomena that specifically pertain to Asian Americans. "Yellow fever," which in medical parlance refers to a hemorrhagic disease transmitted by tropical mosquitos (also known as "yellow jack" and "yellow rainer"), has also come to denote the sexual fetish that certain non-Asians have for Asians, similar to "jungle fever," which could refer to any number of tropical diseases, such as malaria, but also means a white person's sexual attraction to a black person, as made famous by Spike Lee's 1991 film *Jungle Fever*.

Yellowface, akin to blackface, applies specifically to yellow minstrelsy, in which white entertainers in film and on stage don costumes and facial prosthetics to evoke Asianness, such as white actor Jonathan Pryce's performance of the part of a mixed-race Vietnamese in the Broadway musical *Miss Saigon* (Marchetti 1993; Jane Park 2010). David Henry Hwang's 2007 play *Yellow Face* is a theatrical rendering of this controversial practice. Similarly, Han Tang's 2010 documentary film *Yellow Face* focuses on the controversy surrounding the casting of white actors in the film version of *The Last Airbender*. Among the many scholarly works to address this issue is Krystyn Moon's *Yellowface* (2005), which examines the development of the Chinese figure in American popular culture between the 1850s and 1920s. Despite the profuse criticism levied against it, yellowface has proved resilient and long lasting. This minstrel practice, which appeared on screen as far back as 1915, when Mary Pickford played the role of the tragic Cio-Cio San in a version of *Madam Butterfly*, forcefully reemerged in 2012, when a number of non-Asian actors donned facial prosthetics to portray Asian characters in the film *Cloud Atlas*.

As is periodically the case with negative epithets that persist over time, "yellow" has been reclaimed by some Asian Americans to evoke pride in their subaltern status. (A notable example of this reappropriation process is the word "queer," which was chiefly used derogatorily to mean a gay man but is now employed affirmatively, as in "queer studies.") *Yellow Pearl*, a collection of poems, drawings, and songs compiled within an LP-sized yellow box, was published in 1972 for this purpose by Basement Workshop, among the earliest Asian American arts and culture organizations formed in New York City. The box set was inspired by the song "Yellow Pearl" by Chris Iljima and Nobuko Miyamoto, who, together with "Charlie" Chin, collaborated on the 1973 musical album *A Grain of Sand: Music for the Struggle by Asians in America*. Both the song and the box set simultaneously play on and subvert the term "yellow peril" to express not the danger posed by Asia to America but the emerging consciousness of Asians in America. Akin to the Black Power movement that emerged during this time, the Yellow Power movement sought dignity, pride, and self-determination for Asian Americans by co-opting "yellow" as a positive term (Wei 1993; Maeda 2011).

The embracement of yellow as either a neutral or positive symbol of Asian American identity has persisted. The legal scholar Frank Wu's collection of essays, *Yellow: Race in America beyond Black and White* (2002), addresses the particularities of yellow as a racial marker by contemplating the intermediacy of Asian Americans, who are politically constructed as neither white nor black. In the realm of fiction, Korean American author Don Lee has penned *Yellow: Stories* (2001), which features characters who are Japanese American, Korean American, and Chinese American—in other words people who are yellow—living in a multicolored America.

Bibliography

aapi nexus. 2009a. "Special Issue on K–12 Education." 7 (1).

———. 2009b. "Special Issue on Higher Education." 7 (2).

———. 2010. "Special Issue on Intersections of Education." 8 (1).

———. 2011. "Forging the Future: The Role of New Research, Data, & Policies for Asian Americans, Native Hawai'ians, & Pacific Islanders" (special issue). 9 (1 and 2).

Abelmann, Nancy. 2009. *The Intimate University: Korean American Students and the Problem of Segregation*. Durham, NC: Duke University Press.

Abelmann, Nancy, and John Lie. 1997. *Blue Dreams: Korean Americans and the Los Angeles Riots*. Cambridge, MA: Harvard University Press.

Abraham, Margaret. 2000. *Speaking the Unspeakable: Marital Violence among South Asian Immigrants in the United States*. New Brunswick, NJ: Rutgers University Press.

Abrahamian, Ervand. 2013. *The Coup: 1953, the CIA, and the Roots of Modern U.S.-Iranian Relations*. New York: New Press.

Adachi, Jeff, dir. 2006. *The Slanted Screen*. San Francisco: Asian American Media Mafia Productions.

Adams, Brian E., and Ping Ren. 2006. "Asian Americans and Campaign Finance in Municipal Elections." *Social Science Journal* 43 (4): 597–615.

Agamben, Giorgio. 1998. *Homo Sacer: Sovereign Power and Bare Life*. Palo Alto, CA: Stanford University Press.

———. 2002. "What Is a Paradigm?" Lecture at European Graduate School, Leuk-Stadt, Switzerland. August. <http://www.egs.edu/faculty/giorgio-agamben/articles/what-is-a-paradigm/>.

Aguilar-San Juan, Karin. 1994a. "Linking the Issues: From Identity to Activism." In *The State of Asian America: Activism and Resistance in the 1990s*, edited by Karin Aguilar-San Juan, 1–18. Boston: South End Press.

———, ed. 1994b. *The State of Asian America: Activism and Resistance in the 1990s*. Boston: South End Press.

———. 2009. *Little Saigons: Staying Vietnamese in America*. Minneapolis: University of Minnesota Press.

Alba, Richard, and Victor Nee. 1997. "Rethinking Assimilation Theory for a New Era of Immigration." *International Migration Review* 31 (4): 826–74.

Alcantara, Ruben. 1981. *Sakada: Filipino Adaptation in Hawai'i*. Washington, DC: University Press of America.

Alexander, Meena. 1996. "The Shock of Arrival: Body, Memory, Desire in Asian-American Art." In *The Shock of Arrival: Reflections on Postcolonial Experience*, by Meena Alexander, 152–64. Boston: South End Press.

Alexander, Michelle. 2010. *The New Jim Crow: Mass Incarceration in the Age of Colorblindness*. New York: New Press.

Alimi, Eitan Y. 2011. "Relational Dynamics in Factional Adoption of Terrorist Tactics: A Comparative Perspective." *Theory and Society* 40 (1): 95–118.

Althusser, Louis. 1971. *Lenin and Philosophy and Other Essays*. Translated by Ben Brewster. New York: Monthly Review Press.

Amendment to the Japanese-American Evacuation Claims Act of 1948: Hearings on H. R. 7435, before the Committee on the Judiciary, 83rd Cong. (1954). ("Amendment" in text.)

American Veterans Center. 2012. "WWII: The Japanese American Experience." <http://www.americanveteranscenter.org/avq/avq-issue-ii/wwii-the-japanese-american-experience/?doing_wp_cron=1376599724>.

Ancheta, Angelo N. 2006. *Race, Rights, and the Asian American Experience*, second edition. New Brunswick, NJ: Rutgers University Press.

Anderson, Benedict R. O'G. (1983) 1991. *Imagined Communities: Reflections on the Origin and Spread of Nationalism*. London: Verso.

Anderson, Terry H. 1995. *The Movement and the Sixties*. New York: Oxford University Press.

Anderson, Wanni W., and Robert G. Lee, eds. 2005. *Displacements and Diasporas: Asians in the Americas*. New Brunswick, NJ: Rutgers University Press.

Ang, Ien. 2001. *On Not Speaking Chinese. Living between Asia and the West*. London: Routledge.

Appadurai, Arjun, ed. 1986. *The Social Life of Things: Commodities in a Cultural Perspective*. Cambridge, UK: Cambridge University Press.

———, ed. 2000. "Globalization." *Public Culture* 12 (1).

Appadurai, Arjun, and Carol A. Breckenridge. 1995. "Public Modernity in India." In *Consuming Modernity: Public Culture in a South Asian World*, edited by Carol A. Breckenridge, 1–20. Minneapolis: University of Minnesota Press.

Arendt, Hannah. 1968. *The Origins of Totalitarianism*. San Diego, CA: Harcourt Brace Jovanovich.

Armstrong, Bruce. 1989. "Racialisation and Nationalist Ideology: The Japanese Case." *International Sociology* 4 (3): 329–43.

Asato, Noriko. 2005. *Teaching Mikadoism: The Attack on Japanese Language Schools in Hawai'i, California, and Washington, 1919–1927*. Honolulu: University of Hawai'i Press.:. Honolulu: University of Hawai'i Press.

Ashcroft, Bill. 1989. *The Empire Writes Back: Theory and Practice in Post-colonial Literatures*. London: Routledge.

Ashcroft, John D., and Viet D. Dinh. 2011. "Liberty, Security, and the USA Patriot Act." In *Confronting Terror: 9/11 and the Future of American National Security*, edited by Dean Reuter and John Yoo, 187–201. Jackson, TN: Encounter Books.

Asian American Studies Department. 2009. *At 40: Asian American Studies @ San Francisco State: Self-Determination, Community, Student Service*. San Francisco: Asian American Studies Department, College of Ethnic Studies, San Francisco State University.

Asian American Women Artists Association. 2007. *Cheers to Muses: Contemporary Works by Asian American Women*. San Francisco: Asian American Women Artists Association.

Asian Community Center Archive Group. 2009. *Stand Up: An Archive of the Bay Area Asian American Movement, 1968–1974*. Berkeley, CA: Eastwind Books.

Aslan, Reza. 2010. "European Islamophobia Finds a Home in the U.S." *All Things Considered*. National Public Radio, August 23. <http://www.npr.org/templates/story/story.php?storyId=129381552>.

August, Tim. 2012. "The Contradictions in Culinary Collaboration: Reading Vietnamese American Bodies in Top Chef and Stealing Buddha's Dinner." *MELUS* 37 (3): 97–115.

Austin, J. L. 1962. *How to Do Things with Words*. Oxford: Clarendon Press.

Azuma, Eiichiro. 2005. *Between Two Empires: Race, History, and Transnationalism in Japanese America*. New York: Oxford University Press.

Bailey, Paul. 1972. *City in the Sun: The Japanese Concentration Camp at Poston, Arizona*. Los Angeles: Westernlore Press.

Baldoz, Rick. 2011. *The Third Asiatic Invasion: Empire and Migration in Filipino America, 1898–1946*. New York: New York University Press.

Balthazar, Gabe. 2012. *If It Swings, It's Music: The Autobiography of Hawai'i's Gabe Balthazar, Jr*. Honolulu: University of Hawai'i Press.

Bambu. 2012. *One Rifle per Family*. CD. Los Angeles: Beatrock Music.

Banks, Tyra, Kenya Barris, and Ken Mok, creator/developers. 2003. *America's Next Top Model*. Hollywood, CA: UPN and CW.

Bao, Quang, and Hanya Yanagihara, eds. 2000. *Take-Out: Queer Writings from Asian Pacific America*. New York: Asian American Writers Workshop.

Bao, Xiang. 2007. *Global "Body Shopping": An Indian Labor System in the Information Technology Industry*. Princeton, NJ: Princeton University Press.

Bao, Xiaolan. 2001. *Holding Up More than Half the Sky: Chinese Women Garment Workers in New York City, 1948–1992*. Urbana: University of Illinois Press.

Barnes, P. M., P. F. Adams, and E. Powell-Griner. 2008. *Health Characteristics of the Asian Adult Population: United States, 2004–2006*. Hyattsville, MD: U.S. Department of Health and Human Services, Centers for Disease Control and Prevention, National Center for Health Statistics.

Barth, Gunther. 1964. *Bitter Strength: A History of the Chinese in the United States, 1850–1970*. Cambridge, MA: Harvard University Press.

Bascara, Victor. 2006. *Model-Minority Imperialism*. Minneapolis: University of Minnesota Press.

Basch, Linda G., Nina Glick Schiller, and Cristina Szanton Blanc, eds. (1993) 1994. *Nations Unbound: Transnational Projects, Postcolonial Predicaments, and Deterritorialized*

Nation-States. New York: Gordon and Breach Science Pubishers.

Baynton, Douglas. 1996. *Forbidden Signs: American Culture and the Campaign against Sign Language*. Chicago: University of Chicago Press.

Bayoumi, Moustafa. (2008) 2009. *How Does It Feel to Be a Problem? Being Young and Arab in America*. New York: Penguin.

Beechert, Edward D. 1985. *Working in Hawai'i: A Labor History*. Honolulu: University of Hawai'i Press.

Beinin, Joel. 2003. "Is Terrorism a Useful Term in Understanding the Middle East and the Palestinian-Israeli Conflict?" *Radical History Review* 85: 12–23.

Bell, Chris. 2006. "Introducing White Disability Studies: A Modest Proposal." In *The Disability Studies Reader*, second edition, edited by Lennard J. Davis, 275–82. New York: Routledge.

Berlet, Chip, and Mathew N. Lyons. 2000. *Right-Wing Populism in America: Too Close for Comfort*. New York: Guilford Press.

Binder, Guyora. 2010. "Critical Legal Studies." In *A Companion to Philosophy of Law and Legal Theory*, second edition, edited by Dennis Patterson, 267–78. Oxford: Blackwell Publishing.

Bishoff, Tonya, and Jo Rankin, eds. 1997. *Seeds from a Silent Tree: An Anthology by Korean Adoptees*. San Diego, CA: Pandal Press.

Bix, Brian. 2013. "John Austin." In *The Stanford Encyclopedia of Philosophy*, edited by Edward N. Zalta. <http://plato.stanford.edu/archives/spr2013/entries/austin-john/>.

Blauner, Robert. 1975. *Internal Colonialism and Ghetto Revolt*. Indianapolis: Bobbs-Merrill.

Blenstrup, Angelika. 2007. *They Made It! How Chinese, French, German, Indian, Iranian, Israeli, and Other Foreign-Born Entrepreneurs Contributed to High-Tech Innovation in Silicon Valley, the United States, and Overseas*. Cupertino, CA: HappyAbout.com.

Blow, Charles M. 2012. "The Meaning of Minority." *New York Times*, December 12. <http://www.nytimes.com/2012/12/13/opinion/blow-the-meaning-of-minority.html>.

Bobo, Kimberly, Jackie Kendall, and Steve Max. 2010. *Organizing for Social Change: Midwest Academy Manual for Activists*. Santa Anna, CA: Forum Press.

Bodnar, John. 1987. *The Transplanted: A History of Immigrants in Urban America*. Bloomington: Indiana University Press.

Bogdan, Robert. 1990. *Freak Show: Presenting Human Oddities for Amusement and Profit*. Chicago: University of Chicago Press.

Bonacich, Edna. 1973. "A Theory of Middleman Minorities." *American Sociological Review* 38 (5): 583–94.

Bonacich, Edna, and Lucie Cheng, eds. 1984. *Labor Immigration under Capitalism: Asian Workers in the United States before World War II*. Berkeley: University of California Press.

Bonacich, Edna, and John Modell. 1980. *The Economic Basis of Ethnic Solidarity: Small Business in the Japanese American Community*. Berkeley: University of California Press.

Bonilla-Silva, Eduardo. 2008. "What Is the Social Significance of Barack Obama?" *Contexts*, August 8. <http://contexts.org/obama/#comments-list>.

———. 2010. *Racism without Racists: Color-Blind Racism and the Persistence of Racial Inequality in the United States*, third edition. Lanham, MD: Rowman & Littlefield.

Bonus, Rick. 2000. *Locating Filipino Americans: Ethnicity and the Cultural Politics of Space*. Philadelphia: Temple University Press.

Boot, Max. 2002. *The Savage Wars of Peace: Small Wars and the Rise of American Power*. New York: Basic Books.

Boris, Eileen, and Rhacel Salazar Parreñas, eds. 2010. *Intimate Labors: Cultures, Technologies, and the Politics of Care*. Stanford, CA: Stanford University Press.

Borshay Liem, Deann, dir. 2000. *First Person Plural*. San Francisco: Center for Asian American Media.

———, dir. 2010. *In the Matter of Cha Jung Hee*. Harriman, NY: New Day Films.

Borstelmann, Thomas. 2003. *The Cold War and the Color Line: American Race Relations in the Global Arena*. Cambridge, MA: Harvard University Press.

Borzutsky, Silvia. 2007. "The Politics of Impunity: Cold War, State Terror, Trauma, Trials and Reparations in Argentina and Chile." *Latin American Research Review* 42 (1): 167–85.

Bosworth, Allan. 1967. *America's Concentration Camps*. New York: W. W. Norton.

Bow, Leslie. 2001. *Betrayal and Other Acts of Subversion: Feminism, Sexual Politics, Asian American Women's Literature*. Princeton, NJ: Princeton University Press.

———. 2010. *Partly Colored: Asian Americans and Racial Anomaly in the Segregated South*. New York: New York University Press.

Braziel, Jana Evans, and Anita Mannur. 2003. "Nation, Migration, Globalization: Points of Contention in Diaspora Studies." In *Theorizing Diaspora: A Reader*, edited by Jana Evans Braziel and Anita Mannur, 1–22. Oxford: Blackwell Publishing.

Brian, Kristi. 2012. *Reframing Transracial Adoption: Adopted Koreans, White Parents, and the Politics of Kinship*. Philadelphia: Temple University Press.

Brooks, Charlotte. 2012. *Alien Neighbors, Foreign Friends: Asian Americans, Housing, and the Transformation of Urban California*. Chicago: University of Chicago Press.

Broom, Leonard, and Ruth Reimer. 1949. *Removal and Return*. Berkeley: University of California Press.

Brown, Michael D. 1992. *Views from Asian California: 1920–1965; An Illustrated History*. San Francisco: Michael Brown.

Brown v. Board of Education, 347 U.S. 483 (1954).

Buchanan, Ian. 2012. *A Dictionary of Critical Theory*. Oxford: Oxford University Press.

Burgett, Bruce, and Glenn Hendler, eds. 2007. *Keywords for American Cultural Studies*. New York: New York University Press.

Burgorgue-Larsen, Laurence, and Amaya Úbeda de Torres. 2011. "'War' in the Jurisprudence of the Inter-American Court of Human Rights." *Human Rights Quarterly* 33 (1): 148–74.

Burns, Lucy Mae San Pablo. 2012. *Puro Arte: Filipinos on the Stages of Empire*. New York: New York University Press.

Bush, Michael L. 2000. *Servitude in Modern Times*. Cambridge, UK: Polity Press.

Bush, Roderick D. 2009. *The End of White World Supremacy: Black Internationalism and the Problem of the Color Line*. Philadelphia: Temple University Press.

Busto, Rudy V. 1996. "The Gospel According to the Model Minority?: Hazarding an Interpretation of Asian American Evangelical College Students." *Amerasia Journal* 22 (1): 133–47.

Butler, Judith. 1988. "Performative Acts and Gender Constitution: An Essay in Phenomenology and. Feminist Theory." *Theatre Journal* 40 (4): 519–31.

———. 1990. *Gender Trouble: Feminism and the Subversion of Identity*. New York: Routledge.

Cacho, Lisa Marie. 2012. *Social Death: Racialized Rightlessness and the Criminalization of the Unprotected*. New York: New York University Press.

Cain, Bruce E., D. Roderick Kiewiet, and Carole Uhlaner. 1991. "The Acquisition of Partisanship by Latinos and Asian Americans." *American Journal of Political Science* 35: 390–422.

Cainkar, Louise. 2002. "Special Registration: A Fervor for Muslims." *Journal of Islamic Law and Culture* 7 (2): 73–101.

———. 2009. *Homeland Insecurity: The Arab American and Muslim American Experience after 9/11*, first edition. New York: Russell Sage Foundation.

Camacho, Keith. 2011. *Cultures of Commemoration: The Politics of War, Memory, and History in the Mariana Islands*. Honolulu: University of Hawai'i Press.

Camacho, Keith, and Setsu Shigematsu, eds. 2010. *Militarized Currents: Toward a Decolonized Future in Asia and the Pacific*. Minneapolis: University of Minnesota Press.

"Cambodia Tribunal Monitor." 2011. Documentation Center of Cambodia and Center for International Human Rights at Northwestern School of Law. <www.cambodiatribunal.org>.

Campomanes, Oscar V. 1997. "New Formations in Asian American Studies and the Question of U.S. Imperialism." *Positions: East Asia Cultures Critique* 5 (2): 523–50.

Canaday, Margot. 2009. *The Straight State: Sexuality and Citizenship in Twentieth-Century America*. Princeton, NJ: Princeton University Press.

Capino, Jose. 2010. *Dream Factories of a Former Colony: American Fantasies, Philippine Cinema*. Minneapolis: University of Minnesota Press.

Carby, Hazel V. 1980. "Multi-Culture." *Screen Education* 34: 62–70.

CARE National Commission on Asian American and Pacific Islander Research in Education. 2010. *Federal Higher Education Policy Priorities and the Asian American and Pacific Islander Community*. New York: CARE. ("CARE" in text.)

———. 2011. *The Relevance of Asian Americans & Pacific Islanders in the College Completion Agenda*. New York: CARE.

———. 2013. *iCount: A Data Quality Movement for Asian Americans and Pacific Islanders in Higher Education*. New York: CARE.

Carnes, Tony, and Fenggang Yang, eds. 2004. *Asian American Religions: The Making and Remaking of Borders and Boundaries*. New York: New York University Press.

Caruth, Cathy. 1996. "Unclaimed Experience: Trauma and the Possibility of History." In *Unclaimed Experience: Trauma, Narrative and History*, edited by Cathy Caruth, 10–24. Baltimore: Johns Hopkins University Press.

Carruthers, Susan L. 2005. "Between Camps: Eastern Bloc 'Escapees' and Cold War Borderlands." *American Quarterly* 57 (3): 911–42.

Casey, Steven. 2001. *Cautious Crusades: Franklin D. Roosevelt, American Public Opinion, and the War against Nazi Germany*. New York: Oxford University Press.

Castelnuovo, Shirley. 2008. *Soldiers of Conscience: Japanese American Military Resisters in World War II*. Westport, CT: Praeger Publishers.

Castleman, Bruce A. 1994. "California's Alien Land Laws." *Western Legal History* 9 (Winter/Spring): 25–68.

Cha, Marn J. 2010. *Koreans in Central California (1903–1957): A Study of Settlement and Transnational Politics*. Lanham, MD: University Press of America.

Chae Chan Ping v. United States, 130 U.S. 581 (1889).

Chan, Jeffery, Frank Chin, Lawson Fusao Inada, and Shawn Wong, eds. 1991. *The Big Aiiieeeee!: An Anthology of Chinese American and Japanese American Literature*. New York: Meridan.

Chan, Kenyon S. "Rethinking the Asian American Studies Project: Bridging the Divide between 'Campus' and 'Community.'" *Journal of Asian American Studies* 3 (1): 17–36.

Chan, Sucheng. (1986) 1989. *This Bittersweet Soil: The Chinese in California Agriculture, 1860–1910*. Berkeley: University of California Press.

———. 1991. *Asian Americans: An Interpretive History*. Boston: Twayne Publishers.

———. 1994. "The Exclusion of Chinese Women, 1870–1943." In *Entry Denied: Exclusion and the Chinese Community in America, 1882–1943*, edited by Sucheng Chan, 94–146. Philadelphia: Temple University Press.

———, ed. 2003. *Not Just Victims: Conversations with Cambodian Community Leaders in the United States*. Urbana: University of Illinois Press.

———. 2004. *Survivors: Cambodian Refugees in the United States*. Urbana: University of Illinois Press.

———. 2006. *The Vietnamese American 1.5 Generation: Stories of War, Revolution, Flight, and New Beginnings*. Philadelphia: Temple University Press.

———. 2014. "Alien Land Laws." In *Encyclopedia of Asian American History*, edited by Xiaojian Zhao and Edward J. W. Park. Santa Barbara, CA: ABC-Clio Press.

———. Forthcoming. "Asian American Economic and Labor History." In *The Oxford Handbook of Asian American History*, edited by David K. Yoo and Eiichiro Azuma. New York: Oxford University Press.

Chang, Alexandra. 2008. *Envisioning Diaspora: Asian American Visual Arts Collectives from Godzilla, Godzookie, to the Barnstormers*. Beijing and Shanghai: Timezone 8 Editions.

Chang, E., L. C. Fung, C. S. Li, T. C. Lin, L. Tam, C. Tang, and E. Tong. 2013. "Offering Acupuncture as an Adjunct for Tobacco Cessation: A Community Clinic Experience." *Health Promotion Practice* 14 (5 suppl.): 80S–87S. doi:10.1177/1524839913485756.

Chang, Gordon H. 2008. "Emerging from the Shadows: The Visual Arts and Asian American History." In *Asian American Art: A History, 1850–1970*, edited by Gordon H. Chang, Mark Dean Johnson, and Paul J. Karlstrom, ix–xv. Palo Alto, CA: Stanford University Press.

Chang, Gordon H., Mark Dean Johnson, and Paul J. Karlstrom, eds. 2008. *Asian American Art: A History, 1850–1970*. Palo Alto, CA: Stanford University Press.

Chang, Juliana. 2012. *Inhuman Citizenship: Traumatic Enjoyment and Asian American Literature*. Minneapolis: University of Minnesota Press.

Chang, Shenglin. 2006. *The Global Silicon Valley Home: Lives and Landscapes within Taiwanese American Trans-Pacific Culture*. Palo Alto, CA: Stanford University Press.

Chang, Yoonmee. 2010. *Writing the Ghetto: Class, Authorship, and the Asian American Ethnic Enclave*. New Brunswick, NJ: Rutgers University Press.

Chanse, Samantha, ed. 2008. *Activist Imagination: Is an Exhibition and Series of Discussions Investigating, Exploring, and Imagining the Past, Present, and Future of Activism. Artists: Bob Hsiang, Donna Keiko Ozawa, Christine Wong Yap*. Exh. cat. San Francisco: Kearny Street Workshop Press.

Char, Tin-Yuke. 1975. *The Sandalwood Mountains: Readings and Stories of the Early Chinese in Hawai'i*. Honolulu: University Press of Hawai'i.

Chau, Monica. 1994. "Picturing Asian America: Communities, Culture, Difference." In *Picturing Asian America: Communities, Culture, Difference*. Exh. cat. Houston: Houston Center for Photography.

Chaudhuri, Una. 2001. "Theater and Cosmopolitanism: New Stories, Old Stages." In *Cosmopolitan Geographies: New Locations in Literature and Culture*, edited by Vinay Dharwadker, 171–96. New York: Routledge Press.

Cheah, Pheng. 1998. "Introduction Part II: The Cosmopolitical-Today." In *Thinking and Feeling Beyond the Nation*, edited by Pheng Cheah and Bruce Robbins, 20–44. Minneapolis: University of Minnesota Press.

Chen, David. 2012. "Campaign Finance Lessons for Disillusioned Asian-American Group." *New York Times*, March 13. A-24.

Chen, Edith Wen-Chu, and Shirley Hune. 2011. "Asian American Pacific Islander Women from Ph.D. to Campus President: Gains and Leaks in the Pipeline." In *Women of Color in Higher Education: Changing Directions and New Perspectives*, edited by G. Jean-Marie and B. Lloyd-Jones, 163–90. Bingley, UK: Emerald Publishing.

Chen, Edith Wen-Chu, and Grace J. Yoo, eds. 2010. *Encyclopedia of Asian American Issues Today*. Santa Barbara, CA: ABC-CLIO.

Chen, Mel. 2012. *Animacies: Biopolitics, Racial Mattering, and Queer Affect*. Durham, NC: Duke University Press.

Chen, Tina. 2005. *Double Agency: Acts of Impersonation in Asian American Literature and Culture*. Palo Alto, CA: Stanford University Press.

Chen, Yong. 2000. *Chinese San Francisco, 1850–1943: A Trans-Pacific Community*. Palo Alto, CA: Stanford University Press.

Cheng, Anne. 2001. *The Melancholy of Race: Psychoanalysis, Assimilation, and Hidden Grief*. London: Oxford University Press.

Cheng, Lucie, and Philip Q. Yang. 2000. "The 'Model Minority' Deconstructed." In *Contemporary Asian America: A Multidisciplinary Reader*, edited by Min Zhou and James V. Gatewood, 449–58. New York: New York University Press.

Cheng Hirata, Lucy. 1979. "Free, Indentured, Enslaved: Chinese Prostitutes in Nineteenth-Century America." *Signs* 5 (1): 3–29.

Cherokee Nation v. Georgia, 30 U.S. 1 (1831).

Cheung, King-Kok. 1990. "*The Woman Warrior* versus *The Chinaman Pacific*: Must a Chinese American Critic Choose between Feminism and Heroism?" In *Conflicts in Feminism*, edited by Marianne Hirsch and Evelyn Fox Keller, 234–54. New York: Routledge.

———. 1997. "Re-viewing Asian American Literary Studies." In *An Interethnic Companion to Asian American Literature*, edited by King-Kok Cheung, 1–38. New York: Cambridge University Press.

Chhuon, Vichet, and Cynthia Hudley. 2008. "Factors Supporting Cambodian American Students' Successful Adjustment into the University." *Journal of College Student Development* 49 (1): 15–30.

Chiang, Connie Y. 2008. *Shaping the Shoreline: Fisheries and Tourism on the Monterey Coast*. Seattle: University of Washington Press.

———. 2010. "Imprisoned Nature: Toward an Environmental History of the World War II Japanese American Incarceration." *Environmental History* 15: 236–67.

Chiang, Mark. 2009. *The Cultural Capital of Asian American Studies: Autonomy and Representation in the University*. New York: New York University Press.

Chin, Frank, Jeffery Paul Chan, Lawson Fusao Inada, and Shawn Wong, eds. (1974) 1979. *Aiiieeeee! An Anthology of Asian-American Writers*. Washington, DC: Howard University Press.

Chin, Margaret M. 2005. *Sewing Women: Immigrants and the New York Garment Industry*. New York: Columbia University Press.

Chiswick, Barry R., ed. 2011. *High-Skilled Immigration in a Global Labor Market*. Washington, DC: American Enterprise Institute for Public Policy Research.

Chiu, Melissa. 2006. *Breakout: Chinese Art outside China*. Milano: Edizioni Charta.

Chiu, Melissa, Karin Higa, and Susette S. Min, eds. 2006. *One Way or Another: Asian American Art Now*. Exh. cat. New York: Asia Society in association with Yale University Press.

Chiu, Ping. 1967. *Chinese Labor in California, 1850–1880: An Economic Study*. Madison: State Historical Society of Wisconsin.

Cho, W. K. T. 2002. "Tapping Motives and Dynamics behind Campaign Contributions: Insights from the Asian American Case." *American Politics Research* 30 (4): 347–83.

Choi, Chungmoo, ed. 1997. "The Comfort Women: Colonialism, War and Sex." *Positions: East Asia Cultures Critique* 5 (1).

Chong, Sylvia Sin Huey. 2012. *The Oriental Obscene: Violence and Racial Fantasies in the Vietnam Era*. Durham, NC: Duke University Press.

Chow, Rey. 2005. "'Have You Eaten?'—Inspired by an Exhibit." *Amerasia Journal* 31 (1): 19–22.

Choy, Catherine Ceniza. 2003. *Empire of Care: Nursing and Migration from Filipino American History*. Durham, NC: Duke University Press.

———. 2013. *Global Families: A History of Asian International Adoption in the United States*. New York: New York University Press.

Choy, Christine, and Renee Tajima-Pena, dirs. 1987. *Who Killed Vincent Chin?* New York: Third World Newsreel.

Chua, Amy L. 2011. *Battle Hymn of the Tiger Mother*. New York: Penguin Press.

Chuh, Kandice. 2003. *Imagine Otherwise: On Asian Americanist Critique*. Durham, NC: Duke University Press.

Chuman, Frank. 1976. *The Bamboo People: The Law and Japanese Americans*. Del Mar, CA: Publisher's Inc.

Chun, Wendy, and Lynne Joyrich, eds. 2009. "Feminism, Culture, and Media Studies: Race and/as Technology." *Camera Obscura* 24 (1).

Chung, Angie Y. 2007. *Legacies of Struggle: Conflict and Cooperation in Korean American Politics*. Palo Alto, CA: Stanford University Press.

Chung, Sue Fawn. 2011. *In Pursuit of Gold: Chinese American Miners and Merchants in the American West*. Urbana: University of Illinois Press.

Civil Rights Congress. (1951) 1970. *We Charge Genocide: The Historic Petition to the United Nations for Relief from a Crime of the United States Government against the Negro People*. New York: Civil Rights Congress.

Clarke, Kamari Maxine, and Deborah A. Thomas, eds. 2006. *Globalization and Race: Transformations in the Cultural Production of Blackness*. Durham, NC: Duke University Press.

Clifford, James. 1997. "Diasporas." In *Routes: Travel and Translation in the Late Twentieth Century*, by James Clifford, 244–77. Cambridge, MA: Harvard University Press.

Cockcroft, Eva, John Weber, and Jim Cockcroft, eds. 1977. *Toward a People's Art: The Contemporary Mural Movement*. New York: E.P. Dutton.

Cohen, Lucy M. 1984. *Chinese in the Post-Civil War South: A People without a History*. Baton Rouge: Louisiana State University Press.

Cohen, Robin. 1997. *Global Diasporas: An Introduction*. Seattle: University of Washington Press.

Cole, David. 2009. *The Torture Memos: Rationalizing the Unthinkable*. New York: New Press.

Collet, Christian, and Pei-Te Lien. 2009. "The Transnational Politics of Asian Americans: Controversies, Questions, Convergence." In *The Transnational Politics of Asian Americans*, edited by Christian Collet and Pei-Te Lien, 1–22. Philadelphia: Temple University Press.

Collier, Malcolm, and Daniel Phil Gonzales. 2009. "Origins: People, Time, Place, Dreams." In *At 40: Asian American Studies @ San Francisco State: Self-Determination, Community, Student Service*, by Asian American Studies Department, 7–18. San Francisco: Asian American Studies Department, College of Ethnic Studies, San Francisco State University.

Commission on Wartime Relocation and Internment of Civilians. 1997. *Personal Justice Denied*. Seattle: University of Washington Press. ("Commission" in text.)

Considine, Austin. 2011. "For Asian American Stars, Many Web Fans." *NewYorkTimes.com*, July 21. <http://www.nytimes.com/2011/07/31/fashion/for-asian-stars-many-web-fans.html?_r=0>.

Constable, Nicole. 2003. *Romance on a Global Stage: Pen Pals, Virtual Ethnography, and "Mail Order" Marriages*. Berkeley: University of California Press.

Coolidge, Mary Roberts. 1909. *Chinese Immigration*. New York: Henry Holt and Company.

Cooper, Frederick, Thomas C. Holt, and Rebecca Scott, eds. 2000. *Beyond Slavery: Explorations of Race, Labor, and Citizenship in Postemancipation Societies*. Chapel Hill: University of North Carolina Press.

Cordova, Fred. 1983. *Filipinos: Forgotten Asian Americans*. Dubuque, IA: Kendall-Hunt.

Cornell, Daniell, and Mark Dean Johnson, eds. 2008. *Asian/American/Modern Art: Shifting Currents, 1900–1970*. Exh. cat. San Francisco: Fine Arts Museums of San Francisco with University of California Press.

Cornell, Michiyo. 1996. "Living in Asian America: An Asian American Lesbian's Address before the Washington Monument (1979)." In *Asian American Sexualities: Dimensions of the Gay and Lesbian Experience*, edited by Russell Leong, 83–84. New York: Routledge.

Crenshaw, Kimberlé. 1989. "Demarginalizing the Intersection of Race and Sex: A Black Feminist Critique of Antidiscrimination Doctrine, Feminist Theory, and Antiracist Politics." *University of Chicago Legal Forum* (1989): 139–67.

de Crèvecoeur, J. Hector St. John. (1792) 2007. *Letters from an American Farmer*. Carlisle, MA: Applewood.

Cunningham, David. 2008. "Truth, Reconciliation, and the Ku Klux Klan." *Southern Cultures* 14 (3): 68–87.

Curtain, Michael, and Hemant Shah, eds. 2011. *Re-orientating Global Communication: India and Chinese Media Beyond Borders*. Chicago: University of Illinois Press.

DaCosta, K. 2008. "Viewpoint: Is Barack Obama Black?" *BBC News*, November 18. <http://news.bbc.co.uk/2/hi/americas/us_elections_2008/7735503.stm>.

Danico, Mary, and Franklin Ng. 2004. *Asian American Issues*. Westport, CT: Greenwood Press.

Daniels, Roger. 1966. "Westerners from the East: Oriental Immigrants Reappraised." *Pacific Historical Review* 35 (November): 375.

———. 1972. *Concentration Camps U.S.A: The Japanese Americans and World War II*. New York: Holt, Rinehart and Wilson.
1972. New York: Holt, Rinehart and Wilson.

———. (1962) 1977. *The Politics of Prejudice: The Anti-Japanese Movement in California and the Struggle for Japanese Exclusion*. Berkeley: University of California Press. (1962) 1977. Berkeley: University of California Press.

———. 2005. "Words Do Matter: A Note on Inappropriate Terminology and the Incarceration of the Japanese Americans." In *Nikkei in the Pacific Northwest*, edited by Louis Fiset and Gail M. Nomura, 190–214. Seattle: University of Washington Press.

Das Gupta, Monisha. 2006. *Unruly Immigrants: Rights, Activism, and Transnational South Asian Politics in the United States*. Durham, NC: Duke University Press.

Dasgupta, Shamita Das, ed. 2007. *Body Evidence: Intimate Violence against South Asian Women in America*. New Brunswick, NJ: Rutgers University Press.

Daulatzai, Sohail. 2012. *Black Star, Crescent Moon: The Muslim International and Black Freedom beyond America*. Minneapolis: University of Minnesota Press.

Davé, Shilpa. 2013. *Indian Accents: Brown Voice and Racial Performance in American Television and Film*. Chicago: University of Illinois Press.

Davé, Shilpa, Pawan Dhingra, Sunaina Maira, Partha Mazumdar, Lavina Dhingra Shankar, Jaideep Singh, and Rajini Srikanth. 2000. "De-Privileging Positions: Indian Americans, South Asian Americans, and the Politics of Asian American Studies." *Journal of Asian American Studies* 3 (1): 67–100.

Davé, Shilpa, Leilani Nishime, and Tasha G. Oren, eds. 2005. *East Main Street: Asian American Popular Culture*. New York: New York University Press.

Davidson, Arnold I. 2001. *The Emergence of Sexuality: Historical Epistemology and the Formation of Concepts*. Cambridge, MA: Harvard University Press.

Davis, Lawrence-Minh Bùi, Gerald Maa, Tyrone Nagai, and Alicia Upano, eds. 2011. *Asian American Literary Review* 2 (5).

Davis, Lennard J. 1995. *Enforcing Normalcy: Disability, Deafness, and the Body*. New York: Verso Press.

Davis, Peter, dir. 1974. *Hearts and Minds*. Los Angeles: BBS Productions.

Deleuze, Gilles, and Félix Guattari. 1986. *Kafka: Toward a Minor Literature*. Translated by Dana Polan. Minneapolis: University of Minnesota Press.

Delmendo, Sharon. 2004. *The Star-Entangled Banner: One Hundred Years of America in the Philippines*. New Brunswick, NJ: Rutgers University Press.

Deloria, Vine. 1983. *American Indians, American Justice*. Austin: University of Texas Press.

Desai, Jigna. 2004. *Beyond Bollywood: The Cultural Politics of South Asian Diasporic Film*. New York: Routledge.

DeSouza, Allan. 1997. "The Flight of/from the Authentic Primitive." In *Memories of Overdevelopment: Philippine Diaspora in Contemporary Art*, edited by Wayne Baerwaldt, 117–42. Irvine: University of California/Irvine Art Gallery.

Deutsch, Nathaniel. 2001. "'The Asiatic Black Man': An African American Orientalism?" *Journal of Asian American Studies* 4 (3): 193–208.

DeVotta, Neil. 2011. "Sri Lanka: From Turmoil to Democracy." *Journal of Democracy* 22 (2): 130–44.

DeWind, Josh, and Philip Kasinitz. 1997. "Everything Old Is New Again? Processes and Theories of Immigrant Incorporation." *International Migration Review* 31 (4): 1096–1111.

De Witt, Howard. 1976. *Anti-Filipino Movements in California: A History, Bibliography, and Study Guide*. San Francisco: R and E Research Associates.

———. 1978. "The Filipino Labor Union: The Salinas Lettuce Strike of 1934." *Amerasia Journal* 5 (2): 1–21.

———. 1980. *Violence in the Fields: California Farm Labor Unionization during the Great Depression*. Saratoga, CA: Century Twenty One.

Dharwadker, Vinay. 2001. "Introduction: Cosmopolitan and its Time and Place." In *Cosmopolitan Geographies: New Locations in Literature and Culture*, edited by Vinay Dhadwadker, 1–14. New York: Routledge.

Dhingra, Pawan. 2012. *Life behind the Lobby: Indian American Motel Owners and the American Dream*. Palo Alto, CA: Stanford University Press.

Diaz, Maria-Elena D. 2012. "Asian Embeddedness and Political Participation: Social Integration and Asian American Voting Behavior in the 2000 Presidential Election." *Sociological Perspectives* 55 (1): 141–66.

Dibblin, Jane. 1990. *Day of Two Suns: U.S. Nuclear Testing and the Pacific Islanders*. New York: New Amsterdam Press.

Dickerson, Debra J. 2007. "Colorblind." *Salon.com*, January 22. <http://www.salon.com/opinion/ feature/2007/01/22/obama/>.

Diep, Kane, dir. 2012. *Uploaded: The Asian American Movement*. Los Angeles: TPF Films.

Dinnerstein, Leonard, and David M. Reimers. 1999. *Ethnic Americans: A History of Immigration*. New York: Columbia University Press.

Dirlik, Arif. 1996. "Asians on the Rim: Transnational Capital and Local Community in the Making of Contemporary Asian America." *Amerasia Journal* 22 (3): 1–24.

Dorow, Sara K. 2006. *Transnational Adoption: A Cultural Economy of Race, Gender, and Kinship*. New York: New York University Press.

Drinnon, Richard. 1989. *Keeper of Concentration Camps: Dillon S. Myer and American Racism*. Berkeley: University of California Press.

Dubal, Veena. 2011. "Police Accused of Violating Muslims' Civil Rights." *National Public Radio*. KQED News, March 29. <http://www.kqed.org/a/kqednews/RN201103291730/a>.

DuBois, Thomas A. 1993. "Constructions Construed: The Representation of Southeast Asian Refugees in Academic, Popular, and Adolescent Discourse." *Amerasia Journal* 19 (3): 1–25.

Du Bois, W.E.B. 1897. *The Conservation of Races*. American Negro Academy Occasional Papers, No. 2.

———. (1903) 2008. *The Souls of Black Folk*. Rockville, MD: Arc Manor.

Dudziak, Mary. 2011. *Cold War Civil Rights: Race and the Image of American Democracy* Princeton, NJ: Princeton University Press.

Dunning, Bruce. 1989. "Vietnamese in America: The Adaptation of the 1975–1979 Arrivals." In *Refugees as Immigrants: Cambodians, Laotians, and Vietnamese in America*, edited by David. W. Haines, 55–85. Lanham, MD: Rowman & Littlefield.

Duong, Lan P. 2012. *Treacherous Subjects: Gender, Culture and Trans-Vietnamese Feminism*. Philadelphia: Temple University Press.

Duong, Lan P., and Isabelle Pelaud. 2012. "Vietnamese American Art and Community Politics: An Engaged Feminist Perspective." *Journal of Asian American Studies* 15 (3): 241–69.

Dutton, Michael. 2008. "Passionately Governmental: Maoism and the Structured Intensities of Revolutionary Governmentality." *Postcolonial Studies* 11 (1): 99–112.

Duus, Masayo Umezawa. 1999. *The Japanese Conspiracy: The Oahu Sugar Strike of 1920*. Berkeley: University of California Press.

Dye, Bob. 1997. *Merchant Prince of the Sandalwood Mountains: Afong and the Chinese in Hawaiʻi*. Honolulu: University of Hawaiʻi Press.

Eagleton, Terry. 2000. *The Idea of Culture*. Malden, MA: Blackwell Publishers.

Eaton, Allen. 1952. *Beauty behind Barbed Wire: The Arts of the Japanese in Our War Relocation Camps*. New York: Harper.

Ebron, Paula, and Anna Tsing. 1995. "From Allegories of Identity to Sites of Dialogue." *Diaspora* 4 (2): 125–51.

Eck, Diana. 2002. *A New Religious America: How a "Christian Country" Has Become the World's Most Religiously Diverse Nation*. San Francisco: Harper.

Edwards, Blake, dir. 1961. *Breakfast at Tiffany's*. Hollywood, CA: Paramount Pictures.

Elbaum, Max. 2002. *Revolution in the Air: Sixties Radicals turn to Lenin, Mao and Che*. London: Verso.

———. 2002. "What Legacy from the Radical Internationalism of 1968?" *Radical History Review* 82: 37–64.

Enders, Walter, and Todd Sandler. 2002. "Patterns of Transnational Terrorism, 1970–1999: Alternative Time-Series Estimates." *International Studies Quarterly* 46 (2): 145–65.

———. 2006. *The Political Economy of Terrorism*. Cambridge, UK: Cambridge University Press.

Eng, David. 1997. "Out Here and Over There: Queerness and Diaspora in Asian American Studies." *Social Text* 52/53: 31–52.

———. 2001. *Racial Castration: Managing Masculinity in Asian America*. Durham, NC: Duke University Press.

———. 2010. *The Feeling of Kinship: Queer Liberalism and the Racialization of Intimacy*. Durham, NC: Duke University Press.

Eng, David, Judith Halberstam, and José Esteban Muñoz. 2005. "What's Queer about Queer Studies Now." *Social Text* 84–85 (3–4): 1–17.

Eng, David, and Alice Hom, eds. 1998. *Q & A: Queer in Asian America*. Philadelphia: Temple University Press.

Espiritu, Augusto Fauni. 2005. *Five Faces of Exile: The Nation and Filipino American Intellectuals*. Palo Alto, CA: Stanford University Press.

Espiritu, Yến Lê. 1992. *Asian American Panethnicity: Bridging Institutions and Identities*. Philadelphia: Temple University Press.

———. 1999. "Gender and Labor in Asian Immigrant Families." *American Behavioral Scientist* 42: 628–47.

———. 2003. *Home Bound: Filipino American Lives across Cultures, Communities, and Countries*. Berkeley: University of California Press.

———. 2008. *Asian American Women and Men: Labor, Laws, and Love*, second edition. Lanham, MD: Rowman & Littlefield.

Evan B. Donaldson Adoption Institute. 2013. "International Adoption Facts." <http://www.adoptioninstitute.org/research/internationaladoption.php>.

Fadiman, Anne. 1997. *The Spirit Catches You and You Fall Down*. New York: Farrar, Straus and Giroux.

Faist, Thomas. 2010. "Diaspora and Transnationalism: What Kind of Dance Partners?" In *Diaspora and Transnationalism: Concepts, Theories and Methods*, edited by Thomas Faist and Rainer Baubock, 9–34. Amsterdam: Amsterdam University Press.

Fajardo, Kale Bantigue. 2011. *Filipino Crosscurrents: Oceanographies of Seafaring, Masculinities, and Globalization*. Minneapolis: University of Minnesota Press.

Fanon, Frantz. (1961) 2005. *The Wretched of the Earth*. New York: Grove Press.

Farver, Jane. 1997. "Inside and Out of India: Contemporary Art of the South Asian Diaspora." In *Out of India: Contemporary Art of the South Asian Diaspora*, edited by Jane Farver and Radha Kumar, 12–21. Exh. cat. New York: Queens Museum of Art.

Farver, Jane, Young Chul Lee, Elaine H. Kim, Minne Jung-Min Hong, and Sae June Kim. 1993. *Across the Pacific: Contemporary Korean and Korean American Art*. Exh. cat. New York: Queens Museum of Art.

Feng, Peter X. 2002. *Identities in Motion: Asian American Film and Video*. Durham, NC: Duke University Press.

Ferguson, Niall. 2003. *Empire: The Rise and Demise of the British World Order and the Lessons for Global Power*. New York: Basic Books.

Ferguson, Roderick A. 2004. *Aberrations in Black: Toward a Queer of Color Critique*. Minneapolis: University of Minnesota Press.

———. 2012a. *The Reorder of Things: The University and Its Pedagogies of Minority Difference*. Minneapolis: University of Minnesota Press.

———. 2012b. "On the Specificities of Racial Formation: Gender and Sexuality in Historiographies of Race." In *Racial Formation in the Twenty-First Century*, edited by Daniel Martinez HoSang, Oneka LaBennett, and Laura Pulido, 44–56. Berkeley: University of California Press.

File, Thom, and Sarah Crissey. 2012. *Voting and Registration in the Election of November 2008*. U.S. Census Bureau Report P20–562RV. U.S. Department of Commerce: Economics and Statistics Administration.

Foner, Eric. (1970) 1995. *Free Soil, Free Labor, Free Men: The Ideology of the Republican Party before the Civil War*. New York: Oxford University Press.

Fong, Timothy. 2006. *The Contemporary Asian American Experience: Beyond the Model Minority*. Upper Saddle River, NJ: Prentice Hall.

Foucault, Michel. 1977. *Language, Counter-memory, Practice: Selected Essays and Interviews*. Ithaca, NY: Cornell University Press.

———. (1978) 1990. *The History of Sexuality*. Translated by Robert Hurley. New York: Vintage Books.

———. 1982. "The Subject and Power." *Critical Inquiry* 8 (4): 777–95.

———. 2003. *"Society Must Be Defended": Lectures at the Collège de France, 1975–1976*. Translated by Arnold I. Davidson. New York: Picador.

Francisco, Luzviminda. 1973. "The First Vietnam: The U.S.-Philippine War of 1899." *History Is a Weapon*. <www.historyisaweapon.com/defcom1/franciscofirstviernam.html>.

Frank, Andre Gunder. 1998. *ReOrient: Global Economy in the Asian Age*. Berkeley: University of California Press.

Frank, Caroline. 2011. *Objectifying China, Imagining America: Chinese Commodities in Early America*. Chicago: University of Chicago Press.

Frasure, Lorrie, Matt Barreto, Sylvia Manzano, Ange-Marie Hancock, Ricardo Ramirez, Karthick Ramakrishnan, Gabriel Sanchez, and Janelle Wong. 2008. Collaborative Multiracial Post-election Study (CMPS). Unpublished dataset. <http://www.cmpstudy.com/index.html>.

Freeman, James A. 1989. *Hearts of Sorrow: Vietnamese-American Lives*. Palo Alto, CA: Stanford University Press.

Freud, Sigmund. (1914) 1976. "Remembering, Repeating, and Working Through." *The Complete Psychological Works of Sigmund Freud (Standard Edition)*, Volume 12. New York: W. W. Norton.

Friday, Chris. 1994. *Organizing Asian American Labor: The Pacific Coast Canned Salmon Industry, 1870–1942*. Philadelphia: Temple University Press.

Friis-Hansen, Dana, Alice G. Guillermo, and Jeff Baysa. 1998. *At Home and Abroad: 20 Contemporary Filipino Artists*. Exh. cat. San Francisco: Asian Art Museum of San Francisco.

Fujikane, Candace. 2000. "Sweeping Racism under the Rug of 'Censorship': The Controversy over Lois-Ann Yamanaka's *Blu's Hanging*." *Amerasia Journal* 26 (2): 158–94.

———. 2005. "Foregrounding Native Nationalisms: A Critique of Antinationalist Sentiment in Asian American Studies." In *Asian American Studies After Critical Mass*, edited by K. A. Ono, 73–97. Oxford: Blackwell Publishing.

———. 2008. "Introduction: Asian Settler Colonialism in the U.S. Colony of Hawai'i." In *Asian Settler Colonialism: From Local Governance to the Habits of Everyday Life in Hawai'i*, edited by Candace Fujikane and Jonathan Y. Okamura, 1–42. Honolulu: University of Hawai'i Press.

Fujikane, Candace, and Jonathan Y. Okamura, eds. 2008. *Asian Settler Colonialism: From Local Governance to the Habits of Everyday Life in Hawai'i*. Honolulu: University of Hawai'i Press.

Fujino, Diane. 2005. *Heartbeat of Struggle: The Revolutionary Life of Yuri Kochiyama*. Minneapolis: University of Minnesota Press.

———. 2008. "Who Studies the Asian American Movement?: A Historiographical Analysis." *Journal of Asian American Studies* 11: 127–69. doi:10.1353/jaas.0.0003.

———. 2012. *Samurai among Panthers: Richard Aoki on Race, Resistance, and a Paradoxical Life*. Minneapolis: University of Minnesota Press.

Fujitani, T. 2011. *Race for Empire: Koreans as Japanese and Japanese as Americans during World War II*. Berkeley: University of California Press.

Fujita-Rony, Dorothy B. 2003. *American Workers, Colonial Power: Philippine Seattle and the Transpacific West*. Berkeley: University of California Press.

Fulbeck, Kip. 2006. *Part Asian, 100% Hapa*. San Francisco: Chronicle Books.

Furumoto, Warren, ed. 2003. "Special Issue: Pedagogy, Social Justice, and the State of Asian American Studies." *Amerasia Journal* 29 (2).

Gamblin, Noriko, and Long Beach Museum of Art. 1992. *Relocations and Revisions: The Japanese-American Internment Reconsidered*. Long Beach, CA: Long Beach Museum of Art.

Gardner, Martha. 2009. *The Qualities of a Citizen: Women, Immigration, and Citizenship, 1870–1965*. Princeton, NJ: Princeton University Press.

Garland-Thomson, Rosemarie. 1997. *Extraordinary Bodies: Figuring Physical Disability in American Culture and Literature*. New York: Columbia University Press.

Gee, Deborah, dir. 1988. *Slaying the Dragon*. San Francisco: National Asian American Telecommunications Association (NAATA).

Gee, Emma, ed. 1976. *Counterpoint: Perspectives in Asian America*. Los Angeles: University of California Los Angeles Asian American Studies Center.

Gee, G. C., and N. Ponce. 2010. "Associations between Racial Discrimination, Limited English Proficiency, and Health-

Related Quality of Life among 6 Asian Ethnic Groups in California." *American Journal of Public Health* 100 (5): 888–95.

Gee, G. C., M. S. Spencer, J. Chen, and D. Takeuchi. 2007. "A Nationwide Study of Discrimination and Chronic Health Conditions among Asian Americans." *American Journal of Public Health* 97 (7): 1275–82.

Gee, Jennifer. 2003. "Housewives, Men's Villages, and Sexual Respectability: Gender and the Interrogation of Asian Women at the Angel Island Immigration Station." In *Asian/Pacific Islander American Women: A Historical Anthology*, edited by Shirley Hune and Gail M. Nomura, 90–105. New York: New York University Press.

Geiger, Andrea. 2011. *Subverting Exclusion: Transpacific Encounters with Race, Caste, and Borders, 1885–1928*. New Haven, CT: Yale University Press.

Gellately, Robert, and Ben Kiernan, eds. 2003. *The Specter of Genocide: Mass Murder in Historical Perspective*. Cambridge, UK: Cambridge University Press.

George, David. 1979. "Shakespeare in Minneapolis." *Shakespeare Quarterly* 30 (2): 219–21.

Gesensway, Deborah, and Mindy Roseman. 1987. *Beyond Words: Images from America's Concentration Camps*. Ithaca, NY: Cornell University Press.

Ghosh, Chandak. 2003. "Healthy People 2010 and Asian Americans/Pacific Islanders: Defining a Baseline of Information." *American Journal of Public Health* 93 (12): 2093–98.

Gibney, Matthew, and Randall Hansen, eds. 2005. *Immigration and Asylum: From 1900 to the Present*. Santa Barbara, CA: ABC-CLIO.

Gilman, Sander. 1985. *Difference and Pathology: Stereotypes of Race, Sexuality, and Madness*. Ithaca, NY: Cornell University Press.

———. 1996. *Seeing the Insane: A Cultural History of Psychiatric Illustration*. Lincoln: University of Nebraska Press.

Gilmore, Ruth Wilson. 2007. *Golden Gulag: Prisons, Surplus, Crisis, and Opposition in Globalizing California*. Berkeley: University of California Press.

Gilroy, Paul. 1993. *The Black Atlantic: Modernity and Double-Consciousness*. Cambridge, MA: Harvard University Press.

Glenn, Evelyn Nakano. 1983. "Split Household, Small Producer and Dual Wage Earner: An Analysis of Chinese-American Family Strategies." *Journal of Marriage and Family* 45 (1): 35–46.

———. 1988. *Issei, Nisei, War Bride: Three Generations of Japanese American Women in Domestic Service*. Philadelphia: Temple University Press.

———. 2004. *Unequal Freedom: How Race and Gender Shaped American Citizenship and Labor*. Cambridge, MA: Harvard University Press.

Glick, Clarence E. 1980. *Sojourners and Settlers: Chinese Migrants in Hawai'i*. Honolulu: University Press of Hawai'i.

Go, Julian. 2011. *Patterns of Empire: The British and American Empires, 1688 to the Present*. Cambridge, UK: Cambridge University Press.

Goffman, Erving. 1959. *The Presentation of Self in Everyday Life*. New York: Doubleday.

Goldberg, David Theo. 1993. *Racist Culture: Philosophy and the Politics of Meaning*. Malden, MA: Blackwell Publishers.

Goldmacher, Shane. 2012. "The Power of the Asian-American Vote Is Growing—And It's Up for Grabs." *National Journal*, October 25. <http://www.nationaljournal.com/magazine/the-power-of-the-asian-american-vote-is-growing-and-it-s-up-for-grabs-20121025>.

Gomez, S. L., A. M. Noone, D. Y. Lichtensztajn, S. Scoppa, J. T. Gibson, L. Liu, and B. A. Miller. 2013. "Cancer Incidence Trends among Asian American Populations in the United States, 1990–2008." *Journal of the National Cancer Institute* 105 (15): 1096–1110.

Gong Lum v. Rice, 275 U.S. 78 (1927).

Gonzalves, Theodore. 2010. *The Day the Dancers Stayed: Performing in the Filipino/American Diaspora*. Philadelphia: Temple University Press.

Goodwin, Jeff. 2006. "A Theory of Categorical Terrorism." *Social Forces* 84 (4): 2027–46.

Gopinath, Gayatri. 2005. *Impossible Desire: Queer Diasporas and South Asian Public Cultures*. Durham, NC: Duke University Press.

Gordon, Avery. 1997. *Ghostly Matters: Haunting and the Sociological Imagination*. Minneapolis: University of Minnesota Press.

Gordon, Avery, and Christopher Newfield, eds. 1996. *Mapping Multiculturalism*. Minneapolis: University of Minnesota Press.

Gouldner, Alvin. 1960. "The Norm of Reciprocity: A Preliminary Statement." *American Sociological Review* 25 (2): 161–78.

Grabias, David, dir. 2006. *Sentenced Home*. DVD. Sentenced Home Productions.

Gramsci, Antonio. 1971. *Selections from the Prison Notebooks*. Edited and translated by Quintin Hoarc and Geoffrey Nowell-Smith. London: Lawrence and Wishart.

Grewal, Inderpal, and Caren Kaplan. 1994. "Introduction: Transnational Feminist Practices and Questions of Post-modernity." In *Scattered Hegemonies: Postmodernity and Transnational Feminist Practices*, edited by Inderpal Grewal and Caren Kaplan, 1–33. Minneapolis: University of Minnesota Press.

Grodzins, Morton. 1949. *Americans Betrayed: Politics and the Japanese Evacuation*. Chicago: University of Chicago Press.

Groening, Matt, creator. 1989. *The Simpsons*. Los Angeles: Fox Broadcasting.

Guevarra, Anna Romina. 2010. *Marketing Dreams, Manufacturing Heroes: The Transnational Labor Brokering of Filipino Workers*. New Brunswick, NJ: Rutgers University Press.

Guralnik, David B., and Joseph H. Friend, eds. 1968. *Webster's New World Dictionary of the American Language, College Edition*. Cleveland: World Publishing Company.

Guterl, Matthew Pratt. 2003. "After Slavery: Asian Labor, the American South, and the Age of Emancipation." *Journal of World History* 14 (June): 209–42.

Gyory, Andrew. 1998. *Closing the Gate: Race, Politics, and the Chinese Exclusion Act*. Chapel Hill: University of North Carolina Press.

Habal, Estella. 2007. *San Francisco's International Hotel: Mobilizing the Filipino American Community in the Anti-Eviction Movement*. Philadelphia: Temple University Press.

Haddad, John R. 2013. *First Adventure in China: Trade, Treaties, Opium, and Salvation*. Philadelphia: Temple University Press.

Haenni, Sabine. 2008. *The Immigrant Scene: Ethnic Amusements in New York, 1880–1920*. Minneapolis: University of Minnesota Press.

Haines, David W. 1989. "Introduction." In *Refugees as Immigrants: Cambodians, Laotians, and Vietnamese in America*, edited by David W. Haines, 14–23. Lanham, MD: Rowman & Littlefield.

Halbwachs, Maurice. 1992. *On Collective Memory*. Chicago: University of Chicago Press.

Hall, Stuart. 1973. *Encoding and Decoding in the Television Discourse*. Birmingham, UK: Centre for Contemporary Cultural Studies.

———. 1992. "What Is This 'Black' in Black Popular Culture?" In *Black Popular Culture: A Project by Michele Wallace*, edited by Gina Dent, 21–33. Seattle: Bay Press.

Hall, Stuart, and David Held. 1989. "Left and Rights." *Marxism Today* (June): 16–23.

Hallmark, Kara Kelly. 2007. *Encyclopedia of Asian American Artists*. Westport, CT: Greenwood Press

Halter, Marilyn. 2000. *Shopping for Identity: The Marketing of Ethnicity*. New York: Schocken Books.

Hamamoto, Darrell. 1994. *Monitored Peril: Asian Americans and the Politics of TV Representation*. Minneapolis: University of Minnesota Press.

Hamamoto, Darrell, and Sandra Liu. 2000. *Countervisions: Asian American Film Criticism*. Philadelphia: Temple University Press.

Hamid, Mohsin. 2007. "Interview with Terry Gross." *National Public Radio*. "Fresh Air," April 3.

Hamilton-Merritt, Jane. 2008. *Tragic Mountains: The Hmong, the Americans, and the Secret Wars for Laos*. Indianapolis: Indiana University Press.

Handlin, Oscar. 1951. *The Uprooted: The Epic Story of the Great Migrations that Made the American People*. New York: Little, Brown and Company.

Harris, Cheryl I. 1995. "Whiteness as Property." In *Critical Race Theory: The Key Writings that Formed the Movement*, edited by K. Crenshaw, N. Gotanda, G. Peller, and K. Thomas, 276–91. New York City: New Press.

Harvey, David. 1989. *The Condition of Postmodernity: An Enquiry into the Origins of Cultural Change*. Malden, MA: Blackwell Publishers.

———. 2007. *A Brief History of Neoliberalism*. Oxford: Oxford University Press.

Harvey, William S. 2008. "Brain Circulation? British and Indian Scientists in Boston, Massachusetts, U.S.A." *Asian Population Studies* 4 (3): 294–309.

Hayashi, Robert T. 2007a. "Beyond Walden Pond: Asian American Literature and the Limits of Ecocriticism." In *Coming into Contact: Explorations in Ecocritical Theory and Practice*, edited by Annie Merrill Ingram, Ian Marshall, Daniel J. Philippon, and Adam W. Sweeting, 58–75. Atlanta: University of Georgia Press.

———. 2007b. *Haunted by Waters: A Journey through Race and Place in the American West.* Iowa City: University of Iowa Press.

Hedges, Chris. 2002. *War Is a Force that Gives Us Meaning.* New York: Public Affairs.

Herberg, Will. 1960. *Protestant, Catholic, Jew.* New York: Doubleday.

Hernandez, Kelly Lytle. 2010. *Migra!: A History of the U.S. Border Patrol.* Berkeley: University of California Press.

Herzig-Yoshinaga, Aiko. 2009. "Words Can Lie or Clarify: Terminology of the World War II Incarceration of Japanese Americans" (last modified 2010). *NPS.gov.* <http://www.nps.gov/tule/forteachers/loader.cfm?csModule=security/getfile&PageID=373742>.

Higa, Karin. 1992. *The View from Within: Japanese American Art from the Internment Camps, 1942–1945.* Exh. cat. Los Angeles: Japanese American National Museum.

Higa, Karin, with contributing authors Ian Buruma et al. 1999. *Bruce and Norman Yonemoto: Memory, Matter, and Modern Romance.* Exh. cat. Los Angeles: Japanese American National Museum.

Higashide, Seiichi. 2000. *Adios to Tears: The Memoirs of a Japanese-Peruvian Internee in U.S. Concentration Camps.* Seattle: University of Washington Press.

Higginbotham, Leon. 1980. *In the Matter of Color: Race and the American Legal Process.* New York: Oxford University Press.

Hildebrand, Lorraine. 1977. *Straw Hats, Sandals, and Steel: The Chinese in Washington State.* Tacoma: Washington State American Revolution Bicentennial Commission.

Hing, Bill Ong. 1993. *Making and Remaking Asian America through Immigration Policy, 1850–1990.* Palo Alto, CA: Stanford University Press.

———. 2006. *Deporting Our Souls: Values, Morality, and Immigration Policy.* Cambridge, UK: Cambridge University Press.

Hirabayashi, James A. 1994. "'Concentration Camp,' or 'Relocation Center': What's in a Name?" *Japanese American National Museum Quarterly* 9 (3): 5–10.

Hise, Greg. 2004. "Border City: Race and Social Distance in Los Angeles." *American Quarterly* 56 (3): 545–58.

Ho, Christine. 1989. "'Hold the Chow Mein, Gimme Soca': Creolization of the Chinese in Guyana, Trinidad and Jamaica." *Amerasia* 15 (2): 3–25.

Ho, Jennifer, and James Kyung-Jin Lee, eds. 2013. "The State of Illness and Disability in Asian America." *Amerasia Journal* 39 (1).

Ho v. San Francisco Unified School District, 147 F. 3d 854 (9th Cir. 1998).

Hobsbawm, E. J. 1992. "Introduction: The Invention of Tradition." In *The Invention of Tradition*, edited by E. J. Hobsbawm and T. O. Ranger, 1–14. New York: Cambridge University Press.

Hoefte, Rosemarijn. 1998. *In Place of Slavery: A Social History of British Indian and Javanese Laborers in Suriname.* Gainesville: University Press of Florida.

Höhn, Maria, and Seungsook Moon, eds. 2010. *Over There: Living with the U.S. Military Empire from World War Two to the Present.* Durham, NC: Duke University Press.

Hom, L. D. 2013. "Early Chinese Immigrants Organizing for Health Care: The Establishment of the Chinese Hospital in San Francisco." In *Handbook of Asian American Health*, edited by Grace J. Yoo, Mai-Nhung Le, and Alan Oda, 353–62. New York: Springer Publishing.

Hong, Grace Kyungwon. 2006. *The Ruptures of American Capital: Women of Color Feminism and the Culture of Immigrant Labor.* Minneapolis: University of Minnesota Press.

Hong, Grace Kyungwon, and Roderick A. Ferguson. 2011. *Strange Affinities: The Gender and Sexual Politics of Comparative Racialization.* Durham, NC: Duke University Press.

hooks, bell. 1992. *Black Looks: Race and Representation.* Cambridge, MA: South End Press.

Houston, Velina Hasu. 2002. "Notes from a Cosmopolite." In *The Color of Theater: Race, Culture, and the Contemporary Performance*, edited by Roberta Uno and Lucy Burns, 83–90. New York: Continuum.

Hsien, Theodore, and Victor Hwang. 2000. "Charged with Being Ethnic Chinese." *ChinaNews.* <http://www.sinomania.com/CHINANEWS/case_of_wen_ho_lee.htm>.

Hsu, Madeline. 2000. *Dreaming of Gold, Dreaming of Home: Transnationalism and Migration between the United States and Southern China, 1882–1943.* Palo Alto, CA: Stanford University Press.

———. 2008. "From Chop Suey to Mandarin Cuisine: Fine Dining and the Refashioning of Chinese Ethnicity during the Cold War Era." In *Chinese Americans and the Politics of Race and Culture*, edited by Sucheng Chan and Madeline Y. Hsu, 173–93. Philadelphia: Temple University Press.

———. 2012. "The Disappearance of America's Cold War Chinese Refugees." *Journal of American Ethnic History* 31 (4): 12–33.

Huang, Eddie. 2013. *Fresh Off the Boat.* New York: Spiegel & Grau.

Huang, Guiyou, and Wu Bing, eds. 2008. *Global Perspectives on Asian American Literature.* Beijing: Foriegn Language Teaching and Research Press.

Hubinette, Tobias. 2006. *Comforting an Orphaned Nation: Representations of International Adoption and Adopted Koreans in Korean Popular Culture.* Seoul: Jimoondang.

Hu-DeHart, Evelyn. 1992. "Chinese Coolie Labor in Cuba and Peru in the Nineteenth Century: Free Labor or Neoslavery." *Journal of Overseas Chinese* 2 (2): 149–82.

———. 1999. "Asian American Formation in the Age of Globalization." In *Across the Pacific: Asian Americans and Globalization,* edited by Evelyn Hu-DeHart, 1–28. Philadelphia: Temple University Press.

———. 2005. "Concluding Commentary: On Migration, Diasporas, and Transnationalism in Asian American History." *Journal of Asian American Studies* 8: 309–12. doi:10.1353/jaas.2005.0049.

Hughes, John, dir. 1984. *Sixteen Candles.* Universal City, CA: Universal Pictures.

Hum, Tarry. 2014. *Making a Global Immigrant Neighborhood: Brooklyn's Sunset Park.* Philadelphia: Temple University Press.

Humanities Institute. 1987. "Caribbean Diaspora: Processes of Migration and Settlement." Third Annual Conference of the CUNY Association of Caribbean Studies. March 6–7.

Hune, Shirley. 1989. "Expanding the International Dimension of Asian American Studies." *Amerasia* 15 (2): xix–xxiv.

———. 2011. "Asian American Women Faculty: Navigating Student Resistance and (Re)Claiming Authority and Their Rightful Place." In *Women of Color in Higher Education: Turbulent Past, Promising Future,* edited by G. Jean-Marie and B. Lloyd-Jones, 307–35. Bingley, UK: Emerald Publishing.

Hune, Shirley, and David T. Takeuchi. 2008. *Asian Americans in Washington State: Closing Their Hidden Achievement Gaps.* Seattle: Washington State Commission on Asian Pacific American Affairs.

Hune, Shirley, and Jeomja Yeo. 2010. "How Do Pacific Islanders Fare in U.S. Education?: A Look inside Washington State Public Schools with a Focus on Samoans." *aapi nexus* 8 (1): 1–16.

Hurh, Won Moo, and Kwang Chung Kim. 1984. *Korean Immigrants in America: A Structural Analysis of Ethnic Confinement and Adhesive Adaptation.* Rutherford, NJ: Fairleigh Dickinson University Press.

Ichihashi, Yamato. (1932) 1969. *Japanese in the United States: A Critical Study of the Problems of the Japanese Immigrants and Their Children.* Palo Alto, CA: Stanford University Press.

Ichioka, Yuji. 1988. *The Issei: The World of the First Generation Japanese Immigrants in the United States, 1885–1924.* New York: Free Press.

———. 2000. "A Historian by Happenstance." *Amerasia Journal* 26 (1): 32–53.

Iijima, Chris K. 1997. "The Era of We-Construction: Reclaiming the Politics of Asian Pacific American Identity and Reflections on the Critique of the Black/White Paradigm." *Columbia Human Rights Law Review* 29: 47–90.

Iijima, Chris K., Nobuko Miyamoto, and Charlie Chin. 2003. *A Grain of Sand.* CD. San Francisco: Paredon Records.

International Commission of Jurists. 2009. "Assessing Damage, Urging Action." *UN.org.*<http://www.un.org/en/sc/ctc/specialmeetings/2011/docs/icj/icj-2009-ejp-execsumm.pdf>.

Irick, Robert. 1982. *Ch'ing Policy toward the Coolie Trade, 1847–1878.* Taipei: Chinese Materials Center.

Iron Chef. 1993–1999. Tokyo: Fuji Television Network and Television Food Network.

Isaac, Allan Punzalan. 2006. *American Tropics: Articulating Filipino America.* Minneapolis: University of Minnesota Press.

Isaac, Benjamin H. 2004. *The Invention of Racism in Classical Antiquity.* Princeton, NJ: Princeton University Press.

Ishizuka, Karen L. 2006. *Lost and Found: Claiming the Japanese American Incarceration.* Champaign: University of Illinois Press.

Islam, N. S., S. Khan, S. Kwon, D. Jang, M. Ro, and C. Trinh-Shevrin. 2010. "Methodological Issues in the Collection, Analysis, and Reporting of Granular Data in Asian American Populations: Historical Challenges and Potential Solutions." *Journal of Health Care for the Poor and Underserved* 21 (4): 1354.

Iwamura, Jane. 2010. *Virtual Orientalism: Asian Religions and American Popular Culture.* New York: Oxford University Press.

Iwamura, Jane, and Paul Spickard, eds. 2003. *Revealing the Sacred in Asian and Pacific America*. New York: Routledge.

Iwata, Masakazu. 1992. *Planted in Good Soil: A History of the Issei in United States Agriculture*. New York: Peter Lang.

Jackson, Kim, and Heewon Lee with Jae Ran Kim, Kim Park Nelson, and Wing Young Huie. 2010. *Here: A Visual History of Adopted Koreans in Minnesota*. St. Paul, MN: Yeong & Yeong Book Company.

Jacobs, Gary, creator. 1994–1995. *All-American Girl*. New York: ABC Television Network

Jacobson, Matthew Frye. 2000. *Barbarian Virtues: The United States Encounters Foreign Peoples at Home and Abroad, 1876–1917*. New York: Hill and Wang.

———.1999. *Whiteness of a Different Color: European Immigrants and the Alchemy of Race*. Cambridge, MA: Harvard University Press.

———. 2006. *Roots Too: White Ethnic Revival in Post–Civil Rights America*. Cambridge, MA: Harvard University Press.

James, Jennifer. 2007. *A Freedom Bought with Blood: African American War Literature from the Civil War to World War II*. Chapel Hill: University of North Carolina Press.

James, Jennifer, and Cynthia Wu, eds. 2006. "Race, Ethnicity, Disability, and Literature: Intersections and Interventions." *MELUS* 31 (3).

Jang, D., and H. L. Tran. 2009. "Health Policy Advocacy." In *Asian American Communities and Health*, edited by C. Shevrin, N. Islam, and M. Rey, 589–609. San Francisco: Jossey-Bass.

JanMohamed, Abdul R., and David Lloyd. 1990. "Introduction: Toward a Theory of Minority Discourse: What Is to Be Done?" In *The Nature and Context of Minority Discourse*, edited by Abdul R. JanMohamed and David Lloyd, 1–16. New York: Oxford University Press.

Jenkins, Henry. 1992. *Textual Poachers: Television Fans and Participatory Culture*. New York: Routledge.

———. 2006. *Convergence Culture: Where Old and New Media Collide*. New York: New York University Press.

Jenkins, Henry, Sam Ford, and Joshua Green. 2013. *Spreadable Media: Creating Value and Meaning in a Networked Culture*. New York: New York University Press.

Jensen, Joan M. 1988. *Passage from India: Asian Indian Immigrants in North America*. New Haven, CT: Yale University Press.

Johnson, Mark Dean. 2013. "Introduction." In *The Moment for Ink*, edited by Mark Dean Johnson, Patricia Wakida, and Sharon E. Bliss, 12–27. Exh. cat. San Francisco: San Francisco State University.

Jordan, Don, and Michael Walsh. 2007. *White Cargo: The Forgotten History of Britain's White Slaves in America*. New York: New York University Press.

Joshi, Khyati Y. and Jigna Desai, eds. 2013. *Asian Americans in Dixie: Race and Migration in the South*. Champaign: University of Illinois Press.

Journal of Asian American Studies. 2012. Editor's Forum: "Has Asian American Studies Failed?" 15 (3): 327–46.

Jung, John. 2007. *Chinese Laundries: Tickets to Survival on Gold Mountain*. Cypress, CA: Yin and Yang Press.

Jung, Marilyn, Monica Chau, and Margo Machida. 1997. *Uncommon Traits: Re/Locating Asia*. Exh. cat. Buffalo, NY: CEPA Gallery.

Jung, Moon-Ho. 2006. *Coolies and Cane: Race, Labor, and Sugar in the Age of Emancipation*. Baltimore: John Hopkins University Press.

Kaling, Mindy, creator. 2012–. *The Mindy Project*. Los Angeles: Fox Broadcasting.

Kang, Jerry. 2002. "Thinking through Internment: 12/7 and 9/11." In *Asian Americans on War and Peace*, edited by Russell Leong and Don Nakanishi, 55–62. Los Angeles: UCLA Asian American Studies Center Press.

Kang, Laura Hyun Yi. 2002. *Compositional Subjects: Enfiguring Asian/American Women*. Durham, NC: Duke University Press.

Kang, Miliann. 2010. *The Managed Hand: Race, Gender, and the Body in Beauty Service Work*. Berkeley: University of California Press.

Kaplan, Amy, and Donald E. Pease, eds. 1993. *Cultures of United States Imperialism*. Durham, NC: Duke University Press.

Kaplan, Carla. 2007. "Identity." In *Keywords for American Cultural Studies*, edited by Bruce Burgett and Glenn Hendler, 123–27. New York: New York University Press.

Kashima, Tetsuden. 2003 *Judgment without Trial*. Seattle: University of Washington Press.

Kauanui, J. Kēhaulani. 2008a. "Colonialism in Equality: Hawai'ian Sovereignty and the Question of U.S. Civil Rights." *South Atlantic Quarterly* 107 (4): 635–50.

———. 2008b. *Hawai'ian Blood: Colonialism and the Politics of*

Sovereignty and Indigeneity. Durham, NC: Duke University Press.

Kelley, David E., creator. 1997–2002. *Ally McBeal*. Los Angeles: Fox Broadcasting.

Kelly, Gail. 1986. "Coping with America: Refugees from Vietnam, Cambodia, and Laos in the 1970s and 1980s." *Annals of the American Academy of Political Science* 486 (1): 138–49.

Kerkvliet, Melina Tria. 2002. *Unbending Cane: Pablo Manlapit, a Filipino Labor Leader in Hawai'i*. Honolulu: University of Hawai'i Office of Multicultural Student Services.

Khan, Aisha. 2004. *Callaloo Nation: Metaphors of Race and Religious Identity among South Asians in Trinidad*. Durham, NC: Duke University Press.

Khandelwal, Madhulika S. 2002. *Becoming American, Being Indian: An Immigrant Community in New York City*. Ithaca, NY: Cornell University Press.

Kiang, Peter Nien-Chu. 1991. "About Face: Recognizing Asian & Pacific American Vietnam Veterans in Asian American Studies." *Amerasia Journal* 17 (3): 22–40.

———. 2006. "Policy Challenges for Asian Americans and Pacific Islanders in Education." *Race Ethnicity and Education* 9 (1): 103–15.

Kibria, Nazli. 2003. *Becoming Asian American: Second Generation Chinese and Korean American Identities*. Baltimore: Johns Hopkins University Press

———. 1995. *Family Tightrope: The Changing Lives of Vietnamese Americans*. Princeton, NJ: Princeton University Press.

Kiernan, Ben. 1996. *The Pol Pot Regime: Race, Power, and Genocide in Cambodia under the Khmer Rouge, 1975–1979*. New Haven, CT: Yale University Press.

Kieu, Tram. 2013. "Why Immigration Is an Asian American Issue." *Center for American Progress*, May 28. <http://www.americanprogress.org/issues/immigration/news/2013/05/28/64474/why-immigration-is-an-asian-american-issue/>.

Kim, Claire Jean. 2000. *Bitter Fruit: The Politics of Black-Korean Conflict in New York City*. New Haven, CT: Yale University Press.

Kim, David Kyuman. 2003. "Enchanting Diasporas, Asian Americans, and the Passionate Attachment of Race." In *Revealing the Sacred in Asian and Pacific America*, edited by Jane Iwamura and Paul Spickard, 327–40. New York: Routledge.

Kim, Elaine H. 1982. *Asian American Literature: An Introduction to the Writings and Their Social Context*. Philadelphia: Temple University Press.

———. 1990. "'Such Opposite Creatures': Men and Women in Asian American Literature." *Michigan Quarterly Review* 29 (1): 68–93.

———. 2003. "Interstitial Subjects: Asian American Visual Art as a Site for New Cultural Conversations," In *Fresh Talk/Daring Gazes*, edited by Elaine H. Kim, Margo Machida, and Sharon Mizota, 40–41. Berkeley and Los Angeles: University of California Press.

———. 2010. "Coordinator's Reports: New Directions for Asian American Studies." *Veritaas: The UC Berkeley Asian American Studies Newsletter* 1 (1): 1, 5. <http://ethnicstudies.berkeley.edu/documents/veritaas01.pdf>.

———, dir. 2011. *Slaying the Dragon: Reloaded*. San Francisco: Asian Women United of California.

Kim, Elaine H., Margo Machida, and Sharon Mizota, eds. 2003. *Fresh Talk/Daring Gazes: Conversations on Asian American Art*. Berkeley and Los Angeles: University of California Press.

Kim, Eleana Jean. 2010. *Adopted Territory: Transnational Korean Adoptees and the Politics of Belonging*. Durham, NC: Duke University Press.

Kim, Hyung-chan. 1994. *A Legal History of Asian Americans, 1700–1990*. Westport, CT: Greenwood Press.

Kim, Jina. 2014. "'People of the Apokalis': Spatial Disability and the Bhopal Disaster." *Disability Studies Quarterly* 34 (3): n.p. <http://dsq-sds.org/article/view/3795>.

Kim, Jodi. 2009. "An 'Orphan' with Two Mothers: Transnational and Transracial Adoption, the Cold War, and Contemporary Asian American Cultural Politics." *American Quarterly* 61 (4): 855–80.

———. 2010. *Ends of Empire: Asian American Critique and the Cold War*. Minneapolis: University of Minnesota Press.

Kim, Nadia Y. 2007. "Critical Thoughts on Asian American Assimilation in the Whitening Literature." *Social Forces* 86 (2): 561–74.

———. 2008. *Imperial Citizens: Koreans and Race from Seoul to LA*. Palo Alto, CA: Stanford University Press.

Kim, Richard S. 2011. *The Quest for Statehood: Korean Immigrant Nationalism and U.S. Sovereignty, 1905–1945*. New York: Oxford University Press.

Kim, Sun-Jung, ed. 2000. *KOREAMERICAKOREA*. Exh. cat. Seoul: Artsonje Center.

Kina, Laura, and Wei Ming Dariotis, eds. 2013. *War Baby/Love Child: Mixed Race Asian American Art*. Seattle and London: University of Washington Press.

King-O'Riain, Rebecca Chiyoko. 2006. *Pure Beauty: Judging Race in Japanese American Beauty Pageants*. Minneapolis: University of Minnesota Press.

Kiong, Tong Chee, and Yong Pit Kee. 1998. "Guanxi Bases, Xinyong and Chinese Business Networks." *British Journal of Sociology* 49 (1): 75–96.

Kipling, Rudyard. 1899. "The White Man's Burden." *McClure's Magazine* 12 (4): 290.

Klarman, Michael. 2004. *From Jim Crow to Civil Rights: The Supreme Court and the Struggle for Racial Equality*. New York: Oxford University Press.

Klein, Christina. 2003. *Cold War Orientalism: Asia in the Middlebrow Imagination, 1945–1961*. Berkeley: University of California Press.

Kochin, Peter. 1987. *Unfree Labor: American Slavery and Russian Serfdom*. Cambridge, MA: Belnap Press.

Kolko, Gabriel. 1976. *Main Currents in Modern American History*. New York: Harper & Row.

Kondo, Dorinne. 1997. *About Face: Performing Race in Fashion and Theater*. New York: Routledge.

Korematsu v. United States, 323 U.S. 214 (1944).

Koshy, Susan. 2004. *Sexual Naturalization: Asian Americans and Miscegenation*. Palo Alto, CA: Stanford University Press.

Kramer, Paul. 2006. *The Blood of Government: Race, Empire, the United States, & the Philippines*. Chapel Hill: University of North Carolina Press.

Kraut, Alan M. 1995. *Silent Travelers: Germs, Genes, and the "Immigrant Menace."* Baltimore: Johns Hopkins University Press.

Ku, Robert Ji-Song. 2014. *Dubious Gastronomy: The Cultural Politics of Eating Asian in the USA*. Honolulu: University of Hawai'i Press.

Kuo, Gwen, ed. 2009. *Present Tense Biennial: Chinese Character*. Exh. cat. San Francisco: Chinese Culture Foundation of San Francisco.

Kuper, Leo. 1981. *Genocide*. New Haven, CT: Yale University Press.

Kurashige, Lon. 2002. *Japanese American Celebration and Conflict: A History of Ethnic Identity and Festival, 1934–1990*. Berkeley: University of California Press.

Kurashige, Scott. 2008. *The Shifting Grounds of Race: Black and Japanese Americans in the Making of Multiethnic Los Angeles*. Princeton, NJ: Princeton University Press.

Kwon, Soo Ah. 2013. *Uncivil Youth: Race, Activism, and Affirmative Governmentality*. Durham, NC: Duke University Press.

Kwong, Paul C. K. 1991. "Immigration and Manpower Shortage." In *The Other Hong Kong Report 1990*, edited by R. Y. C. Wong and J. Y. S. Cheng, 297–338. Hong Kong: Chinese University Press.

Kwong, Peter. 1979. *Chinatown, N.Y.: Labor and Politics, 1930–1950*. New York: Monthly Review Press.

———. (1988) 1996. *The New Chinatown*. New York: Hill and Wang.

Kwong, Peter, and Dušanka Miščević. 2005. *Chinese America: The Untold Story of America's Oldest New Community*. New York: New Press.

Kydd, Andrew H., and Barbara F. Walter. 2006. "Strategies of Terrorism." *International Security* 31 (1): 49–79.

Lacouture, Jean. 1977. "The Bloodiest Revolution" (review of *Cambodge, année zero* by François Ponchaud). *New York Review of Books*, March 31.

Laguerre, Michel S. 2000. *The Global Ethnopolis: Chinatown, Japantown, and Manilatown in American Society*. New York: Palgrave Macmillan.

Lai, James S. 2011. *Asian American Political Action: Suburban Transformations*. Boulder, CO: Lynn Reinner Publishers.

Lai, James S., Wendy K. Tam Cho, Thomas P. Kim, and Okiyoshi Takeda. 2001. "Asian Pacific-American Campaigns, Elections, and Elected Officials." *Political Science and Politics* 3: 611–17.

Lai, James S., and Kim Geron. 2006. "When Asian Americans Run: The Suburban and Urban Dimensions of Asian American Candidates in California Local Politics." *California Politics & Policy* 10 (1): 62–88.

Lai, Mark Him. 1991. "The Kuomintang in Chinese American Communities before World War II." In *Entry Denied: Exclusion and the Chinese Community in America, 1882–1943*, edited by Sucheng Chan, 170–212. Philadelphia: Temple University Press.

Lai, Walton Look. 1993. *Indentured Labor, Caribbean Sugar: Chinese and Indian Migrants to the British West Indies, 1838–1918*. Baltimore: Johns Hopkins University Press.

Lawrence, Adria. 2010. "Triggering Nationalist Violence:

Competition and Conflict in Uprisings against Colonial Rule." *International Security* 35 (2): 88–122.

Le, Viet, Alice Ming Wai Jim, and Linda Trinh Võ. 2005. *Charlie Don't Surf: 4 Vietnamese American Artists*. Exh. cat. Vancouver: Vancouver International Centre for Contemporary Asian Art.

Le, Viet, and Yong Soon Min, eds. 2008. *transPOP: Korea Vietnam Remix*. Exh. cat. Seoul: Arko Art Center, Arts Council of Korea.

Lee, Anthony W. 2001. *Picturing Chinatown: Art and Orientalism in San Francisco*. Berkeley: University of California Press.

———, ed. 2003. *Yun Gee: Poetry, Writings, Art, Memories*. Seattle and London: University of Washington Press.

Lee, Christopher. 2005. "Diaspora, Transnationalism, and Asian American Studies: Positions and Debates." In *Displacements and Diasporas: Asians in the Americas*, edited by Wanni Anderson and Robert G. Lee, 23–38. New Brunswick, NJ: Rutgers University Press.

Lee, Erika. 2003. "Exclusion Acts: Chinese Women during the Chinese Exclusion Era, 1882–1943." In *Asian/Pacific Islander American Women: A Historical Anthology*, edited by Shirley Hune and Gail M. Nomura, 77–89. New York: New York University Press.

———. (2003) 2004. *At America's Gates: Chinese Immigration during the Exclusion Era, 1882–1943*. Chapel Hill: University of North Carolina Press.

———. 2005. "Orientalisms in the Americas: A Hemispheric Approach to Asian American History." *Journal of Asian American Studies* 8: 235–56. doi:10.1353/jaas.2005.0051.

Lee, Erika, and Naoko Shibusawa. 2005. "Guest Editor's Introduction: What Is Transnational Asian American History?: Recent Trends and Challenges." *Journal of Asian American Studies* 8: vii–xvii. doi:10.1353/jaas.2005.0050.

Lee, Erika, and Judy Yung. 2010. *Angel Island: Immigrant Gateway to America*. Oxford: Oxford University Press.

Lee, Esther Kim. 2006. *A History of Asian American Theatre*. Cambridge, UK: Cambridge University Press.

Lee, Grace, dir. 2005. *The Grace Lee Project*. DVD. New York: Women Make Movies.

Lee, Jennifer. 2002. *Civility in the City: Blacks, Jews, and Koreans in Urban America*. Cambridge, MA: Harvard University Press.

Lee, Josephine. 1997. *Performing Asian America*. Philadelphia: Temple University Press.

———. 2010. *The Japan of Pure Invention: Gilbert and Sullivan's The Mikado*. Minneapolis: University of Minnesota Press.

Lee, Kapson Yim. 1997. "Sa-ee-gu (April 29) Was a Riot, Not 'Civil Unrest.'" *Korea Times*, English edition, March 26–April 29: 3–4.

Lee, Luchia Meihua. 2004. *Nexus: Taiwan in Queens*. Exh. cat. New York: Queens Museum of Art.

Lee, Rachel. 1999. *The Americas of Asian American Literature: Gendered Fictions of Nation and Transnation*. Princeton, NJ: Princeton University Press.

Lee, Robert G. 1999. *Orientals: Asian Americans in Popular Culture*. Philadelphia: Temple University Press.

Lee, Shelley Sang-Hee. 2013. *A New History of Asian America*. New York: Routledge.

Lee, Stacey J. 1996. *Unraveling the "Model Minority" Stereotype: Listening to Asian American Youth*. New York: Teachers College Press.

———. 2005. *Up against Whiteness: Race, School, and Immigrant Youth*. New York: Teachers College Press.

Lee, Taeku. 2000. "The Backdoor and the Backlash: Campaign Finance and the Politicization of Chinese Americans." *Asian American Policy Review* 9: 30–55.

Lee, Thomas. 2000. "Forum Charges Racial Profiling in Lee Case." *AsianWeek* 21: 6. <http://www.asianweek.com/2000_05_04/news_vroomanspeaks.html>.

Lee, Yan Phou. 1889. "The Chinese Must Stay." *North American Review* 149: 476–83.

Lee-Loy, Anne-Marie. 2010. *Searching for Mr. Chin: Constructions of Nation and the Chinese in West Indian Literature*. Philadelphia: Temple University Press.

Leighton, Alexander. 1945. *The Governing of Men: General Principles and Recommendations Based on Experience at a Japanese Relocation Camp*. Princeton, NJ: Princeton University Press.

Leiner, Danny, dir. 2004. *Harold and Kumar Go to White Castle*. Los Angeles: New Line Cinema.

Lemkin, Raphael. 1944. *Axis Rule in Occupied Europe: Laws of Occupation, Analysis of Government Proposals for Redress*. Washington, DC: Carnegie Endowment for International Peace, Division of International Law.

Lenin, V. I. 1939. *Imperialism: The Highest Stage of Capitalism*. New York: International Publishers.

Leonard, Karen I. 1992. *Making Ethnic Choices: California's Punjabi Mexican Americans*. Philadelphia: Temple University Press.

Leong, Karen. 2000. "'A Distinct and Antagonistic Race': Constructions of Chinese Manhood in the Exclusion Debates, 1869–1978." In *Across the Great Divide: Cultures of Manhood in the American West*, edited by Matthew Basso, Laura McCall, and Dee Garceau, 131–48. New York: Routledge.

———. 2005. *The China Mystique: Pearl S. Buck, Anna May Wong, Mayling Soong, and the Transformation of American Orientalism*. Berkeley: University of California Press.

Leong, Russell. 1989. "Asians in the Americas: Interpreting the Diaspora Experience." *Amerasia* 15 (2): vii–xvii.

———, ed. (1991) 1992. *Moving the Image: Independent Asian Pacific American Media Arts*. Los Angeles: UCLA Asian American Studies Center and Visual Communications, Southern California Asian American Studies Central.

———, ed. 1996. *Asian American Sexualities: Dimensions of the Gay and Lesbian Experience*. New York: Routledge.

Levitt, Peggy. 2009. "Roots and Routes." *Journal of Ethnic and Migraton Studies* 35 (7): 1225–42.

Levitt, Peggy, and Mary Waters. 2006. *The Changing Faces of Home: The Transnational Lives of the Second Generation*. New York: Russell Sage Foundation.

Lew, Jamie. 2006. *Asian Americans in Class: Charting the Achievement Gap among Korean American Youth*. New York: Teachers College Press.

Li, David. 2000. "Can Asian American Studies Abandon 'Nation'?" In *Navigating Islands and Continents: Conversations and Contestations in and around the Pacific*, edited by Cynthia Franklin, Ruth Hsu, and Suzanne Kosanke, 101–14. Honolulu: University of Hawai'i Press.

Li, Wei. 2009. *Ethnoburb: The New Ethnic Community in Urban America*. Honolulu: University of Hawai'i Press.

Lien, Pei-te. 1997. *The Political Participation of Asian Americans: Voting Behavior in Southern California*. New York: Garland Publishing.

———. 2008. "Homeland Origins and Political Identities among Chinese in Southern California." *Ethnic and Racial Studies* 31: 1381–1403. doi:10.1080/01419870701682253.

Lien, Pei-te, M. Margaret Conway, and Janelle Wong. 2004. *The Politics of Asian America: Diversity and Community*. New York: Routledge.

Lieu, Nhi T. 2011. *The American Dream in Vietnamese*. Minneapolis: University of Minnesota Press.

Light, Ivan. 1972. *Ethnic Enterprise in America*. Berkeley: University of California Press.

Light, Ivan, and Edna Bonacich. 1988. *Immigrant Entrepreneurs: Koreans in Los Angeles, 1965–1982*. Berkeley: University of California Press.

Lim, Shirley Geok-lin. 1993. "Feminist and Ethnic Literary Theories in Asian American Literature." *Feminist Studies* 19 (3): 570–95.

Lim, Shirley Geok-lin, and Amy Ling, eds. 1992. *Reading the Literatures of Asian America*. Philadelphia: Temple University Press.

Lim, Zi Heng. 2013. "For Asian Undocumented Immigrants, a Life of Secrecy." *Atlantic*, May 14. <http://www.theatlantic.com/national/archive/2013/05/for-asian-undocumented-immigrants-a-life-of-secrecy/275829/>.

Lin, Jan. 1998. *Reconstructing Chinatown: Ethnic Enclave, Global Exchange*. Minneapolis: University of Minnesota Press.

———. 2011. *The Power of Urban Ethnic Places: Cultural Heritage and Community Life*. New York: Routledge.

Lin, Justin, dir. 2003. *Better Luck Tomorrow*. DVD. Hollywood, CA: Paramount.

Ling, Huping. 2011. *Chinese Chicago: Race, Transnational Migration, and Community since 1870*. Palo Alto, CA: Stanford University Press.

Ling, Jinqi. 1998. *Narrating Nationalisms: Ideology and Form in Asian American Literature*. Oxford: Oxford University Press.

Lionnet, Françoise, and Shu-mei Shih. 2005. "Introduction: Thinking through the Minor, Transnationally." In *Minor Transnationalism*, edited by Françoise Lionnet and Shu-mei Shih, 1–23. Durham, NC: Duke University Press.

Lippard, Lucy. 1990. *Mixed Blessings: New Art in a Multicultural America*. New York: Pantheon.

Lippert, Randy. 1999. "Governing Refugees: The Relevance of Governmentality to Understanding the International Refugee Regime." *Alternatives: Global, Local, Political* 24 (3): 295–328.

Lipset, Seymour Martin. 1996. *American Exceptionalism: A Double-Edged Sword*. New York: W. W. Norton.

Liu, Haiming. 2005. *The Transnational History of a Chinese Family: Immigrant Letters, Family Business, and Reverse Migration*. New Brunswick, NJ: Rutgers University Press.

——. 2009. "Chop Suey as Imagined Authentic Chinese Food: The Culinary Identity of Chinese Restaurants in the United States." *Journal of Transnational American Studies* 1 (1): 1–24.

Liu, Haiming, and Lianlian Lin. 2009. "Food, Culinary Identity, and Transnational Culture: Chinese Restaurant Business in Southern California." *Journal of Asian American Studies* 12: 135–62. doi:10.1353/jaas.0.0039.

Liu, Lisong. 2012. "Return Migration and Selective Citizenship: A Study of Returning Chinese Professional Migrants from the United States." *Journal of Asian American Studies* 15: 35–68.

Liu, Michael, Kim Geron, and Tracy Lai. 2008. *The Snake Dance of Asian American Activism: Community, Vision, and Power*. Lanham, MD: Lexington Books.

Liu, Robyn. 2002. "Governing Refugees 1919–1945." *Borderlands* 1 (1).

Loewen, James W. (1971) 1988. *The Mississippi Chinese: Between Black and White*. Cambridge, MA: Harvard University Press.

Logan, Enid. 2008. "What Is the Social Significance of Barack Obama?" *Contexts*, August 8. <http://contexts.org/obama/#comments-list>.

López, Kathleen. 2013. *Chinese Cubans: A Transnational History*. Chapel Hill: University of North Carolina Press.

Louie, Andrea. 2009. "'Pandas, Lions, and Dragons, Oh My!': How White Adoptive Parents Construct Chineseness." *Journal of Asian American Studies* 12 (3): 285–320.

Louie, Miriam Ching Yoon. 2001. *Sweatshop Warriors: Immigrant Women Workers Take on the Global Factory*. Cambridge, MA: South End Press.

Louie, Reagan, and Carlos Villa, eds. 1994. *Worlds in Collision: Dialogues on Multicultural Art Issues*. San Francisco: San Francisco Art Institute and International Scholars Publications.

Louie, Steve, and Glenn K. Omatsu, eds. 2001. *Asian Americans: The Movement and the Moment*. Los Angeles: UCLA Asian American Studies Center Press.

Louie, Vivian S. 2004. *Compelled to Excel: Immigration, Education, and Opportunity among Chinese Americans*. Palo Alto, CA: Stanford University Press.

Lowe, Donald. 1995. *The Body in Late-Capitalist USA*. Durham, NC: Duke University Press.

Lowe, Lisa. 1991a. *Critical Terrains: French and British Orientalisms*. Ithaca, NY: Cornell University Press.

——. 1991b. "Heterogeneity, Hybridity, Multiplicity: Marking Asian American Differences." *Diaspora: A Journal of Transnational Studies* 1 (1): 24–44.

——. 1996. *Immigrant Acts: On Asian American Cultural Politics*. Durham, NC: Duke University Press.

——. 1998. "The International within the National: American Studies and Asian American Critique." *Cultural Critique* 40: 29–47.

——. 2006. "The Intimacies of Four Continents." In *Haunted by Empire: Geographies of Intimacy in North American History*, edited by Ann Laura Stoler, 191–212. Durham, NC: Duke University Press.

Lowe, Lisa, and David Lloyd. 1997. *The Politics of Culture in the Shadow of Capital*. Durham, NC: Duke University Press.

Lowe, Pardee. 1943. *Father and Glorious Descendent*. Boston: Little, Brown and Company.

Luibhéid, Eithne. 2002. *Entry Denied: Controlling Sexuality at the Border*. Minneapolis: University of Minnesota Press.

Luibhéid, Eithne, and Lionel Cantu, Jr, eds. 2005. *Queer Migrations: Sexuality, U.S. Citizenship, and Border Crossings*. Minneapolis: University of Minnesota Press.

Lydon, Sandy. 1985. *Chinese Gold: The Chinese in the Monterey Bay Region*. Santa Cruz, CA: Capitola.

Lye, Colleen. 2004. *America's Asia: Racial Form and American Literature, 1893–1945*. Princeton, NJ: Princeton University Press.

——. 2008. "Racial Form." *Representations* 104 (1): 92–101.

Lyon, Cherstin M. 2012. *Prisons and Patriots: Japanese American Wartime Citizenship, Civil Disobedience, and Historical Memory*. Philadelphia: Temple University Press.

Ma, L. Eve Armentrout. 1990. *Revolutionaries, Monarchists, and Chinatowns: Chinese Politics in the Americas and the 1911 Revolution*. Honolulu: University of Hawai'i Press.

Mabalon, Dawn Bohulano. 2013. *Little Manila Is in the Heart: The Making of the Filipina/o American Community in Stockton, California*. Durham, NC: Duke University Press.

MacFarquhur, Roderick, and Michael Schoenhals. 2009. *Mao's Last Revolution*. Cambridge, MA: Harvard University Press.

Machida, Margo. 2008. "Art and Social Consciousness: Asian American and Pacific Islander Artists in San Francisco: 1965–1980." In *Asian American Art: A History, 1850–1970*, edited by Gordon H. Chang, Mark Dean Johnson, and Paul J. Karlstrom, 257–79. Palo Alto, CA: Stanford University Press.

———. 2009. *Unsettled Visions: Contemporary Asian American Artists and the Social Imaginary*, 1–6, 17–56, 283–84. Durham, NC, and London: Duke University Press.

Maeda, Daryl Joji. 2009. *Chains of Babylon: The Rise of Asian America*. Minneapolis: University of Minnesota Press.

———. (2011) 2012. *Rethinking the Asian American Movement*. New York: Routledge.

Mahan, Sue, and Pamela L. Griset. 2008. *Terrorism in Perspective*. Thousand Oaks, CA: Sage Publications.

Maira, Sunaina. 2000. "Henna and Hip Hop: The Politics of Cultural Production and the Work of Cultural Studies." *Journal of Asian American Studies* 3 (1): 329–69.

———. 2002. *Desis in the House: Indian American Youth Culture in New York City*. Philadelphia: Temple University Press.

———. 2007. "Indo-Chic: Late Capitalist Orientalism and Imperialist Culture." In *Alien Encounters: Popular Culture in Asian America*, edited by Mimi Thi Nguyen and Thuy Linh Nguyen Tu, 221–47. Durham, NC: Duke University Press.

———. 2008. "Belly Dancing: Arab-Face, Orientalist Feminism, and U.S. Empire." *American Quarterly* 60 (2): 317–45.

———. (2009) 2010. *Missing: Youth, Citizenship, and Empire after 9/11*. Durham, NC: Duke University Press.

Maira, Sunaina, and Magid Shihade. 2006. "Meeting Asian/Arab American Studies: Thinking Racism, Empire, and Zionism in the U.S." *Journal of Asian American Studies* 9 (2): 117–40.

Malkki, Liisa. 1995. "Refugees and Exile: From 'Refugee Studies' to the National Order of Things." *Annual Review of Anthropology* 24: 495–523.

Manalansan, Martin F., IV. 2003. *Global Divas: Filipino Gay Men in the Diaspora*. Durham, NC: Duke University Press.

———. 2005. "Race, Violence, and Neoliberal Spatial Politics in the Global City." *Social Text* 84–85 (3–4): 141–55.

———. 2006a. "Immigrant Lives and the Politics of Olfaction in the Global City." In *The Smell Culture Reader*, edited by Jim Drobnick, 41–52. New York: Berg.

———. 2006b. "Queer Intersections: Sexuality and Gender in Migration Studies." *International Migration Review* 40 (1): 224–49.

———. 2007. "Cooking up the Senses: A Critical Embodied Approach to the Study of Food and Asian American Tele-

vision Audiences." In *Alien Encounters: Popular Culture in Asian America*, edited by Thuy Linh Nguyen Tu and Mimi Nguyen, 179–93. Durham, NC: Duke University Press.

Manderson, Lenore, and Margaret Jolly, eds. 1997. *Sites of Desire, Economies of Pleasure: Sexualities in Asia and the Pacific*. Chicago: University of Chicago Press.

Mangaoang, Gil. 1996. "From the 1970s to the 1990s: Perspective of a Gay Filipino American Activist." In *Asian American Sexualities*, edited by Russell Leong, 101–11. New York: Routledge.

Mannur, Anita. 2005. "'Peeking Ducks' and 'Food Pornographers': Commodifying Culinary Chinese Americanness." In *Culture, Identity Commodity*, edited by Tseen Khoo and Kam Louie, 19–38. Hong Kong: Hong Kong University Press.

———. 2006. "Asian American Food-Scapes." *Amerasia* 32 (2): 1–5.

———. 2010. *Culinary Fictions: Food in South Asian Diasporic Cultures*. Philadelphia: Temple University Press.

Maramba, Dina C., and Rick Bonus, eds. 2013. *The "Other" Students: Filipino Americans, Education, and Power*. Charlotte, NC: Information Age Publishing.

Marchetti, Gina. (1993) 1994. *Romance and the "Yellow Peril": Race, Sex and Discursive Strategies in Hollywood*. Berkeley: University of California Press.

Martini, Edwin A. 2013. *Agent Orange: History, Science, and the Politics of Uncertainty*. Amherst: University of Massachusetts Press.

Marx, Karl. 1887. *Capital: A Critique of Political Economy*, Volume One. Translated by Samuel Moore and Edward Aveling. Edited by Frederick Engels. *Marxists.org*. <http://www.marxists.org/archive/marx/works/download/pdf/Capital-Volume-I.pdf>.

———. (1852) 1951. *The Eighteenth Brumaire of Louis Bonaparte*. Volume XXXV of *Marxist Library: Works of Marxism-Leninism*. New York: International Publishers.

———. 1978. *The Marx-Engels Reader*, second edition. Edited by Robert C. Tucker. New York: W. W. Norton.

Masequesmay, Gina, and Sean Metzger, eds. 2009. *Embodying Asian/American Sexualities*. Lanham, MD: Lexington Books.

Masquelier, Adeline. 2006. "Why Katrina's Victims Aren't Refugees: Musings on a 'Dirty' Word." *American Anthropologist* 108 (4): 735–43.

Massey, Douglas, and Nancy Denton. 1993. *American Apartheid: Segregation and the Making of the Underclass*. Cambridge, MA: Harvard University Press.

Mathews, Biju. 2005. *Taxi! Cabs and Capitalism in New York City*. New York: New Press.

Mathur, Shubh. 2006. "Surviving the Dragnet: 'Special Interest' Detainees in the U.S. after 9/11." *Race and Class* 47 (3): 31–46.

Matsuda, Mari. 1991. "Standing by My Sister, Facing the Enemy: Legal Theory out of Coalition." *Stanford Law Review* 43: 1183.

———. 2001. "Planet Asian America." *Asian Law Journal* 8: 169.

———. 2002. "Beyond, and Not Beyond, Black and White, Deconstruction Has a Politics." In *Crossroads, Directions, and a New Critical Race Theory*, edited by Francisco Valdes, Jerome McCristal Culp, and Angela Harris, 393–98. Philadelphia: Temple University Press.

———. 2010. "Poem for Armenian Genocide Day and Rules for Postcolonials." *Journal of Asian American Studies* 13 (3): 359–69.

Mathew, Biju, and Vijay Prashad. 2000. "The Protean Forms of Yankee Hindutva." *Ethnic and Racial Studies* 23 (3): 516–35.

Matsumoto, Valerie J. 1993. *Farming the Home Place: A Japanese American Community in California, 1919–1982*. Ithaca, NY: Cornell University Press.

Matthews, Julie. 2007. "Eurasian Persuasions: Mixed Race, Performativity and Cosmopolitanism." *Journal of Intercultural Studies* 28 (1): 41–54.

Mayer, Arno J. 2000. *The Furies: Violence and Terror in the French and Russian Revolutions*. Princeton, NJ: Princeton University Press.

Mazumdar, Sucheta. 1984. "Colonial Impact and Punjabi Emigration to the United States." In *Labor Immigration under Capitalism: Asian Workers in the United States before World War II*, edited by Lucie Cheng and Edna Bonacich, 316–36. Berkeley: University of California Press.

———. 1991. "Asian American Studies and Asian Studies: Rethinking Roots." In *Asian Americans: Comparative and Global Perspectives*, edited by Shirley Hune, Hyung-chan Kim, Stephen S. Fugita, and Amy Ling, 29–44. Pullman: University of Washington Press.

———. 2003. "'What Happened to the Women': Chinese and Indian Male Migration to the United States in Global Perspective." In *Asia/Pacific Islander American Women: A Historical Anthology*, edited by Shirley Hune and Gail M. Nomura, 58–76. New York: New York University Press.

Mbembe, Achille. 2001. *On the Postcolony*. Berkeley: University of California Press.

McAlister, Melani. 2001. *Epic Encounters: Culture, Media and U.S. Interests in the Middle East since 1945*. Berkeley: University of California Press.

McCormack, Gavan. 2003. "Reflections on Modern Japanese History in the Context of the Concept of 'Genocide.'" In *The Specter of Genocide: Mass Murder in Historical Perspective*, edited by Robert Gellately and Ben Kiernan, 265–87. Cambridge, UK: Cambridge University Press.

McGranahan, Carole. 2005. "Truth, Fear, and Lies: Exile Politics and Arrested Histories of the Tibetan Resistance." *Cultural Anthropology* 20 (4): 570–600.

McLuhan, Marshall. 1964. *Understanding Media: The Extensions of Man*. New York: New American Library.

Mehta, D. H., and R. S. Phillips. 2007. "Use of Complementary and Alternative Therapies by Asian Americans: Results from the National Health Interview Survey." *Journal of General Internal Medicine* 22 (6): 762–67.

Melamed, Jodi. 2011. *Represent and Destroy: Rationalizing Violence in the New Racial Capitalism*. Minneapolis: University of Minnesota Press.

Melendy, H. Brett. 1977. *Asians in America: Filipinos, Koreans, and East Indians*. Boston: Twayne Publishers.

Meyerowitz, Joanne. 2004. *How Sex Changed: A History of Transexuality in the United States*. Cambridge, MA: Harvard University Press.

Michaels, Walter Benn. 2011. "Model Minorities and the Minority Model—The Neoliberal Novel." In *The Cambridge History of the American Novel*, edited by Leonard Cassuto, Clare Virginia Eby, and Benjamin Reiss, 1016–30. Cambridge, UK: Cambridge University Press.

Mignolo, Walter. 2000. "The Many Faces of Cosmo-polis: Border Thinking and Critical Cosmopolitanism." *Public Culture* 13 (3): 721–48.

Mills, Charles W. 1997. *The Racial Contract*. Ithaca, NY: Cornell University Press.

Mills, Cynthia, Lee Glazer, and Amela A. Goerlitz, eds. 2012. *East-West Interchanges in American Art: A Long and Tumultu-*

ous Relationship. Washington, DC: Smithsonian Institution Scholarly Press.

Mimura, Glen. 2009. *Ghostlife of Third Cinema: Asian American Film and Video*. Minneapolis: University of Minnesota Press.

Min, Pyong Gap. 1996. *Caught in the Middle: Korean Communities in New York and Los Angeles*. Berkeley: University of California Press.

———, ed. 2006. *Asian Americans: Contemporary Trends and Issues*. Thousand Oaks, CA: Sage Publications.

———. 2008. *Ethnic Solidarity for Economic Survival: Korean Greengrocers in New York City*. New York: Russell Sage Foundation.

Min, Pyong Gap, and Jung Ha Kim, eds. 2002. *Religions in Asian America: Building Faith Communities*. Walnut Creek, CA: Alta Mira.

Min, Susette S. 2006. "The Last Asian American Exhibition in the Whole Entire World." In *One Way or Another*, edited by Melissa Chiu, Karin Higa, and Susette S. Min, 34–41. Exh. cat. New York: Asia Society in association with Yale University Press.

Min, Yong Soon. 2002. "Certain Latitudes." In *Gwangju Biennale 2002, THERE: Sites of Korean Diaspora*, 10–59. Exh. cat. Gwangju, Korea: Gwangju Biennale Foundation.

Minich, Julie. 2013. *Accessible Citizenships: Disability, Nation, and the Cultural Politics of Greater Mexico*. Philadelphia: Temple University Press.

Miyoshi, Masao. 1993. "A Borderless World? From Colonialism to Transnationalism and the Decline of the Nation-State." *Critical Inquiry* 19: 726–51.

Molina, N. 2006. *Fit to Be Citizens?: Public Health and Race in Los Angeles, 1879-1939*. Berkeley: University of California Press.

Monberg, Terese. 2008. "Listening for Legacies, or How I Began to Hear Dorothy Laigo Cordova, the Pinay behind the Podium Known as FAHNS." In *Representations: Doing Asian American Rhetoric*, edited by Luming Mao and Morris Young, 83–105. Logan: Utah State University Press.

Moon, Katharine H. S. 1997. *Sex among Allies: Military Prostitution in U.S.-Korea Relations*. New York: Columbia University Press.

Morgan, Edmund. 2013. *American Slavery, American Freedom*. New York: W. W. Norton.

Morley, David, and Kevin Robins. 1995. *Spaces of Identity: Global Media, Electronic Landscapes and Cultural Boundaries*. London: Routledge.

Mullen, Bill. 2004. *Afro-Orientalism*. Minneapolis: University of Minnesota Press.

Muller, Eric L. 2001. *Free to Die for Their Country: The Story of Japanese American Draft Resisters in World War II*. Chicago: University of Chicago Press.

Mullings, Leith. 2005. "Interrogating Racism: Toward an Antiracist Anthropology." *Annual Review of Anthropology* 34: 667–93.

———. 2008. "Race and Globalization: Racialization from Below." In *Transnational Blackness: Navigating the Global Color Line*, edited by M. Marable and V. Agard-Jones, 11–18. New York: Palgrave Macmillan.

Murphy-Shigematsu, Stephen. 2012. *When Half Is Whole*. Palo Alto, CA: Stanford University Press.

Museus, Samuel D., ed. 2009. *Conducting Research on Asian Americans in Higher Education: New Directions for Institutional Research*. San Francisco: Jossey Bass.

Museus, Samuel D., Dina C. Maramba, and Robert T. Teranishi, eds. 2013. *The Misrepresented Minority: New Insights on Asian Americans and Pacific Islanders and Their Implications for Higher Education*. Sterling, VA: Stylus.

Naber, Nadine Christine. 2012. *Arab America: Gender, Cultural Politics, and Activism*. New York: New York University Press.

Nadarajah, Suthakaran, and Dhananjayan Sriskandarajah. 2005. "Politics of Naming the LTTE." *Third World Quarterly* 26 (1): 87–100.

Nagai, Tyrone. 2010. "Multiracial Identity and the U.S. Census." *Proquest Discovery Guides*. <http://www.csa.com/discoveryguides/census/review.pdf>.

Nair, Mira, dir. 1992. *Mississippi Masala*. New York: Samuel Goldwyn Company.

———, dir. 2007. *The Namesake*. Hollywood, CA: Fox Searchlight.

Najita, Susan Y. 2006. *Decolonizing Cultures in the Pacific: Reading History and Trauma in Contemporary Fiction*. New York: Taylor and Francis.

Nakagawa, Mako. n.d. "The Power of Words." *NPS.gov*. <http://www.nps.gov/tule/forteachers/upload/Power_of_Words.pdf>.

Nakamura, Lisa. 2002. *Cybertypes: Race, Ethnicity and Identity on the Internet*. London: Routledge.

———. 2007. *Digitizing Race: Visual Cultures of the Internet*. Minneapolis: University of Minnesota Press.

Nakamura, Tadashi, dir. 2009. *A Song for Ourselves*. Los Angeles: TRT.

Nakanishi, Don. 1991. "The Next Swing Vote? Asian Pacific Americans and California Politics." In *Racial and Ethnic Politics in California*, edited by Byran O. Jackson and Michael B. Preston, 25–54. Berkeley: IGS Press, Institute of Governmental Studies, University of California at Berkeley.

———. 2011. "A Growing Political Presence: The Participation and Representation of Asian Pacific Americans in American Politics." In *2011–2012 National Asian Pacific American Political Almanac*, edited by Don Nakanishi and James Lai, 2–3. Los Angeles: UCLA Asian American Studies Center Press.

Nakanishi, Don, and James S. Lai. 2003. "Historical Forms of Civic Engagement and Protest." In *Asian American Politics*, edited by James Lai and Don Nakanishi, 19–22. Boulder, CO: Rowman & Littlefield.

Nakashima, Cynthia. 1992. "An Invisible Monster: The Creation and Denial of Mixed-Race People in America." In *Racially Mixed People in America*, edited by Maria P. P. Root, 162–80. Thousand Oaks, CA: Sage Publications.

Naone, Nicole. 2013. Twitter post. June 12, 8:08 p.m. <https://twitter.com/nicoleforever>.

Nee, Victor, and Brett de Bary Nee. 1986. *Longtime Californ': A Documentary Study of an American Chinatown*. Palo Alto, CA: Stanford University Press.

Neilsen, Kim. 2012. *A Disability History of the United States*. Boston: Beacon Press.

New York City Profiling Collaborative et al. 2012. "In Our Own Words: Narratives of South Asian New Yorkers Affected by Racial and Religious Profiling." *SAALT.org*, March. <http://saalt.org/wp-content/uploads/2012/09/In-Our-Own-Words-Narratives-of-South-Asian-New-Yorkers-Affected-by-Racial-and-Religious-Profiling.pdf>.

New York Times. 2013. "Drone Strikes under Scrutiny" (editorial). February 7. <http://www.nytimes.com/2013/02/07/opinion/drone-strikes-under-scrutiny.html>.

Ng, Franklin. 1987. "The Sojourner, Return Migration, and Immigration History." *Chinese America: History and Perspectives* 1: 53–67.

Ngai, Mae. 2000. "American Orientalism." *Reviews in American History* 28: 408–15.

———. (2003) 2004a. *Impossible Subjects: Illegal Aliens and the Making of Modern America*. Princeton, NJ: Princeton University Press.

———. 2004b. "Transnationalism and the Transformation of the 'Other': Response to the Presidential Address." *American Quarterly* 57 (1): 59–65.

———. 2006. "Asian American History—Reflections on the Decentering of the Field." *Journal of American Ethnic History* 25 (4): 97–108.

———. 2010. *The Lucky Ones: One Family and the Extraordinary Invention of Chinese America*. Boston: Houghton Mifflin Harcourt.

———. 2015. "Chinese Gold Miners, the Coolie Question, and the Propaganda of History." *Journal of American History* 101 (4).

Ngô, Fiona I. B., Mimi Thi Nguyen, and Mariam B. Lam. 2012. "Southeast Asian American Studies Special Issue: Guest Editors' Introduction." *Positions: East Asia Cultures Critique* 20 (3): 671–84.

Nguyen, Mimi Thi. 2012. *The Gift of Freedom: War, Debt and Other Refugee Passages*. Durham, NC: Duke University Press.

Nguyen, Mimi Thi, and Thuy Linh Nguyen Tu, eds. 2007. *Alien Encounters: Popular Culture in Asian America*. Durham, NC: Duke University Press.

Nguyen Tan Hoang. 2004. "The Resurrection of Brandon Lee: The Making of a Gay Asian American Porn Star." In *Porn Studies*, edited by Linda Williams, 223–70. Durham, NC: Duke University Press.

———. 2014. *A View from the Bottom: Asian American Masculinity and Sexual Representation*. Durham, NC: Duke University Press.

Nguyen, Viet Thanh. 2002. *Race and Resistance: Literature and Politics in Asian America*. Oxford: Oxford University Press.

———. 2009. "Remembering War, Dreaming Peace: On Cosmopolitanism, Compassion and Literature." *Japanese Journal of American Studies* 20: 149–74.

———. 2012. "Refugee Memories and Asian American Critique." *Positions: East Asia Cultures Critique* 20 (3): 911–42.

———. 2013. "Just Memory: War and the Ethics of Remembrance." *American Literary History* 25 (1): 144–63.

Nguyen, Viet Thanh, and Tina Chen. 2000. "Editor's Introduction: Postcolonial Asian America." *Jouvert* 4 (3).

Nomura, Gail M., Russell Endo, Stephen H. Sumida, and Russell C. Leong, eds. 1989. *Frontiers of Asian American Studies:*

Writing, Research and Commentary. Seattle: University of Washington Press.

Nonini, Donald M. 2001. "Diaspora Chinese in the Asia-Pacific: Transnational Practices and Structural Inequalities." In *Chinese Populations in Contemporary Southeast Asian Societies: Identities, Interdependence and International Influence*, edited by M. Jocelyn Armstrong et al., 237–63. Richmond, VA: Curzon Press.

Northrup, David. 1995. *Indentured Labor in the Age of Imperialism, 1834–1922*. New York: Cambridge University Press.

Norton, Ann W. 2002. *The Spirit of Cambodia . . . a Tribute*. Exh. cat. Providence, RI: Providence College.

O'Brien, Robert W. 1949. *The College Nisei*. Palo Alto, CA: Pacific Books.

Office of Refugee Resettlement. n.d. "Annual Refugee Arrival Data by Resettlement State and Country of Origin." Washington, DC: U.S. Department of Health and Human Services.

Oh, Arissa H. 2012. "From War Waif to Ideal Immigrant: The Cold War Transformation of the Korean Orphan." *Journal of American Ethnic History* 31 (4): 34–55.

Okada, John. 1976. *No-No Boy*. Seattle: University of Washington Press.

Okamura, Jonathan Y. 2003. "Asian American Studies in the Age of Transnationalism: Diaspora, Race, Community." *Amerasia Journal* 29 (2): 171–93.

Okamura, Raymond. 1982. "The American Concentration Camps: A Cover-Up through Euphemistic Terminology." *Journal of Ethnic Studies* 10 (3): 95–109.

Okihiro, Gary Y. 1991. *Cane Fires: The Anti-Japanese Movement in Hawai'i, 1865–1945*. Philadelphia: Temple University Press.

———. 1994. *Margins and Mainstreams: Asians in American History and Culture*. Seattle: University of Washington Press.

Okihiro, Gary Y., Shirley Hune, Arthur A. Hansen, and John M. Liu, eds. 1968. *Reflections on Shattered Windows: Promises and Prospects for Asian American Studies*. Pullman: Washington State University Press.

Okubo, Miné. (1946) 1983. *Citizen 13660*. Seattle: University of Washington Press.

Olick, Jeffrey K., Vered Vinitzky-Seroussi, and Daniel Levy, eds. 2011. "Introduction." In *The Collective Memory Reader*, edited by Jeffrey Olick, Vered Vinitzky-Seroussi, and Daniel Levi, 1–62. New York: Oxford University Press.

Omatsu, Glenn. 1994. "The 'Four Prisons' and the Movements of Liberation: Asian American Activism from the 1960s to the 1990s." In *The State of Asian America*, edited by Karin Aguilar-San Juan, 19–70. Boston: South End Press.

———. 2000. "The 'Four Prisons' and the Movements of Liberation: Asian American Activism from the 1960s to the 1990s." In *Asian American Studies: A Reader*, edited by Jean Yu-Wen Shen Wu and Min Hyoung Song, 164–96. New Brunswick, NJ: Rutgers University Press.

———. 2003. "The 'Four Prisons' and the Movements of Liberation: Asian American Activism from the 1960s to the 1990s." In *Asian American Politics*, edited by James Lai and Don Nakanishi, 135–62. Boulder, CO: Rowman & Littlefield.

———. 2008. "Immigrant Workers Take the Lead: A Militant Humility Transforms Koreatown." In *Immigrant Rights in the Shadows of Citizenship*, edited by Rachel I. Buff, 266–82. New York: New York University Press.

Omi, Michael, and Howard Winant. (1986) 1994. *Racial Formation in the United States: From the 1960s to the 1990s*. New York: Routledge.

Ong, Aihwa. 1987. *Spirits of Resistance and Capitalist Discipline: Factory Women in Malaysia*. Albany: State University of New York Press.

———. 1999. *Flexible Citizenship: The Cultural Logics of Transnationality*. Durham, NC: Duke University Press.

———. 2003. *Buddha Is Hiding: Refugees, Citizenship, the New America*. Berkeley: University of California Press.

Ong, Paul, Edna Bonacich, and Lucie Cheng, eds. 1994. *The New Asian Immigration in Los Angeles and Global Restructuring*. Philadelphia: Temple University Press.

Ong, Paul, and Don Nakanishi. 1996. "Becoming Citizens, Becoming Voters: The Naturalization and Political Participation of Asian Pacific Immigrants." In *The State of Asian Pacfic America: Reframing the Immigration Debate*, edited by Bill Ong Hing and Ronald Lee, 275–330. Los Angeles: LEAP and UCLA.

Ongiri, Amy. 2002. "'He Wanted to Be Just Like Bruce Lee': African Americans, Kung Fu Theater and Cultural Exchange at the Margins." *Journal of Asian American Studies* 5 (1): 31–40.

Ono, Kent, and Vincent Pham. (2008) 2009. *Asian Americans and the Media*. Malden, MA: Polity.

Oosterhuis, Harry. 2000. *Stepchildren of Nature: Krafft-Ebing, Psychiatry, and the Making of Sexual Identity*. Chicago: University of Chicago Press.

Ordona, Trinity A. 2003. "Asian Lesbians in San Francisco: Struggles to Create a Safe Space, 1970s–1980s." In *Asian/Pacific Islander American Women: A Historical Anthology*, edited by Shirley Hune and Gail M. Nomura, 319–34. New York: New York University Press.

O'Reilly, Bill. 2012. "The White Establishment Is Now the Minority." *Fox Nation* video, November 7. <http://nation.foxnews.com/bill-oreilly/2012/11/07/bill-o-reilly-white-establishment-now-minority>.

Orellana, M. F., B. Thorne, and W. Lam. 2001. "Transnational Childhoods: The Participation of Children in Processes of Family Migration." *Social Problems* 48: 572–91.

Orentlicher, Diane F. 2007. "Genocide." In *Crimes of War 2.0*, edited by Anthony Dworkin, Roy Gutman, and David Rieff, 191–95. New York: W. W. Norton.

Osajima, Keith. 1993. "The Hidden Injuries of Race." In *Bearing Dreams, Shaping Visions: Asian Pacific American Perspectives*, edited by Linda A. Revilla, Gail M. Nomura, Shawn Wong, and Shirley Hune, 81–91. Pullman: Washington State University Press.

———. 2007. "Replenishing the Ranks: Raising Critical Consciousness among Asian Americans." *Journal of Asian American Studies* 10 (1): 59–83.

Painter, Nell Irvin. 2010. *The History of White People*. New York: W. W. Norton.

Palmieri, Victor H. 1980. "United States: The Refugee Act of 1980 and Its Implementation." *International Legal Materials* 19 (3): 700–25.

Palumbo-Liu, David. 1999. *Asian/American: Historical Crossings of a Racial Frontier*. Palo Alto, CA: Stanford University Press.

Park, Clara C., A. Lin Goodwin, and Stacey J. Lee, eds. 2003. *Asian American Identities, Families, and Schooling*. Greenwich, CT: Information Age Publishing.

Park, Edward J. W. 1999. "Friends or Enemies?: Generational Politics in the Korean American Community." *Qualitative Sociology* 22 (2): 161–75.

Park, Edward J. W., and John S. W. Park. 2005. *Probationary Americans: Contemporary Immigration Policies and the Shaping of Asian American Communities*. New York: Routledge.

Park, Jane. 2010. *Yellow Future: Oriental Style in Hollywood Cinema*. Minneapolis: University of Minnesota Press.

Park, John S. W. 2004. *Elusive Citizenship: Immigration, Asian Americans, and the Paradox of Civil Rights*. New York: New York University Press.

Park, Kyeyoung. 1997. *The Korean American Dream: Immigrants and Small Business in New York City*. Ithaca, NY: Cornell University Press.

Park, Lisa Sun-Hee. 2005. *Consuming Citizenship: Children of Asian Immigrant Entrepreneurs*. Palo Alto, CA: Stanford University Press.

———. 2008. "Continuing Significance of the Model Minority Myth: The Second Generation." *Social Justice* 35 (2): 134–44.

———. 2011. *Entitled to Nothing: The Struggle for Immigrant Health Care in the Age of Welfare Reform*. New York: New York University Press.

Park, Robert. 1914. "Racial Assimilation in Secondary Groups with Particular Reference to the Negro." *American Journal of Sociology* 19 (5): 606–23.

———. 1950. *Race and Culture*. Glencoe, IL: Free Press.

Park, Robert, and E. W. Burgess. 1925. *The City*. Chicago: University of Chicago Press.

———. (1921) 1969. *Introduction to the Science of Sociology*. Chicago: University of Chicago Press.

Parker, Andrew, and Eve Kosofsky Sedgwick. 1995. *Performance and Performativity*. New York: Routledge.

Parreñas, Rhacel Salazar. 2001. *Servants of Globalization: Women, Migration, and Domestic Work*. Palo Alto, CA: Stanford University Press.

———. 2005. *Children of Global Migration: Transnational Families and Gendered Woes*. Palo Alto, CA: Stanford University Press.

———. 2008. *The Force of Domesticity: Filipina Migrants and Globalization*. New York: New York University Press.

Pascoe, Peggy. 2009. *What Comes Naturally: Miscegenation Law and the Making of Race in America*. Oxford: Oxford University Press.

Peffer, George Anthony. 1999. *If They Don't Bring Their Women Here: Chinese Female Immigration before Exclusion*. Urbana: University of Illinois Press.

Pelaud, Isabelle Thuy. 2011. *This Is All I Choose to Tell: History and Hybridity in Vietnamese American Literature*. Philadelphia: Temple University Press.

Pew Forum on Religion and Public Life. 2012. "Asian Americans: A Mosaic of Faiths." *Pew Forum on Religion and Life.* <http://www.pewforum.org/Asian-Americans-A-Mosaic-of-Faiths-religious-affiliation.aspx>.

Pfaelzer, Jeanne. (2007) 2008. *Driven Out: The Forgotten War against Chinese Americans.* Berkeley: University of California Press.

Plessy v. Ferguson, 163 U.S. 537 (1896).

Ponce, Martin Joseph. 2011. "José Garcia Villa's Modernism and the Politics of Queer Diasporic Reading." *GLQ: A Journal of Lesbian and Gay Studies* 17 (4): 575–602.

———. 2012. *Beyond the Nation: Diasporic Filipino Literature and Queer Reading.* New York: New York University Press.

Ponchaud, François. 1978. *Cambodia: Year Zero.* New York: Henry Holt and Company.

Poon, Irene. 2001. *Leading the Way: Asian American Artists of the Older Generation.* Wenham, MA: Gordon College.

Poon, OiYan A. 2013. "'Think About It as Decolonizing Our Minds': Spaces for Critical Race Pedagogy and Transformative Leadership Development." In *The Misrepresented Minority: New Insights on Asian Americans and Pacific Islanders and Their Implications for Higher Education,* edited by Samuel D. Museus, Dina C. Maramba, and Robert T. Teranishi, 294–310. Sterling, VA: Stylus.

Poon, OiYan A., Linda Tran, and Paul M. Ong. 2009. *The State of Asian American Businesses.* Los Angeles: University of California Los Angeles Asian American Studies Center. <http://www.academia.edu/220955/The_State_of_Asian_American_Businesses>.

Portes, Alejandro, and Rubén G. Rumbaut. 2001. *Legacies: The Story of the Immigrant Second Generation.* Berkeley: University of California Press.

Portes, Alejandro, and Min Zhou. 1992. "Gaining the Upper Hand: Economic Mobility among Immigrant and Domestic Minorities." *Ethnic and Racial Studies* 15 (4): 491–522.

———. 1993. "The New Second Generation: Segmented Assimilation and Its Variants." *Annals of the American Academy of Political and Social Science* 530 (1): 74–96.

Poshyananda, Apinan. 2004. "Desperately Diasporic." In *Over Here, International Perspectives on Art and Culture,* edited by Gerardo Mosquera and Jean Fisher, 182–90. New York: New Museum of Contemporary Art.

Postman, Neil. 1985. *Amusing Ourselves to Death: Public Discourse in the Age of Show Business.* New York: Penguin Books.

Prashad, Vijay. 2000. *The Karma of Brown Folk.* Minneapolis: University of Minnesota Press.

———. (2001) 2002. *Everybody Was Kung Fu Fighting: Afro-Asian Connections and the Myth of Cultural Purity.* Boston: Beacon Press.

———. 2005. "How the Hindus Became Jews: American Racism after 9/11." *South Atlantic Quarterly* 104 (3): 583–606.

———. 2007. "Orientalism." In *Keywords in American Cultural Studies,* edited by Bruce Burgett and Glenn Hendler, 174–76. New York: New York University Press.

———. 2008. *The Darker Nations: A People's History of the Third World.* New York: New Press.

———. 2009. *Uncle Swami: South Asians in America Today.* New York: New Press.

———. 2013. *The Poorer Nations: A Possible History of the Global South.* New York: Verso.

Price, Lorna, ed. 1996. *Who's Afraid of Freedom: Korean-American Artists in California.* Exh. cat. Newport Harbor, CA: Newport Harbor Art Museum.

Prochaska, David. 2003. "That Was Then, This Is Now: The Battle of Algiers and After." *Radical History Review* 85: 133–49.

Puar, Jasbir. 2007. *Terrorist Assemblages: Homonationalism in Queer Times.* Durham, NC: Duke University Press.

Pulido, Laura. 2006. *Black, Brown, Yellow, and Left: Radical Activism in Los Angeles.* Berkeley: University of California Press.

Purkayastha, Bandana. 2005. *Negotiating Ethnicity: Second-Generation South Asian Americans Traverse a Transnational World.* New Brunswick, NJ: Rutgers University Press.

———. 2010. "Interrogating Intersectionality: Contemporary Globalisation and Racialised Gendering in the Lives of Highly Educated South Asian Americans and Their Children." *Journal of Intercultural Studies* 31: 29–47.

Qian, Zhijian, ed. 2009. *Here + Now: Chinese Artists in New York.* New York: Museum of Chinese in America.

Race Ethnicity and Education. 2006. "Asian Americans and Pacific Islanders: The State of Research" (special issue). 9 (1).

Rafael, Vicente L., ed. 1995. *Discrepant Histories: Translocal Essays on Filipino Cultures.* Philadelphia: Temple University Press.

———. 2000. *White Love and Other Events in Filipino History*. Durham, NC: Duke University Press.

Rajan, Gita, and Shailja Sharma, eds. 2006. *New Cosmopolitanisms: South Asians in the U.S.* Palo Alto, CA: Stanford University Press.

Ramakrishnan, Karthick, Jane Junn, Taeku Lee, and Janelle Wong. 2008. "National Asian American Survey." Ann Arbor, MI: Inter-university Consortium for Political and Social Research. doi:10.3886/ICPSR31481.v2.

Ramakrishnan, Karthick, and Taeku Lee. 2012. "The Policy Priorities and Issue Preferences of Asian Americans and Pacific Islanders." *National Asian American Survey*, September 25 (updated October 16). <http://www.naasurvey.com/resources/Home/NAAS12-sep25-issues.pdf>.

Rana, Junaid. 2002. "Muslims across the Brown Atlantic: The Position of Muslims in the U.K. and the U.S." *Samar* 15 (Summer/Fall).

———. 2011. *Terrifying Muslims: Race and Labor in the South Asian Diaspora*. Durham, NC: Duke University Press.

Razack, Sherene. 2007. *Casting Out: The Eviction of Muslims from Western Law and Politics*. Toronto: University of Toronto Press.

Reddy, Chandan. 2011. *Freedom with Violence: Race, Sexuality, and the US State*. Durham, NC: Duke University Press.

Regents of the University of California v. Bakke, 438 U.S. 265 (1978).

Reinecke, John E. 1996. *The Filipino Piecemeal Sugar Strike of 1924–1925*. Honolulu: University of Hawai'i Social Research Institute.

Reiss, Benjamin. 2008. *Theaters of Madness: Insane Asylums and Nineteenth-Century American Culture*. Chicago: University of Chicago Press.

Rembis, Michael. 2011. *Defining Deviance: Sex, Science, and Delinquent Girls, 1890–1960*. Champaign: University of Illinois Press.

Renan, Ernest. 1882. "What Is Nation?" Paper presented at the Sorbonne, Paris, March 11.

Rindfleisch, Jan. 1988. "Art of the Refugee Experience." In *Art of the Refugee Experience*, by Jan Rindfleisch, 7–10. Exh. cat. Cupertino, CA: De Anza College.

Robertson, Roland, and Kathleen White, eds. 2002. *Globalization*. London: Routledge.

Robinson, Cedric J. 1983. *Black Marxism: The Making of the Black Radical Tradition*. London: Zed Books.

Robinson, Courtland. 1998. *Terms of Refuge*. London: Zed Books.

Robinson, Greg. 2001. *By Order of the President: FDR and the Internment of Japanese Americans*. Cambridge, MA: Harvard University Press.

———. 2009. *A Tragedy of Democracy: Japanese Confinement in North America*. New York: Columbia University Press.

Robinson, Greg, and Elena Tajima Creef, eds. 2008. *Miné Okubo: Following Her Own Road*. Seattle and London: University of Washington Press.

Robison, Kristopher K., Edward M. Crenshaw, and Craig J. Jenkins. 2006. "Ideologies of Violence: The Social Origins of Islamist and Leftist Transnational Terrorism." *Social Forces* 84 (4): 2009–26.

Robles, Rowena. 2006. *The Shifting Politics of Race: The Dismantling of Affirmative Action at an Elite Public High School*. New York: Routledge.

Rodríguez, Dylan. 2005. "Asian-American Studies in the Age of the Prison Industrial Complex: Departures and Renarrations." *Review of Education, Pedagogy, and Cultural Studies* 27: 241–63.

———. 2006. *Forced Passages: Imprisoned Radical Intellectuals and the U.S. Prison Regime*. Minneapolis: University of Minnesota Press.

———. (2009) 2010. *Suspended Apocalypse: White Supremacy, Genocide, and the Filipino Condition*. Minneapolis: University of Minnesota Press.

Rodriguez, Robyn Magalit. 2010. *Migrants for Export: How the Philippine State Brokers Labor to the World*. Minneapolis: University of Minnesota Press.

Roediger, David R. 1991. *The Wages of Whiteness: Race and the Making of the American Working Class*. New York: Verso.

———. 2008. *How Race Survived U.S. History: From Settlement and Slavery to the Obama Phenomenon*. New York: Verso.

Rondilla, Joanne L. 2002. "The Filipino Question in Asia and the Pacific: Rethinking Regional Origins in Diaspora." In *Pacific Diaspora: Island Peoples in the United States and across the Pacific*, edited by Paul Spickard, Joanne L. Rondilla, and Debbie Hippolite Wright, 56–66. Honolulu: University of Hawai'i Press.

Rondilla, Joanne L., and Paul Spickard. 2007. *Is Lighter Better? Skin Tone Discrimination among Asian Americans*. Lanham, MD: Rowman & Littlefield.

Rooks, Michael, ed. 2006. *Alimatuan: The Emerging Artist as American Filipino*. Exh. cat. Honolulu: Contemporary Museum.

Root, Maria, ed. 1996. *The Multiracial Experience: Racial Borders as the New Frontier*. Thousand Oaks, CA: Sage Publications.

———. 2001. *Love's Revolution: Interracial Marriage*. Philadelphia: Temple University Press.

Ropp, Steven Masami. 2000. "Secondary Migration and the Politics of Identity for Asian Latinos in Los Angeles." *Journal of Asian American Studies* 3 (2): 219–29. doi:10.1353/jaas.2000.0025.

Rosaldo, Renato. 1994. "Cultural Citizenship in San Jose, CA." *PoLAR: Political and Legal Anthropological Review* 17 (2): 57–64.

Roxworthy, Emily. 2008. *The Spectacle of Japanese American Trauma: Racial Performativity and World War II*. Honolulu: University of Hawai'i Press.

Roy, Arundhati. 2003. "Confronting Empire." Paper presented at the World Socialist Forum, Porto Alegre, Brazil, January 28.

———. 2004. *An Ordinary Person's Guide to Empire*. Cambridge, MA: South End Press.

Rudruppa, Sharmila. 2004. *Ethnic Routes to Becoming American: Indian Immigrants and the Cultures of Citizenship*. New Brunswick, NJ: Rutgers University Press.

Ruiz, Neil G., and Jill H. Wilson. 2013. "The 2014 H-1B Visa Race Begins Today." *Brookings Institution*, April 1. <http://www.brookings.edu/blogs/up-front/posts/2013/04/01-2014-h1b-visas-ruiz-wilson>.

Safran, William. 1991. "Diasporas in Modern Societies: Myths of Homeland and Return." *Diaspora* 1 (1): 83–99.

Said, Edward. 1978. *Orientalism*. New York: Vintage Books.

———. 1981. *Covering Islam: How the Media and the Experts Determine How We See the Rest of the World*. New York: Pantheon Books.

———. 1994. *Culture and Imperialism*. New York: Vintage Books.

Saito, Leland T. 1998. *Race and Politics: Asian Americans, Latinos, and Whites in a Los Angeles Suburb*. Urbana: University of Illinois Press.

Sakoda, James. 1989. "The 'Residue': The Unsettled Minidokans, 1943–1945." In *The View from Within*, edited by Yuji Ichioka, 247–81. Los Angeles: Asian American Studies Center Press.

Saleem, Mohammed M., and Michael K. Thomas. 2011. "The Reporting of the September 11 Terrorist Attacks in American Social Studies Textbooks: A Muslim Perspective." *High School Journal* 95 (1): 15–33.

Salyer, Lucy. 1995. *Laws Harsh as Tigers: Chinese Immigrants and the Shaping of Modern Immigration Law*. Chapel Hill: University of North Carolina Press.

Sanchez, George J. 1993. *Becoming Mexican American: Ethnicity, Culture and Identity in Chicano Los Angeles, 1900–1945*. Oxford: Oxford University Press.

Sanders, Jimmy, and Victor Nee. 1992. "Problems in Resolving the Enclave Economy Debate." *American Sociological Review* 57 (3): 415–18.

San Juan, E., Jr. 1995. *On Becoming Filipino: Selected Writings of Carlos Bulosan*. Philadelphia: Temple University Press.

———. 2005. "We Charge Genocide: A Brief History of US in the Philippines." *Political Affairs*, November 28. <http://www.politicalaffairs.net/we-charge-genocide-a-brief-history-of-us-in-the-philippines/>.

Saunders, Kay. 1982. *Workers in Bondage: The Origins and Bases of Unfree Labour in Queensland, 1824–1916*. St. Lucia, Australia: University of Queensland Press.

Saxenian, AnnaLee. 1990. *Silicon Valley's New Immigrant Entrepreneurs*. San Francisco: Public Policy Institute of California.

Saxton, Alexander. (1971) 1975. *The Indispensable Enemy: Labor and the Anti-Chinese Movement in California*. Berkeley: University of California Press.

Schechner, Richard. 2002. *Performance Studies: An Introduction*. New York: Routledge.

Schein, Louisa. 2008. "Neoliberalism and Hmong/Miao Transnational Media Ventures." In *Privatizing China*, edited by Aihwa Ong and Li Zhang, 103–19. Ithaca, NY: Cornell University Press.

Schlund-Vials, Cathy J. 2012a. "Cambodian American Memory Work: Justice and the 'Cambodian Syndrome.'" *Positions: East Asia Cultures Critique* 20 (3): 805–30.

———. 2012b. *War, Genocide, and Justice: Cambodian American Memory Work*. Minneapolis: University of Minnesota Press.

Schumacher, Frank. 2006. "'Marked Severities': The Debate over Torture during America's Conquest of the Philippines, 1899–1902." *Amerikastudien/American Studies* 51 (4): 475–98.

Schweik, Susan. 2010. *The Ugly Laws: Disability in Public*. New York: New York University Press.

Scott, Joan W. 1986. "Gender: A Useful Category of Historical Analysis." *American Historical Review* 91 (5): 1053–75.

Sedgwick, Eve Kosofsky. 1990. *Epistemology of the Closet*. Berkeley: University of California Press.

See, Sarita. 2009. *The Decolonized Eye: Filipino American Art and Performance*. Minneapolis: University of Minnesota Press.

Sexton, Jared. 2008. *Amalgamation Schemes: Antiblackness and the Critique of Multiculturalism*. Minneapolis: University of Minnesota Press.

Shah, Nayan. 2001. *Contagious Divides: Epidemics and Race in San Francisco's Chinatown*. Berkeley: University of California Press.

———. (2011) 2012. *Stranger Intimacy: Contesting Race, Sexuality and the Law in the North American West*. Berkeley: University of California Press.

Shah, Sonia. 1997. *Dragon Ladies: Asian American Feminists Breathe Fire*. Boston: South End Press.

Shankar, Lavina Dhingra, and Rajini Srikanth. 1998. *A Part, Yet Apart: South Asian Americans in Asian America*. Philadelphia: Temple University Press.

Shankar, Shalini. 2008. *Desiland: Teen Culture, Class, and Success in Silicon Valley*. Durham, NC: Duke University Press.

Sharma, Miriam. 1984. "Labor Migration and Class Formation among the Filipinos in Hawai'i, 1906–1946." In *Labor Immigration under Capitalism: Asian Workers in the United States before World War II*, edited by Lucie Cheng and Edna Bonacich, 579–616. Berkeley: University of California Press.

Sharma, Nitasha Tamar. 2001. "Rotten Coconuts and Other Strange Fruit." *SAMAR* 14 (Fall/Winter): 30–32.

———. 2010. *Hip Hop Desis: South Asian Americans, Blackness, and a Global Race Consciousness*. Durham, NC: Duke University Press.

———. 2013. "Rap, Race, Revolution: Post-9/11 Brown and a Hip Hop Critique of Empire." In *AudibleEmpire: Music, Global Politics, Critique*, edited by Ronald Radano and Teju Olaniyan. Durham, NC: Duke University Press.

Shaw, Angel Velasco, and Luis H. Francia, eds. 2002. *Vestiges of War: The Philippine-American War and the Aftermath of an Imperial Dream, 1899–1999*. New York: New York University Press.

Shibusawa, Naoko. 2006. *America's Geisha Ally: Reimagining the Japanese Enemy*. Cambridge, MA: Harvard University Press.

Shimakawa, Karen. 2002. *National Abjection: The Asian American Body Onstage*. Durham, NC: Duke University Press.

Shimizu, Celine Parreñas. 2007. *The Hypersexuality of Race: Performing Asian/American Women on Screen and Scene*. Durham, NC: Duke University Press.

Shin, Hyunjoon. 2009. "Have You Ever Seen the Rain? And Who'll Stop the Rain?: The Globalizing Project of Korean Pop (K-pop)." *Inter-Asia Cultural Studies* 10: 507–23. doi:10.1080/14649370903166150.

Shinagawa, Larry Hajime, and Gin Yong Pang. 1996. "Asian American Panethnicity and Intermarriage." *Amerasia Journal.* 22 (2): 127–52.

Shukla, Sandhya. 2003. *India Abroad: Diasporic Cultures of Postwar America and England*. Princeton, NJ: Princeton University Press.

Siebers, Tobin. 2009. *Disability Theory*. Ann Arbor: University of Michigan Press.

Silva, Denise Ferreira da. 2007. *Toward a Global Idea of Race*. Minneapolis: University of Minnesota Press.

Simmonds, Yussuf J., and Jennifer Bihm. 2012. "Race and Rage: L.A. Civil Unrest 20 Years Later." *Los Angeles Sentinel*, April 26. <http://www.lasentinel.net/index.php?option=com_content&view=article&id=641:race-and-rage-l-a-civil-unrest-20-years-later&catid=80&Itemid=170>.

Singh, Nikhil Pal. 2004. *Black Is a Country: Race and the Unfinished Struggle for Democracy*. Cambridge, MA: Harvard University Press.

———. 2012. "Racial Formation in the Age of Permanent War." In *Racial Formation in the Twenty-First Century*, edited by Daniel Martinez HoSang, Oneka LaBennett, and Laura Pulido, 276–301. Berkeley: University of California Press.

Sinn, Elizabeth. 1997. "Xin Xi Guxiang: A Study of Regional Associations as a Binding Mechanism in the Chinese Diaspora. The Hong Kong Experience." *Modern Asian Studies* 31 (2): 375–97.

Siu, Lok C. D. 2005. *Memories of a Future Home: Diasporic Citizenship of Chinese in Panama*. Palo Alto, CA: Stanford University Press.

———. 2013. "Twenty-First-Century Food Trucks: Mobility, Social Media, and Urban Hipness." In *Eating Asian America*, edited by Robert Ku, Martin Manalansan, and Anita Mannur, 231–44. New York: New York University Press.

Siu, Paul C. P. 1952. "The Sojourner." *American Journal of Sociology* 58 (1): 34–44.

———. (1953) 1987. *The Chinese Laundryman: A Study in Social Isolation*. Edited by John Kuo Wei Tchen. New York: New York University Press.

Skrentny, John D., Stephanie Chan, Jon Fox, and Denis Kim. 2007. "Defining Nations in Asia and Europe: A Comparative Analysis of Ethnic Return Migration Policy." *International Migration Review* 41: 793–825. doi:10.1111/j.1747-7379.2007.00100.x.

Slaughter, Sheila, and Gary Rhoades. 2004. *Academic Capitalism and the New Economy: Markets, State, and Higher Education*. Baltimore: Johns Hopkins University Press.

Smith, Michael P., and Luis Guarnizo. 1998. *Transnationalism from Below*. New Brunswick, NJ: Transaction Publishers.

Smith, Robert. 2005. *Mexican New York: Transnational Lives of New Immigrants*. Berkeley: University of California Press.

Snow, Hilary K., ed. 2000. *Shifting Perceptions: Contemporary L.A. Visions*. Exh. cat. Pasadena, CA: Pacific Asia Museum.

Soguk, Nevzat. 1999. *States and Strangers: Refugees and Displacement of Statecraft*. Minneapolis: University of Minnesota Press.

Soh, C. Sarah. 2008. *The Comfort Women: Sexual Violence and Postcolonial Memory in Korea and Japan*. Chicago: University of Chicago Press.

Sohi, Seema. 2014. *Echoes of Mutiny: Race, Surveillance, and Indian Anticolonialism in North America*. New York: Oxford University Press.

Sollors, Werner. 1988. *The Invention of Ethnicity*. New York: Oxford University Press.

Sommers, Samuel R., Evan P. Apfelbaum, Kristin N. Dukes, Negin Toosi, and Elsie J. Wang. 2006. "Race and Media Coverage of Hurricane Katrina: Analysis, Implications, and Future Research Questions." *Analyses of Social Issues and Public Policy* 6 (10): 39–55.

Spann, Girardeau. 2000. *The Law of Affirmative Action: Twenty-Five Years of Supreme Court Decisions on Race and Remedies*. New York: New York University Press.

Spencer, Rainier. 2009. "Mixed-Race Chic." *Chronicle of Higher Education*, May 19. <http://chronicle.com/article/Mixed-Race-Chic/44266/>.

Spickard, Paul. 1997. "What Must I Be?" *Amerasia Journal* 23: 43–60.

———. 2001. "Who Is Asian? Who Is Pacific Islander? Monoracialism, Multiracial People, and Asian American Communities." In *The Sum of Our Parts: Mixed-Heritage Asian Americans*, edited by Teresa Williams-León and Cynthia L. Nakashima, 11–25. Philadelphia: Temple University Press.

———. 2007. "Whither the Asian American Coalition?" *Pacific Historical Review* 76: 585–604.

Spielman, Ed, creator. 1972–1975. *Kung Fu*. New York: ABC Television Network.

Spivak, Gayatri Chakravorty. 1996. *The Spivak Reader*. Edited by Donna Landry and Gerald MacLean. New York: Routledge.

———. 2008. *Other Asias*. Malden, MA: Blackwell Publishers.

Springer, Richard. 2012. "Bengali-Language Voters Faced Election Day Barriers." *IndiaWest*, December 8. <http://www.indiawest.com/news/global_indian/bengali-language-voters-faced-election-day-barriers/article_9109ebe0-b5ee-50fa-b9e8-1ad8aba3a4cf.html>.

Srikanth, Rajini. 2004. *The World Next Door: South Asian American Literature and the Idea of America*. Philadelphia: Temple University Press.

———. 2012. *Constructing the Enemy: Empathy/Antipathy in U.S. Literature and Law*. Philadelphia: Temple University Press.

Srinivasan, Priya. 2011. *Sweating Saris: Indian Dance as Transnational Labor in the U.S.* Philadelphia: Temple University Press.

Steen, Shannon, ed. 2006. *AfroAsian Encounters: Culture, History, Politics*. New York: New York University Press.

Steinfeld, Robert J. 1991. *The Invention of Free Labor: The Employment Relation in English and American Law and Culture, 1350–1870*. Chapel Hill: University of North Carolina Press.

———. 2001. *Coercion, Contract, and Free Labor in the Nineteenth Century*. New York: Cambridge University Press.

Sternbach, David, and Joseph N. Newland, eds. 1994. *Asia/America: Identities in Contemporary Asian American Art*. Exh. cat. New York: Asia Society Galleries and New Press.

Stryker, Susan. 2009. *Transgender History*. Berkeley, CA: Seal Press.

Sturdevant, Saundra Pollock, and Brenda Stoltzfus, eds. 1992. *Let the Good Times Roll: Prostitution and the U.S. Military in Asia*. New York: New Press.

Su, Julie, and Chanchanit Martorell. 2001. "Exploitation

and Abuse in the Garment Industry: The Case of the Thai Slave-Labor Compound in El Monte." In *Asian and Latino Immigrants in a Restructuring Economy: The Metamorphosis of Southern California*, edited by Marta López-Garza and David R. Diaz, 21–45. Palo Alto, CA: Stanford University Press.

Sueyoshi, Amy. 2012. *Queer Compulsions: Race, Nation, and Sexuality in the Affairs of Yone Noguchi*. Honolulu: University of Hawai'i Press.

Suh, Sharon A. 2004. *Being Buddhist in a Christian World: Gender and Community in a Korean American Temple*. Seattle: University of Washington Press.

Sze, Julie. 2007. *Noxious New York: The Racial Politics of Urban Health and Environmental Justice*. Cambridge, MA: MIT Press.

———. 2011. "Asian American, Immigrant and Refugee Environmental Justice Activism Under Neoliberal Urbanism." *Asian American Law Journal* 18: 5–23.

Tachiki, Amy, Eddie Wong, Franklin Odo, and Buck Wong, eds. 1971. *Roots: An Asian American Reader*. Los Angeles: University of California, Los Angeles, Asian American Studies Center.

Tadiar, Neferti Xina M. 2003. *Fantasy-Production: Sexual Economies and Other Philippine Consequences for the New World Order*. Hong Kong: Hong Kong University Press.

Tajima-Pena, Renee, dir. 1997. *My America . . . or Honk if You Love Buddha*. San Franciso: Independent Television Service (ITVS).

Takagi, Dana. (1992) 1993. *The Retreat from Race: Asian American Admissions and Racial Politics*. New Brunswick, NJ: Rutgers University Press.

———. 1994. "Maiden Voyage: Excursion into Sexuality and Identity Politics in Asian America." *Amerasia Journal* 20 (1) 1–17.

———. 1996. "Maiden Voyage: Excursion into Sexuality and Identity Politics in Asian America." In *Asian American Sexualities: Dimensions of the Gay and Lesbian Experience*, edited by Russell Leong, 21–36. New York: Routledge.

Takaki, Ronald. 1979. *Iron Cages: Race and Culture in 19th-Century America*. London: Oxford University Press.

———. 1983. *Pau Hana: Plantation Life and Labor in Hawai'i, 1835–1920*. Honolulu: University of Hawai'i Press.

———. 1989. *Strangers from a Different Shore: A History of Asian Americans*. Boston: Little, Brown and Company.

Takao Ozawa v. United States, 260 U. S. 178, 43 Sup. Ct. 65, 67 L. Ed (1922).

Tam, Augie, ed. 2000. "Is There an Asian American Aesthetics?" In *Contemporary Asian America: A Multidisciplinary Reader*, edited by Min Zhou and James V. Gatewood, 627–35. New York: New York University Press.

Tam, Wendy. 1995. "Asians—A Monolithic Voting Bloc?" *Political Behavior* 17: 223–49.

Tarrow, Sidney G. 1994. *Power in Movement: Social Movements and Contentious Politics*, third edition. New York: Cambridge University Press.

Taylor, Charles. 2003. *Modern Social Imaginaries*. Durham, NC: Duke University Press.

Taylor, Diana. 2003. *The Archive and the Repertoire: Performing Cultural Memory in the Americas*. Durham, NC: Duke University Press.

Taylor, Paul, et al. 2012. "The Rise of Asian Americans." June 19. Washington, DC: Pew Social & Demographic Trends.

Tchen, John Kuo Wei. (1999) 2001. *New York before Chinatown: Orientalism and the Shaping of American Culture, 1776–1882*. Baltimore: Johns Hopkins University Press.

———. 2007. "Asian." In *Keywords for American Cultural Studies*, edited by Bruce Burgett and Glenn Hendler, 22–25. New York: New York University Press.

tenBroek, Jacobus, et al. 1954. *Prejudice, War and the Constitution*. Berkeley: University of California Press.

Teranishi, Robert T. 2010. *Asians in the Ivory Tower: Dilemmas of Racial Inequality in American Higher Education*. New York: Teachers College.

Thai, Hung C. 2008. *For Better or for Worse: Vietnamese International Marriages in the New Global Economy*. New Brunswick, NJ: Rutgers University Press.

Thomas, Dorothy S., and Richard S. Nishimoto. 1946. *The Spoilage*. Berkeley: University of California Press.

Ting, Jennifer P. 1995. "Bachelor Society: Deviant Heterosexuality and Asian American Historiography." In *Positions: The Sites of Asian American Studies*, edited by Gary Y. Okihiro, Marilyn Alquizola, Dorothy Fujita-Rony, and K. Scott Wong, 271–79. Pullman: Washington State University Press. 1995.

———. 1998. "The Power of Sexuality." *Journal of Asian American Studies* 1: 65–82.

Tinker, Hugh. 1974. *A New System of Slavery: The Export of Indian Labour Overseas, 1830–1920*. Oxford: Oxford University Press.

Tiongson, Antonio T., Jr., Ricardo Gutierrez, and Edgardo Gutierrez, eds. 2006. *Positively No Filipinos Allowed: Building Communities and Discourse*. Philadelphia: Temple University Press.

Tölölyan, Khachig. 1991. "The Nation-State and Its Others." *Diaspora* 1 (1): 3–7.

Toronto Hakka Heritage and Culture Conference. 2000. December 29–30.

Tran, GB. 2010. *Vietnamerica*. New York: Villard Books.

Trask, Hauani-Kay. 2008. "Settlers of Color and 'Immigrant' Hegemony: 'Locals' in Hawai'i." In *Asian Settler Colonialism: From Local Governance to the Habits of Everyday Life in Hawai'i*, edited by Candace Fujikane and Jonathan Y. Okamura. Honolulu: University of Hawai'i Press.

Trenka, Jane Jeong. 2003. *The Language of Blood: A Memoir*. St. Paul: Minnesota Historical Society.

———. 2009. *Fugitive Visions: An Adoptee's Return to Korea*. St. Paul: Graywolf Press.

Trent, James. 1995. *Inventing the Feeble Mind: A History of Mental Retardation in the United States*. Berkeley: University of California Press.

Trinh, Minh-ha T. 1992. *Framer Framed*. New York: Routledge.

———, dir. 2005. *Surname Viet Given Name Nam*. New York: Women Make Movies.

Tsai, Shih-shan H. 1976. "American Involvement in the Coolie Trade." *American Studies* 6: 49–66.

———. 1983. *China and the Overseas Chinese in the United States, 1869–1911*. Fayetteville: University of Arkansas Press.

Tsang, Daniel C. 2000. "Losing Its Soul? Reflections on Gay and Asian Activism." In *Legacy to Liberation: Politics and Culture of Revolutionary Asian Pacific America*, edited by Fred Ho, 59–64. San Francisco: Big Red Media and AK Press.

———. 2001. "Slicing Silence: Asian Progressives Come Out." In *Asian Americans: The Movement and the Moment: History through Word and Image 1965–2001*, edited by Steve Louie and Glenn K. Omatsu, 221–39. Los Angeles: UCLA Asian American Studies Center Press.

Tsutakawa, Mayumi, ed. 1994. *They Painted from Their Hearts: Pioneer Asian American Artists*. Exh. cat. Seattle: Wing Luke Asian Museum.

Tsutakawa, Mayumi, and Alan Chong Lau, eds. 1982. *Turning Shadows into Light: Art and Culture of the Northwest's Early Asian/Pacific Community*. Seattle: Young Pine Press and Asian Multi-Media Center.

Tu, Thuy Linh Nguyen. 2010. *The Beautiful Generation: Asian Americans and the Cultural Economy of Fashion*. Durham, NC: Duke University Press.

Tu, Thuy Linh Nguyen, and Alondra Nelson, eds. 2001. *Technicolor: Race, Technology and Everyday Life*. New York: New York University Press.

Tuan, Mia. 1999. *Forever Foreigners or Honorary Whites? The Asian Ethnic Experience Today*. New Brunswick, NJ: Rutgers University Press.

Tuan, Mia, and Jiannbin Lee Shiao. 2011. *Choosing Ethnicity, Negotiating Race: Korean Adoptees in America*. New York: Russell Sage Foundation.

Tunc, Tanfer Emin, Elisabetta Marino, and Daniel Y. Kim. 2012. "Redefining the American in Asian American Studies: Transnationalism, Diaspora, and Representation." *Journal of Transnational American Studies* 4 (1). <http://www.escholarship.org/uc/item/53c6c1kp>.

Twain, Mark. 1901. "To the Person Sitting in Darkness." *North American Review* 172 (531): 161–76.

Um, Khatharya. 2006. "Refractions of Home: Exile, Memory and Diasporic Longing." In *Expressions of Cambodia: The Politics of Tradition, Identity and Change*, edited by Leakthina Tollier and Timothy Winter, 86–100. New York: Routledge.

———. 2012. "Exiled Memory: History, Identity and Remembering in Southeast Asia and Southeast Asian Diaspora." *Positions: East Asia Cultures Critique* 20 (3): 831–50.

Umemoto, Karen. 1989. "'On Strike!' San Francisco State College Strike, 1968–69: The Role of Asian American Students." *Amerasia Journal* 15: 3–41.

———. 2000. "'On Strike!' San Francisco State College Strike." In *Contemporary Asian America: A Multidisciplinary Reader*, edited by Min Zhou and James V. Gatewood, 43–104. New York: New York University Press.

Ung, Luong. 2006. *Lucky Child*. New York: Harper Perennial.

U.N. General Assembly. 1948. Resolution 260. "Convention on the Prevention and Punishment of the Crime of Genocide." December 9. <http://www.un.org/ga/search/view_doc.asp?symbol=A/RES/260(iii)>.

———. 1951. "Convention Relating to the Status of Refugees." July 28. <http://www.un.org/millennium/law/v-14.htm>.

United States v. Bhagat Singh Thind, 261 U.S. 204 (1923).

Uno, Edison. 1974. "Concentration Camps American-Style." *Pacific Citizen*, December 20–27.

USA Patriot Act. 2001. *GPO.gov*. <http://www.gpo.gov/fdsys/pkg/PLAW-107publ56/pdf/PLAW-107publ56.pdf>.

Valverde, Kieu-Linh Caroline. 2012. *Transnationalizing Viet Nam: Community, Culture, and Politics in the Diaspora*. Philadelphia: Temple University Press.

Vang, Chia Youyee. 2010. *Hmong America: Reconstructing Community in Diaspora*. Urbana: University of Illinois Press.

Vann Woodward, C. 1966. *The Strange Career of Jim Crow*. New York: Oxford University Press.

Varma, Roli. 2006. *Harbingers of Global Change: India's Techno-Immigrants in the United States*. Lanham, MD: Lexington Books.

Vergara, Benito Manalo. 2009. *Pinoy Capital: The Filipino Nation in Daly City*. Philadelphia: Temple University Press.

Võ, Linda Trinh. 2004. *Mobilizing an Asian American Community*. Philadelphia: Temple University Press.

Võ, Linda Trinh, and Rick Bonus, eds. 2002. *Contemporary Asian American Communities: Intersections and Divergences*. Philadelphia: Temple University Press.

Volkman, Toby Alice. 2005. "Embodying Chinese Culture: Transnational Adoption in North America." In *Cultures of Transnational Adoption*, edited by Toby Alice Volkman, 81–115. Durham, NC: Duke University Press.

Volpp, Leti. 2002. "The Citizen and the Terrorist." *UCLA Law Review* 49 (5): 1575–1600.

———. 2005. "Divesting Citizenship: On Asian American History and the Loss of Citizenship through Marriage." *UCLA Law Review* 53 (2): 405–83.

Waldinger, Roger, and David Fitzgerald. 2004. "Transnationalism in Question." *American Journal of Sociology* 109 (5): 1177–95.

Wang, Karen. 2006. "Move Over, Telenovelas: Korean Dramas Are Next." *Television Week*, December 11.

Wang, L. Ling-chi. 1998. "Race, Class, Citizenshp, and Extraterritoriality: Asian Americans and the 1996 Campaign Finance Scandal." *Amerasia Journal* 24 (1): 1–21.

Wang, Oliver. 2006. "These Are the Breaks: Hip-Hop and AfroAsian Cultural (Dis)connection." In *AfroAsian Encounters: Culture, History, Politics*, edited by Heike Raphael-Hernandez and Shannon Steen, 146–66. New York: New York University Press.

———. 2007. "Rapping and Repping Asian: Race, Authenticity and the Asian American MC." In *Alien Encounters: Popular Culture in Asian America*, edited by Mimi Nguyen and Thuy Linh Nguyen Tu, 35–68. Durham, NC: Duke University Press.

———. 2013. "Learning from Los Kogi Angeles: A Taco Truck and Its City." In *Eating Asian America*, edited by Robert Ku, Martin Manalansan, and Anita Mannur, 78–97. New York: New York University Press.

Wang, ShiPu. 2011. *Becoming American? The Art and Identity Crisis of Yasuo Kuniyoshi*. Honolulu: University of Hawai'i Press.

Wang, Wayne, dir. 1993. *The Joy Luck Club*. Burbank, CA: Buena Vista Pictures.

Wat, Eric. 2002. *The Making of a Gay Asian Community: An Oral History of Pre-AIDS Los Angeles*. Lanham, MD: Rowman & Littlefield.

Wechsler, Jeffrey, ed. 1997. *Asian Traditions/Modern Expressions: Asian American Artists and Abstraction 1945–1970*. New York: Harry N. Abrams, in association with the Jane Voorhees Zimmerli Art Museum, Rutgers, State University of New Jersey.

Wei, William. 1993. *The Asian American Movement*. Philadelphia: Temple University Press.

Whelchel, Toshio. 1999. *From Pearl Harbor to Saigon: Japanese American Soldiers and the Vietnam War*. London: Verso.

Wiesel, Elie. 1999. "The Perils of Indifference." Millennial Speech at White House, Washington, D.C., April 12.

Wilcox, Fred A., and Noam Chomsky. 2011. *Scorched Earth: Legacies of Chemical Warfare in Vietnam*. New York: Seven Stories Press.

Williams, Raymond. 1978. *Marxism and Literature*. London: Oxford University Press.

———. 1979. *Culture and Society: 1780–1950*. New York: Columbia University Press.

———. (1976) 1985. *Keywords: A Vocabulary of Culture and Society*. New York: Oxford University Press.

Williams, Raymond Brady. 1988. *Religions of Immigrants from India and Pakistan: New Threads in the American Tapestry*. Cambridge, UK: Cambridge University Press.

Williams-León, Teresa, and Velina Hasu Houston, eds. 1997. "No Passing Zone." *Amerasia Journal* 23 (1).

Williams-León, Teresa, and Cynthia L. Nakashima, eds. 2001a. *The Sum of Our Parts: Mixed- Heritage Asian Americans.* Philadelphia: Temple University Press.

———. 2001b. "Reconfiguring Race, Rearticulating Ethnicity." In *The Sum of Our Parts: Mixed-Heritage Asian Americans,* edited by Teresa Williams-León and Cynthia L. Nakashima, 3–10. Philadelphia: Temple University Press.

Wilson, William Julius. 1987. *The Truly Disadvantaged: The Inner City, the Underclass, and Public Policy.* Chicago: University of Chicago Press.

Wimmer, Andreas, and Nina Glick Schiller. 2003. "Methodological Nationalism, the Social Sciences, and the Study of Migration: An Essay in Historical Epistemology." *International Migration Review* 37 (3): 576–610.

Winant, Howard. 1994. *Racial Conditions.* Minneapolis: University of Minnesota Press.

———. 2001. *The World Is a Ghetto: Race and Democracy since World War II.* New York: Basic Books.

———. 2002. "The Modern World Racial System." *Souls: A Critical Journal of Black Politics, Culture, and Society* 4 (3): 17–30.

Wirth, Louis. 1945. "The Problem of Minority Groups." In *The Science of Man in the World Crisis,* edited by Ralph Linton, 347–72. New York: Columbia University Press.

Wong, Bernard P. 2006. *The Chinese in Silicon Valley: Globalization, Social Networks, and Ethnic Identity.* Lanham, MD: University Press of America.

Wong, Jade Snow. 1945. *Fifth Chinese Daughter.* New York: Scholastic Books.

Wong, Janelle. 2006. *Democracy's Promise: Immigrants and American Civic Institutions.* Ann Arbor: University of Michigan Press.

Wong, Janelle, Karthick Ramakrishnan, Taeku Lee, and Jane Junn. 2011. *Asian American Political Participation: Emerging Constituents and Their Political Identities.* New York: Russell Sage Foundation.

Wong, Kent. 2003. "Building an Asian Pacific Labor Alliance: A New Chapter in Our History." In *Asian American Politics,* edited by James Lai and Don Nakanishi, 421–30. Boulder, CO: Rowman & Littlefield.

Wong, K. Scott. 2005. *Americans First: Chinese Americans and the Second World War.* Cambridge, MA: Harvard University Press.

———. 2009. "Introduction: Transnationalism, Race, and the Links between Asian and Asian American Studies." *Journal of American-East Asian Relations* 16: 135–37. doi:10.1163/187656109793645643.

Wong, K. Scott, and Sucheng Chan, eds. 1998. *Claiming America: Constructing Chinese American Identities during the Exclusion Era.* Philadelphia: Temple University Press.

Wong, Marie Rose. 2004. *Sweet Cakes, Long Journey: The Chinatowns of Portland, Oregon.* Seattle: University of Washington Press.

Wong, Morrison. 2006. "Chinese Americans." In *Asian Americans: Contemporary Trends and Issues,* edited by Pyong Gap Min, 110–45. Thousand Oaks, CA: Pine Forge Press.

Wong, Sau-ling Cynthia. 1992. "Ethnicizing Gender: An Exploration of Sexuality as Sign in Chinese American Immigrant Literature." In *Reading the Literatures of Asian America,* edited by Shirley Geok-lin Lim and Amy Ling, 111–30. Philadelphia: Temple University Press.

———. 1993. *Reading Asian American Literature.* Princeton, NJ: Princeton University Press.

———. 1995. "Denationalization Reconsidered: Asian American Cultural Criticism at a Theoretical Crossroads." *Amerasia Journal* 21 (1–2): 1–27.

Wong, Yutian. 2010. *Choreographing Asian America.* Middleton, CT: Wesleyan University Press.

Wu, Cynthia. 2012. *Chang and Eng Reconnected: The Original Siamese Twins in American Culture.* Philadelphia: Temple University Press.

Wu, Frank. 2003. *Yellow: Race in America beyond Black and White.* New York: Basic Books.

Wu, Jean Yu-Wen Shen, and Min Hyoung Song, eds. 2000. *Asian American Studies: A Reader.* New Brunswick, NJ: Rutgers University Press.

Wu, Judy Tzu-Chun. 2003. "Asian American History and Racialized Compulsory Deviance." *Journal of Women's History* 15 (3): 58–62.

———. 2005. *Doctor Mom Chung of the Fair-Haired Bastards: The Life of a Wartime Celebrity.* Berkeley: University of California Press.

———. 2013. *Radicals on the Road: Internationalism, Orientalism, and Feminism during the Vietnam Era.* Ithaca, NY: Cornell University Press.

Xu, Wenying. 2008. *Eating Identities: Reading Food in Asian American Literature*. Honolulu: University of Hawai'i Press.

Yamashita, Karen Tei. 1997. *Tropic of Orange*. St. Paul, MN: Coffee House.

Yanagisako, Sylvia. 1995. "Transforming Orientalism: Gender, Nationality, and Class in Asian American Studies." In *Naturalizing Power: Essays in Feminist Cultural Analysis*, edited by Sylvia Yanagisako and Carol Delaney, 275–98. New York: Routledge.

Yanagisako, Sylvia. 1995. "Transforming Orientalism: Gender, Nationality, and Class in Asian American Studies." In, edited by Sylvia Yanagisako and Carol Delaney, 275–98. New York: Routledge.

Yang, Alice. 1998. "Why Asia?" In *Why Asia? Contemporary Asian and Asian American Art*, edited by Jonathan Hay and Mimi Young, 103–6. New York: New York University Press.

Yang, Kao Kalia. 2008. *The Latehomecomer: A Hmomg Family Memoir*. Minneapolis: Coffee House Press.

Ying, Chris, ed. 2012. "Chinatown Edition." *Lucky Peach* 5.

Yoneyama, Lisa. 1999. *Hiroshima Traces: Time, Space, and the Dialectics of Memory*. Berkeley: University of California Press.

Yoo, David, ed. 1999. *New Spiritual Homes: Religion and Asian Americans*. Honolulu: University of Hawai'i Press.

Yoo, Grace J., Mai-Nhung Le, and Alan Oda, eds. 2013. *Handbook of Asian American Health*. New York: Springer Publishing.

Yoo, John. 2011. "Interrogation." In *Confronting Terror: 9/11 and the Future of American National Security*, edited by Dean Reuter and John Yoo, 157–73. Jackson, TN: Encounter Books.

Yoon, Injin. 1997. *On My Own: Korean Businesses and Race Relations in America*. Chicago: University of Chicago Press.

Yoshiaki, Yoshimi. (1995) 2000. *Comfort Women: Sexual Slavery in the Japanese Military during World War II*. Translated by Suzanne O'Brien. New York: Columbia University Press.

Yoshihara, Mari. 2003. *Embracing the East: White Women and American Orientalism*. New York: Oxford University Press.

———. 2007. *Musicians from a Different Shore: Asians and Asian Americans in Classical Music*. Philadelphia: Temple University Press.

Yoshikawa, Yoko. 1994. "The Heat Is on *Miss Saigon* Coalition: Organizing across Race and Sexuality." In *The State of Asian America: Activism and Resistance in the 1990s*, edited by Karin Aguilar-San Juan, 275–94. Boston: South End Press.

Yoshimoto, Midori. 2005. *Into Performance: Japanese Women Artists in New York*. New Brunswick, NJ: Rutgers University Press.

Young, Iris Marion. 1990. *Justice and the Politics of Difference*. Princeton, NJ: Princeton University Press.

Young, James. 1993. *The Texture of Memory*. New Haven, CT: Yale University Press.

Young, Louis, ed. 1990. *The Decade Show: Frameworks of Identity in the 1980s*. Exh. cat. New York: Museum of Contemporary Hispanic Art, New Museum of Contemporary Art, and Studio Museum in Harlem.

Young, Marilyn B. 1991. *The Vietnam Wars, 1945–1990*. New York: Harper Perennial.

Yu, Henry. (2001) 2002. *Thinking Orientals: Migration, Contact, and Exoticism in Modern America*. New York: Oxford University Press.

Yu, Renqiu. 1992. *To Save China, to Save Ourselves: The Chinese Hand Laundry Alliance of New York*. Philadelphia: Temple University Press.

Yuh, Ji-Yeon. 2002. *Beyond the Shadow of Camptown: Korean Military Brides in America*. New York: New York University Press.

———. 2005. "Moved by War: Migration, Diaspora, and the Korean War." *Journal of Asian American Studies* 8 (3): 277–91.

Yun, Lisa. 2008. *The Coolie Speaks: Chinese Indentured Laborers and African Slaves in Cuba*. Philadelphia: Temple University Press.

Yung, Judy. 1995. *Unbound Feet: A Social History of Chinese Women in San Francisco*. Berkeley: University of California Press.

Zeleny, Jeff. 2010. "Reid Apologizes for Racial Remarks about Obama." *New York Times*, January 9. <http://thecaucus.blogs.nytimes.com/2010/01/09/reid-apologizes-for-racial-remarks-about-obama/>.

Zhao, Xiaojian. 2002. *Remarking Chinese America: Immigration, Family, and Community, 1940–1965*. New York: Routledge.

———. 2010. *The New Chinese America: Class, Economy, and Social Hierarchy*. New Brunswick, NJ: Rutgers University Press.

Zhou, Min. (1992) 1995. *Chinatown: The Socioeconomic Potential of an Urban Enclave*. Philadelphia: Temple University Press.

———. 1998. "'Parachute Kids' in Southern California: The Educational Experience of Chinese Children in Transnational Families." *Educational Policy* 12: 682–704. doi:10.1177/0895904898012006005.

———. 2004. "The Role of the Enclave Economy in Immigrant Adaptation and Community Building: The Case of New York's Chinatown." In *Immigrant and Minority Entrepreneurship: The Continuous Rebirth of American Communities*, edited by John S. Butler and George Kozmetsky, 37–60. Westport, CT: Praeger.

———. 2007. "Are Asian Americans Becoming White?" In *Contemporary Asian America: A Multidisciplinary Reader*, second edition, edited by Min Zhou and J. V. Gatewood, 354–59. New York: New York University Press.

Zhou, Min, and Carl L. Bankston III. 1998. *Growing Up American: How Vietnamese Children Adapt to Life in the United States*. New York: Russell Sage Foundation.

———. 2006. "Delinquency and Acculturation in the Twenty-First Century: A Decade's Change in a Vietnamese American Community." In *Immigration and Crime: Ethnicity, Race, and Violence*, edited by Ramiro Martinez Jr. and Abel Valenzuela Jr. New York: New York University Press.

Zhou, Min, and J. V. Gatewood. 2007. "Transforming Asian American: Globalization and Contemporary Immigration to the United States." In *Contemporary Asian America: A Multidisciplinary Reader*, second edition, edited by Min Zhou and J. V. Gatewood, 217–59. New York: New York University Press.

Zhou, Min, and Susan S. Kim. 2006. "Community Forces, Social Capital, and Educational Achievement: The Case of Supplementary Education in the Chinese and Korean Immigrant Communities." *Harvard Educational Review* 76 (1): 1–28.

Zinn, Howard. 1980. *A People's History of the United States*. New York: Harper & Row.

Žižek, Slavoj. 2001. "Revolutionary Terror from Robespierre to Mao." *Positions: East Asia Cultures Critique* 19 (3): 671–706.

About the Contributors

Rick Bonus is Associate Professor of American Ethnic Studies at the University of Washington, Seattle. He co-edited (with Linda Trinh Võ) *Contemporary Asian American Communities: Intersections and Divergences* (2002) and is author of *Locating Filipino Americans: Ethnicity and the Cultural Politics of Space* (2000).

Lucy Mae San Pablo Burns is Associate Professor of Asian American Studies at the University of California, Los Angeles. She is the author of *Puro Arte: Filipinos on the Stages of Empire* (NYU Press, 2012).

Sucheng Chan is Professor Emerita of Asian American Studies and Global Studies at the University of California, Santa Barbara. She is author of *In Defense of Asian American Studies: The Politics of Teaching and Program Building* (2005), *Asian Americans: An Interpretive History* (1991), *Survivors: Cambodian Refugees in the United States* (2004), and *This Bittersweet Soil: The Chinese in California Agriculture, 1860–1910* (1989). She also edited *The Vietnamese American 1.5 Generation: Stories of War, Revolution, Flight and New Beginnings* (2006), *Chinese American Transnationalism: The Flow of People, Resources and Ideas between China and America during the Exclusion Era* (2005), *Hmong Means Free: Life in Laos and America* (1994), *Quiet Odyssey: A Pioneer Korean Woman in America* (1990), and several other books.

Kornel Chang is Associate Professor of History and American Studies at Rutgers University, Newark. He is author of *Pacific Connections: The Making of the U.S.-Canadian Borderlands* (2012).

Yoonmee Chang is Associate Professor of English at George Mason University. She received her Ph.D. from the University of Pennsylvania and is the author of *Writing the Ghetto: Class, Authorship, and the Asian American Enclave* (2010). Chang's current research focuses on North Korea and disability studies; she also writes poetry.

Sylvia Shin Huey Chong is Director of the Asian Pacific American Studies minor and Associate Professor of English and American Studies at the University of Virginia. Her most recent book is *The Oriental Obscene: Violence and Racial Fantasies in the Vietnam Era* (2012).

Catherine Ceniza Choy is Professor of Ethnic Studies at the University of California, Berkeley. She is the author of *Empire of Care: Nursing and Migration in Filipino American History* (2003) and *Global Families: A History of Asian International Adoption in America* (NYU Press, 2013).

Monisha Das Gupta is Associate Professor of Ethnic Studies and Women's Studies at the University of Hawai'i at Mānoa. She is the author of *Unruly Immigrants: Rights, Activism, and Transnational South Asian Politics in the United States* (2006), which won awards in 2008 from the Association of Asian American Studies and the American Sociological Association's section on Asia and Asian America.

Shilpa Davé is Assistant Professor of Media Studies and American Studies at the University of Virginia. She is the author of *Indian Accents: Brown Voice and Racial Performance in American Television and Film* (2013) and co-editor (with Leilani Nishime and Tasha G. Oren) of the collection *East Main Street: Asian American Popular Culture* (NYU Press, 2005).

Jigna Desai is Professor in the Department of Gender, Women, and Sexuality Studies and the Program of Asian American Studies at the University of Minnesota. She is the author of *Beyond Bollywood: The Cultural Politics of South Asian Diasporic Film* (2004) and co-editor of *Bollywood: A Reader* (2009), *Transnational Feminism and Global Advocacy in South Asia* (2012), and *Asian Americans in Dixie: Race and Migration in the South* (2013).

Pawan Dhingra is Chair and Professor of Sociology and American Studies at Tufts University. He co-curated the Smithsonian Institution exhibition *Beyond Bollywood* (2014). He also has authored two award-winning monographs: *Managing Multicultural Lives: Asian American Professionals and the Challenge of Multiple Identities* (2007) and *Life behind the Lobby: Indian American Motel Owners and the American Dream* (2012). He recently co-authored *Asian America: Sociological and Interdisciplinary Perspectives* (2014).

Lan P. Duong is Associate Professor in the Media and Cultural Studies Department at the University of California, Riverside. She is author of *Treacherous Subjects: Gender, Culture, and Trans-Vietnamese Feminism* (2012).

Yến Lê Espiritu is Professor of Ethnic Studies at the University of California, San Diego. She has published widely on Asian American panethnicity, gender, and migration, and U.S. colonialism and wars in Asia. Her most recent book is *Body Counts: The Vietnam War and Militarized Refuge(es)* (2014).

Evelyn Nakano Glenn is Professor of Gender and Women's Studies and Ethnic Studies and Founding Director of the Center for Race and Gender at the University of California, Berkeley. She is the author of *Issei, Nisei, War Bride: Three Generations of Japanese American Women in Domestic Service* (1988), *Unequal Freedom: How Race and Gender Shaped American Citizen and Labor* (2004), and *Forced to Care: Coercion and Caregiving in America* (2012); she is also editor of *Mothering: Ideology, Experience and Agency* (1993) and *Shades of Difference: Why Skin Color Matters* (2009).

Vernadette Vicuña Gonzalez is Associate Professor of American Studies at the University of Hawai'i, Mānoa. She is author of *Securing Paradise: Tourism and Militarism in Hawai'i and the Philippines* (2013).

Neil Gotanda is Professor of Law at Western State College of Law in Fullerton, California. He has published in numerous law journals and co-edited (with Kimberlé Crenshaw, Gary Peller, and Kendall Thomas) *Critical Race Theory: Key Writings That Formed the Movement* (1995).

Robert T. Hayashi is Associate Professor and Chair of American Studies at Amherst College. He is author of *Haunted by Waters: A Journey through Race and Place in the American West* (2007) and is currently writing a book that explores the intersections of sports, race, and class in Pittsburgh, Pennsylvania.

Bill Ong Hing is Professor of Law at the University of San Francisco School of Law. He has authored *Ethical Borders:*

NAFTA, Globalization, and Mexican Migration (2010), *Deporting Our Souls: Morality, Values, and Immigration Policy* (2005), *Defining America through Immigration Policy* (2004), *To Be an American: Cultural Pluralism and the Rhetoric of Assimilation* (NYU Press, 1997), and *Making and Remaking Asian America through Immigration Policy* (1993).

Lane Ryo Hirabayashi is Professor of Asian American Studies, and holds the George and Sakaye Aratani Endowed Chair at the University of California, Los Angeles. He is co-author of *A Principled Stand: The Story of Hirabayashi v. United States* (2013), and the author of *Japanese American Resettlement through the Lens: Hikaru Carl Iwasaki and the WRA's Photographic Section* (2009), among other books. Lane has also written a series of articles with Marilyn Alquizola on the Filipino writer and activist Carlos Bulosan, including "Carlos Bulosan's Final Defiant Acts" in *Amerasia Journal* (2012), as well as a new introduction to the reissue of Bulosan's classic book *America Is in the Heart* (2014).

Jennifer Ho is Associate Professor in the Department of English & Comparative Literature at the University of North Carolina, Chapel Hill. She is author of *Racial Ambiguity in Asian American Culture* (forthcoming 2015).

Evelyn Hu-DeHart is Professor of History and American Studies and the Director of Ethnic Studies at Brown University. She has authored *Missionaries, Miners, and Indians: History of Spanish Contact with the Yaqui Indians of Northwestern Spain, 1533–1830* (1981) and *Yaqui Resistance and Survival: Struggle for Land and Autonomy, 1821–1910* (1984). She edited *Across the Pacific: Asian Americans and Globalization* (1999) and (with Khun Eng Kuah-Pearce) *Voluntary Associations in the Chinese Diaspora* (2006).

Shirley Hune is Professor of Educational Leadership and Policy Studies at the University of Washington, Seattle, and Professor Emerita of Urban Planning, UCLA. She has published extensively in the areas of Asian American historiography and critical race, women's, and gender studies, and on the challenges experienced by Asian American and Pacific Islander students, faculty, and administrators in higher education.

Allan Punzalan Isaac is Associate Professor of American Studies and English at Rutgers University–New Brunswick. His book, *American Tropics: Articulating Filipino America* (2006), was the recipient of the Association for Asian American Studies Cultural Studies Book Award.

Helen Heran Jun is Associate Professor in the English Department and the African American Studies Department at the University of Illinois, Chicago. She is author of *Race for Citizenship: Black Orientalism and Asian Uplift from Pre-Emancipation to Neoliberal America* (NYU Press, 2011).

Moon-Ho Jung is Associate Professor and the Walker Family Endowed Professor of History at the University of Washington, Seattle. He is author of *Coolies and Cane: Race, Labor, and Sugar in the Age of Emancipation* (2006) and editor of *The Rising Tide of Color: Race, State Violence, and Radical Movements across the Pacific* (2014). His current project is *The Unruly Pacific: Race and the Politics of Empire and Revolution, 1898–1941* (forthcoming).

David Kyuman Kim is Associate Professor of Religious Studies and American Studies at Connecticut College, where he also served as the Inaugural Director of the Center for the Comparative Study of Race and Ethnicity. He is author of *Melancholic Freedom: Agency and the Spirit* of *Politics* (2007) and co-editor of *The Post-Secular in Question* (NYU Press, 2012), and co-edits the book series RaceReligion.

Richard S. Kim is Chair and Associate Professor in the Department of Asian American Studies at the University of California, Davis. He is the author of *The Quest for Statehood: Korean Immigrant Nationalism and U.S. Sovereignty, 1905–1945* (2011).

Rebecca Chiyoko King-O'Riain is Senior Lecturer of Sociology at National University of Ireland Maynooth. Her most recent book is *Global Mixed Race* (NYU Press, 2014).

Robert Ji-Song Ku is Associate Professor of Asian American Studies at Binghamton University of the State University of New York. He is the author of *Dubious Gastronomy: The Cultural Politics of Eating Asian in the USA* (2014) and co-editor of *Eating Asian America: A Food Studies Reader* (NYU Press, 2013).

James Kyung-Jin Lee is Associate Professor and Chair of Asian American Studies at the University of California, Irvine. A former associate editor of *American Quarterly*, he is author of *Urban Triage: Race and Fictions of Multiculturalism* (2004).

Josephine Lee is Professor of English and Asian American Studies at the University of Minnesota. She is author of *The Japan of Pure Invention: Gilbert and Sullivan's* The Mikado (2010) and *Performing Asian America: Race and Ethnicity on the Contemporary Stage* (1997). She has co-edited (with R. A. Shiomi and Don Eitel) *Asian American Plays for a New Generation* (2011) and (with Imogene Lim and Yuko Matsukawa) *Re/collecting Early Asian America: Essays in Cultural History* (2002).

Robert G. Lee is Associate Professor of American Studies at Brown University. He edited *Dear Miye, Letters Home from Japan 1939–1946* (1995), which received the 1996 Special Book Award from the Association for Asian American Studies. He is author of *Orientals: Asian Americans in Popular Culture* (1999), which received awards from the Northeast Popular Culture/American Culture Association, the American Political Science Association, and the American Studies Association.

Shelley Sang-Hee Lee is Associate Professor of Comparative American Studies and History at Oberlin College. She is author of *Claiming the Oriental Gateway: Seattle and Japanese America, 1900–1942* (2011) and *A New History of Asian America* (2013).

Karen Leong is Associate Professor of Women and Gender Studies and Asian Pacific American Studies in the School of Social Transformation at Arizona State University. She is the author of *The China Mystique: Pearl S. Buck, Anna May Wong, Mayling Soong Chiang and the Transformation of American Orientalism* (2005).

Nhi T. Lieu is an independent scholar and author of *The American Dream in Vietnamese* (2011). Her published works have appeared in *Alien Encounters: Popular Culture in Asian America*, *Frontiers: A Journal of Women Studies*, and *Journal of Asian American Studies*.

Andrea Louie is Associate Professor in the Department of Anthropology at Michigan State University and is also the Director of the institution's Asian Pacific American Studies program. She is author of *Chineseness across Borders: Renegotiating Chinese Identities in China and the United* States (2004), which won the Social Science Book Award from the Association for Asian American Studies. Her most recent book is *How Chinese Are You? Adopted*

Chinese Youth and Their Families Negotiate Identity and Culture (forthcoming 2015).

Margo Machida is Professor of Art History and Asian American Studies at the University of Connecticut. Her most recent monograph is *Unsettled Visions: Contemporary Asian American Artists and the Social Imaginary* (2009), which was the recipient of the Cultural Studies Book Award from the Association for Asian American Studies. She also co-authored (with Elaine H. Kim and Sharon Mizota) *Fresh Talk/ Daring Gazes: Conversations on Asian American Art* (2005).

Daryl Joji Maeda is Associate Professor of Ethnic Studies at the University of Colorado, Boulder. He is the author of *Rethinking the Asian American Movement* (2012) and *Chains of Babylon: The Rise of Asian America* (2009).

Martin F. Manalansan IV is Associate Professor of Asian American Studies and Anthropology at the University of Illinois, Urbana-Champaign. He is author of *Global Divas: Filipino Gay Men in the Diaspora* (2003). He has edited the following collections: (with Robert Ku and Anita Mannur) *Eating Asian America: A Food Studies Reader* (NYU Press, 2013), (with Arnaldo Cruz-Malave) *Queer Globalizations: Citizenship and the Afterlife of Colonialism* (NYU Press, 2002), and *Cultural Compass: Ethnographic Explorations of Asian America* (2000).

Anita Mannur is Associate Professor of English and Asian/Asian American Studies at Miami University. She is author of *Culinary Fictions: Food in South Asian Diasporic Culture* (2010) and co-edited (with Martin Manalansan and Robert Ku) *Eating Asian America: A Food Studies Reader* (NYU Press, 2013) and (with Jana Evans) *Theorizing Diaspora: A Reader* (2003).

Mari Matsuda is Professor of Law in the William S. Richardson School of Law at the University of Hawai'i at Manoa. She is co-author (with Charles Lawrence) of *We Won't Go Back: Making the Case for Affirmative Action* (1997) and *Words That Wound: Critical Race Theory, Assaultive Speech, and the First Amendment* (1993). She is also author of *Where Is Your Body?: Essays on Race, Gender, and the Law* (1996) and edited *Called from Within: Early Women Lawyers of Hawai'i* (1992).

Viet Thanh Nguyen is Associate Professor of English and American Studies and Ethnicity at the University of Southern California. He is author of *Race and Resistance: Literature and Politics in Asian America* (2002) and the novel *The Sympathizer* (forthcoming 2015).

Crystal Parikh is Associate Professor of English and Social and Cultural Analysis at New York University. Her monograph, *An Ethics of Betrayal: The Politics of Otherness in Emergent U.S. Literature and Culture* (2009), received the MLA Prize in United States Latina and Latino and Chicana and Chicano Literary and Cultural Studies.

Edward J. W. Park is a Professor in the Asian Pacific American Studies Program at Loyola Marymount University in Los Angeles. He co-authored (with John S. W. Park) *Probationary Americans: Contemporary Immigration Policies and the Shaping of Asian American Communities* (2005).

John S. W. Park is Chair and Professor of Asian American Studies at the University of California, Santa Barbara, and he serves as the Associate Director for the UC Center for New Racial Studies. He is the co-author (with Edward J. W. Park) of *Probationary Americans* (2005), and his two other books are *Elusive Citizenship* (NYU Press, 2004) and *Illegal Migrations and the Huckleberry Finn Problem* (2013).

Lisa Sun-Hee Park is Professor of Sociology and Asian American Studies at the University of Minnesota. She has authored *Entitled to Nothing: The Struggle for Immigrant Health Care in the Age of Welfare Reform* (NYU Press, 2011) and *Consuming Citizenship: Children of Asian Immigrant Entrepreneurs* (2005), which was awarded the American Sociological Association's Outstanding Book Award (Asia and Asian America Section) in 2006. She also co-authored two books with David Naguib Pellow: *The Slums of Aspen: Immigrants vs. the Environment in America's Eden* (NYU Press, 2011) and *The Silicon Valley of Dreams: Immigrant Labor, Environmental Injustice, and the High Tech Global Economy* (NYU Press, 2002).

Martin Joseph Ponce is Associate Professor of English at The Ohio State University. He is the author of *Beyond the Nation: Diasporic Filipino Literature and Queer Reading* (NYU Press 2012).

Junaid Rana is Associate Professor of Asian American Studies at the University of Illinois, Urbana-Champaign. He is the author of *Terrifying Muslims: Race and Labor in the South Asian Diaspora* (2011).

Greg Robinson is Professor of History at l'Université du Québec à Montréal and author of *By Order of the President: FDR and the Internment of Japanese Americans* (2001), *A Tragedy of Democracy: Japanese Confinement in North America* (2009), which was the recipient of the 2009 History Book Prize of the Association for Asian American Studies, and *After Camp: Portraits in Midcentury Japanese American Life and Politics* (2012), which won the 2013 Caroline Bancroft History Prize. He also

edited *Pacific Citizens: Larry and Guyo Tajiri and Japanese America Journalism in the World War II Era* (2012).

Robyn Magalit Rodriguez is Associate Professor of Asian American Studies at the University of California, Davis. She is author of *Migrants for Export: How the Philippine State Brokers Labor to the World* (2010) and co-author, with Pawan Dhingra, of *Asian America: Sociological and Interdisciplinary Perspectives* (2014).

Cathy J. Schlund-Vials is Associate Professor in English and Asian/Asian American Studies at the University of Connecticut (Storrs). She is currently the Director for the UConn Asian American Studies Institute and is the author of two monographs: *Modeling Citizenship: Jewish and Asian American Writing* (2011) and *War, Genocide, and Justice: Cambodian American Memory Work* (2012). She is also a series editor (with David Palumbo-Liu, Linda Trinh Võ, and K. Scott Wong) for Temple University Press's Asian American History and Culture series.

Nitasha Tamar Sharma is Associate Professor of African American Studies and Asian American Studies at Northwestern University. She is author of *Hip Hop Desis: South Asian Americans, Blackness and Global Race Consciousness* (2010).

Min Hyoung Song is Professor of English at Boston College and the former editor of the *Journal of Asian American Studies*. He is the author of *Strange Future: Pessimism and the 1992 Los Angeles Riots* (2005) and *The Children of 1965: On Writing, and Not Writing, as an Asian American* (2013). He also co-edited (with Jean Wu) *Asian American Studies: A Reader* (2000), and is co-editing (with Rajini Srikanth) *The Cambridge History of Asian American Literature*.

Rajini Srikanth is Professor of English, affiliated faculty in the Asian American Studies Program, and Dean of the Honors College at the University of Massachusetts, Boston. She has authored two monographs, *Constructing the Enemy: Empathy/Antipathy in U.S. Literature and Law* (2012) and *The World Next Door: South Asian American Literature and the Idea of America* (2004), and co-edited several collections, including *White Women in Racialized Spaces: Imaginative Transformation and Ethical Action in Literature* (2002).

Khatharya Um is Associate Professor of Ethnic Studies and Chair of Peace and Conflict Studies at the University of California, Berkeley. She is co-editor of *Southeast Asian Migration: People on the Move in Search of Work, Marriage and Refuge* (forthcoming 2015), author of *From the Land of Shadows* (forthcoming 2015), and has published articles in *Positions, Southeast Asian Affairs, Refuge,* and *Amerasia Journal.*

Linda Trinh Võ is Associate Professor in the Department of Asian American Studies at the University of California, Irvine. She is the author of *Mobilizing an Asian American Community* (2004) and co-editor of *Contemporary Asian American Communities: Intersection and Divergences* (2002), *Asian American Women: The "Frontiers" Reader* (2004), and *Labor versus Empire: Race, Gender, and Migration* (2004). She is a series editor for the Asian American History and Culture series published by Temple University Press and is president of the Association for Asian American Studies.

Janelle Wong is Associate Professor of Political Science and Asian American Studies at the University of Maryland, where she also serves as the Director of the Asian American Studies Program. She is author of *Democracy's Promise: Immigrants and American Civic Institutions* (2006) and co-authored (with S. Karthick Ramakrishnan, Taeku Lee, and Jane Junn) *Asian American Political Participation: Emerging Constituents and Identities* (2011) and (with Pei-te Lien and M. Margaret Conway) *The Politics of Asia America: Diversity and Community* (2004).

K. Scott Wong is James Phinney Baxter III Professor of History and Public Affairs at Williams College, where he teaches a variety of courses in Asian American history, comparative immigration history, history and memory, and the history of race and ethnicity in American culture. In addition to numerous articles in journals and anthologies, he co-edited, with Sucheng Chan, *Claiming America: Constructing Chinese American Identities during the Exclusion Era* (1998), and he is the author of *"Americans First": Chinese Americans and the Second World War* (2005). He is a series editor for the Asian American History and Culture series published by Temple University Press.

Cynthia Wu is Assistant Professor of American Studies at the State University of New York, Buffalo. She is author of *Chang and Eng Reconnected: The Original Siamese Twins in American Culture* (2012).

Judy Tzu-Chun Wu is Professor of Asian American Studies at the University of California, Irvine. She is the author of *Dr. Mom Chung of the Fair-Haired Bastards: The Life of a Wartime Celebrity* (2005) and *Radicals on the Road: Internationalism, Orientalism, and Feminism during the Vietnam Era* (2013). She is also the co-editor of *Frontiers: A Journal of Women's Studies* and *Women's America: Refocusing the Past,* 8th Edition (forthcoming 2015).

Grace J. Yoo is Professor and Chair of Asian American Studies at San Francisco State University. She recently co-authored (with Barbara Kim) *Caring across Generations: The Linked Lives of Korean American Families* (NYU Press, 2014), co-edited (with Mai-Nhung Le and Alan Oda) *Handbook of Asian American Health* (2013), and edited *Koreans in America: History, Identity and Community* (2012). She also co-edited (with Edith Chen) *Encyclopedia of Asian American Issues Today* (2010).